PRESIDENTIAL TRANSITIONS

PRESIDENTIAL TRANSITIONS

Eisenhower Through Reagan

CARL M. BRAUER

New York   Oxford
OXFORD UNIVERSITY PRESS
1986

Oxford University Press

Oxford   New York   Toronto
Delhi   Bombay   Calcutta   Madras   Karachi
Petaling Jaya   Singapore   Hong Kong   Tokyo
Nairobi   Dar es Salaam   Cape Town
Melbourne   Auckland

and associated companies in
Beirut   Berlin   Ibadan   Nicosia

Published by Oxford University Press, Inc.
200 Madison Avenue, New York, New York 10016

Oxford is the registered trademark of Oxford University Press

Library of Congress Cataloging-in-Publication Data

Brauer, Carl M., 1946–
Presidential transitions: Eisenhower through Reagan.

Bibliography: p.
Includes index.
1. Presidents—United States—Transition periods.
2. United States—Politics and government—1945–
I. Title.
JK518.B73   1986   353.03'1   85-30983
ISBN 0-19-504051-1

Printing (last digit): 9 8 7 6 5 4 3 2 1

Printed in the United States of America

To
Nancy Jay Schieffelin
Jacob Schieffelin Brauer
Peter Schieffelin Brauer

PREFACE

This book was commissioned by and written at the Institute of Politics of the John F. Kennedy School of Government, Harvard University. The Institute of Politics has a long interest in Presidential transitions and a commitment to their improvement. Richard Neustadt, who in 1960 was a professor at Columbia University, advised John F. Kennedy on his transition. The Institute of Politics was subsequently established as a living memorial to President Kennedy and in 1966, Neustadt, who had come to Harvard, became its first director. In 1968 the IOP organized a Faculty Study Group on Presidential Transition to advise whomever might become President; the President-elect turned out to be Richard Nixon, and Henry Kissinger was a member of that Faculty Study Group. In 1976 and 1980, reconstituted Faculty Study Groups, under Ernest May's chairmanship, provided materials for and advised the transitions of Jimmy Carter and Ronald Reagan.

In part, these Faculty Study Groups were providing incoming administrations with historical materials about what had happened in previous transitions, but the materials were incomplete and there had been little scholarship on this subject in recent years. The IOP therefore sought funding to underwrite the costs of writing an analytical history of modern Presidential transitions. The Ford Foundation and the Alfred P. Sloan Foundation generously underwrote those costs—and we are very grateful to them for doing so. Ernest

May gave me the opportunity to write this history and I am very grateful to him for that and for all his help.

The Institute of Politics provided a wonderful home to this project. The IOP's mission is to serve as a link between Harvard and the world of politics. It does this in such a lively and stimulating manner that I sometimes found myself distracted or diverted from the task at hand. At the same time, I think this is a better book for having been written in its environment and I know that I was a happier author for having worked in it. Jonathan Moore, its director, deserves high praise for making the IOP such a special place. I thank him for including me in its activities and for much besides, and I am grateful for the many friends I have made among the IOP's staff, fellows, and student associates.

Although the Institute of Politics commissioned this book and the Faculty Study Group on Presidential Transition advised me on it, they are in no way responsible for its contents. I am solely responsible for them. At the same time, I am grateful for the help I received from the Institute of Politics and from the Faculty Study Group, whose members this time were Ernest May, chairman, Graham Allison, Phillip Areeda, Jonathan Moore, Richard Neustadt, and Don Price. Other Harvard faculty members took the time to read and comment on portions of this work in progress and so did certain former government officials and I wish to thank each of them: David Bell, Hale Champion, Elliot Cutler, John Ehrlichman, Hugh Heclo, Franklin Lindsay, John Meyer, William G. Miller, Elliot Richardson, Gregory Treverton, James Verdier, Raymond Vernon, Harrison Wellford, and Adam Yarmolinsky. This book could not have been written without the assistance of many participants in this history who consented to be interviewed. They are too numerous to be listed here and some would prefer to remain unnamed; I am grateful to them all. I am indebted to the many archivists around the country who assisted me, and I owe special thanks to Malcom Hamilton and his staff at the Kennedy School's library.

I have had the benefit of criticism and support from friends and relatives, including Barbara and Arthur Powell, Melanie Billings-Yun, Marni Clippinger, Thomas Axworthy, Heather and Charles Campion, Martin Linsky, Mark Ramee, William Mayer, and, especially, David Whitman, Richard Margolis and my wife, Nancy Schieffelin. Winthrop Knowlton, Director of Harvard's Center for Business and Government, where I now work, generously allowed me to take time away from my current endeavor so I could complete the final stages of publication. He and Maxine Groffsky, my agent, gave me encouragement and sympathy when I needed them most. Sheldon Meyer and Leona Capeless of Oxford University Press provided sound editorial advice. I had able research assistance from Stephen Bates and Andrew Robertson, and for shorter durations, from Jennifer Laurendeau and Robert Yarbrough. To all of these good people I give my sincere thanks.

Cambridge, Massachusetts   C. M. B.
November 1985

CONTENTS

Introduction

American Presidential election campaigns take greater effort, cost more, and last longer than ever before, but they do not yield a more enlightening debate or noticeably better Presidents. No sooner does an election occur than everyone begins to speculate on who the likely candidates will be in four years' time. In fact, even before the results of the first exit poll have been broadcast or the last ballot counted, future Presidential aspirants have begun to lay plans and map strategies. Observers and participants alike have, with considerable justification, criticized the Presidential selection process for its excessive cost, length, and superficiality, for its resemblance to a horse race, beauty contest, marketing campaign, or marathon.

Candidates, the press, and the public pay, by comparison, relatively little attention to what happens after someone has actually won this quadrennial competition. How do Preidents-elect prepare to assume command of the largest, most complex, and important institution in the world? Whom do they choose for the Cabinet, sub-Cabinet, and other high offices and how do they choose them? What are their priorities, and how do they go about implementing them? How do they persuade others to follow them? Which inherited policies do they adopt, which do they abandon? How do they organize their staffs, and how do they relate to their Cabinets, to Congress, and to career officials? In short, by what manner and means do they try to govern and toward what ends?

This book treats Presidential transitions, by which I mean the passage newly elected Presidents travel from successful candidacy to established incumbency. The approximately ten weeks that elapse between election and inauguration are often referred to as *the* transition, but they are more accurately an interregnum. Though formal authority continues to reside in the occupant of the White House, his political power is small compared with that of his successor. The focus of attention is on the person about to become President, not on the person about to vacate the office. During these very busy weeks, Presidents-elect choose the highest officials of the executive branch, plan their initial policies, calculate the meaning of their mandates, and establish relations with the outgoing administration, with the new Congress, and with some career officials. They even begin to talk to foreign leaders, either personally, through emissaries, or by public statement.

After they acquire formal authority, newly inaugurated Presidents put their plans into action. They enunciate their public policy priorities and seek to get them implemented, either by executive fiat or with the approval of Congress. They gain operational control of foreign policy, begin to work closely with their top appointees and with career officials, and set into place their system for operating the White House. They establish a tone for governing and for public life. They begin to find out how their initial decisions are going to fare and they grow accustomed to being President. Within about six months of taking office—there is no arbitrary date—they are well under way, and their transitions can be said to be over.

Transitions are filled with peril and with opportunity. The ability of newly elected Presidents to avoid the former and make the most of the latter goes a long way toward determining their success in office and affects a great deal besides that. Newly elected Presidents have ended wars or prolonged them. They have demonstrated acumen or ineptitude on national security and foreign policy issues. They have maximized their mandates and led Congress, or squandered their mandates and failed to lead Congress. They have inspired or failed to inspire the public through their statements and actions. They have established economic and social policies with widely varying results. They have wisely or imprudently adopted or discarded inherited policies. They have appointed people who helped them achieve their goals and who graced public service and others whom they came to regard as liabilities and mistakes.

In view of the many potential pitfalls, it is striking that nonincumbents typically enter their transitions with confidence bordering on arrogance and hopefulness bordering on innocence. After

months and years of arduous and single-minded work, the successful candidate and his entourage have reached the pinnacle of American politics. It is a heady time. Although new Presidents in the
nuclear age may be humbled by the sudden awesome weight of their
war-making capability, humility about prospects of governing effectively is rarely in evidence. They tend to believe they can do things
much differently and much better than their immediate predecessors
did, especially because in every case since 1952 they defeated either
the incumbent or the candidate of his choice. Yet we know that
frequently they do things about the same or worse.

book
© 1986

This book aims to provide Presidential aspirants, Presidents-
elect, the press, and the public with an understanding of how the
newly elected Presidents since 1952—Eisenhower, Kennedy, Nixon,
Carter, and Reagan—dealt with their transitions from candidacy to
incumbency. Although there are abundant writings about each of
these men and their administrations—memoirs, scholarly works,
and reportage—no one has addressed their transitions as a distinct
subject. Political scientists, led by Richard Neustadt, have discussed
transitions, but the only book to treat them systematically has been
Laurin Henry's *Presidential Transitions* which was published in
1960. It covered Eisenhower's transition, but Henry did not have
available the rich sources about it that are now available. I am also
less interested in providing a comprehensive narrative than Henry
was and more interested in analysis; I am much more inclined to
judge decisions retrospectively.

This book begins with Eisenhower largely because he was the
first nonincumbent to assume office under the Twenty-second
Amendment, which moved up the inauguration date by two
months. (The last previous transition by a nonincumbent was in
1932–33, when Franklin D. Roosevelt succeeded Herbert Hoover.
Frank Freidel treats this transition authoritatively in the fourth volume of his Roosevelt biography, *Launching the New Deal*.) Eisenhower was also the first newly elected nonincumbent to take office
since the advent of nuclear weapons. I do not treat the successions
of Truman, Johnson, or Ford, or second-term transitions following
the election of incumbents in 1948, 1956, 1964, 1972, and 1984.
Although some problems found in successions and second-term
transitions parallel those of first-term transitions, they also differ
enough to warrant separate treatment. In addition, five transitions
seemed sufficient for one book.

Newly elected Presidents and their advisers have sometimes
shown curiosity about how their predecessors handled their transi-

tions and have sought information about them. Occasionally they have acted on false notions of what their predecessors, particularly immediate ones, did and with what effects. Always newly elected Presidents find that they have to make decisions at a rapid rate, often more haphazardly and less deliberately, more on faith and intuition and less on certainty and information, than they would like. Always, too, they are thrown back upon their own prior experiences in executive and political or military positions other than the Presidency, which none of them (except Grover Cleveland a hundred years ago) ever occupied before. This book seeks to broaden future, newly elected Presidents' experience by providing information and analysis about how five of their predecessors handled their assumption of power. It proceeds from the premise that an understanding of the past inevitably shapes policy and that better understanding can lead to better policy.

Equally important, I hope this book will increase public understanding of this important phenomenon. We rightly take pride as a nation in the orderly transfer of authority that takes place when the Presidency changes hands. Indeed, a Presidential inauguration has become a ritualized celebration of the stability of our system of government. Yet the hopefulness and optimism that are engendered by an inauguration too often give way to disappointment and pessimism, if not defeatism, over the longer run. A better understanding of transitions, I hope, will temper excessive optimism with an antidote of realism. I assume that a well-informed public will make better choices than a disillusioned one.

I am a historian and this is a history, which I have striven to make objective and dispassionate. I have tried to examine as many relevant sources as I could. In the cases of Eisenhower and Kennedy that meant rich manuscript and oral-history collections and the writings of historians. The very richness of these sources largely explains why the first two chapters are longer than the others. In the cases of Nixon, Carter, and Reagan, none of whose Presidential records were open at the time I did the research, I have relied more heavily on memoirs and reportage. But for each of the chapters I have conducted as many interviews with informed individuals as I could obtain and were practical to do. I am grateful to the many individuals who gave me their time and shared their memories and thoughts. I have not quoted from these interviews but I have cited them when the interviewee was willing. These citations indicate where I got certain information and how I came to certain opinions, but they do not mean to suggest that my sources agree with what I have written.

The five chapters describing individual transitions treat certain recurrent topics, functions, and problems. Most everything can be subsumed under one of three categories: personnel, policy, and organization. But because I wanted the chapters to be readable and because I am wary of categorization, I wrote them essentially as narratives that respect chronology and that consider context and personality. I hope there is enough analysis to whet the appetites of more theoretically minded readers, but I know they will not be able to make a meal of it. I hope even more that people who are involved in transitions not of the Presidential variety—at the state and local levels, in profit-seeking, nonprofit and government organizations, wherever—will find interesting ideas and useful analogies here.

Interspersed through the five narrative chapters are certain recurring patterns which I elaborate upon in the concluding chapter. These patterns include the important role played by a new President's own background or biography; the trap of overconfidence and hopefulness; misunderstandings that frequently occur between old and new administrations; problems caused by false expectations of Cabinet government; the enormous difficulty of making the right appointments; and the risks and rewards of both continuity and discontinuity in policy. From these recurring patterns, I derive certain broad lessons, suggestions, and warnings. I do not believe that history can provide people a road map to future success, but it can both inspire and instruct them and it can spare them from repeating past mistakes.

PRESIDENTIAL TRANSITIONS

1

EISENHOWER

☆ ☆ ☆

Prior to resigning his military commission in 1952 to seek the Republican Presidential nomination, Dwight D. Eisenhower spent most of his adult life in the United States Army. He became a World War II hero by virtue of commanding the Normandy invasion of 1944, one of the most complex undertakings in history, and by personally accepting German surrender the following year. As Supreme Commander of the Allied Expeditionary Force, he demonstrated organizational and diplomatic skills of a high order, effectively working with larger and touchier egos than his own while harmonizing conflicting national interests. He possessed great vitality and charm and exuded self-confidence and sincerity. "He has the power of drawing the hearts of men towards him as a magnet attracts the bits of metal," British Field Marshal Bernard Montgomery wrote. "He merely has to smile at you, and you trust him at once." Eisenhower appreciated the important role of public opinion in waging war and took pains to ensure favorable public relations. The public, the press, and his troops admired him for his lack of military swagger and for his common touch, symbolized by the simple "Eisenhower jacket."[1]

To his keen disappointment as a young West Point graduate, Eisenhower never saw combat in World War I, remaining in this country to train others to fight. After the war, he served primarily in a staff capacity. As an aide to Army Chief of Staff Douglas MacArthur, he helped disperse the Bonus Army of protesting veterans that descended upon Washington in the Great Depression. Later he accompanied MacArthur to the Philippines. His prominent World War II command grew directly out of staff work he did for Army Chief of Staff George C. Marshall, who elevated him over 366 more senior officers.

His military career impressed upon Eisenhower the virtues of effective organization, while also making him aware of how ill-managed organizations produced costly inefficiencies and of how special-interest groups threatened the general good. He acquired a certain dislike for politics, a word he often used pejoratively and synonymously with selfishness. Imbued with a soldierly ideal of duty, he wanted people to put aside their selfish interests and work cooperatively and voluntarily for a common purpose. Such cooperation was the secret, he believed, of American success in World War II.

As a professional soldier, Eisenhower avoided politics, register-ing in no political party and refraining from voting. Uncomfortable when military officers such as MacArthur involved themselves in politics, Eisenhower was firmly devoted to the doctrine that the President was Commander-in-Chief of the military. After he became president of Columbia University in 1948, his political philosophy began to emerge, characterized by the phrase, "the middle way," which expressed his hope that government could harmonize the differences between capital and labor, between rugged individual-ism and the welfare state, and between the parties. "Gad, how I wish that both parties had the courage to go out for militant advo-cacy to the middle of the road," he confided to his diary in 1949, "and choose some issues outside of the nation's economy to fight out elections." More specifically, though, his middle way often meant preventing expansion of the federal government's role in the nation's economy or social welfare.[2]

On foreign affairs Eisenhower derived from World War II firm lessons that the United States must remain active in the world and that both isolationism and appeasement were folly. Although he voiced idealistic notions about creating world order, he thought that American policy should also be guided by real economic inter-ests. He regarded communism as a menace, but like Truman, he preferred containing it to conquering it. Like Truman, too, and unlike a faction of the Republican party, he believed that Europe, not Asia, should be the focus of America's containment efforts. Accordingly, he agreed to take leave from Columbia in 1951 to assume command of NATO forces in Europe.[3]

Others sought Eisenhower for the Presidency more than he sought it himself. Interestingly, the first serious draft movement came from nervous liberal Democrats who wanted to replace Truman, seemingly a certain loser to the Republicans, with Eisenhower in 1948, an idea that Truman himself had already broached to Eisenhower privately. When Eisenhower showed no interest and when Truman decided to seek the nomination himself, the movement collapsed. The next year, Thomas E. Dewey, the Republican nominee who had unexpectedly lost to Truman, told Eisenhower that only he could "save this country from going to hades in the handbasket of paternalism, socialism, dictatorship." Eisenhower protested that he did not want to enter politics or seek a vote, but he left the door ajar by saying that he *doubted* whether he could ever be convinced that he had a duty to seek political office. Over the next several years, Dewey and his allies in the party strove to convince the general that he had such a duty. Eisenhower, fussing and ambivalent all the way, finally succumbed. No one, not even Eisenhower, becomes President against his will. But in modern times only Eisenhower could have become President as a Republican or as a Democrat.[4]

Although there was a powerful draft movement for Eisenhower in 1952, he did have to seek the nomination, for had he not done so, it would have gone to Ohio Senator Robert A. Taft, who actively sought it and who had a very significant following in the party. Following its defeat in 1948, the Republican party suffered from internal recriminations and from a bitter division between Taft and Dewey factions. Taft, whose following centered in the Midwest, was sometimes called an isolationist in foreign affairs, though unilateralist would have described his positions more accurately. Indeed, he and, to an even greater degree, his sympathizers were ardent interventionists when it came to Asia. They fretted about entangling alliances in Europe, about NATO, and about the high costs of foreign aid, but they bitterly attacked the Democrats for "losing" China after the Communists wrested control from the Nationalists in 1949 and Chiang Kai-shek and his army fled to Taiwan. The Dewey wing, numerically strongest in the East, was internationalist and pro-NATO. Its members often supported Truman on foreign policy, adhering to the bipartisanship that had been forged during World War II and which Taftites repudiated after 1948.

Eisenhower's philosophic agreement with the Dewey wing on foreign-policy issues—he did not differ significantly with Taft on domestic issues—proved decisive in convincing him to contest the

Senator for the nomination. Eisenhower's great popularity, the fear that Taft could not win the general election, and adroit convention maneuvering by Eisenhower's managers gave him the nomination. Although Eisenhower quickly extended himself personally to his opponent, and although he soon made certain rhetorical concessions, internal party divisions over foreign policy along with unhealed factional wounds saddled his administration in its early years.[5]

In many ways, the general election in November turned on the Korean war, which had started in June 1950, when Communist North Korea invaded anti-Communist South Korea. Responding quickly, the United States had gotten the United Nations to send troops, though Americans bore the brunt of the fighting. After UN forces threatened to reunify Korea in the fall of 1950, Communist China intervened. Negotiations toward a peaceful resolution of the conflict began in the summer of 1951, but without progress, and the war ground on, with neither side gaining an upper hand. The war cost Truman his popularity at home, particularly after he fired General Douglas MacArthur for insubordination in the spring of 1951. MacArthur favored a policy of victory, not containment, which had become Truman's objective after he was chastened by Chinese intervention, and MacArthur conveyed his views directly to Congress and the press. Public ambivalence toward the war showed up in the short-and long-term response to MacArthur. Given a hero's welcome at first, he failed to convert his popularity into votes the following year; his quest for the Republican nomination fell far short.

General Eisenhower, by contrast, profited politically from Korea. He aroused no fears that he would expand the war, first emphasizing that South Koreans should bear a greater burden of the fighting, then equivocally endorsing MacArthur's plan of bombing bases beyond the Yalu River in Manchuria. The last several weeks of his campaign were climaxed by his promise to go to Korea in order possibly to bring the war to an early honorable end. How precisely he would end the war, he did not say, but his pledge to visit Korea reassured the public because of his enormous prestige as a military leader. His Democratic opponent, Governor Adlai E. Stevenson of Illinois, challenged him to spell out his positions, on the important issue of prisoner repatriation, for example. But while Stevenson endorsed Truman's Korean policies, implying indefinite continuation of the war, Eisenhower held out hope of ending the war.

At the same time, Eisenhower embraced the anti-Communist rhetoric of the Republican right, calling for the "liberation" of the "captive peoples" of Eastern Europe and a repudiation of the Yalta agreements and promising to root Communists and security risks out of government. Although certain right-wing Republicans such as Senators Joseph McCarthy of Wisconsin and William Jenner of Indiana privately disgusted Eisenhower, he publicly favored their reelection and failed to repudiate their demagogic methods. Bowing to political caution, he deleted planned remarks in Wisconsin defending his mentor, George C. Marshall, from McCarthy's wild charges of disloyalty. The Republican campaign capitalized on scandals that had occurred under Truman; its anticorruption theme was only temporarily set back by revelation of a private fund that Eisenhower's running mate, Senator Richard M. Nixon, had to help pay his expenses. On domestic issues such as civil rights, economic controls, tidelands oil, and social welfare measures, Eisenhower ran well to the right of Stevenson, advocating states' rights, decontrol, and individualism.

Eisenhower won in a landslide, with 55 percent to Stevenson's 44 percent, 39 states and 442 electoral votes to his opponent's 9 states and 89 electoral votes, which were confined to the South and West Virginia. Eisenhower ran ahead among all income groups and among most ethnic groups. His coattails carried in Republicans in both houses of Congress, by ten seats in the House and a bare majority in the Senate. Opinion surveys showed that the outcome reflected public discontent with the party in power more than it did positive support for the Republicans. Indeed, by a 47 to 27 margin, voters still classified themselves as Democrats. Very few people who voted for Eisenhower cited party allegiance as their reason; rather, they pointed to his experience and personal qualities. Nowhere did the very personal nature of Eisenhower's victory show up more clearly than on the problem that most troubled the voters, Korea. Although public opinion was fractured on what should be done about the war, 75 percent of the public believed that Eisenhower would be able to end the war more quickly than Stevenson.[6]

On election night Eisenhower asked three men to serve as a committee to screen high-level appointees and the next day left for a ten-day golfing holiday in Georgia, consulting with them by phone. The committee's composition and Eisenhower's use of it characterized both his approach to administration and certain problems he faced as a newly elected President. It consisted of Lucius D. Clay, a retired general, lifetime friend and colleague during the war who had become chairman of the Continental Can Company; Herbert Brownell, Jr., a Wall Street lawyer and close Dewey associate who had played a central role in Eisenhower's nomination and campaign; and Thomas E. Coleman, a manufacturing executive and prominent Wisconsin Republican, who had led Joseph McCarthy's first campaign for the Senate in 1946 and who was Taft's floor manager at the 1952 convention.

Thus, the committee had two Eisenhower men and one Taft man, two industrialists and one corporate lawyer, two politicians and one soldier. Although its members had considerable experience—none was remotely a callow youth—their backgrounds did not include any Cabinet or White House service, the absence of which largely reflected the long hiatus in Republican control of the White House. Some Republicans had served under Roosevelt and Truman, including Robert Lovett, the incumbent Secretary of Defense, but in the highly partisan atmosphere of the day, Eisenhower and his subordinates generally regarded them with suspicion and did not want their service or their advice, thus denying themselves a valuable resource.

Coleman, the Taftite, quickly declined to serve, however, on the grounds that he was the wrong person for the job since he was unsympathetic with Eisenhower's views. Brownell considered it a selfless act, which it may have been, but it also illustrated the severity of the party's internal wound. Brownell consulted Taft by phone about some prospective appointees, but few Taft preferences were accepted, and Taft was sometimes distressed at Eisenhower's selections. He was also upset that Eisenhower initially violated the traditional courtesy of consulting Republican Senators, himself included, about prospective appointees from their own states and complained about the "indecent haste with which all the Eisenhower supporters seem to be demanding and obtaining jobs." He wondered about Eisenhower's intelligence and about his seeming unwillingness to read anything; the general preferred oral briefings.[7]

Accustomed to the military chain of command, Eisenhower believed in the practice of delegating authority. From an administrative standpoint, it became *the* central feature of his Presidency. It spawned controversy then over whether Eisenhower made decisions himself or merely ratified decisions that had been made by subordinates, whether he was an active or passive President. The controversy continues to this day, fueled rather than smothered by the opening of vast quantities of his papers and of oral histories about him. It has often overlooked the fact that when Eisenhower was interested in a problem, such as selecting high-level personnel, making major foreign or defense policies, or balancing the federal budget, he became so intimately involved in his delegates' work that one has to conclude that they made decisions together, but with Eisenhower as the dominant personality and the final arbiter.[8]

Eisenhower worked closely with Clay and Brownell on personnel selection. He established certain guidelines for them to use. Above all, he wanted men of character and ability, which he ranked ahead of expertise in particular areas. For the heads of Defense and Treasury, he wanted men from business and finance. He strongly preferred businessmen generally and he sought people who did not want or need to serve, but for whom service was a duty and a sacrifice. Political experience was unimportant to him and, if anything, a handicap. He told Clay and Brownell to be on the lookout for a woman and for a Democrat and labor leader, whose inclusion would foster national unity. Eisenhower downplayed religious affiliation, though Clay and Brownell hoped to find a Catholic for the Cabinet.

Eisenhower wanted to fill the top posts before he left for Korea approximately three weeks after his election, so appointments proceeded unusually fast. Eisenhower himself casually filled the first slot on election day when he asked Brownell to be his chief of staff. Brownell demurred on the grounds that his life was in the law, prompting Eisenhower to offer him Attorney General. Brownell accepted, though the announcement was put off for two weeks. Believing it was wrong to have military men in high positions (with the evident exception of the Presidency), Clay had earlier made Eisenhower promise that he would not offer him a position. Thus, neither of his principal advisers on personnel was angling for a job himself. Eisenhower also quickly named two men to serve as his liaison with the Truman administration: Henry Cabot Lodge, who had just been defeated for reelection to the Senate in Massachusetts by John F. Kennedy and who had played a central role in getting Eisenhower the nomination; and Joseph M. Dodge, a Detroit banker whom Eisenhower had known from his fiscal work during the American occupation of Germany in 1945.

For each position Clay and Brownell gathered a large number of names before narrowing down the choice. Sherman Adams, the New Hampshire governor who had been a top Eisenhower campaign aide, provided staff assistance. The operation was spared outside pressure because its creation was not announced publicly. Frequently Eisenhower opposed a recommendation initially to test how strongly its proponent favored someone. In sifting prospective Cabinet officers, the screening committee came up with candidates for second-tier positions. Sometimes these names were simply passed along to the secretary-designate. Other times the secretary-designate was asked to accept certain subordinates; no one refused to do so. Clay and Brownell took care that Eisenhower never saw any candidate who would turn him down. Dewey, a logical contender for several top posts, emphatically took himself out of the running, but was consulted about certain prospective appointees. Often Eisenhower saw only the leading candidate for a position and he apparently never rejected a person who had gotten that far.[9]

Intimates of Eisenhower, including Clay; Brownell; Milton Eisenhower, his brother and confidant; and C. D. Jackson, a staff assistant; have given differing versions of John Foster Dulle's appointment as Secretary of State. There is no way of establishing the degree of Eisenhower's initial enthusiasm for the appointment. It is certain that Dulles, a preeminent Wall Street lawyer, was the first-ranking and most experienced Republican expert and spokesman on foreign policy. He was an internationalist who had played an important role in bipartisanship after the war, even negotiating the Japanese peace treaty. In 1952 he had trimmed sail, accommodating to Taft's desire for less expensive policies by advocating the development of military means by which we could retaliate instantly against open Communist aggression. Responding to right-wing frustrations over policies of merely containing communism, he called for the liberation of Eastern Europe, though without spelling out how this could be done.

While privately favoring Eisenhower's nomination, he had written the Republican platform on foreign policy, which gave offense to neither wing of the party. Importantly, Taft found Dulles completely acceptable as Secretary of State. Eisenhower had had several conversations with Dulles before he was elected, and he was impressed with Dulle's sincerity, loyalty, and expertise, and with the orderliness of his mind. When Dulles spoke, Eisenhower recalled, it was "almost like a printed page." Eisenhower also recollected how during the campaign he had discovered an omission in a speech Dulles had given about this country's readiness to use all means to liberate the captive nations of Eastern Europe. Eisenhower pointed out to Dulles that he had inadvertently left out the word "peaceful" before "means." Dulles agreed at once. The exchange forecast both Eisenhower's dominance of Dulles and Eisenhower's more cautious rhetoric on international politics.[10]

For Defense, several men were considered, all industrialists.

Through Lodge, Robert Lovett advised against this course. Industrial experience was useful, he affirmed, but not as important as knowledge of Congress, the armed services, and world conditions. Lovett cautioned that he knew a number of leading industrialists who had failed in Washington because things were done so differently there from what they were used to. Eisenhower brushed aside Lovett's advice, telling Lodge that we had tried "an investment banker [James Forrestal], a politician [Louis Johnson], a military man [General Marshall] and an investment banker with wide experience in the Executive Branch [Lovett] and none of them had been able to get unification." Perhaps an industrialist could. The Secretary of Defense had to exert great leadership, in Eisenhower's well-schooled view, and had to demand dedication to the country ahead of dedication to one particular service.[11]

Several industrialists were considered, including David Sarnoff, the head of RCA, who was ruled out because he was regarded as being too close to the Truman administration. Clay recommended Charles E. Wilson, the president of General Motors, who enjoyed an excellent reputation as an industrial leader but who lacked government experience. Eisenhower had met him several times since the war, and after a long conversation with him, the job was his. Lodge immediately registered his doubts with Eisenhower about Wilson's ability to handle Congressional and public relations. Eisenhower responded that he personally would handle such things, but Lodge doubted Eisenhower would have the time. With his wealth of military experience, Eisenhower clearly intended to involve himself in running the Defense Department. It was not a design for great leadership by the Secretary. One also has to wonder what Eisenhower and Wilson talked about in their long conversation since Eisenhower asked *Lodge* to tell Wilson what he needed to do.[12]

The Treasury Department also went to an industrialist, George M. Humphrey, the president of Mark Hanna, a mining, manufacturing, shipping, and financial concern. Clay knew Humphrey and thought that he and Eisenhower would get along well. Indeed, they got along famously, becoming close friends and enjoying the same recreational pursuits. Neither Wilson's nor Humphrey's appointment pleased Taft, who worried about the ability of big businessmen to cope with problems of government. For Treasury he had strongly favored Senator Harry Byrd of Virginia, a conservative Democrat, as a means of constructing an alliance between Republicans and Southern Democrats in Congress.[13]

Three other Cabinet posts went to businessmen as well, though ones with some political experience. Geography played an important part in the selection of a Secretary of Interior. Eisenhower wanted someone from the West since much of Interior's activities were concentrated there, but neither Governor Earl Warren of California nor Governor Arthur Langlie of Washington was interested. Eisenhower settled on Douglas McKay, who was completing a term as governor of Oregon after having been an auto dealer. Sinclair Weeks, a Massachusetts manufacturer who had served an interim term in the Senate, became Commerce Secretary after first declining the chairmanship of the Republican National Committee. Arthur Summerfield, the incumbent party chairman and a car dealer from Michigan, became Postmaster General, though Eisenhower insisted that he resign as party chairman. Ezra Taft Benson of Utah, a leader of the Mormon church with a background in farm cooperatives and agricultural marketing, became Secretary of Agriculture. Party unity played an important role here because he had been a supporter of Robert Taft (no relation). "You will be the only member of the Cabinet," Taft wrote Benson, "who openly supported me before the Convention."[14]

The final department head to be chosen was Labor. Eisenhower and his advisers hoped that they could reestablish the good relations that had once existed between the Republican party and labor unions but which had soured in the 1930s. Governor Alfred Driscoll of New Jersey was an early possibility until he decided to enter private business. Eisenhower turned to Martin Durkin, whose name had been put forward by Harold Stassen, a former governor of Minnesota who had worked for Eisenhower during the fall campaign. Durkin was president of the American Federation of Labor's plumber's union, a Democrat who had supported Stevenson, and a former labor commissioner in Illinois. In his meeting with Eisenhower, Durkin seemed worried about how his appointment would fare. When he agreed to take the job, he informed Eisenhower that his union was holding his old position open for a year in the event that things did not work out. It probably should have been clear to Eisenhower that Durkin simply did not fit in his administration ("eight millionaires and a plumber," Democrats quipped), but Eisenhower's lack of experience with labor apparently allowed him to substitute unrealistic hopes for sound judgment. (Moreover, the final decision was rushed, coming only hours before Eisenhower left for Korea.)[15]

Although certain Republicans, such as Lodge, regarded Durkin an inspired choice, Robert Taft was shocked, publicly declaring it "incredible." Durkin had advocated repeal of the Taft-Hartley law, a broad 1947 enactment that he would have to enforce as Secretary. Privately Taft fumed that it was like naming Dean Acheson Secretary of State. In Taft's view, the appointment constituted a repudiation of Eisenhower's campaign promises and his personal commitments to Taft. "I don't know whether he realizes that," Taft acidly wrote, "but if he doesn't he is very stupid indeed."[16]

Eisenhower wanted a woman in the Cabinet. He did not get one, but he accorded Oveta Culp Hobby Cabinet rank when he named her to head the Federal Security Agency, which oversaw a variety of social welfare responsibilities and which Eisenhower hoped Congress would soon convert into a department. Eisenhower knew her from the war when she had headed the Women's Army Corps. She was a Houston publisher and a Democrat-for-Eisenhower. At the start of his administration he also regularly invited seven other appointees to sit with the Cabinet: Henry Cabot Lodge, Ambassador to the United Nations; Harold Stassen, Mutual Security Director; Joseph Dodge, Budget Director; Sherman Adams, the top White House assistant; General Robert Cutler, a Boston banker and campaign aide who administered the National Security Council; C. D. Jackson, a magazine publisher who served as an assistant for psychological warfare; and Arthur Flemming, a university president who directed Defense Mobilization and worked on problems of government organization.[17]

In his memoir, Eisenhower recalled how his military background, which had taught him organizational skills, and his prior observations of White House operations caused him to pay particular attention to the selection of a chief of staff, who was given the title "Assistant to the President," and whom newspapers soon referred to as "The Assistant to the President." Eisenhower wanted a "competent administrator and a good friend . . . who would be close to and trusted by me." Several military officers who had worked for Eisenhower before would have been naturals for the job, but Eisenhower was persuaded that such a person, teamed with him, "would create in many quarters a suspicion of excessive military influence." After Brownell declined the post, Adams and Lodge became the front-runners, but Lodge much preferred the UN ambassadorship, which left Adams.[18]

Eisenhower and Adams have given conflicting accounts as to whether Eisenhower spelled out Adams's duties at the time of his appointment, though it is certain what the job became. "Eisenhower simply expected me to manage a staff that would boil down,

simplify and expedite the urgent business that had to be brought to
his personal attention," Adams wrote, "and to keep as much work
of secondary importance as possible off his desk." Dour, tactiturn,
and extremely hardworking, Adams gave no time to social ame-
nites. Even "Beetle" Smith, Eisenhower's chief of staff during the
war and himself a tough customer, was impressed in late 1952
when he met this chunk of "New Hampshire granite." Although
Adams acquired a reputation as an empire builder, in reality he was
Eisenhower's "no" man and simply carried out the President's desires. One of the advantages of delegation that Eisenhower had
learned in the military was that a commanding officer could always
have a subordinate do the dirty work of relieving someone or reject-
ing their plans.[19]

Eisenhower personally selected several other staff members, including James Hagerty as press secretary, General Wilton B. Persons
who had done Congressional liaison work for the Pentagon and
who worked in a similar capacity for Eisenhower, Emmet Hughes
as chief speech writer, and Thomas Stephens as appointment secretary. The last post was to have gone to Arthur Vandenburg, Jr. His
security check evidently revealed some kind of impropriety, however, and he left the staff. His departure was publicly attributed to a
blood disorder. Eisenhower doubted that he needed Gabriel Hauge
as an economic adviser—and he feared that Hauge would get in the
way of Arthur Burns, who became chairman of the Council of
Economic Advisers—but Adams persuaded him to hire Hauge for
his versatility. (Hauge and Burns, were close friends who did work
well together.) Bernard Shanley became counsel to the President,
which entailed giving legal and political advice, not the policy making and speech writing that several of his predecessors had done. All
of these men and most of Eisenhower's other assistants in the White
House had traveled with him on the campaign train, and many of
them had been associated with Dewey in the years before that. Only
after Taft's death the following summer did one of Taft's assistants
join the White House staff, in Congressional liaison work. It was a
politically seasoned staff unusually devoted to its boss.[20]

One of the most sensitive and potentially significant things that
occurs after the election of a new President is liaison between the
incoming and outgoing administration. Office-leavers invariably
want to feel that they have done their best to prepare their successors for their new responsibilities and often believe that their successors are not up to the task. All transitions, as distinct from
successions, since 1932 have involved a change in party, at the

least implying popular rejection of an incumbent administration, so incoming officials have a mandate for their view that they can do a superior job to that done by their predecessors. They are the winners and the people in office the losers; they fear taking the losers' advice lest they become trapped in their failed policies. All transitions include ritualized public statements about the orderly transfer of authority that is taking place in a democracy, though in fact relations may be antagonistic, strained, or nonexistent. Public-spirited office-leavers give generously of their time and disinterestedly of their experience to their heirs; wise office-takers profit from their predecessors' assistance and advice.

At the Presidential level in 1952 formal correctness faintly disguised outright hostility. The warm personal relations that had once existed between Truman and Eisenhower fell victim to partisanship, blunt talk, and thin skin. The onus for the deterioration falls on Truman. In August, Truman invited Eisenhower and Stevenson for a White House briefing, which Eisenhower, evidently fearing a political trap, courteously declined. Rather than let the matter rest, Truman wrote Eisenhower that he had simply intended a continuation of bipartisan foreign policy. "Partisan politics should stop at the boundaries of the United States," Truman admonished Eisenhower, "I am extremely sorry that you have allowed a bunch of screwballs to come between us. You have made a bad mistake and I'm hoping it won't injure this great Republic." To a soldier like Eisenhower the suggestion that he might hurt his country was an insult, and Truman, who hated nothing more than to have his own patriotism impugned, should have known better. Displaying greater self-control and style, Eisenhower wrote back by hand thanking Truman for the courtesy of his note.[21]

Things got worse during the fall. The Republicans ran harder against Truman and his Secretary of State Dean Acheson than they did against Stevenson. Truman was angered in particular by Republican exploitation of the Korean war and by Eisenhower's failure to defend George Marshall in Wisconsin. At the same time, he prided himself on his administrative conscientiousness and had felt deprived of adequate briefing when he suddenly became President upon Franklin D. Roosevelt's death. His anger and his desire to effectuate an orderly transfer manifested themselves in his congratulatory telegram to Eisenhower on the morning after the election. He said he was required to present the 1954 budget to Congress before January 15 and advised Eisenhower to have a representative meet with the Director of the Budget Bureau immediately. He then offered Eisenhower the Presidential airplane "if you still desire to go to Korea." Truman's insulting implication infuriated Eisenhower, but he responded cordially in declining the offer of a plane—any suitable military transport would be satisfactory to him. Truman cabled back immediately, this time without insult, inviting Eisenhower to the White House in the near future "to discuss the problem of this transition period, so that it may be clear that this nation is united in its struggle for freedom and peace."[22]

On November 18 Eisenhower, accompanied by Lodge and Dodge, met with Truman and some of his Cabinet officers in the White House. Truman recorded in his diary that when Eisenhower first came into his office "he had a chip on his shoulder." Truman wrote that he told Eisenhower that he was only interested in having an orderly transfer. When Truman offered him certain pictures and a globe, Eisenhower seemed to him curt and ungracious. Eisenhower asked if Truman had a chief of staff. No, Truman replied; although John Steelman coordinated differences between Cabinet officers, they were free to see him at any time. Truman then offered advice on staff functioning. "I think all this went into one ear and out the other," he reflected. Then he took Eisenhower to the Cabinet Room for a briefing on Korea and foreign affairs. "Gen. Eisenhower," Truman thought, "was overwhelmed when he found what he faced." In his memoir Eisenhower wrote that "this meeting added little to my knowledge, nor did it affect my planning for the new administration, but I did thank the President sincerely for his cooperation."[23]

Secretary of State Acheson briefed Eisenhower on pressing foreign issues, mainly Korea, Iran, the European Defense Community, and Southeast Asia. Acheson was particularly concerned about Korean negotiations. He feared an Indian plan for creating a commission to deal with the problem of prisoner repatriation that was winning support among our allies. (Approximately 83,000 North Korean and Chinese prisoners of war did not want to return home.) He hoped Eisenhower would agree to a joint statement on the "utmost importance to preserve the principle that prisoners of war shall not be forcibly repatriated," but Eisenhower did not want to have his hands tied. The communiqué simply said that Truman and Eisenhower were cooperating, but that the Constitution required the incumbent to "exercise his functions until he leaves office, and his successor cannot be asked to share or assume the responsibilities of the Presidency until he takes office." No substance appeared in the statement; even an assertion about the need to preserve our allies' confidence was removed. The next day, however, Eisenhower authorized Senator Alexander Wiley, ranking Republican on the Foreign Relations Committee and a delegate to the United Nations, to say that he favored the principle of "non-forcible repatriation."[24]

Liaison between the Truman and Eisenhower staffs was also limited. Adams spent a little time at the White House at John Steelman's invitation. Steelman even allowed Adams and his assistant for operations Roger Steffan to begin making changes in office layout, but when Truman heard the carpenters he asked what was going on. When he was told, Adams recalled, he cursed and reminded everyone that he was running the Executive Branch until January 20, not the damned Republicans. It was only after the inauguration that Adams discovered that the career White House staff, such as the clerks and ushers, were totally reliable sources on operations and procedures, making Steffan somewhat superfluous. Steelman himself stayed on after the inauguration for several months as a consultant on procedures, but it was was an arrangement that neither Adams nor Steelman remembered positively. Adams recalled Steelman's briefings on certain aspects of White House operations as useful, but in general thought it had been a mistake to keep him. Steelman reflected that a holdover either has to get out after a few weeks or stay permanently and be taken in as a full member.[25]

Liaison within the departments and agencies varied widely. At the Budget Bureau it proceeded extremely well. Joseph Dodge had considerable government experience and was concerned about how to get things done in Washington. He was respected not only by Eisenhower, but by Truman. Within days of his designation, he was attending Budget Bureau sessions. Truman's people and the civil servants at the Bureau hid nothing from him. He listened to all the deliberations that were occuring between the Bureau and the various agencies and departments over the makeup of Truman's last budget. This gave Dodge invaluable information about current fiscal matters while bolstering his confidence in the professionalism of the career officers, with whom he developed an excellent relationship. The Bureau staff took pride in the fact that two months after Truman's budget was submitted to Congress they substantially revised it in accordance with instructions from Eisenhower and Dodge. In the process, any remaining political suspicions of the Budget Bureau were allayed and Dodge retained its professionals. He also named a deputy and three assistant directors who shared his predisposition to work easily with career officials. Morale remained high at the Bureau and Eisenhower's interests were well served.[26]

The Budget Bureau also provided incoming Cabinet and agency heads with useful briefings which sometimes headed off potential problems and misunderstandings. For example, the Bureau informed Sinclair Weeks that both parties were committed to the St. Lawrence seaway and that Congress looked to the Secretary of Commerce to provide leadership on it. Weeks, however, was on record against the project; that was going to create problems for him. With good humor, Weeks acknowledged the dilemma, dropped his opposition, and set the department's wheels in motion for preparing legislation to create the seaway, which proved to be an early legislative accomplishment of the Eisenhower administration.[27]

Liaison at the Treasury Department also went smoothly. George Humphrey had complete freedom to name his top subordinates, and he wasted no time in naming several businessmen and lawyers with whom he was well acquainted and who were familiar with Washington and with the issues they would attempt to manage. By early December they were in the capital, preparing for the takeover. Humphrey and his subordinates knew and trusted the incumbent Treasury Secretary John Snyder and had confidence in what he told them. They also regarded the principal civil servants as trustworthy and competent. Although some difficult dealings with Congress lay ahead, a cohesive Treasury team was formed early, strengthened by effective liaison with incumbent officials.[28]

Liaison at the State Department was not as successful. On the one hand, Dulles personally knew many of the department's top personnel, from Acheson on down. The State Department made an office available to him and Acheson kept him informed, though they met only briefly. Dulles sought Acheson's views on the appointment of a High Commissioner for Germany and followed Acheson's advice against naming a certain career officer to that post. Dulles also asked David K. E. Bruce, Acheson's Under Secretary, for his general appraisals of people, and Bruce stayed on for several weeks after the inauguration to assist him. Dulles talked as well to numerous other officials, including Assistant Secretaries and returning ambassadors.[29]

On the other hand, in a foretaste of Dulle's conduct of the office he was about to assume, it was a top-heavy operation. Caring only about policy, Dulles abhorred administration. At the same time, he lacked a facility for picking good administrators to work under him, and he was a reluctant delegator besides. In effect, he did not want to administer the State Department, but he jealously guarded his powers, making it difficult for anyone else to administer it either. Two further keys to understanding Dulle's conduct of office are that he believed the Secretary of State should be the President's counselor or lawyer on foreign affairs and therefore must maintain the President's confidence and that a Secretary of State could not afford to alienate Congressional or public opinion. He had witnessed his uncle, Secretary of State Robert Lansing, lose the confidence of President Woodrow Wilson, and he had observed Dean Acheson's loss of Congressional confidence over internal security matters. He was determined not to let a similar fate befall him.[30]

For unknown reasons, Dulles and Eisenhower (and here it is interesting to note that Eisenhower was involved in making higher echelon State Department appointments) did not fill the Under Secretary's position until January and then they divided the job in two, naming General Walter Bedell Smith Under Secretary and Donald B. Lourie Under Secretary for Administration. Smith had been Eisenhower's chief of staff during the war and he was now CIA Director. He was close to Eisenhower, and Dulles apparently welcomed the appointment for that reason and because he hoped Smith would relieve him of administrative duties. Smith's appointment also freed up the CIA directorship, which Eisenhower gave to Allen Dulles, then a deputy director and Foster's younger brother. Dulles never was comfortable with Smith's desire to be his chief of staff through whom everything would be screened, and Smith resigned his post within a year.[31]

Lourie, who was president of the Quaker Oats Company, initially declined to serve because, as he told Dulles, he knew nothing about foreign relations. Dulles, who had not known Lourie before, reassured him that he would not have to know anything about foreign relations, that he was hiring him simply to reorganize the department and to remove the many operational bureaus that had been accumulating within it. In his year as Under Secretary, Lourie achieved some success in carrying out this mandate, but he also committed foolish errors reflecting his political innocence and his ignorance of Washington and the State Department. He hired Scott McLeod to administer the department's internal security program, which proved to be a poor appointment. In order to reduce expenses, he tried to disallow the use of the diplomatic pouch for personal mail by Foreign Service employees, which would have had the effect of allowing all mail in Moscow to be read by Soviet officials.[32]

Lourie's innocence of the jungles of Washington is illustrated by a story that one of Dulles's personal assistants later told. Right after the first staff meeting, Bedell Smith invited Lourie in for a cup of coffee. "One lump, please," replied Lourie. "Here," said Smith. "Now, Lourie, I want you to be very clear on just one thing. There's only one Under Secretary in this Department! Is that clear?" "Yes, sir," Lourie meekly responded.[33]

Dulles named a small group of retired Foreign Service officers to recommend high-level career appointments. In principle it was a good idea, but the group had not been close to the Foreign Service for many years. They were so far out of date that two of the people they recommended turned out to be dead. The top appointments and diplomatic posts generally went to seasoned diplomats, lawyers, and businessmen. Two appointees Dulles relied heavily on were fellow lawyers: Robert Bowie, who came from the Harvard law faculty to direct policy planning; and Herman Phleger, a prominent San Francisco lawyer, who became the department's legal adviser. The politically sensitive position of Assistant Secretary for the Far East went to Walter Robertson, a Richmond banker with Chinese experience and a devotion to Chiang.[34]

Liaison between officials at the Defense Department and their replacements left much to be desired. Although Charles Wilson had no government experience, he was a supremely confident industrialist who believed that GM's organizational principles of decentralized operations and centralized policy and control could be readily transposed to the Defense Department. Wilson met only cursorily with Lovett. Roger Kyes, whom he brought from GM as his Deputy Secretary, turned a deaf ear to his counterpart William C. Foster's advice—perhaps not even knowing that Eisenhower had great confidence in Foster—and he later swept out Foster's entire staff indiscriminately. Lovett suggested that if they did retain anyone, it should be the comptroller, which they did, but in reorganizing the department in their first year they placed several "vice presidents" above him and therefore lost out on his unique understanding of their budget.

Working out of a Washington hotel room, Wilson and Kyes summoned Assistant Secretaries and others before them for information and appraisal. In the end they retained several incumbents but they also let go of several they should have kept. Historically, the Defense Department and its predecessor, the War Department, had a shortage of high-ranking civilian officials, so Wilson and Kyes were inadvertently placing themselves even more at the mercy of the many military officers whose first loyalty lay with their individual services, not with the department. The service secretaries meanwhile were chosen by Eisenhower, Clay, and Brownell, though Wilson was given veto power over these appointments, which he apparently did not exercise. The whole process did not bode well for Eisenhower's desired goals of economy and unification in the military.[35]

Incumbent officials in Defense and elsewhere prepared briefing books for their successors which varied in usefulness. New officials also benefitted from studies done by independent sources, particularly from reports prepared under John Corson's supervision by McKinsey and Company, a management consulting firm. These reports, which had been commissioned in May by Harold Talbott, a businessman who became Secretary of the Air Force, informed appointees about the positions they could fill under them, usually only a small fraction of the jobs in their department of agency. Many of the expenses of the Eisenhower transition, much of which was quartered at the Commodore Hotel in New York and had a staff of about 120 people, were borne by the Republican National Committee. Wealthy new officials also sometimes paid expenses out of their own pockets.[36]

In early December, Eisenhower vindicated his dramatic campaign pledge by visiting Korea for three days. Great care was taken to keep the visit secret until after he had safely left Korea so as to minimize the risk of assassination. It "was one of the few secrets of any consequence that I know of that was ever kept," remarked Wilton Persons, his friend and aide who accompanied him. On the other hand, the visit was extremely well publicized just as soon as it was over. "We found ourselves preparing one elaborate plan to safeguard the President-elect," Mark W. Clark, the American UN commander recalled, "and another to help the press corps tell the world about every phase of his visit."[37]

Eisenhower received numerous briefings, visited troops, observed forward positions, saw his son John, an officer, and got a better feel for the immediate problems of fighting there. Field commanders told him that if negotiations did not succeed fairly soon, Eisenhower recalled, "our only recourse would eventually be to mount an all-out attack regardless of the risks." "Under the circumstances of the moment," he further reflected, "decisions of this kind could not even be made; but discussion was valuable. My conclusion as I left Korea was that we could not stand forever on a static front and continue to accept casualities without any visible results. Small attacks on small hills would not end this war."[38]

For Clark, however, Eisenhower's visit had a further meaning. Clark had prepared a detailed estimate of what would be required to obtain a military victory should the new administration decide to seek one. "To me the most significant thing about the visit of the President-elect was that I never had the opportunity to present this estimate for his consideration. The question of how much it would take to win the war was never raised," Clark wrote. "It soon became apparent, in our many conversations, that he would seek an honorable truce." Clark apparently did not know that in his briefing at the Pentagon several weeks before, Eisenhower had been offered two options: let the war drag on as before or seek a military victory by conventional means. Eisenhower had declared both options "intolerable." As Persons observed, the trip merely reinforced Eisenhower's view that the war had to be ended as quickly as possible and in an honorable way. The trip simply redeemed an important campaign pledge which could not have been dropped. Eisenhower's cautious public statements on Korea meanwhile reassured America's allies of his prudence.[39]

Eisenhower's cautiousness manifested itself in his relations with South Korean President Syngman Rhee, who wanted victory over his Communist foes, not peace with them. Eisenhower avoided the large public demonstrations and meetings that Rhee planned for him. He had only two brief courtesy calls with Rhee, who even then warned Eisenhower that anything short of throwing the Communists out of Korea would store up woe for future generations. Rhee also showed himself adept at publicity. Late in the afternoon of Eisenhower's departure, Clark informed Rhee that Eisenhower would come by at 5:45 p.m. for a few minutes to return Rhee's call and say goodbye. When Eisenhower arrived at the appointed time, he was subjected to large crowds of officials and many photographers. After many introductions, handshakes, and photographs, Eisenhower left the house. "But he didn't get away from ceremony that easily," Clark recalled. Outside "were huge floodlights, an ROK Army, Navy and Air Force Honor Guard, bands and photographers. It looked like a Hollywood opening night. Rhee had really laid it on." The lesson was there, though there is no indication that Eisenhower drew it, that Rhee would become a very formidable opponent of the peace he sought.[40]

After flying to Guam, Eisenhower transferred to the cruiser *Helena*. He had been accompanied in Korea by Wilson, Brownell, and three of his own aides. Near Wake Island, Wilson flew on to Hawaii for consultations, and a helicopter delivered other guests aboard ship, Dulles, Humphrey and McKay, Dodge and Clay, and speech writers C. D. Jackson and Emmet Hughes. For three days until they landed in Hawaii, they held concentrated discussions about what they should do about such pressing problems as appointments, getting control over the budget, and wage and price controls. Occasionally they took time out for skeet-shooting and swimming. It was a unique opportunity for all aboard to get to know one another. "By the time we finished that trip," Humphrey later recalled, "we knew each other pretty well and knew pretty well what each of us thought and what each of the others thought about the things we were about to do." (The only other President-elect to have a retreat for new Cabinet officers was Jimmy Carter).[41]

During Eisenhower's visit to Korea, Douglas MacArthur gave a speech in which he said he had a plan to end the war which he would be willing to give to Eisenhower. The speech prompted discussion on the *Helena* as to how Eisenhower should respond. Eisenhower did not like his former boss, but some of his advisers urged him to see MacArthur for political reasons. MacArthur after all remained an important spokesman for military victory in Asia. (In January 1953 a Gallup poll indicated that Americans admired him second only to Eisenhower among all living persons.) Swallowing his pride, Eisenhower cabled MacArthur that he would like to meet with him. The only cost of such a meeting was a further deterioration in Eisenhower's relations with Truman. When word of Eisenhower's cable was released, Truman revived his campaign charge that Eisenhower's trip was demagoguery and announced that "if anyone has a reasonable plan for ending the Korean fighting in an honorable way, in a way that will not lead directly to a great war, that plan should be presented at once to the President. If we can cut this fighting short by one day we should do so."[42]

Shortly after returning to New York, Eisenhower and Dulles got together with MacArthur at Dulles's home. MacArthur proposed that Eisenhower meet with Soviet Premier Josef Stalin to discuss Korea and the world situation. At this conference, MacArthur suggested, the President should warn Stalin that if Korea were not reunited under a form of government to be popularly determined, it would be our intention to clear North Korea of enemy forces, which could be accomplished through atomic bombing, the sowing of a radioactive strip, and amphibious landings in the North. Stalin should also be informed that in such an eventuality "it would probably become necessary to neutralize Red China's capability to wage modern war," which he optimistically forecast "could be accomplished by the destruction of Red China's limited airfields and industrial and supply basis, the cutting of her tenuous supply lines from the Soviet Union and the landing of China's Nationalist forces in Manchuria near the mouth of the Yalu, with limited continuing logistical support until such time as the communist government has fallen."[43]

Eisenhower later privately recounted listening in silence to MacArthur, then commenting that if the United States was going to extend the war, it would need its allies' consent. Eisenhower recalled Dulles afterward telling him that he was certain that we were fighting only to assure the integrity of South Korea, not to reunite the Koreans. In his memoir Eisenhower both endorsed the idea of an atomic threat and enumerated reasons for not using atomic weapons, including the risk of a wider war and our allies' opposition. It seems clear that Eisenhower entered office with two minds about nuclear threats. The ambivalence manifested itself in his first months as President and endured into his post-Presidential explanation of how the Korean armistice was achieved.[44]

Within a week of seeing MacArthur, Eisenhower met with another onetime superior, former President Herbert Hoover. "One of the men I've admired extravagantly is Herbert Hoover," Eisenhower recorded in his diary the previous year, but on account of Hoover's isolationism and fortress-America concept he had been "forced to believe he's getting senile." At their preinaugural conference, they discussed, not foreign policy, but the less controversial issue of government reorganization, about which Eisenhower had already appointed a three-man committee consisting of his brother Milton, Arthur Flemming, and Nelson Rockefeller. Like the MacArthur conference, this meeting demonstrated Eisenhower's willingness to confer with various Republican spokesmen. It may well have been at this time, not soon after the inauguration as Eisenhower reports in his memoir, that Hoover warned him that he would be caught between groups wanting new welfare programs and others wanting a rollback. "All you can do," Eisenhower quoted Hoover, "is to try to turn away gradually from the path leading to paternalism, until it takes a central course, and then stick with it. And both sides will dislike you." Eisenhower told Hoover he understood and "expressed the hope that occassionally he would have an admonitory word for those who were not so understanding as he."[45]

In early January, Eisenhower met with another elder statesman, this one returned to power the previous year, Prime Minister Winston Churchill of Great Britain. The meeting with Churchill was not unusual in that Eisenhower and Dulles had also seen other foreign officials, including ones from Mexico, Brazil, Australia, and India.

Some of these meetings included substantive talk. For example, when he saw Anthony Eden, Britain's Foreign Secretary, in November, Eisenhower indicated his support for British opposition to that country's immediate entry into the pending European Defense Community. In doing so, Eisenhower effectively reversed Truman administration policy, though he apparently failed to inform Acheson and Truman of the fact. On the Indian plan for prisoner repatriation in Korea, Eden in his memoirs reported Eisenhower to be "guarded" but "helpful." Here, too, it appears that Eisenhower steered his own course and hardly upheld Truman policy against the Indian resolution.[46]

Churchill and Eisenhower had worked closely and well together during the war, and Churchill evidently hoped to parlay their friendship into a special partnership between the two countries. Eisenhower, however, kept his distance. He believed that when it was in our interest to have prior understandings with the British, we should do so, such as in our Asian problems, but even in those cases it would be better to "treat, publicly, every country as a sovereign equal." "To do otherwise," Eisenhower confided to his diary, "would arouse resentment and damage the understandings we are trying to promote." He assured Churchill that he stood ready to communicate with him personally, but said that official agreements would have to be made through normal channels. He also emphasized to him the importance of European cohesion, and he criticized recent United States-British efforts to settle a serious British-Iranian dispute.

Eisenhower probably correctly suspected Churchill of trying to recreate the personal diplomacy of the war when Churchill and Roosevelt had tried to rule the world from "some rather Olympian platform." "In the present international complexities," Eisenhower reflected, "any hope of establishing such a relationship is completely fatuous," because nationalism was on the march, exploited by world Communism for all it was worth. "Much as I hold Winston in my personal affection and much as I admire him for his past accomplishments and leadership," Eisenhower observed, "I wish that he would turn over leadership of the British Conservative party to younger men."

Clearly, Eisenhower was right at home in international diplomacy, which he began conducting in a limited way before taking office. Clearly, too, despite all Churchill's hopes, United States–British relations would not fit neatly into place under Eisenhower. On the other hand, the leaders' hopes and friendship and their

nations' alliance and similar cultures may have prevented Eisenhower and Churchill from openly acknowledging and discussing
differences that would only grow in the next several years. Apparently Eisenhower saved his frankest words for his diary.[47]

Problems with Congress were variously prevented, neglected,
and sown during the weeks immediately preceding the inauguration. Wisely, Eisenhower remained nominally neutral as House and
Senate Republicans chose their leaders. In the Senate this meant
doing nothing to stand in the way of Taft's selection as majority
leader. Taft posed obvious dangers to Eisenhower, and his charac-
terization of Durkin's selection as "incredible" made some of the
President-elect's allies wonder about his loyalty in the future. But to
have opposed Taft would have meant certain trouble. Congress
resents Presidential interference in its own affairs, and opposing
Taft would have exacerbated the party's internal rift and would
have probably failed anyway. It was better to accept the inevitable
and hope for the best.

Eisenhower had an early opportunity to demonstrate his good
faith. Taft asked Frank Carlson of Kansas, one of Eisenhower's best
Senate friends, to ascertain Eisenhower's opinion prior to Taft's declaration of candidacy. After talking with Eisenhower, Carlson called
a press conference and endorsed Taft, leaving the implication that
Eisenhower did, too. Even before his formal selection, Taft demonstrated his loyalty by promising to do all in his power to have the
Senate quickly confirm Eisenhower's Cabinet designees, including
Durkin. Before long Eisenhower was relying on Taft and regarding
him as a friend, though differences in viewpoint endured.[48]

Eisenhower disliked such practices as dispensing patronage appointments and giving legislators the authority to block appointees
from their own states, but he reluctantly accepted the inevitable
here as well. He wanted to work with Congress and with his party,
not reform them. In December he conferred with Congressional and
party leaders, with the dominant themes being harmony and cooperation. He also created the first substantial Congressional liaison
office in the White House. Yet, from the start, many Congressional
leaders were unimpressed with Eisenhower's devotion to such tasks.
Leverett Saltonstall of Massachusetts, the GOP Senate whip, later
told of the time that House Speaker Joe Martin, also of Massachusetts, said in Eisenhower's presence that the only patronage request
he had made was a postmastership in a small town in his district,
and it was disregarded.[49]

A Congressional liaison oversight at this time caused difficulty in the months ahead. Although Eisenhower met with many Congressional leaders, he failed to see Daniel A. Reed of New York. After long service in the House, Reed was about to become chairman of the powerful, tax-writing Ways and Means Committee. When Marion Folsom, the new Deputy Secretary of the Treasury, first talked to Reed he realized that he was peeved at not being invited to see Eisenhower. Reed proceeded independently to introduce a general tax reduction bill, which had the honor of being listed H. R. 1. Undoubtedly his motive was not merely pique, for he believed that Democrats had made taxes excessively high. In principle, Eisenhower and his financial advisors agreed, but their first priority was reduction of the projected budget deficit. Tax reduction would, in their view, have to follow deficit reduction. This was the start of a protracted battle with Reed over taxes, in which Eisenhower did not prevail until July. The battle might have been avoided or at least toned down by elementary staff work during the transition, such as having Eisenhower simply see Reed.[50]

Eisenhower's failure to develop a substantial legislative program constituted a significant strategic error. Without a Presidentially backed program to keep it busy, Congress found it much easier in 1953 to get into controversial, negative, or largely symbolic issues in which the Eisenhower administration often found itself in holding actions, trying to prevent a weakening of the Presidency or a repudiation of existing foreign policies. There is no telling what would have happened had Eisenhower presented a positive legislative program. Given strong partisan feelings on such issues as the Yalta resolutions and the Bricker amendment and given Congressional Republican customs of attacking the executive branch, long held by the Democrats, perhaps the 1953 Congressional session would have turned out the same. On the other hand, Eisenhower did assume office with a great personal mandate which might have been translated into effective leadership on the Hill for a Presidential program—if he had one. The opportunity, at least, existed, but Eisenhower failed to seize it.

The reasons were several. In his newness to politics, Eisenhower was naïve about what was likely to happen if Congress were left to its own devices. He entered office as well with a very traditional notion of the separation of powers and did not believe that a President should press Congress too much. In addition, the Republicans were against certain world developments and domestic trends that had occurred during Democratic administrations and they had built the GOP platform around these positions. Eisenhower, once again the newcomer to politics, felt obligated to carry out campaign promises. Several months later he had discovered how mischievous some of these promises were to his own conduct of office. With his party having been out of power for so long, Eisenhower intended "to use 1953 largely as a period of study and formulation of programs." "We have always felt," he wrote his brother Milton in November of that year, "that the 'Administration Bible' would be brought out for publication in the 1954 Message to the Congress."

In early 1953 Eisenhower had not decided what problems, if any, the federal government should be doing more to solve. Here he soon discovered that his erstwhile and purportedly more conservative foe, Robert Taft, in fact had more "liberal" views than his own. The one thing Eisenhower was adamantly for was a balanced budget, but Dodge early gave him pessimistic reports on the outlook for achieving one. Projected deficits of $10 billion were anathema to Eisenhower, yet many parts of the budget had already been appropriated or involved largely uncontrollable obligations such as debt service and military spending. The budget had relatively little "give" in it, which is why Eisenhower was forced to oppose tax reductions initially even though the Republican platform had also called for them.[51]

All this may seem to justify Eisenhower's failure to produce a legislative program, but it does not, for his inaction gave right-wing forces in Congress far too much leeway to pursue their own agenda. Under the circumstances, almost any Presidential program would have been better than none. Indeed, Eisenhower might even have been better off taking the leadership for a program of reaction, so as better to control it. But since his own views tended toward the center, he should have led Congress in that direction from the outset. He might, for example, have sought Congressional authorization for the kinds of housing and education programs that Taft favored, while deferring appropriations for such programs until budget deficits were eliminated. At least he should have patched together the various legislative requests his administration did make in its first several months, label it *his* program, and implore Congress to give it top priority.

A week before his inauguration, Eisenhower held two preliminary Cabinet meetings at the Commodore. At the first he read a draft of his inaugural address and was greeted by an ovation. Eisenhower told the Cabinet that he had read the speech for its criticisms, not applause. Although his listeners gradually offered minor suggestions and criticisms, the meeting was marked by Eisenhower's dominance. Only

Charles Wilson demonstrated the personal force to challenge Eisenhower in a discussion of trade with the Communists, though Eisenhower had much the better of the argument. Like the Cabinet meetings that were to take place with great regularity in the years ahead, major parts of the discussion, such as one involving the Congressional role in government reorganization, could have been just as easily conducted by smaller subgroups. For an administration that took pride in its businesslike efficiency, Cabinet meetings were, from the start, generally inefficient forums of communication and seldom instruments of decision making or implementation. They gave policy making the appearance of being planned and corporate, when in fact it was often ad hoc and proprietary.[52]

Several days before the inauguration on January 20, Charles Wilson ran into confirmation difficulties at the Senate Armed Services Committee when he refused to sell his stock in General Motors, which did a lot of business with the Defense Department. Wilson resisted selling his shares because of the large capital-gains taxes he would have to pay, but the committee was concerned about a possible conflict of interest. It came as a surprise to Eisenhower that opposition to Wilson came not just from partisan Democrats, but from Republicans and from Harry Byrd of Virginia, a conservative Democrat who had supported Eisenhower's election. Wilson's problems derived in large part from his style, for he had a predilection for lecturing to Congress. By contrast, George Humphrey, who also owned stock in companies where there was a potential conflict of interest, handled his hearings with finesse and did not dispose of any of his stock. Two days after the inauguration, Wilson finally agreed to sell his stock, after Eisenhower personally insisted.[53]

When Wilson's confirmation hearings were released, they contained a passage that quickly became a major public-relations blunder. Wilson was asked whether he would make a decision adverse to GM, and he replied that he had long "thought what was good for the country was good for General Motors and vice versa." For years afterward Wilson's gaffe was compounded by misquotation into "what is good for General Motors is good for the country." Still, opponents of the Eisenhower administration would not have had a field day with Wilson's remarks if he had not provided the field. Lodge's initial estimate of Wilson's inability to handle Congressional and public relations received early confirmation. Elie Abel, a reporter who covered the Pentagon in 1953, recalled how the press had a friendly, joshing relationship with Wilson. "Certain of the newsmen would frame the most outrageous comments and ask, did he agree or disagree." Very often he would agree and the newspapers would have another headline. "It wasn't malicious," Abel reflected. "It was on the whole a kindly, almost warm personal relationship. It was perfectly obvious the man had no sophistication and shouldn't have been there really."[54]

Although Eisenhower placed his own holdings in a blind, irrevocable trust while he was President, he did not require his subordinates to do likewise. Apparently legal advisers did not deem it necessary, and business appointees who were used to controlling their assets resisted such a course. But the episode should have demonstrated that conflicts of interest posed serious political problems, particularly for an administration heavily populated by businessmen. Eisenhower, who was prepared to believe the best about his appointees' ethics, dismissed too easily the doubts of Congressmen. He feared that the application of an extreme standard would result in Washington jobs going exclusively to "business failures, college professors, and New Deal lawyers," all of whom "would jump at the chance to get a job that a successful businessman has to sacrifice very much to take." As things turned out, Eisenhower's faith in his appointees' ethics did on several occasions prove misplaced. Conflict-of-interest controversies, moreover, plagued his administration; the Wilson case was merely the first. They involved significant legal, ethical, and public relations issues which Eisenhower, from the beginning, showed a reluctance to manage and resolve.[55]

Inauguration day was bright and sunny, in contrast to the Eisenhower-Truman relationship, which had become a feud. Eisenhower avoided the ritual of going into the White House to meet the outgoing President, and he declined Truman's invitation to lunch. Custom decreed that they ride down Pennsylvania Avenue together to the Capitol for the swearing-in. In his diary for that day, Truman recalled Eisenhower's saying that the Secretary of the Army tried to order him home in 1948 for Truman's inaugural but Eisenhower would not come "because half the people cheering me at that time had told him they were for him." Truman shot back: "Ike I didn't ask you to come—or you'd been here." "The only comment of any consequence that I can recall," Eisenhower wrote in *his* account, "was asking the President the identity of the person who had ordered my son back from the combat area to be present at the inauguration. The President replied, 'I did,' and I thanked him sincerely for his thoughtfulness." Truman was never invited to the

White House while Eisenhower was President, and this was their last conversation until they were ex-Presidents and the feud was ended.[56]

Eisenhower worked over and worried about his Inaugural Address considerably. It was not a great speech. Although Eisenhower was more articulate and cared more about words than is often thought, he was never an outstanding speaker. His popularity always rested less on how he sounded or on what he said, than on who he was, what he did, and even how he looked—he was a handsome man with a radiant smile. The speech began with a prayer, written by Eisenhower alone at the last moment, and the speech concentrated almost exclusively on the international situation, the struggle between good and evil, free and Communist. "Freedom is pitted against slavery," he declared, "lightness against dark."

Peace was the responsibility of statesmanship, asserted Eisenhower, and it could be achieved through sufficient strength to deter aggression. At the same time, he stood "ready to engage with any and all others in joint effort to remove the causes of mutual fear and distrust among nations, so as to make possible drastic reduction in armaments." He emphasized the importance of religious faith, of individualism, and of economic health, and he called upon his fellow citizens to accept sacrifices to protect their liberty. "We must be ready to dare all for our country," he declared. "We must be willing, individually and as a Nation, to accept whatever sacrifices may be required of us." It is interesting to note that eight years later John F. Kennedy would voice almost identical views in his Inaugural Address. Kennedy was the more forceful speaker and his words the more eloquent and stirring, but the two speeches read side by side reflect how little American views of the world changed in the 1950s.[57]

The opening prayer and Eisenhower's emphasis on religious faith indicated that his adminstration would place significant emphasis on civic piety. Although there is no reason to doubt Eisenhower's sincerity at the moment he started this trend, there are signs that the mixture of religion and politics did not always sit easily with him. He formally joined a church (Presbyterian) for the first time when he became President. "We were scarcely home before the fact was being publicized, by the pastor, to the hilt," he fumed in his diary. The pastor had promised him there would be no publicity, and Eisenhower felt like changing to another church within the denomination. Eisenhower also established the practice of having a silent prayer start each Cabinet meeting. Once, however, his Cabinet secretary slipped him a note reminding him that the prayer had been overlooked. "Oh, goddammit," Eisenhower exclaimed, "we forgot the silent prayer."[58]

Eisenhower probably experienced less of a jolt at actually becoming President than most other modern Presidents have. As he noted in his diary after his first full day at the desk: "Plenty of worries and difficult problems. But such has been my position for a long time—the result is that this just seems (today) like a continuation of all I've been doing since July 1941—even before that." Yet not even Eisenhower went unaffected. "There had been dramatic events in my life before—but none surpassed, emotionally, crossing the threshold to an office of such awesome responsibility," he wrote in his memoir. When Omar Bradley, one of his oldest and closest friends, addressed him over the phone as "Mr. President," he felt a sense of separation from friends. The loneliness of command exceeded his wartime experience.[59]

Although at times Eisenhower felt alone, he, in fact, sustained an impressive number of friendships as President, many with people outside Washington (usually from business or the military) and several with current officeholders, such as George Humphrey and Robert Cutler. His brother Milton was his confidant and also played a significant role as an adviser, both unofficially and officially. Milton, a former government official who was president of Pennsylvania State University in 1953 (and later of Johns Hopkins University), spent many weekends at the White House. Eisenhower often revealed his private feelings and thoughts in letters to trusted friends and to his brothers. In addition, he spent time with close friends who shared his love of golf, fishing, and bridge.[60]

At the very start of his administration, Eisenhower disposed of the Presidential yacht, the *Williamsburg,* and gave up Presidential quarters the Navy maintained in Key West, Florida. Truman had used them as escapes and Eisenhower wanted a public display of his own commitment to "economy, bordering on or approaching austerity," as he explained to one of his oldest friends. Even though he recognized their importance, he felt they symbolized "luxury in the public mind that would tend to defeat some of the purposes I was trying to accomplish." "I have kept only the camp up in the Catoctins," which he renamed Camp David after his only grandson. "Shangri-La" (FDR's name for it), he wrote, was "just a little fancy for a Kansas farm boy."

Yet Eisenhower evidently soon regretted these economy moves

because they made it harder to escape the White House, at least at first. During a May weekend he spent trying to relax and fish with Milton in State College, Pennsylvania, he was constantly scrutinized and interrupted. Afterward his military aide asked about the trip, and he replied that he could understand why the *Williamsburg* had been kept around. The private retreats of rich friends, the Augusta National Golf Club, and eventually a farm he acquired in Gettysburg, Pennsylvania, filled the void left by his rejection of Presidential perquisites. Later, Eisenhower's golfing became a public-relations problem for him. (Presidents need to get away and to relax, but they must not appear to get away too often or to relax too much.)[61]

Eisenhower entered office determined to improve White House efficiency. For him that meant having a staff system that carried out his orders and kept less important problems away from him, while gathering information on more important ones. On inauguration day, the chief White House usher was surprised when Eisenhower upbraided him for delivering a sealed envelope. "Never bring me a sealed envelope," he reportedly said, "that's what I've got aides for." Eisenhower preferred oral briefings to written ones, and he disliked doing business over the phone, often delegating that task to a staff member. Although Eisenhower was reluctant to acknowledge it, Adams controlled the flow of Cabinet members into the Oval office. Dulles successfully challenged Adam's authority at the outset, and Humphrey learned to get around Adams by going through another office, but Eisenhower's allowance of these exceptions only confirmed his tacit approval of Adams's more usual role.[62]

The system naturally required time to shake down. "It took a while for some members of the Cabinet and other high-ranking government executives to accept me as a spokesman of Eisenhower's viewpoints," Adams later wrote, but after a year the President felt he had reached that position. In the administration's early months, Adams held frequent staff meetings and went over a variety of concerns, from office deportment to assignments. By contrast, Truman had conducted his own staff meetings. But the White House operated less rigidly, and Adams was less powerful than sometimes appeared. Adams could not, for example, ward off unwanted pressure on Eisenhower that came in personal meetings with people; nor did he play a large role in the national security or foreign policy areas. To Eisenhower's benefit, Adams did become a whipping-boy, safer to attack than the President himself. Right-wing Republicans eventually accused Adams of insulating the President from the Republican organization, of establishing, in Joe McCarthy's phrase, a "palace guard."[63]

Eisenhower entered office with an enormous reservoir of popular good will which he did nothing to dissipate in his first six months in office. Indeed, he left the White House eight years later with his popularity largely intact, a feat unmatched by any President since Franklin D. Roosevelt. This accomplishment has been interpreted in conflicting ways, basically either as a reflection of Eisenhower's success and acuity or of his failure to exercise genuine leadership. Thus Eisenhower either correctly understood the inherent limitations of the Presidency and carefully husbanded his reputation to bring about the things he thought most important—the "middle way," a financially solvent government, military security, and peace—or he failed to appreciate and use the Presidency's potential for good, accepting and reinforcing the status quo at home and abroad, excelling above all in knowing how to protect himself politically. Such things will be debated for years to come because the debaters themselves have widely differing premises and values and because Eisenhower made it difficult either to ascertain his motives or to know how calculated his actions were. Perhaps he was just very lucky.

Like any President, Eisenhower from the start faced hard decisions with incalculable consequences. He discovered that nothing in his vast prior experience as an executive adequately prepared him for what he now confronted. "This is because of the infinite variety of problems presented," he wrote an intimate friend in July, "and the rapidity with which they are placed in front of the responsible individual for action." Eisenhower's method was to "apply common sense—to reach an average solution." Into that average of course went certain personal attitudes and beliefs about the proper course of government. Into it, too, invariably went a multitude of other things, including "selfish interests," which Eisenhower abhorred. If the "average solutions" Eisenhower favored were not necessarily comprised of all relevant considerations or the best ones, they were widely and soundly enough based to escape popular rejection. Staying off limbs, Eisenhower clung to the trunk of politics.[64]

Eisenhower's espousal of "common sense" solutions and his avoidance of controversy help account for his high public esteem. They enhanced his preferred image of being above politics, a good soldier merely serving his country. The give and take of the electoral campaign inevitably tarnished that image, at least slightly, but his public statements during his first six months as President polished it up again. In addition to the State of the Union message, he gave only three speeches that could be categorized as major, his "Chance for Peace" speech to the American Society of Newspaper Editors, a radio address on national security, and an informal television report in which he shared the stage with four Cabinet members, Humphrey, Hobby, Benson, and Brownell. Most of his speeches were merely brief welcoming or inspirational remarks before groups in Washington or nearby. Even his rare forays outside Washington, which included several appearances before Republican groups, eschewed controversy and partisanship. His speeches were sometimes platitudinous, never fiery.

In his first six months as President, he averaged two news conferences a month. Here, too, he avoided controversy and repeatedly emphasized his common sense, nonpartisan approach to problems. At his first news conference, he expressed incredulity about speculation that he and the press would develop an antagonistic relationship. "I feel that no individual has been treated more fairly and squarely over the past many years now," he flattered the journalists, "than I have by the press. Through the war years and ever since, I have found nothing but a desire to dig at the truth, so far as I was concerned, and be open-handed and forthright about it. That is the kind of relationship I hope we can continue." The press indulged his frequent admissions of ignorance, his acknowledgments that he was still learning, and his reluctance to talk about certain subjects. Eisenhower did not dazzle the press, nor did he offend it. He respected individual journalists, and he kept his criticisms of the press—of its inaccuracy, for example—private.[65]

Eisenhower's posture and performance in office clearly pleased the public. According to a Gallup poll, his approval rating remained in the seventies during his first half-year in office. In June, Gallup found that only 16 percent of the public disapproved of anything Eisenhower had said or done thus far. The same month Gallup asked people to rate Eisenhower according to a numbering system that went from plus five at the top to minus five at the bottom. Fifty-seven percent rated him plus five, 11 percent plus four, 13 percent plus three. Only something over 3 percent rated him at negative one or below while 5 percent had no opinion. Not only did Eisenhower have many admirers among the public, he had few detractors.[66]

All newly elected Presidents come to office having made certain promises and having stood for certain beliefs. In the process of getting elected they take pains to differentiate themselves from their opponents. If their opponent is the incumbent or belongs to the incumbent's party, as has been the case whenever a nonincumbent has been elected President between 1932 and 1980, newly elected Presidents have opposed certain policies associated with their immediate predecessors. After getting elected, however, they have to decide which of their promises and beliefs to implement immediately, which to postpone temporarily, which to vitiate, and which to bury. This is necessary because new Presidents soon discover—if they did not already know—that they simply cannot do everything they said in their campaigns, certainly not immediately and possibly not ever. The responsibilities of office as well as information they acquire there force them to set limits. New Presidents have to make choices, to decide on priorities, and to control for resultant political damages when they do, because broken promises and unfulfilled commitments trigger disappointment and resentment.

Rarely do new Presidents acknowledge, even after the fact, that their policies differ from their earlier promises. Eisenhower was not that rarity. In his memoir he recounted his first meeting after becoming President with Congressional Republican leadership. "To my astonishment," he wrote, "I discovered that some of the men in the room could not seem to understand the seriousness with which I regarded our platform's provisions, and were amazed by my uncompromising assertion that I was going to do my best to fulfill every promise to which I had been a party." If Eisenhower truly believed that he could or did carry out every promise, he was fooling himself and may have been causing himself unnecessary difficulty. In practice, of course, he, like any President, made choices and watered down, delayed, or abandoned certain promises. Evaluating his choices from the incomparable advantage of hindsight, some of them appear excellent, others good or indifferent, and still others poor.[67]

Eisenhower was persuaded to spell out his policies in detail and in person before Congress. The occasion was his State of the Union Address on February 2. In his diary that day he recorded his misgivings: "I feel it a mistake for a new administration to be talking so soon after inauguration; basic principles, expounded in an inaugural talk, are one thing, but to begin talking concretely about a great array of specific problems is quite another. Time for study, exploration, and analysis is necessary. But, the Republicans have been so long out of power they want, and probably need, a pronouncement from their President as a starting point." Eisenhower hoped and prayed "that it does not contain blunders that we will later regret." Work on the speech actually began on the *Helena,* and in the next two months, Eisenhower, his speechwriters and several Cabinet members, including Dulles and Brownell, worked on eight drafts of it. Eisenhower himself went over it with Republican Congressional leaders.[68]

The speech contained few surprises. Indeed most of it reflected Republican platform promises or reiterated Eisenhower's well-known views, in favor of mutual security in Europe, for example. Consequently it did not generate controversy, and the blunders that Eisenhower worried about were not immediately, at least, apparent. The speech's big news was Eisenhower's announcement that he was removing the Seventh Fleet from the waters around Formosa, a fleet that had been placed there to prevent Chiang from invading Red China as well as to protect him from a Red Chinese invasion. Republicans and many newspapers hailed the "unleashing" of Chiang, but Eisenhower's tactic proved insignificant in the short run since neither Chiang nor his adversaries budged. Over the long run, it encouraged Nationalist hopes and complicated our relations with Chiang.[69]

Eisenhower also announced before Congress his decision to remove wage and price controls in an orderly manner and not to seek a renewal of control authority when existing legislation expired at the end of April. Eisenhower thus honored a campaign promise early and decisively. He did so after extensive consultations, beginning on the *Helena,* about precisely how the controls were to be lifted. He chose a slower, more cautious approach than some of his advisers recommended, but one which still allowed him to remove most controls immediately, the remainder within several months. Eisenhower thereby struck early blows for a free-market economy and for frugality in government, the control mechanisms having incurred direct costs in 1952 of $101 million. Naturally he took credit for the ensuing stability of prices and wages, without mentioning that stability had been the rule in the last quarter of 1952 when controls were in force and may have remained so under him in part because of the Federal Reserve Board's tight money policy and a softening of the economy in mid-1953. Temporarily, though, inflationary fears were quieted, later to be replaced by recessionary ones.[70]

In his State of the Union Address, Eisenhower made clear his preference for a balanced budget over reduced taxes. "Reduction of taxes will be justified," he declared, "only as we show we can

succeed in bringing the budget under control." This preference encountered difficulties on Capitol Hill. At a meeting with Congressional leaders on April 30, Eisenhower emphasized the high costs of
national security, but Taft, who had favored postponing tax reductions, sharply challenged military spending. The administration, he
charged, had adopted Truman's policies, and one result would be
the election of a Democratic Congress in 1954. He recalled that
General Omar Bradley had said in 1950 that $13.5 billion was
adequate for defense, but was now saying that $50 billion was not
enough, which made Taft lack confidence in the experts Eisenhower
had around him. His tone and comments infuriated Eisenhower,
who wisely bit his tongue so as not to lose his temper. After some
further discussion Eisenhower quietly reviewed the essentials of
American global strategy, which he patronizingly termed "not difficult to understand." By the time of their next meeting, however,
good relations were restored and the previous clash treated with
humor. Taft remained loyal.[71]

Eisenhower's disagreement with Daniel Reed, chairman of the
House Ways and Means Committee, on the other hand, became
public as Reed tried first to reduce taxes across the board and then
opposed the administration's efforts to extend the excess-profits
tax. Although Reed won early skirmishes in his own committee,
Eisenhower's emphatic stand and that of the Republican leadership
in the House overwhelmed Reed and his business allies. Eisenhower's triumph on tax policy was facilitated by his recommendations of $10 billion in budget reductions, half of which were to fall
in Defense. Some cuts came hard, as when the Defense Department
tried to close a base in a Republican district, but they were substantially accepted by Congress. Truman's projected budget deficit was
ultimately trimmed by nearly $3 billion, leaving red ink of $7 billion. Ironically, Eisenhower's fiscal mastery was rewarded by a recession in mid-1953, the product in significant measure of his very
success, which retarded demand. Sometimes when a President appears to win, he may in fact be losing.[72]

In the fall campaign, Eisenhower unambiguously supported
states' rights over federal rights to tidelands oil. It was a controversy that had raged for years. Shortly after Eisenhower took office,
a senior Republican Senator advised him to stay on the sidelines
while Congress battled it out. Eisenhower followed the advice and
in May signed the Submerged Lands Act, which gave to the states
the rights to submerged oil deposits out to three miles from their
shores and permitted litigation for certain additional historic claims.

Ironically, though the legislation appeared to be a victory for the affected states, it proved the opposite over time, for the richest deposits lay in the outer continental shelf, where the federal government retained its rights. No one knew about the richness of those resources in 1953; nor did the technology to extract them exist.[73]

Eisenhower began making good or another campaign pledge when he signed his first executive order on January 29, establishing the President's Advisory Committee on Government Organization, whose members were Nelson Rockefeller, chairman, Arthur Flemming, and Milton Eisenhower. Dwight Eisenhower had promised to overhaul the federal bureaucracy, and this committee, which drew on the staff and ideas of several earlier groups devoted to bureaucratic reform, facilitated his sending to Congress ten plans for executive branch reorganization between March and June. Earlier, Congress had approved an extension of legislation, which gave the President authority to reorganize the executive branch subject only to its disapproval. None of Eisenhower's plans was disapproved in 1953, in part because important Congressional preferences were incorporated into them before their submission. It is beyond the scope of this study to analyze the plans department-by-department, so it is impossible to generalize about their effects except to say that like most institutional reorganizations, they failed to attract popular attention.[74]

The first reorganization plan Eisenhower submitted mildly violated the indifference rule because it created a new department, Health, Education and Welfare. This step symbolized Eisenhower's recognition of a permanent, legitimate federal role in the social welfare area, even though he proposed no important new programs or expansions of old ones in his first year in office. Presidents going back to Warren Harding had futilely sought to create such a department. In recent years constituent groups, particularly in medicine and education, had fought off a department because they preferred having their own independent agencies to being submerged in a larger department.

The plan's easy acceptance under Eisenhower resulted from letting certain agencies and offices retain much of their independence and authority within the structure of the department, which was merely the Federal Security Agency in a higher status. It resulted, too, from careful behind-the-scenes work, led by Oveta Culp Hobby, the Secretary-designate. "The effectiveness of Mrs. Hobby's liaison with private groups and Members of Congress become a by-word in the Administration," according to an internal analysis written in May. "Out of her effective selling of the plan came the phrase 'Hobby's Lobby,' and thereafter at Cabinet meetings there was a tendency to suggest that Mrs. Hobby be called in whenever a matter arose which might incur rough going on Capitol Hill."[75]

In the campaign and again in the State of the Union, Eisenhower pledged to remove certain provisions from the Taft-Hartley law that labor unions found particularly objectionable, such as requiring labor leaders alone to take non-Communist oaths. He gave the job of filling in the details to his Labor Secretary, who took an expansive view and saw an opportunity to abolish such labor antipathies as "right to work laws." Opposition to Durkin's views quickly formed in the Commerce Department, which represented business interests just as devotedly as Labor represented those of the union. Less than three weeks into his term, Eisenhower recorded reservations in his diary about the men who led both departments. Weeks, he wrote, "seems so completely conservative in his views that at times he seems to be illogical." Durkin, on the other hand, seemed to "carry a bit of a chip on his shoulder. Whenever he presents anything in the cabinet meetings, it is with an attitude that seems to be just a bit jeering."[76]

Presidential aides tried to resolve the differences but to no avail. Robert Taft told Sherman Adams that he feared the White House would send him two sets of proposals, one from Weeks and another from Durkin. But it was Durkin who was more out of step with the administration. Eisenhower came to regard Durkin as simply a union spokesman, not as his independent adviser on labor matters. At one point he tried to entice Durkin to act independently of his constituency with the guarantee of an excellent job in private industry after he left government. Eisenhower had spoken to two prominent executives and they had assured him of a place for Durkin in their corporations if he demonstrated his independence. Durkin, however, retained his union loyalties; workers would have said he refused to be bought off. At the end of the summer, he submitted his resignation to Eisenhower to reassume his union presidency.

In their parting conversation, Durkin affirmed his lasting friendship and admiration for Eisenhower, but when he announced his resignation he charged two White House aides with "breaking faith," and several days later he told the AFL convention that Eisenhower had broken a promise to him. When Lloyd Mashburn, Under Secretary and a fellow unionist, appeared to Eisenhower to be too much like Durkin, he terminated his experiment in having a labor leader as Secretary. Instead he named James Mitchell, a department-store vice president in charge of labor relations, who served comfortably in this business-oriented administration for its duration. Although Eisenhower's initial idea of reaching out to an important new constituency was adventurous, it simply may not have been realistic, given the large differences between unions and business and his own closeness to business.[77]

Eisenhower, like all Presidents, always said he wanted to appoint the most qualified people he could find, but as the situation at Labor illustrated, he also wanted people who were in general sympathy with his points of view. Other considerations, too, went into appointments, many of which remained to be made long after the inauguration. (As of mid-May only two hundred Presidential appointments had been made.) These considerations included partisan or factional affiliation, friendship, geography, religion, race, and gender. Eisenhower would have been the last to admit that such nonmerit factors were ever germane, but the record is indisputable.[78]

When the Republican National Committee under Leonard Hall (who had been selected by the White House) analyzed Presidential appointments in July, it found that they were "economically, geographically and politically badly out of balance." People with big-business backgrounds and from Eastern seaboard states, particularly New York, were heavily represented, but there was "next to no recognition of our so-called ethnic or minority groups," which created a marked political imbalance. "Our study shows," it candidly concluded, "that our method of appointment has increased the imbalance because of the natural tendency of all of us to pick people or seek people who we personally know, or who are known to friends of ours."[79]

Eisenhower himself occasionally tried to lesson these imbalances. In a telephone conversation with Charles Wilson in January, he asked Wilson to appoint someone from the South as well as a Jew and a Negro, the latter possibly as a special assistant. Adams and Hall made similar appeals to Dulles, who explained that it was difficult for blacks to get security clearances. Dulles told Hall over the phone, "there was practically no negro, even Ralph Bunch[e], who would come through an FBI check lily white, because all of their organizations had been infiltrated at one time or another." Eisenhower only sought a few token appointments of blacks, though he himself did not hire a black staff member above the secretarial level for another two years.[80]

Patronage appointments generated much more pressure than minority appointments. Eisenhower had received only a small percentage of black votes, and civil-rights organizations were far less influential and racial consciousness far less developed in 1953 than they were to become. On the other hand, the Republican party controlled Congress and had state and local organizations around the country that lusted after the many appointive positions now available to them after twenty years in the wilderness. By mid-May over twenty thousand individuals had written the White House or the Republican National Committee to request appointments for themselves. All of these "self starters" were referred back to their state committees for clearance.[81]

The majority of appointive positions existed at the local level, to be filled by the Post Office and Justice Department, reportedly working in conjunction with Republican members of Congress and state party officials. Presidential appointments to independent agencies and commissions were made by the White House, usually without patronage considerations. Department heads made most of their own appointments, though with some "coaching" from the White House, which also often served as "a buffer to protect the Department heads in their choices against counter desires of the Hill," according to an internal report. Most Presidential appointments were initiated at the White House or departments and only then cleared with state and Congressional party members. When Nelson Rockefeller was chosen Under Secretary of HEW, he was cleared politically with no fewer than six party members in Congress and New York. In addition, four Republican leaders of Congress were notified. These procedures often failed to satisfy the party faithful. As of mid-July, Leonard Hall "could not find six members of Congress indebted to the Administration for any patronage they have initiated."[82]

Because the Democrats had been in command of the executive branch for so long, Republicans looked with suspicion at higher-level holdovers. Even Eisenhower, who as a professional military man held career government officials in higher esteem than did many of his governmentally inexperienced subordinates, shared some of these suspicions. He wrote Dulles in March that a civil service officer from a department he did not name told him that "every administrative position in that department is presently held by an individual who believes in the philosophy of the preceding Administration." "Almost without exception," Eisenhower went on, "these individuals reached these high administrative offices through a process of selection *based upon their devotion to the socialistic doctrine and bureaucratic controls practiced over the past two decades."* Eisenhower's informant was worried that if any sizable reductions in the federal workforce occurred before these individuals were removed and new ones appointed to replace them, the result would be "that down through the organization there will be a studied effort to hang onto those believing in the New Deal philosophy and to eliminate those who show any respect for ideals of self-dependence and self-reliance. Eisenhower's own opinion was "that if we are watchful we can prevent any such unfortunate outcome."[83]

In its efforts to promote political loyalty and ideological conformity at the second tier of appointments, the Eisenhower administration sometimes lost the services of excellent career people, damaged morale, and aroused public opposition. Within the Commerce Department, for example, the firing of the head of the National Bureau of Standards provoked such a sharp reaction from the scientific community, from Congress, and from the bureau's scientists, that Weeks reversed himself. Interior Secretary McKay made so many controversial personnel decisions that by the summer Eisenhower insisted on personally scrutinizing all high-level appointments in that department. Personnel changes at the Defense Department, as has been noted, did not generate adverse publicity but did deprive the new leadership of some expertise.[84]

Questions of loyalty—political, ideological, and patriotic—plagued the State Department, which had been under attack by the Republican right for harboring Communists, leftists, and security risks, for selling out Eastern Europe and abandoning China, and for adopting a policy of containing Communism rather than rolling it back. Although Eisenhower and Dulles had generally supported Truman's foreign policies and had helped implement them, in 1952 they had bowed to political realities and accommodated themselves, rhetorically at least, to the Republican right, calling for the liberation of enslaved peoples, not merely the acceptance of the status quo. These accommodations continued after the election in the form of certain appointments, such as Scott McLeod's to oversee internal security, and in early statements and actions.

In his State of the Union Address, Eisenhower declared, to Republican delight, that "we shall never acquiesce in the enslavement of any people in order to purchase fancied gain for ouselves. I shall ask the Congress at a later date to join in an appropriate resolution making clear that this Government recognizes no kind of commitment contained in secret understandings of the past with foreign governments which permit this kind of enslavement." The actual wording of the so-called Yalta or "Captive Nations" resolution was purposely innocuous, however, as Eisenhower took pains to avoid offending Democrats whose support on foreign policy he needed and to deprive the Soviet Union of the opportunity to repudiate agreements it disliked. The resolution went nowhere in 1953 but succeeded in heading off more controversial ones.[85]

Eisenhower's handling of this resolution demonstrated a certain deftness in taking the lead on a potentially explosive right-wing issue and defusing it, but more often he merely responded to un-folding events in this area. Caught between advisers who wanted to mollify right-wingers and others who wanted to stand fast, Eisen-hower alternately did both or he did nothing. His privately declared approach to the loosest cannon on the Republican deck, Joe McCarthy, was to ignore him. Eisenhower explained that Mc-Carthy craved headlines and nothing would draw them as certainly as a confrontation with the President. Although his defenders argue that this approach ultimately worked, in that McCarthy was cen-sured by the Senate in 1954, it is equally possible that things would not have gone that far if Eisenhower had drawn a firm line in 1953 and appointed subordinates who stood shoulder to shoulder with him, not in fear of McCarthy or other right-wingers. Developments in 1953 should have made it clear to Eisenhower that the internal security and loyalty issues required leadership and management, not ignoring.[86]

The administration's handling of the loyalty issue quickly took a heavy toll on Foreign Service morale. One of Dulles's first acts was to call upon the Foreign Service to display "positive loyalty" to the new administration, a message he repeated to senior career diplomats in Europe on his first trip there as Secretary. "The re-mark disgusted some Foreign Service officers, infuriated others, and displeased even those who were looking forward to the new administration," recalled a distinguished senior diplomat. (It so happens that near the end of his term in office, Truman com-plained privately to Acheson about the large number of Taftites in the Foreign Service.) As one Dulles assistant later acknowledged, Dulles was wrong in suspecting the political motives of the Foreign Service; it resisted change, but for essentially bureaucratic, not political, reasons.[87]

Given popular fears of internal subversion and the long-standing exploitation of those fears by Republicans, some internal security program was probably inevitable. So it was that Eisenhower issued an executive order which was government-wide, and by the fall,

Republicans were claiming to have removed 1,456 federal employees (a number that grew to 2,200 by the following January) as security risks. In fact, however, very few of these dismissals resulted from suspicion of disloyalty to the country. The number largely consisted of people about whom derogatory information of a personal, not political, nature had been developed. "Believe it or not, we had, within one year, ninety-nine homos," Donald Lourie later said with dismay; all were separated. Moreover, some of those dismissed resigned without any knowledge of the derogatory information; many resigned to take positions in other government agencies; and some had been appointed by the Republicans themselves.[88]

In the State Department the program should have been administered by someone who was skeptical about the possibility that any Communists remained after several years of intense Congressional investigation and tough executive enforcement, who was sensitive to individual rights and professional morale, and who was loyal to the administration. Instead it was run by Scott McLeod, a zealot with close ties to the Republican right. He and his staff of 350, which included some fellow former FBI men, soon wreaked havoc on professional morale. After successfully passing through his own ordeal by fire, partially started by McLeod's torch, Charles Bohlen, the president of the Foreign Service Association, complained to Eisenhower in Dulles's presence about declining morale that was being caused by the inquisitorial atmosphere. Eisenhower interrupted to say that McLeod's appointment had been an error, but to dismiss him would be a worse error. He also "delivered a homily, saying that having been in the Army for some forty years, he was used to the whims of public opinion, and the only thing to do was to stand firm and let the storm pass." Bohlen could see that there was little value in pressing the matter.[89]

Dulles became personally involved in one loyalty review case he inherited from Acheson, that of John Carter Vincent, a senior Chinese specialist whose sin had been to recognize the inevitability of Mao's triumph over Chiang. Without consulting the blue-ribbon panel Acheson had convened to review Vincent's case and evidently without spending much time reviewing the voluminous file that had been developed, Dulles cleared Vincent of disloyalty but retired him on the grounds that his reporting and advice in the 1940s had not been up to Dulles's standard, which he did not define. The quality of Vincent's work had never been at issue before. Very clearly, Vincent's retirement was a concession to right-wingers, but even so they complained that Vincent had been allowed to have his pension.

Ironically, in his parting conversation with Vincent, Dulles asked about the current situation in China and listened attentively to his expert views. The Vincent retirement was one of a series of bad personnel and policy measures made in the Truman and Eisenhower administrations that blinded America to hard realities on the Asian mainland for a generation. These measures helped bring about America's ill-fated involvement in Vietnam and were not set on the path to correction until the Nixon administration.[90]

Dulles also forced into retirement George Kennan, a Soviet expert who was at the time ambassador to Moscow, though that government had declared him persona non grata because of critical remarks he made about it in Berlin. Kennan was an architect of the containment policy who several days before Eisenhower's inauguration gave a speech criticizing the concept of liberation. Dulles's retirement of Kennan sent a signal to the Foreign Service about the sort of "positive loyalty" he required and about the way loyalty to the department could be rewarded. Like Vincent, Kennan had the odd experience, after being terminated by Dulles, of having Dulles solicit his views. Dulles complimented him for his reply and suggested that he come in and talk to him from time to time. Kennan told his wife that night that it was as if he had said to her: "You know, I'm divorcing you as of today, and you are to leave my bed and board at once. But I love the way you cook scrambled eggs, and I wonder if you'd mind fixing me up a batch of them right now, before you go."[91]

In the Kennan and Vincent affairs, Dulles demonstrated considerable sensitivity to right-wing concerns, but he failed to take them into consideration before Eisenhower nominated Charles Bohlen to be ambassador to Moscow. A career diplomat and Soviet specialist who had been to Yalta with Roosevelt, Bohlen had warned Dulles in advance that his nomination might arouse right-wing ire and suggested that Dulles take soundings in the Senate first. Dulles told him that it had not occurred to him that Bohlen might be asked questions about Yalta and wondered whether he could decline to answer them on the grounds that he had only been an interpreter. Since he had also been an adviser, Bohlen could not see how he could avoid answering the Senate's questions. Apparently Dulles did not take soundings. The reasons are not clear, but only two weeks before, the Senate had unanimously confirmed Bohlen as State Department Counselor, so perhaps he assumed there would be no opposition this time.[92]

He was wrong. First, in his confirmation hearings, Bohlen refused either to minimize his role at Yalta or to repudiate the treaty negotiated there. Problems had resulted not from the treaty, he said, but from Soviet violations of it. This angered right-wingers. Then, McLeod greatly exacerbated the situation when he refused to give Bohlen clearance because the FBI's security check contained a few unsubstantiated rumors of homosexuality. Dulles thought the evidence was flimsy, and after receiving Bohlen's assurance that there was nothing in his past that would embarrass the administration, he overrode his security officer. (Eisenhower knew Bohlen personally and had socialized with Bohlen and his wife.) McLeod and one of his assistants then leaked derogatory information to their Senate allies and to the press, and innuendo soon filled the air. Dulles was furious at McLeod and—with Eisenhower's full backing—threatened to fire him, but McLeod reavowed his loyalty and Dulles relented rather than give the right wing an additional cause.

The three-ring circus continued as Joe McCarthy and his allies demanded to see the raw FBI files and to have McLeod testify. The administration continued its struggle to protect executive privilege and its control of foreign policy machinery. With a great deal on the line, Eisenhower himself came into the picture, publicly defending Bohlen, though without criticizing his accusers. Taft proved the key to victory as he, for the first time, took a strong public stand against McCarthy. When McCarthy demanded that Dulles testify under oath about the contents of the FBI file, Taft bellowed on the Senate floor that Dulles's "statement not under oath" was "just as good as Mr. Dulles's under oath as far as I am concerned." McCarthy's attacks continued, however, and Taft and the administration worked out an arrangement whereby Taft and John Sparkman (an Alabama Democrat) looked at summaries of the files. After they did so, they supported Dulles's view and the Senate finally confirmed Bohlen on March 27, by a vote of 73 to 13. (The minority consisted of eleven Republicans, most of them Taft supporters in 1952, and two Democrats.)[93]

The Bohlen controversy illustrated the risks of not having firm control of one's own adminstration. It would have been much less serious and consumed less time, energy, and political capital if the State Department's security officer had been someone more in line with the administration than McLeod. Political soundings in the Senate, on the other hand, might have deterred the nomination in the first place. Once the adminstration was in a fight with the right wing, the administration demonstrated that it could win and win decisively, so long as Taft was with it, but Taft was with it in part

because he did not think the ambassadorship was sufficiently important to fight about. Neither Taft nor Eisenhower relished intra-
party disputes. Taft's message to the White House afterward was
"no more Bohlens." Troubled by the eleven Republican opponents,
Eisenhower listened to talk of forming a new party dedicated to the
"middle way." "It may come about that this will be forced upon
us," he wrote in his diary, "but the difficulties are vast, and if we
can possibly bring about a great solidarity among Republicans, if
we can get them more deeply committed to teamwork and party
responsibility, this will be much the better way."[94]

In other controversies involving McCarthy, specifically his investigations of the Voice of America and the International Information Agency and his private negotiations to get Greek shipowners to
boycott Communist ports, the administration spoke with conflicting
voices and varying degrees of nerve. Harold Stassen stood up to
McCarthy on the Greek ships, but IIA officials often bowed down
to him. Richard Nixon meanwhile tried futilely to get McCarthy to
be a team player. Eisenhower and Dulles themselves alternately
resisted and mollified McCarthy. For example, after McCarthy promoted the burning of library books written by Communists and
liberals, Eisenhower repudiated book burners in a commencement
speech at Dartmouth College, but a few days later so qualified his
remarks at a press conference that he won McCarthy's praise. A
week later he reversed himself again in a publicly disclosed letter to
the president of the American Library Association. Of such inconsistency are ambiguous policies formed, as the Army-McCarthy
hearings made glaringly apparent the next year.[95]

Eisenhower quickly came to a negative conclusion on the merits
of a constitutional amendment sponsored by Senator John Bricker,
an Ohio Republican, which was directed at restricting Presidential
power to make agreements with foreign governments. In 1953 a
majority of Republicans and many Democrats favored such an
amendment, which derived emotional popular support from suspicions about sordid deals at Yalta and from fears of Presidential
war-making authority in the wake of Korea. Eisenhower personally
believed that the amendment placed unworkable restrictions on a
President's ability to conduct foreign policy, and it could return
America's foreign relations to their sorry condition under the Articles of Confederation. Through the spring of 1953, he kept his
convictions private while trying to persuade Bricker to accept either
an innocuous substitute amendment or a commission to study the
issue. Bricker would not relent, however, and Eisenhower only suc-

ceeded in postponing Senate consideration of the matter until the following February.[96]

At that time Eisenhower had no choice but to oppose Bricker's and similar amendments openly, and the Senate, by the barest of margins, failed to approve one of them. In the series of votes that took place only thirteen Republicans supported Eisenhower's position consistently and only fifteen supported it on the final test, with Democrats providing the other sixteen. It is hard to say whether Eisenhower's postponement of the showdown helped or hurt, but the controversy underlined the ongoing divisions within the Republican party over foreign policy, divisions which had also been evident on trade, foreign aid, and United Nations support legislation in 1953. Often Eisenhower received greater support from Democrats than from Republicans, which reflected both on his nonpartisan style and on his essential agreement with the broad contours of foreign policy developed by his Democratic predecessors.[97]

To be sure, Eisenhower had gone along during the campaign with Republican rhetoric about achieving the liberation of Eastern Europe, perhaps because that rhetoric appealed to Eastern European voters in this country, perhaps because he believed it could be done, though only through peaceful means. Like all new Presidents, he came into office with the hope that he could produce an innovative, coherent, consistent, and clear foreign policy. "We have learned that the free world cannot indefinitely remain in a posture of paralyzed tension, leaving forever to the aggressor the choice of time and place and means to cause greatest hurt to us at least cost to himself," he declared in his State of the Union address. "This administration has, therefore, begun the definition of a new, positive foreign policy." But since Eisenhower also came into office agreeing with the thrust of his predecessors' policies, it is not surprising that he changed them very little.[98]

Eisenhower, in contrast to a significant minority of his party, believed that America's enlightened self-interest demanded close attention to Western Europe and reliance on mutual security. To Eisenhower, whose greatest achievement prior to becoming President had been getting the allies to cooperate militarily in defeating Germany, a go-it-alone or fortress-America philosophy was anathema. Within days of his inauguration, he dispatched Dulles and Stassen as his personal emissaries to assure Western European governments of his continued devotion to mutual security and to urge them, futilely as it turned out, to approve the pending European Defense Community. Such a trip "seemed necessary after the publicized fears, inspired by my trip to Korea, that I would suddenly become obssessed with Asia's problems to the exclusion of Europe," Eisenhower explained to a close military friend in Europe.[99]

Dulles served from the outset as Eisenhower's chief adviser on foreign affairs, as an emissary to foreign governments, and as a spokesman before the public and Congress. Eisenhower relied less heavily on Dulles than Truman had on Acheson. Eisenhower was himself only slightly less expert than Dulles on foreign affairs and far more knowledgeable on military affairs. He gave Dulles considerable leeway on details, but he retained ultimate authority and did not hesitate to overrule him when he thought it important to do so. In early 1953 they were still getting acquainted, which largely meant that Dulles was learning how to work for Eisenhower, such as not sending him reports from Assistant Secretaries, but giving him his own views. In May, Eisenhower recorded in his diary his admiration for Dulles's astuteness on foreign affairs and for his dedication and sincerity, but expressed doubts about his personality. "He is not particularly persuasive in presentation and, at times, seems to have a curious lack of understanding as to how his words and manner may affect another personality," Eisenhower observed.[100]

Dulles evidently helped shape Eisenhower's perception of the Soviet threat. In December 1951 C. L. Sulzburger, the journalist, had dinner with Eisenhower and afterward recorded in his diary that the General believed that the men in the Kremlin either were "dictators who were out to hang on to their jobs and stabilize them; or they were fanatics whose actions could never be predicted and who would inevitably force another war." Eisenhower thought the former to be the case, but by the spring of 1953 he was inclined toward the latter view, which Dulles favored. According to it, Communist ideology was the key, and it dictated expansion. Moscow inevitably called the shots for international communism and was a tactical virtuoso, able to select expediently from among a variety of political and military methods according to the needs of the moment. America therefore had to respond in a similarly skillful fashion. Eisenhower, who had long believed in the value of public relations and propaganda, stepped up the government's reliance on "psychological warfare," by which he meant anything "from the singing of a beautiful hymn up to the most extraordinary kind of physical sabotage." Although this often meant simply making the most out of rhetoric, it also implied an increase in covert intelligence operations, which led to the overthrow of leftist governments in Iran in 1953 and in Guatemala in 1954.[101]

At the same time, Eisenhower had a soldier's abhorrence of war, knew that a war between the United States and the Soviet Union would be devastating, and feared that military spending could become so excessive as to undermine the American economy. As a young officer stationed in Panama, under the tutelage of his learned commanding officer he had studied Clausewitz's *On War* and from it he learned that means had to be subordinated to ends. In Eisenhower's view it would be folly to create a garrison state in a futile search for absolute military security. The purpose of national policy should, according to Eisenhower, be the preservation of the American way of life, including its political and economic institutions. It was a deceptively simple but profound insight.

Eisenhower's "Chance for Peace" speech before the American Society of Newspaper Editors in April well illustrated his personal beliefs and his readiness to set policy by them. Stalin's death in early March set the stage. Eisenhower was frustrated at the lack of any contingency plans for this event. After the presumed heir to Stalin, Georgi Malenkov, launched what Eisenhower perceived as a "peace offensive" in a speech from the Kremlin, Eisenhower began to prepare his own major speech. He cast aside both Dulles's objections to any appearance of conciliation and Churchill's misgivings about timing and scope. Although Eisenhower intended the speech in part as a counteroffensive in the war of words, he also spoke with genuine hope and conviction. When C. D. Jackson, a journalist who advised him on psychological warfare, expressed his doubts about whether Soviet global ambitions would be mollified by "genial, bourgeois talk about schools and hospitals for the ignorant and sick," Eisenhower told of a four-hour conversation he had once had with Stalin. "Damn near all he talked about was the essential things his people needed—homes and food and technical help," Emmet Hughes, his speechwriter, recalled Eisenhower saying. "Hell, those boys have to think in material terms. It's all they believe in."[102]

In his speech, given under great physical stress caused by a stomach disorder, Eisenhower reiterated America's devotion to peace and self-determination and briefly reviewed Soviet reliance on force and fear. The path the world was traveling down, he warned, seemed at worst to be leading to atomic war and at best to a "life of perpetual fear and tension," with a wasteful, onerous arms race that hurt both America and the Soviet Union. "Every gun that is made, every warship launched, every rocket fired signifies, in the final sense," said Eisenhower, "a theft from those who hunger and are not fed, those who are cold and are not clothed." He then described the trade-offs more precisely. The cost of a heavy bomber, for example, was more than that of thirty modern brick schools.

The Soviet Union's new leadership, Eisenhower asserted, had the precious opportunity to help turn the tide of history. He did not know whether they would seize that opportunity, though he was encouraged by recent statements and gestures. The first great step Eisenhower wanted was the "conclusion of an honorable armistice in Korea," to be followed by peace in the embattled countries of Indochina and Malaya. He pledged America's willingness to enter agreements to reduce arms and armies and to establish international controls of atomic energy under United Nations auspices (all of which the Truman administration had sought previously). A substantial percentage of the savings, he promised, would go to a fund for world aid and reconstruction. It was, for its time, a hopeful and bold speech, remarkably free of bellicosity, accusation, and threat.[103]

The speech received unusually full and prominent coverage in the Soviet press. Bohlen cabled from Moscow that this coverage alone constituted an important event that was "unparalleled in the Soviet Union since the institution of the Stalinist dictatorship." The speech was also hailed in the United States and around the world and was a great propaganda triumph. But concrete results proved more elusive. The Korean war did end relatively soon, but it is impossible to say what part the speech played in that. Churchill and Eisenhower's own intelligence estimate had likely been correct that this was not the moment for a general settlement of the great differences separating East and West. Stalin's successors were too preoccupied with deciding vital questions of internal power to permit a grand external settlement. The world continued down the path Eisenhower outlined.[104]

Even so, Eisenhower remained determined that America not spend itself into financial ruin on defense. In a May radio address on the national security and its costs, he stressed costs and repudiated the notion of obtaining maximum military security, for "such security would compel us to imitate the methods of the dictator." "It would compel us," he warned, "to put every able-bodied man in uniform—to regiment the worker, the farmer, the businessman—to allocate materials and to control prices and wages—in short to devote our whole nation to the grim purposes of the garrison state." He observed that short of total mobilization, "we are debating in a realm of speculation—something informed, more often uniformed." He warned that it was "foolish and dangerous for any of us to be hypnotized by magic numbers" in weapons while he assured the public, as he could better than any modern President, because of his unique background, that he had given the subject his personal study and analysis.[105]

In October, Eisenhower's approach to defense policy acquired a name, the "New Look," and a formal internal rationalization, but as early as this radio address its outline was clear: an emphasis on air power (and implicitly on nuclear weapons) over sea power and ground forces. Implementation never came easy. Charles Wilson proved less adept at controlling the military services with their direct ties to Congress than Eisenhower or his Budget Director wished. Still, significant cost reductions were achieved in 1953 and even greater ones the following year. Defense spending as a percentage of the federal budget and as a percentage of gross national product both declined through the Eisenhower years, yet the United States was, if anything, militarily stronger than the Soviet Union at the end of his term than it had been at the beginning. Yet Eisenhower's achievements were often unappreciated as he left office, for by then the New Look was under effective political attack for being both inadequate and dangerous.[106]

To assist him in formulating national security policy, Eisenhower regularly attended frequent meetings of the National Security Council. One hundred fifteen council meetings were held in Eisenhower's first 115 weeks in office. The meetings began with a briefing by the CIA Director and then moved to consideration of a draft policy paper prepared by the council's Planning Board, usually dealing with a single subject. The meetings often included lively debate among the participants, though sometimes high attendance tended to retard frank exchanges among the top officials. Eisenhower used the council as an advisory body or as a sounding board; although he decided some issues right at a meeting, he often reserved or revised his judgment afterward. In September he created an Operations Coordinating Board to oversee policy implementation, often the more difficult task than formulation.[107]

Following Eisenhower's wishes, Robert Cutler, who administered the council and its offshoots, kept a low profile. "No speeches, no public appearances, no talking with reporters," the once outspoken Cutler recalled. When Cutler refused to serve as a pipeline to Joseph Alsop, an old college friend and an influential columnist, Alsop retaliated by treating Cutler critically in his column. Cutler also avoided taking sides in internal debates, striving instead for impartiality and neutrality. In their discretion and neutrality, Cutler and his successors as National Security Adviser under

Eisenhower differed markedly from some of their vocal and partisan successors. But in Eisenhower they had a President with greater confidence and experience in national security affairs than those successors had.[108]

A major review of national security strategy began in the summer of 1953 under the name, Operation Solarium. Each of three teams was assigned to make the strongest case for its assigned option: (1) a continuation of the Truman strategy of containment; (2) deterrence, which was containment with the implied threat of nuclear retaliation; and (3) liberation of Eastern bloc countries through political, psychological, economic, and covert means. Later a fourth option was added, negotiations with the Russians within a strict two-year limit. Strangely enough, George Kennan was invited back to head the containment team. "When the experience was completed," Kennan later gloated, "it was the concept propounded by my team that received the Presidential approval." He delighted in briefing the entire Cabinet and senior officials of the government while at his feet, "in the first row, silent and humble, but outwardly respectful, sat Foster Dulles."[109]

As a historian later pointed out, the administration's strategic concept, the "New Look," in fact "managed to incorporate in one form or another all of the alternatives considered in that exercise." But strategic concept is one thing and policy is another, as Eisenhower well realized. "More important than *what* is planned," Cutler explained, "is that the planners become accustomed to working and thinking together on hard problems; enabling them—when put to the ultimate test—to arrive more surely at a reasonable plan or policy." The policies that Eisenhower actually followed vis-à-vis the Soviet Union differed from Truman's more in public rationalization than they did in fact. Containment remained the operative policy in Europe, and liberation was shown, by the failed popular uprisings in East Germany and Hungary, to be an empty hope. The administration's blustery rhetoric, particularly from Dulles, sometimes masked and distorted Eisenhower's subtlety and prudence. Eisenhower possibly overestimated his ability to lead by example, gave his subordinates too much freedom to speak their own minds, or saw political and diplomatic advantage in their doing so—the right wing was mollified at home while the communists were scared abroad. On critical matters of war and peace, Eisenhower's actions were often more impressive than the rhetoric that accompanied them or the rationalizations that followed, as the ending of the Korean war well illustrated.[110]

It has become part of Republican folklore that the Korean war ended because Eisenhower let the word go out diplomatically that we would not tolerate an endless ground war of attrition, that if the war were not settled soon we would use nuclear weapons and would not confine their use to Korea. As a result of these threats, the story goes, the Communists settled. It was Dulles who first popularized this explanation through an interview with James Shepley, a *Life* magazine reporter. Sherman Adams supported it with Eisenhower's own testimony in his 1961 memoir, and Eisenhower himself incorporated it in his memoir. "We would not be limited by any world-wide gentleman's agreement. In India and in the Formosa Straits area, and at the truce negotiations at Panmunjom, we dropped the word, discreetly, of our intention," Eisenhower wrote. "We felt quite sure it would reach Soviet and Chinese Communist ears. Soon the prospects for armistice negotiations seemed to improve."[111]

This explanation is, in fact, highly speculative. While many, though not all, American government records on the Korean war are now open and reveal much about this government's internal deliberations and motives, no comparable access exists for Pyongyang, Peking, and Moscow. To this day, scholars can only guess about the dynamics that were at work in those capitals, though some of their guesses masquerade as fact. What is strikingly absent from available American records, however, is any verification from the military, the CIA, or the State Department that nuclear blackmail worked or could have worked. Indeed, two critical facts that emerge from internal documents and from the Joint Chiefs of Staff's highly detailed, authorized history are that the key concession by the Communists accepting the principle of nonforcible repatriation *preceded* Dulles's conveyance of the nuclear threat through the Indians and that the United States also made a major concession by accepting the Indian plan for implementing repatriation, which Truman had opposed.[112]

From the start, Eisenhower himself harbored doubts about using nuclear weapons and opposed expanding the war. He told Republican legislative leaders in January that there were no easy solutions in Korea. "The President said U. S. would not get out," according to that meeting's notes, "neither would it go to full mobilization for a war that cannot be won in Korea." At an NSC meeting on February 11, Eisenhower at first authorized Dulles to begin discussion with our allies aimed at either getting them to lift their objections to atomic weapons or to supply three or more additional divisions to drive the Communists back. "In conclusion, however, the President ruled against any discussion with our allies of military plans or weapons of attack." At an NSC meeting on April 8, Dulles said that in view of Communist weakness following Stalin's death and its apparent desire for peace, the United States should now consider abandoning the armistice agreement that had been inherited from Truman which was complete except for the prisoner repatriation issue. If the United States did so, perhaps it would be able to get a much better political settlement than was likely under the incomplete agreement. Eisenhower, by contrast, "stated his belief that it would be impossible to call off the armistice and to go to war again in Korea. The American people would never stand for such a move."[113]

The NSC's planning board listed as many political and military disadvantages as advantages in using atomic weapons and admitted its inability to estimate what the Communists' reaction would be. The Joint Chiefs of Staff were, as Eisenhower reports in his memoir, "pessimistic about the feasibility of using tactical atomic weapons on front-line positions." The place to use them was against strategic targets in China and Manchuria, which would have meant a much wider war, something Eisenhower opposed. As Eisenhower also wrote, the use of atomic weapons not only would create "strong disrupting feelings between ourselves and our allies" (which if the weapons were highly successful would, he believed, repair themselves in time), but that there was no telling what the Soviet Union might do with its own abundant supply of atomic weapons. "Of all the Asian targets which might be subject to Soviet bombing," Eisenhower revealed, "I was most concerned about the unprotected cities of Japan."[114]

It is unlikely that the nuclear threat was even made explicit enough to be heard by the other side. While affirming its existence, Sherman Adams long ago noted that Eisenhower "never suggested that the threat was as specific and as near to being carried out as Dulles estimated it was in his interview with Shepley." Recently, Dulles's own reports of his conversations with India's Prime Minister Nehru, in which the threat was presumably verbalized, have become available; they more than bear out Adams's skepticism. In his first conversation with Nehru, Dulles agreed with Nehru's estimate that

> if the armistice negotiations collapsed, the United States would probably make a stronger rather than a lesser military exertion, and that this might well extend the area of conflict. (*Note:* I

assumed this would be relayed.) I said that we were, however, sincerely trying to get an armistice and that only crazy people could think that the United States wanted to prolong the struggle, which had already cost us about 150,000 casualties and 10 to 15 billion dollars of expenditures.

The next day, "Nehru brought up Korean armistice, referring particularly to my statement of preceding day, that if no (repeat no) armistice occurred hostilities might become more intense," Dulles cabled back to Washington. "[Nehru] said if this happened it [was] difficult to know what end might be." After a discussion of the armistice terms, "[Nehru] brought up again my reference to intensified operations, but I made no (repeat no) comment and allowed the topic to drop." The words Dulles used might simply have been construed as an expansion of conventional warfare. Indeed, such warnings had been conveyed before by Chester Bowles, Truman's ambassador to India. It is also worth noting that Truman himself had publicly stated in late 1950 that atomic weapons were acceptable for use in Korea.[115]

When armistice talks began to show great promise in April and May, Syngman Rhee became a major obstacle to peace. Rhee desperately wanted to reunify Korea and drive the Communists off the peninsula. Correctly seeing that this was not Eisenhower's objective, he raised numerous objections to the terms the Americans were negotiating, threatened to withdraw his military forces from UN command and go it alone, and he rallied public opinion behind him. The American military command and diplomatic officials expended much effort in trying to conciliate and reassure him. Eisenhower pledged a mutual defense treaty and economic aid and invited him to the United States, but Rhee declined to come and did not even answer one Eisenhower letter. When an agreement with the Communists on prisoner repatriation was finally struck in June, Rhee seemed to be on board. But then he played his trump card by releasing 27,000 North Korean prisoners who did not want to be repatriated from stockades which his troops had been guarding. "What Syngman Rhee had done," Eisenhower recollected, "was to sabotage the very basis of the arguments that we had been presenting to the Chinese and North Koreans for all these many months. . . . The Communists asked at this juncture—and, I must confess, with some right— whether the United States was able to live up to any agreement to which the South Koreans might be a party."[116]

Eisenhower cabled Rhee that "unless you are prepared immediately and unequivocally to accept the authority of the UN Command to conduct the present hostilities and to bring them to a close, it will be necessary to effect another arrangement." At a Cabinet meeting Eisenhower emphasized the difficulty "created by the apparent willingness of the South Koreans to undertake suicide." In an interview with Rhee's ambassador, he had asked what the South Koreans would do were American support withdrawn and he had replied simply, "we should die." Eisenhower noted the importance of remembering that Communism was "still our principal enemy in Korea," a point he also made to legislative leaders and in a press conference in coming weeks.[117]

Dulles wrote Rhee a strongly worded letter which was delivered by his and Eisenhower's personal emissary, Assistant Secretary Walter Robertson. In it he reminded Rhee that the United States had come to his country's aid when it was attacked and he asked for our help. "You know full well that we did not come to fight and die in Korea in order to unite it by force, or to liberate by force the North Koreans," he admonished. "It is you who invoked the principle of unity and asked us to pay the price. We have paid it in blood and suffering. Can you now honorably reject the principle which, in your hour of need, you asked us to defend at so high a price?" "Of those one million American boys who have gone to your land, 24,000 died, another 100,000 were wounded. The cost to us in money is counted in the tens of billions of dollars," Dulles wrote. He warned Rhee that if he went his separate way, it would mean a "horrible disaster." Do you now have the moral right to destroy the national life which, at your plea, we helped to save at a great price?" Dulles asked. "Can *you* be deaf when *we* now invoke the plea of unity?"[118]

For the next several weeks, Robertson conducted intensive negotiations with Rhee, during the first part of which he merely let the adamant Korean leader talk. Every day Robertson's route was lined with Koreans holding banners with slogans like "On to the Yalu" and chanting "puk chin, puk chin," which meant "go north, go north." With Eisenhower's blessing, Robertson leaned over backward to meet Rhee's demands and to win his cooperation. He again promised a mutual security pact after the armistice and reported that Dulles, at Eisenhower's direction, had met with Senate leaders and found them willing, provided Rhee would cooperate in the armistice and in the political conference which was to follow. He also pledged economic aid, a buildup of South Korean armed forces, high-level talks in the near future (which meant a Dulles visit to Korea), and to withdraw with the South Koreans from the post-armistice political conference if it proved fruitless (which the United States correctly expected it would).[119]

While Robertson conciliated Rhee, Mark Clark, who as military commander oversaw the armistice talks, let him know by word and deed that we would proceed with an armistice without him. "To show we were in earnest," Maxwell Taylor, commander of the Eighth Army recalled, "we reduced the flow of supplies to Korean forces, particularly ammunition and petroleum products, to a trickle and held back deliveries of equipment for the expansion of the ROK Army. I went about reminding Korean generals of the dependence of their country and their Army on the Americans and the uncertainty of that support if Rhee continued his resistance to the armistice." He also held a press conference to express his confidence that the "UN forces could extricate themselves from the conflict without too much trouble if the ROK's should decide to continue the war alone."[120]

By Robertson's departure on July 12, Rhee had yielded before the American carrot and stick and had agreed to abide by an armistice. Within days a large Communist offensive began and was directed exclusively against his army's positions. In the end, it was repulsed, with American assistance. "One possibly useful result," Eisenhower observed, "was to remind President Rhee of the vulnerability of his forces if deprived of United Nations support." Taylor recalled that the battle was in a sense "a graduation exercise for the ROK Army which had demostrated its ability to recover from a heavy blow and come back fighting. At the same time it reminded Rhee of the formidable strength which the enemy had built up during the long haggling over the armistice, and it certainly convinced his commanders of their inability to break through to the north on their own." Within two weeks, on July 27, a truce was signed, and the Korean war was over.[121]

There was little rejoicing in this country since the end result was a stalemate, not a victory, but there was a great sense of relief. Some senior military men, including Clark, privately regretted Eisenhower's failure to seek victory, and right-wing Republicans complained publicly. But for Eisenhower it was an excellent conclusion to his first six months as President. He had fulfilled his most important campaign promise, to end the war honorably and soon. His achievement was probably not attributable to a nuclear threat, the principal value of which may have been to allow members of the administration to claim some responsibility for the armistice. The war's end likely owed more to Eisenhower's acceptance of Truman's limited political objective and his tolerance of Truman's restrained military tactics, to his handling of our South Korean ally, and to his procedural concessions at the bargaining table which were facilitated by who he was. Almost certainly, if a Democratic President had brought about Eisenhower's armistice in 1953 he would have faced political recriminations. Eisenhower recognized the truce as the significant accomplishment it was, always listing it as his proudest achievement. No President has had a greater transition accomplishment. The sad thing was that few understood how it was done, and Eisenhower himself contributed to a misleading impression which was to bear bitter fruit in the Nixon transition.[122]

2

KENNEDY

☆ ☆ ☆

Like Eisenhower, John F. Kennedy owed his initial political success to wartime heroism, but his heroism was that of a junior officer who saved his men after the PT boat he commanded was sunk by a Japanese destroyer in the South Pacific. His first electoral reward was a Congressional seat from Boston, which he won in 1946 at the age of twenty-nine. Six years later he bucked the Eisenhower landslide to defeat incumbent Senator Henry Cabot Lodge. He was narrowly defeated for the Democratic Vice Presidential nomination in 1956 after it was thrown open to the convention by Governor Adlai Stevenson of Illinois, the Presidential nominee. Immediately after that setback he began laying plans for capturing the Presidential nomination four years later, and his long, methodical campaign for delegates established a precedent that every successful nonincumbent in both parties has since followed.

Jack, as he was known to family and friends, was the son of Joseph P. Kennedy, a self-made multimillionaire who headed the Securities Exchange Commission under Franklin D. Roosevelt. In 1937 Roosevelt made Joe Kennedy Ambassador to Great Britain, which constituted a significant social breakthrough for an Irish Catholic. To Roosevelt's utter dismay, he turned out to sympathize with Prime Minister Neville Chamberlain's appeasement policies toward Nazi Germany. "Who would have thought that the English could take into camp a red-headed Irishman?" Roosevelt remarked. Their friendship soured so badly that Roosevelt refused to give Kennedy a wartime job commensurate with his abilities.[1]

When Joe Kennedy dined with his nine children, political issues were frequently the topic of conversation and sometimes heated debate, while discussion of money was taboo. After they grew up, none of the Kennedy children showed interest in expanding their personal fortunes; rather they devoted themselves to politics, public service, and charity. Joseph P. Kennedy, Jr., the oldest of the four Kennedy boys, manifested the earliest political ambitions, but was killed in the war. Jack's decision to enter politics surprised and delighted his father, for he had seemed more suited to journalism or teaching. As World War II began, he had published to considerable acclaim his revised Harvard senior thesis, *Why England Slept*. At war's end, he covered conferences as a newspaper reporter, an experience that helped persuade him to enter politics.

In 1956, after he was in the Senate, another book, *Profiles in Courage,* appeared under his name. It honored politicians who put the national interest above parochial or self-interest. The book became a best-seller, won a Pulitzer prize, and earned Kennedy a reputation as an intellectual politician. Although Kennedy never manifested an ambition to become a Congressional leader, he had a great drive for power, specifically the Presidential variety. He possessed a quick wit, lacked moral certitude, disliked political piety, and spurned ideological labels. He usually voted with his party's liberals, but certain acts of omission and commission made him acceptable to many Democrats who did not regard themselves as liberal. He was handsome and youthful in appearance, highly energetic, and had insatiable curiosity about people and politics.[2]

Kennedy rode to the Presidency on the wave crest of popular doubts about America's goals and performance. Many Americans wondered whether this country could meet the Soviet technical, educational, and military challenge, vividly symbolized by the launching of *Sputnik* in 1957, the first artificial earth satellite. Congressional hearings popularized the notion that we had a missile gap. People feared that America was too devoted to ephemeral consumer goods and insufficiently committed to public needs in such areas as education, economic development, medical care, and civil rights. Kennedy's speechwriters focused on the theme that we had "to summon every segment of our society . . . to restore America's relative strength as a free nation . . . to regain our security and leadership in a fast changing world menaced by communism."[3]

The wave that Kennedy rode to the Presidency barely carried

him ashore. He won by fewer than 120,000 votes out of nearly 69 million cast. Although he led more comfortably in the electoral college, 303–219, his victory there rested on very thin popular margins in several larger states, which his opponent, Vice President Richard M. Nixon, briefly considered challenging in courts. It constituted less than a ringing endorsement of Kennedy's slogan that it was time "to get American moving again." He could take some comfort in the fact that Nixon often agreed with him that America faced a stiffer challenge abroad and needed to do more at home. His margin of victory would also have been substantially greater had he not lost more Protestant votes than he won Catholic votes on account of his Catholicism. (He was the first and only Catholic President in the nation's history.) On the other hand, Nixon also defended the Eisenhower record and Eisenhower himself remained popular, despite all the implicit criticism of his leadership in the late 1950s and in Kennedy's campaign. Indeed, Nixon likely would have won the election had he asked Eisenhower to campaign earlier and more extensively than he did. If the Twenty-second Amendment had not been ratified, and if Eisenhower had cared to run for a third term, he almost certainly would have defeated Kennedy.

Less ambiguity surrounded the Congressional results. The party taking the Presidency had for the first time in this century failed to gain seats in the Congress. Although Democrats still enjoyed large paper majorities in both houses—65–35 in the Senate and 262–174 in the House—their majorities were smaller by one in the Senate and twenty-two in the House than the immediately previous ones. But even in 1959 and 1960, the conservative coalition of Republicans and Southern Democrats had been able to thwart liberal initiatives, so the prospects for liberal legislation, at least, had not been improved by the election.[4]

Kennedy publicly rejected the notion that he had failed to get a mandate. "The margin is narrow, but the responsibility is clear," he said. "There may be difficulties with the Congress, but a margin of only one vote would still be a mandate." Yet he had won by many fewer votes and states than he had hoped for, a result that he attributed, reasonably enough, to the prevailing sense of peace and prosperity and to anti-Catholic sentiment. The apparent lack of mandate did not paralyze Kennedy as he set about establishing his administration and trying to govern the country, but it both narrowed his options and required that he pay unusually careful attention to building greater public support than he commanded on election day. There is no indication that Kennedy or any of those closest to him identified his lack of a clear mandate as a problem in the days immediately following the election. Their nerves were probably too frayed from the election night ordeal and their minds and bodies too exhausted from the arduous campaign that preceded it to allow for strategic thinking then, but Kennedy's actions in the following months gave implicit recognition to the central importance of the mandate problem.[5]

Kennedy was impressed on the day after the election with how little time he had before he was inaugurated. "Seventy-two days remained," Theodore C. Sorensen, his close aide later wrote, "in which to form an administration, staff the White House, fill some seventy-five key Cabinet and policy posts, name six hundred other major nominees, decide which incumbents to carry over, distribute patronage to the faithful and fix personnel policies for the future." In this same brief period, Sorensen recollected, Kennedy would have to establish liaison with Eisenhower, prepare for the inauguration, formulate concrete domestic and foreign policies, decide on a legislative program, and perform other tasks as well.[6]

Thanks to the Brookings Institution, Kennedy had done some advance planning for his transition. Concerned by the casualness and difficulties of the 1952 transition, Brookings had set up a committee to study transitions. One of its members was James Rowe, a Washington lawyer and Roosevelt administration veteran, who personally urged Kennedy two weeks after his nomination to assign someone to sit with the committee and to begin thinking about what Kennedy should do if he were elected. Kennedy turned to Clark Clifford, once special counsel to President Truman and now a very successful Washington lawyer whom Kennedy himself had used on certain sensitive matters. He trusted Clifford despite the fact that Clifford had worked for one of his convention rivals, Senator Stuart Symington of Missouri, a long-time friend of Clifford's. At the outset, Clifford told Kennedy he would be glad to help, but that he would not take a regular job in his administration. Retrospectively, he regarded this as an extremely important ground rule, for it clarified his role as a disinterested outsider, not someone jockeying for position or favor in competition with Kennedy's own people. Kennedy later quipped that Clifford had asked him for nothing except the right to advertise his law firm on the back of the one-dollar bill.[7]

During the election campaign, Kennedy asked Richard Neustadt, a political scientist who was then at Columbia University and before that a Truman aide, to prepare transition memoranda. Neustadt had published *Presidential Power* in April 1960, and it was already on its way to becoming the most influential book of its time on the Presidency. When Neustadt asked Kennedy how he wanted him to relate to Clifford, Kennedy quickly replied that he did not want him to relate to him. "I can't afford to confine myself to one set of advisers," Kennedy explained. "If I did that, *I* would be on their leading strings." "Once Kennedy said that," Arthur Schlesinger, Jr., the historian and Kennedy assistant, later reflected, "the author of *Presidential Power* was thereafter on *his* leading strings." Like Clifford, Neustadt forswore a job for himself, which made for uncomplicated relations with Kennedy's staff.[8]

The morning after Nixon conceded and two days after the election, Kennedy held a staff meeting in which memos from Clifford and Neustadt as well as one from Brookings were discussed. Clifford pointed out that things would be much different from 1952–53. "Much of the 1952–53 experience is irrelevant," Clifford believed, because the Kennedy administration, in contrast to the incumbent one, would not be suspicious of or hostile to the federal bureaucracy, Eisenhower would make good on his public promise to assist in making the transition a smooth one, an offer that Kennedy should make the most of, and finally, "the President-elect and his associates are well versed in major questions of policy and politics, so that they can avoid the political pitfalls that engulfed the new Administration in 1953." Although Clifford was right about the existence of important differences from 1952–53, he showed little awareness of the similarities or of the possibility that positive lessons could be derived from the earlier transition. For example, the tragic Bay of Pigs debacle in April provided an object lesson precisely in the importance of being suspicious of bureaucratic experts.[9]

Kennedy, of course, was not Eisenhower. He believed in a more activist Presidency and government than Eisenhower did; he followed in the tradition of Franklin D. Roosevelt and Harry Truman. In a speech at the National Press Club early in 1960 he rejected a "restricted concept of the Presidency." The office demanded, he said, that "the President place himself in the very thick of the fight, that he care passionately about the fate of the people he leads, that he be willing to serve them at risk of incurring their momentary displeasure . . . [that he] be prepared to exercise the fullest powers of his office—all that are specified and some that are not."[10]

Typical of newcomers to office, Kennedy and his advisers seized upon a widely perceived mistake of his immediate predecessor and were determined not to repeat it. The conventional wisdom about Eisenhower was that he was passive. It was believed that he merely presided over the government and did not lead it. According to this view, he operated like a chairman of the board who ratified decisions already made by Cabinet officers or his powerful chief of staff. Although the conventional view contained an element of truth, it also underestimated Eisenhower's decisiveness and manipulativeness. It failed to appreciate the many and complex ways Eisenhower used his subordinates, not least of all, to protect himself. The misperception of Eisenhower testifies both to his cunning and to an inherent problem of indirect leadership, for by its very nature it eludes discovery and creates an impression of weakness, aloofness, or indifference.

The advice that Clifford and Neustadt gave Kennedy on organizing his staff was premised on this popular misperception of Eisenhower. At the same time, it gazed back appreciatively at Truman and Roosevelt. Kennedy was particularly fascinated by an appendix Neustadt included on Roosevelt's approach to White House staffing, perhaps because Roosevelt was the Democrats' mythic great President, and Kennedy could identify more easily with an Eastern patrician than he could with Truman, a thoroughly middle-class Midwesterner. Perhaps, too, he was drawn to Roosevelt's staff system because it most resembled his own prior experience in the Senate, where he had operated with a small, versatile, and flexible group, without a chief of staff.[11]

After returning from Palm Beach meetings with Kennedy in December, Neustadt confided to a Brookings staff member that Kennedy wanted to operate like Roosevelt, with one big difference—he was far more calculated and impatient. Where FDR liked to play with a problem and toss ideas around, Kennedy was all business. Others, too, were impressed with Kennedy's ability to get quickly to the heart of a matter, whether he was speed-reading a long memorandum or debriefing an adviser. George Kennan once described Kennedy as "the best listener I've ever seen in high position anywhere." "He was able to resist the temptation, to which so many other great men have yielded, to sound off himself and be admired," Kennan observed. "He asked questions modestly, sensibly, and listened very patiently to what you had to say and did not try, then, to tell jokes, to be laughed at, or to utter sententious statements himself to be admired. This is a rare thing among men who have arisen to very exalted positions. I don't want to name other names, but I can think of some of the greatest with whom it was very hard, indeed, to have a conversation because they tended to monopolize it."[12]

Like many civilians who have served in the armed forces, Kennedy was distinctly unimpressed with military bureaucracy, which had provided the model for Eisenhower's staff system, so there was little chance that he would duplicate Eisenhower's system on that score either. Neustadt, for one, saw merit in there being a "Number-One Boy, serving as a sort of first assistant on general operations, day by day," but he cautioned Kennedy against making him "The Assistant to the President." Neustadt wanted to avoid repeating the Sherman Adams situation or even reminding the public of Sherman Adams; he also anticipated that Kennedy would need several "number-one boys" for different aspects of his work, which is what eventually happened.[13]

Clifford and Neustadt each recommended that Kennedy have a chief adviser on policy, program, and public statements. It would revive the special counsel's position that Roosevelt had created for Samuel Rosenman and which Clifford and Charles Murphy had held under Truman. In the Eisenhower administration, that title had been more narrowly defined as legal counsel. Clifford's and Neustadt's advice, which was put down on paper and elaborated on at some length in person at Palm Beach after the election, also coincided in several other respects as well. Both, for example, stressed the importance of Kennedy's staffing himself in such ways as to meet his own needs. "Presidential staffs," Neustadt perceptively observed, "have evolved in the last twenty years to meet two kinds of needs: on the one hand, needs of Presidents themselves, for help in managing their daily chores, in gaining information, and in keeping control of key government decisions; on the other hand, needs of *other* government officials for backing, support, judgement, or decision, or a borrowing of prestige *from* the President." He urged Kennedy at this stage "to consider only needs of the first sort—your own."[14]

As is customary, Kennedy selected his top transition staff from his campaign staff, and its members then moved into comparable roles in the White House. Two days after the election he named Theodore Sorensen assistant for policy and program (special counsel), Kenneth O'Donnell for administration and appointments, and Pierre Salinger for press relations (press secretary). Like Kennedy himself, who was at forty-three the youngest man ever elected President, all were relatively young—Sorensen, at thirty-two, was the youngest—but all had prior Washington experience, more in fact than some counterparts, including older ones, in other administrations.

Indicative of his brother Robert's importance to him, two of the three had come to work for Jack through Bob. O'Donnell and Bob Kennedy were teammates on the Harvard football team and were close friends. In the 1950s O'Donnell moved back and forth between campaigning for Jack and working for Bob when he was general counsel to the Senate Rackets Committee, which exposed corruption in certain labor unions. Salinger was a former newspaperman in San Francisco who had come to work for Bob Kennedy at the Rackets Committee as an investigator. Sorensen alone of the three did not have a Bob Kennedy connection. After graduating first in his class from the University of Nebraska's law school, he had come to Washington as a lawyer, first for the Federal Security Agency and then on a subcommittee headed by Senator Paul Douglas of Illinois, who recommended him to Kennedy when he entered the Senate. Sorensen became Kennedy's top speechwriter, policy aide, and ghostwriter.[15]

Of the three, Salinger exercised the least influence. He was not a policy adviser as James Hagerty, his predecessor, had been under Eisenhower. But it was during the interregnum that he made one momentous procedural recommendation—that Kennedy allow Presidential press conferences to be televised live. Eisenhower's had only been taped or filmed, and the White House had retained the power to edit them and revise the transcript. It rarely exercised that power, but relatively little of the conferences appeared on television in those days of fifteen-minute network news shows, and what did appear usually failed to show Eisenhower to best advantage.

Salinger's recommendation was opposed by some of Kennedy's top advisers as well as by leading members of the print press. James Reston of the *New York Times* called it "the goofiest idea since the hula hoop." But having done well and profited politically from live campaign debates with Nixon, Kennedy regarded the television medium as an ally, and he dismissed the objection that he might commit an egregious spur-of-the-moment error in the foreign-policy area. Although he had close friends who were newspaper reporters, and alone among recent Presidents had been a reporter himself, Kennedy cared little for preserving the print press's competitive advantage over television, in part because many editors and publishers were Republican. So he accepted Salinger's recommendation, and the decision was announced at the end of December.

Kennedy's hopes of using the live press conference as a way of communicating directly with the public were largely realized. The public heard and saw more of Kennedy through these conferences than any other way, and his personality, wit, and knowledge of government set a standard that his successors have struggled to meet. As of May 1961 three out of four adults had seen at least one of his press conferences, 91 percent of them had a favorable impression of him from them, and only 4 percent had formed an unfavorable one. The conferences had several fringe benefits as well. Preparing for a conference required him and his staff to stay on their toes about a wide variety of matters, not just pending crises. The conferences served as an important method of communicating with his own administration, with Congress, and with foreign governments. In addition, they allowed him to dominate the front pages, generating much more newspaper coverage than the more private sessions of his predecessors, including Franklin D. Roosevelt. Eisenhower had been the first President to appear with some regularity on television, but under Kennedy, television exposure of Presidents greatly increased. But no President since Kennedy has benefited as much from this level and kind of exposure, and several have clearly been hurt by it.[16]

O'Donnell's duties in the White House included general staff administration, arranging Kennedy's appointments, travel, and security, and, as he put it, looking after "any political problem that might be bothering" Kennedy. In the two months after the election, O'Donnell spent more than half his time working with the FBI and the Secret Service on security clearances for the many people who were joining the administration. According to Salinger, who admired him and regarded him as Kennedy's most influential staffer, O'Donnell had only one criterion in carrying out his diverse duties: "Will this action help or hurt the President?" It is worth noting here that Kennedy set a high standard for himself with respect to conflicts of interest, and his administration had relatively few controversies in this area; it never had a Charles Wilson or Sherman Adams case.

O'Donnell had a tough exterior and his job required that he turn away people. He also avoided the press, which therefore regarded him as something of a mystery. "Light-footed, tight-lipped, low-voiced, black-haired, with high cheekbones and a small smile," the journalist Mary McGrory wrote at the time, "he looked for all the world like someone right out of *The Informer* or some other drama of the 'Troubles' of Ireland." Any Presidential aide who "laughed at any scribbler who asked him for any inside information" was bound to receive little or unfavorable treatment in the press. O'Donnell and David F. Powers, who had been with Kennedy since he entered politics, looked after Kennedy's creature comforts and lifted his spirits with their optimism and humor.[17]

Sorensen was less intimate with Kennedy personally, but his policy role was greater. He grabbed hold of the special counsel's position as Clifford and Neustadt had envisaged it. Given the part he had played while Kennedy was in the Senate and on the campaign trail, it was essentially a lateral move. He was assisted by fellow lawyers and Kennedy veterans, Myer Feldman, Lee White, and, until he went to the State Department in November 1961, Richard Goodwin. During the transition the Sorensen group worked with Budget Bureau incumbents and designates on what would be Kennedy's legislative and executive program in his first months in office. At the same time they organized the work of a series of unpaid task forces to report on different policy and organizational areas. These reports did not arrive until after Kennedy's initial course had been set, but the task forces in several areas, such as education, set future agendas, and they also proved useful in uncovering talent or lack of it in prospective appointees. In addition to these responsibilities, Sorensen coordinated Kennedy's speech-writing efforts and wrote the Inaugural Address as well as major parts of a speech Kennedy gave to the Massachusetts legislature.[18]

It must be noted that no one's responsibilities were fixed during the transition. For the most part, people simply continued to work in the same areas that they had labored in during the campaign. Kennedy, who preferred working with a small, fluid, and versatile staff, did not change his habits once he was elected, nor did he rely any less on his brother Robert. During the campaign, John had said about Robert: "I don't even have to think about organization . . . I just show up. Bobby's easily the best man I've ever seen. He's the hardest worker. He's the greatest organizer." As Arthur Schlesinger, Jr., has observed, a myth arose during the campaign that the Kennedys were master political planners; in fact "they were not systematic calculators but brilliant improvisers." "Robert Kennedy's genius as manager," Schlesinger explained, "lay in his capacity to address a specific situation, to assemble an able staff, to inspire and flog them into exceptional deeds and to prevail through sheer force of momentum."[19]

Because the O'Donnell group—which, to Kennedy's annoyance, the press labeled the Irish Mafia—and the Sorensen group had not always gotten along well during the campaign, the Kennedy's perceived a need for a third group, or at least a neutral figure to ease the tension. The person chosen for this role was Frederick G. Dutton, a California lawyer who had served on Governor Edmund Brown's staff and had worked in Kennedy's campaign after he was nominated. Dutton preferred a line position and undertook the assignment reluctantly. His job was not spelled out initially except to stay neutral. After he found out from Bob Kennedy that no one had been named Secretary to the Cabinet, it was agreed that he would take that, only to learn that John Kennedy planned to downgrade the position and to dismantle the formal structure that had surrounded the Cabinet under Eisenhower. Regarded as an outsider by both groups, Dutton never established a distinctive force in the White House and left in November 1961 to run Congressional relations for the State Department.[20]

Some White House assistants such as Arthur Schlesinger, Jr., worked independently of either group, and Ralph Dungan, a veteran Kennedy staffer, kept a foot in both camps. In time a distinctive third group did emerge, though, the one surrounding National Security Assistant McGeorge Bundy and his staff, but like much of what happened, it evolved largely out of particular circumstances, personalities, and the President's needs. Bundy's individual importance was not anticipated or planned during the transition, except insofar as it grew out of the Kennedys' plan to stay flexible and to make changes as need arose.[21]

Although the Kennedy staff was not one big happy family, it would be wrong to characterize it as a set of warring individuals or competing fiefdoms either. Kennedy tolerated and even welcomed disagreements among his staff members. "When you people stop arguing, I'll start worrying," he once commented to Salinger. At the same time, he would not abide courtiers, feuds, or disloyalty once a decision had been made. He never had a staff meeting and "held to the belief," as Salinger put it, "that the productivity of all meetings is in direct inverse ratio to the number of participants."

Kennedy sometimes described himself as the hub of a wheel with a series of spokes, his assistants. Many of those "spokes," including ones that were later moved out of the White House, have commented on Kennedy's unusual ability to maintain an extraordinary number of effective "bilateral" relations with people. A key to that, they have reflected, was that Kennedy always made it clear exactly where they stood with him. The "spokes" sometimes became crossed, the responsibility lost; and all "spokes" were not equal, contrary to what Kennedy sometimes claimed. But for the most part this system worked well for Kennedy because it fit his experience, personality, and needs. Kennedy could not have abided Eisenhower's system any more than Eisenhower could have abided Kennedy's.[22]

The Kennedys thought in terms of people, not structure or organization, and in the weeks immediately after the election they sought to find appropriate roles for all the top campaign people. O'Donnell, Sorensen, and Salinger essentially continued to do what they had been doing in the campaign, but Lawrence O'Brien, another top staffer, took longer to place. Like O'Donnell, he was from Massachusetts and was a political operative and organizer. His immediate task after the election was finding appointive jobs for loyal Democrats, but later he was given the job of handling Kennedy's Congressional relations. Because of O'Brien's lack of experience in this area and because O'Brien tended to be as pessimistic as O'Donnell was optimistic, John Kennedy was slow to be convinced that Congressional relations was the right job for him. When he was later asked why his brother finally relented, Bob Kennedy explained that he and O'Donnell firmly supported O'Brien and that O'Brien wanted the job very much. It was, said Bob Kennedy, "the only natural one for him so we sort of slid him into it." The casualness and intuitiveness of his explanation characterized the way in which the staff was formed, but in this instance as in the other key ones the judgment was sound, for O'Brien proved very able at his assigned role.[23]

Although John Kennedy could fill his own staff with people he knew well from their previous work for him, he could not fill the many top appointive positions of the executive branch in this manner. Kennedy, who had expected that he would enjoy making appointments, quickly discovered that picking the right person was not easy, nor did he know enough people with suitable backgrounds. "For the last four years," he told his aides within weeks of the election, "I spent so much time getting to know people who could help me get elected President that I didn't have any time to get to know people who could help me, after I was elected, to be a good President." His experience had given him a wide knowledge of people in politics, journalism, academics, and labor, but he knew relatively few industrialists, diplomats, bankers, lawyers, military officers, scientists, or foundation executives.

Kennedy interpreted the closeness of his election to mean in part that he should reassure the country of his nonpartisanship and moderation by reappointing certain incumbents and by selecting certain Republicans. By reaching out in particular to New York bankers, financiers, and lawyers such as Robert Lovett and John McCloy, who had served Presidents of both parties, Kennedy sought to augment his narrow mandate. He also believed that men like these had something to contribute. "If I string along exclusively with Galbraith, and Arthur Schlesinger and Seymour Harris and those Harvard liberals, they'll fill Washington with wild-eyed ADA people," he told O'Donnell, "and if I listen to you and Powers and Bailey and Maguire, we'll have so many Irish Catholics that we'll have to organize a White House Knights of Columbus Council. I can use a few smart Republicans. Anyway, we need a Secretary of Treasury who can call a few of those people on Wall Street by their first names."[24]

The process of reassurance began within two days of the election when Kennedy announced that he was retaining Allen Dulles as CIA Director and J. Edgar Hoover as FBI Director. Hoover had headed the FBI since 1924 and was a master bureaucrat who had carefully groomed a reputation as a model public servant and unswerving foe of communism and crime. So great was his reputation and power that it is hard to imagine any President-elect in 1960 relieving him of his duties. "His reappointment seems a matter of course," Neustadt wrote in a pre-election memorandum, "you might as well make the most of it by an early announcement, particularly since you may well find some things you would like him to do for you, quite confidentially before Inauguration." Indeed, at Kennedy's request the FBI conducted investigations of *prospective* appointees. "He didn't have anything against Hoover," Robert Kennedy recalled about his brother in 1964, "and he thought it was well that Hoover stayed and that we didn't cause any internal disruption by firing him and that it would be well to get any speculation about that out of the way." Robert Kennedy also noted that their father thought well of Hoover. Finally, it is possible that John Kennedy feared that were he to fire him, Hoover would disclose derogatory information he had about Kennedy in his files.[25]

Allen Dulles was, of course, the brother of the late Secretary of State, but his intelligence career predated the Eisenhower administration. His espionage work during World War II was legendary. Robert Kennedy later explained his brother's decision to retain Dulles in terms similar to Hoover—that they did not want to cause any internal disruption by firing him, and they wanted to end speculation about their plans quickly. He also recalled that his brother liked and admired Dulles. Neustadt, too, recommended keeping Dulles for the sake of stability, service, and public and personnel relations, though he advised that in Dulles's case as in other retentions, Kennedy should not feel bound to keep him on over the long term. Neustadt also proposed that Kennedy name a personal assistant to the Commander-in-Chief-elect, one of whose jobs would be to watch the intelligence agencies, which Kennedy failed to do. Clark Clifford, too, concurred in Dulles's retention as he did in Hoover's.[26]

Although both reappointments were understandable in context, retrospectively they appear as two of the most questionable decisions that Kennedy made during his transition. As Attorney General, Robert Kennedy had a difficult time getting Hoover to provide the support he needed in organized-crime investigations and civil-rights enforcement. Hoover was too independent of political control and too devoted to his own limited and obsolete agenda of law enforcement. Hoover was rightfully proud of the FBI's lack of corruption, but as investigations after his death later plainly showed, the agency was afflicted by a corruption of power at the very top. When bureaucrats become sacrosanct, it is a good time to retire them, and a change of administrations provides an apposite moment for doing so.[27]

Dulles proved a bad choice in a different way. When he personally endorsed the Bay of Pigs operation to President Kennedy soon after he took office, it became politically dangerous for Kennedy to veto the operation, for he feared that it would become known and he would appear soft since ostensibly similar operations had succeeded under Eisenhower. In other words, at a critical moment early in his administration Kennedy lacked faith in Dulles's loyalty to him. (In his post-Presidential memoirs, Richard Nixon revealed that Dulles criticized Kennedy's behavior to him.) Many people were to blame for the Bay of Pigs debacle, starting with Kennedy himself, but Dulles's role was inordinately weighty because of his reputation and because of his connection with the previous administration. Afterwards Kennedy retained his affection and admiration for Dulles, though, following an appropriate interval, he replaced him. Ironically, the person Kennedy would most likely have appointed to succeed Dulles had he replaced him at the start of his administration was Richard Bissell, the CIA's Deputy Director who ran the Bay of Pigs operation. How Bissell's presence as Director in 1961 would have affected events is impossible to say.[28]

Kennedy fared much better in selecting new people for his administration. He did not get everyone he wanted for the Cabinet, nor did every top appointee fulfill his expectations, but, in general, personnel selection proved to be one of his strong points. A key to his success was that he cast his net broadly, seeking people from diverse backgrounds, and he sought people who shared with him certain important traits. As Sorensen later explained, Kennedy wanted "men who could both think and act," "an outlook more practical than theoretical and more logical than ideological; an ability to be precise and concise; a willingness to learn, to do, to dare, to change; and an ability to work hard and long, creatively, imaginatively, successfully." An important trait that Kennedy's recruiters looked for was "toughness," by which they meant "having the ability to withstand the pressures of one's staff, and to pursue long-range . . . objectives in a practical way in face of all the obstacles that are interposed by the machinery of government." Time would show that when Kennedy's appointees demonstrated these particular qualities to a substantial degree, they acquired his confidence and became influential; when they lacked them to any substantial degree, they failed to win his confidence, lacked influence, and even found themselves in new jobs at a further remove from him.[29]

The selection process was neither as systematic and thorough nor as devoid of political considerations and obligations as was claimed, though such claims habitually accompany transitions. As is also probably inevitable, the process was fairly personal, intuitive, and loose. Kennedy was personally involved in choosing his Cabinet and perhaps several dozen sub-Cabinet, agency, and executive branch officials. In filling these jobs, his most influential advisers were his brother, Robert, his father, his brother-in-law, Sargent Shriver, his personal staff, and certain older former high officials who were not interested in positions for themselves, especially Robert Lovett, but also Clark Clifford, Dean Acheson, and John McCloy. Finally, Kennedy was influenced by members of the press, including Joseph Alsop, Philip Graham, and Walter Lippmann, and by certain politicians. What made Kennedy different from most Presidents-elect was his reliance on family members and journalists.[30]

As the process got under way, Sorensen prepared a list of items for Kennedy's personnel people to keep in mind. He included nine problems to look out for: conflict of interest; compatibility with Kennedy's program; effectiveness in suggesting and implementing policy; Senate confirmation; party factionalism; political clearance and Senatorial courtesy; security clearance and reputation generally; approval of interested organizations and pressure groups; and geographical balance. He told them not to overlook "able men already in Government service, some of whom helped in the campaign or wanted to help" and the "use of patronage in the field as a tool for obtaining passage of the President's program during the first year." In addition, he reminded them of numerous lists of appointive positions that had been prepared, such as those by the Budget Bureau and Civil Service Commission, and he cautioned them to "make certain that all prospective appointees recognize their role and its limits in the selection of their subordinates."[31]

Initially Kennedy asked Shriver to run a talent hunt with O'Brien as his assistant, but somehow this soon changed and each man ran his own operation, with Shriver focusing on recruiting good people and O'Brien concentrating on placing deserving Democrats in good jobs. Both operated out of the Democratic National Committee, and there were some efforts at coordination and cooperation, though a certain amount of competitiveness and friction also developed. Shriver, who got his operation up to speed more quickly, was generally more successful at getting his recruits into prominent positions. "We'll have no trouble competing with Sarge's gang," John Bailey, the future chairman of the Democratic National Committee admitted one day, "if we can just get people who are as good as his people."[32]

Shriver was a Yale Law graduate who was a businessman, not a practicing attorney. Through his salesmanship he had helped make the Merchandise Mart, owned by Joseph P. Kennedy, into a lucrative business. He had also served as president of the Chicago school board and had worked in Jack's campaign, but he lacked Washington experience. A highly able and energetic man, he was known within the Kennedy family as one of its most religiously devout and liberal members. His staff consisted of three other men he had known from the campaign, Adam Yarmolinsky, a lawyer and foundation consultant, Harris Wofford, a lawyer and professor who had worked for the Civil Rights Commission, and Louis Martin, a black newspaperman who was responsible for coming up with black candidates. During the 1960 campaign, Shriver, Wofford, and Martin had promoted and then politically capitalized on John Kennedy's phone call of concern to Martin Luther King's wife after her husband was jailed in Georgia. Their involvement reflected both their civil-rights sympathies and their political savvy.[33]

Shriver and his associates tried to systematize their search methods by drawing up a list of criteria they were looking for in a person, including "judgement, integrity, ability to work with others, industry, devotion to Kennedy's programs, and toughness." They had an IBM executive talk to them about certain systematic search techniques used in business, but after a few days of discussion all agreed that none of them would work in this context. They mainly just got on the telephone and talked to people they knew, and Shriver also flew around the country seeing prospective appointees. "Shriver knew the kind of man Kennedy wanted," Wofford later wrote. "More accurately, since Kennedy worked well with and respected a wide range of types, Shriver knew the kind *not* wanted: the too ideological, too earnest, too emotional, and too talkative—and the dull."

Retrospectively, Wofford detected a bias among their group toward lawyers. Three of them had gone to Yale Law School, and they consulted frequently with its knowledgeable dean, Eugene Rostow. They also enlisted the help of two Washington lawyers, Paul Warnke and Thomas Farmer. Their connections in the foundation and academic worlds were substantial. Shriver had his own contacts in business and a brother on Wall Street, and Wofford's father taught at Columbia University's business school, so Wofford consulted its dean, Courtney Brown. Meanwhile their offices were filled with people looking for jobs, reminding Wofford of stories about Lincoln climbing over office-seekers. It was a terrible experience, Wofford recalled, the worst of his life in terms of dealing with human beings. It "had very few of the exhilarations of the campaign except when somebody like McNamara would be appointed."[34]

Robert McNamara was one of the few Cabinet appointees for whom the Shriver operation could take substantial credit. The Shriver-led talent hunt had greater success at turning up names for the sub-Cabinet and for regulatory commission and agency positions. It also made a significant contribution to the appraisal of candidates at both the Cabinet and sub-Cabinet level. Once a tentative decision had been made about someone by the President or by a Secretary-designate, the Shriver group would make a more intensive check by talking to people who knew the person well and by interviewing the candidate. Interviews were used mainly as a final check to see that the candidate was acceptable to the appointer on a personal basis. In one instance, a potential Secretary of Agriculture killed his chances by failing to give an adequate answer to a basic question about agricultural policy and by putting Kennedy to sleep during the interview.[35]

Kennedy's Cabinet and highest executive branch appointees included several Republicans, Democrats of all stripes, including Kennedy loyalists, politicians, lawyers, academicians, and businessmen.

The median age of Kennedy's department heads and all appointees was four years younger than Eisenhower's. Overall, his appointees were more likely to have had government as their primary or secondary occupation before joining his administration and were substantially less likely to have been Democrats than Eisenhower's were to have been Republicans. The sub-Cabinet was liberally populated by men (there were few women) who had served in the executive branch during the Roosevelt and especially the Truman administrations.

The greater governmental experience of Kennedy's highest-ranking appointees compared with Eisenhower's in part simply reflected the Democrats' shorter absence from the Presidency, only eight years compared with the Republicans' twenty. But is also derived from Kennedy's greater belief in the intrinsic importance of such experience and his lesser faith in businessmen. Kennedy believed that businessmen tended to serve in the government too briefly to become effective and he sought commitments from his appointees to serve at least through his first term as President. His appointees in turn often sought similar assurances from their subordinates. In setting this condition, Kennedy recognized an important problem of governance in Washington—transience—which scholars later highlighted. Among Kennedy's ten department heads, seven served until his death, and he named one of the other three to the Supreme Court. Three of Kennedy's original department heads served through the Johnson adminstration, though their endurance did not necessarily connote stability below them.[36]

Kennedy took several weeks longer than Eisenhower to name his department heads, for he neither delegated as much authority to so few as Eisenhower had, nor did he operate under the deadline of a trip abroad. He had substantially more personnel advisers than Eisenhower had, and he became more involved in the details of searches, in effect doing some of his own staff work. Despite all this, Kennedy, like Eisenhower before him and other Presidents-elect after him, sometimes found himself taking shots in the dark. "I must make the appointment now," he told John Kenneth Galbraith, "a year hence I will know who I really want to appoint." Inevitably some of his shots hit the mark, others went astray; in one instance, State, Kennedy probably did not know who or what he wanted even after a year.[37]

Among the first major new appointments Kennedy made outside the White House was the Director of the Budget Bureau. Clifford, Neustadt, and Galbraith recommended David Bell, who had served in the Bureau under Truman and had worked in economic development and at Harvard since then. Shriver came away from an interview with Bell in Cambridge confident that Kennedy would like him, for he reminded Shriver of one of Kennedy's oldest friends and was "low key, well informed, experienced, unideological, sensitive, quick, somewhat ironic, and good humored." Shriver quickly demonstrated the advantage of having someone who knew a President-elect well conduct personnel searches, for Kennedy took to Bell at their first meeting and offered him the directorship despite his comparative youth—he was forty-one, but Kennedy of course was only forty-three.

Bell cautioned Kennedy that he had never run a big organization and that he lacked familiarity with Congress, but Kennedy reassured him that he had never run a big organization before either and that he and his staff did have substantial experience with Congress and would be able to help out there. Afterward Kennedy praised Shriver for his work, while also cautioning him to improve his briefings prior to an interview. "Next time you bring me an academic who doesn't have a Ph.D. make sure I have the facts straight so I don't sound stupid." Kennedy had mistakenly called Bell "Doctor."

At their first meeting, Kennedy agreed with Bell's view (which was also emphatically Neustadt's) that the Budget Bureau should not simply be the President's accountant as it had under Eisenhower, but that it should provide staff service in the policy field. It should not only say "no" to Cabinet officers' requests but should be able to tell the President when "yes" should be said. Bell also readily got Kennedy's permission to retain Elmer Staats, a career civil servant, as Deputy Director. By early December Bell, who was well known and liked at the Bureau, had, with the approval of incumbent Director Maurice Stans, occupied an office at the Bureau and was getting full briefings. Because his appointment came several weeks later than Dodge's had in 1952, he missed most of the final mark-up sessions on the 1962 budget. As Kennedy named his department heads, Bell briefed them and held discussions on major questions of policy and organization. Probably most important, he worked closely with Sorensen on formulating Kennedy's program. Thus, he was operating at full throttle well before Inauguration and was able to provide Kennedy with invaluable service early in his adminstration. He had also laid the basis, both personally and institutionally, for an influential role in the administration. Because of his great confidence in Bell, Kennedy later asked him to take over the directorship of the troubled foreign aid program.[38]

The first three Cabinet members named were politicians personally known to Kennedy and did not arise from the talent hunt. Governor Abraham Ribicoff of Connecticut had been a loyal supporter of Kennedy since 1956 and Kennedy was anxious to reward him. According to Robert Kennedy and Kenneth O'Donnell, Ribicoff turned down Attorney General because he did not think it would be a good idea politically to have an Irish Catholic President and a Jewish Attorney General enforcing school desegregation in the Protestant South. In addition, Robert Kennedy recalled, Ribicoff aspired to Felix Frankfurter's Supreme Court seat and feared that he would make so many enemies as Attorney General as to jeopardize his confirmation.[39]

Ribicoff instead agreed to take Health, Education and Welfare, which relieved Kennedy of pressure from an intensive campaign to give that post to Michigan Governor G. Mennen Williams, a prominent liberal who had a reputation for financial profligacy. Ribicoff, on the other hand, was known for his prudent financial management, which Kennedy believed would give him greater credibility with Congress. Ribicoff's appointment also laid to rest Shriver's own hopes for a Cabinet position; if Kennedy were to have any relative in the Cabinet, it would be his brother Robert. Simultaneous with the announcement of Ribicoff's appointment came one for Williams as Assistant Secretary of State for Africa. Kennedy realized that Williams's designation prior to the naming of a Secretary of State was odd and could embarrass his future Secretary, but he went ahead with it for his own sake. "Soon as he made that announcement," Clifford observed in early 1961, "that just turned the spiggot off on all of the Williams pressure that had built up over the country."[40]

Political considerations also weighed heavily in the appointment of North Carolina Governor Luther Hodges as Secretary of Commerce. First, Hodges was from the South, and Kennedy wanted Southerners in his administration. Kennedy had previously demonstrated his interest in southern support by taking Lyndon Johnson as his running mate, a move that had paid off handsomely in keeping the South quite solidly Democratic in November. So appointing Southerners to high positions both rewarded an important constituency and encouraged its future loyalty. In 1956 Hodges had supported Kennedy's Vice Presidential candidacy, but he had been an ardent opponent of his Presidential candidacy at the 1960 convention. Like most southern politicians, he had been for Johnson.

Terry Sanford, the Democratic nominee to succeed Hodges, on

the other hand, had backed Kennedy. That did not please Hodges or most of the North Carolina delegation. Robert Kennedy recalled Sanford's coming to his brother and saying should he ever suggest Hodges for any job, Sanford should be thrown out of the office. Yet after Sanford and Kennedy were both elected, Sanford reversed himself because he wanted Hodges out of the state. The Commerce Department mattered little to Kennedy. Hodges had been a businessman and had a good reputation as a governor, so Kennedy offered him the Secretaryship. Their meeting lasted only eight or ten minutes, Hodges recalled, with Kennedy merely emphasizing the importance of expanding exports in order to reduce America's balance of payments problem and Hodges winning Kennedy's consent to name his own staff.[41]

In contrast to the South, Kennedy had few political obligations to the West because he had garnered little support there either for his nomination or his election. Nor did he have much of a program in mind for Interior. At the urging of his brothers Robert and Edward, who had managed his campaign in the West, he decided quickly and easily upon Stewart Udall, a young and able Arizona Congressman who was one of the few western politicians of any prominence to work hard both for Kennedy's nomination and for his election. When Kennedy saw Udall to offer him the top spot, Kennedy picked up the phone, Udall recalled, "doing what he thought was a clever bit of base touching." He called Clinton P. Anderson of New Mexico, who had served as Secretary of Agriculture under Truman and who was now one of the most powerful men in the Senate.

Kennedy flattered Anderson by saying that "of course, if you are interested in the job you would be my first choice." Udall remembered that Anderson practically knocked Kennedy "off his feet by saying, 'I'm interested.' " Within a few days it became clear that Anderson was just playing poker. He wanted to kill the nomination of someone he violently opposed who was rumored to be the new Commissioner of Indian Affairs. Once Anderson had been satisfied on that score, his interest in the Secretaryship died. It was lucky for the Kennedys, who thought Anderson would have wanted to appoint some unsavory people to Interior jobs.[42]

Kennedy also had no trouble deciding on Arthur Goldberg as Secretary of Labor. Both John and Robert knew Goldberg well from their work on labor legislation and labor racketeering. He was their friend and political ally. A lawyer for unions, Goldberg was widely respected for his intelligence, energy, and independence. His name did not appear on the list of candidates submitted by George Meany on behalf of the AFL-CIO, but that did not discourage the Kennedys because the same unions that opposed Goldberg opposed them. They did not want a representative of labor as a Secretary anyway, but a representative to labor. Goldberg dragged his heels in accepting the job, however, because he desired a federal appellate judgeship in his home state of Illinois. The Kennedys promised to consider him for any vacancy there, and President Kennedy of course later topped that by naming him to the Supreme Court.[43]

Agriculture proved more difficult to resolve. "The Kennedys were urban types for whom agricultural policy was a mystery," Schlesinger later wrote. "I don't want to hear about agricultural policy from anyone except you," John Kennedy once told Galbraith, who had started out as an agricultural economist, "and I don't want to hear about it from you." Kennedy wanted someone smart enough and tough enough to take the problems of agriculture, seemingly insoluble, off his shoulders. He went through a series of candidates who failed to impress him as being that person, and finally his search came down to two recently defeated midwestern politicians who had both been his political supporters, George McGovern, a young South Dakota Congressman who had lost his bid for the Senate, and Orville Freeman, the Governor of Minnesota. McGovern was opposed by members of Congress who felt he lacked the seniority to warrant such an appointment. (He became director of a new Food for Peace program in the White House and in 1962 went back to South Dakota and won a Senate seat.)

Having been bloodied in Minnesota's political wars, Freeman initially had little desire to enter the fray at Agriculture, but by the time Kennedy asked him to take the job he had changed his mind. Perhaps fortunately for Freeman he did not have to undergo an interview with Kennedy. In contrast to some of the other candidates, he was a political ally who had given an impressive nominating speech for Kennedy at the 1960 Democratic convention. By the time Kennedy got around to seeing him, it was mid-December, and all of Freeman's competitors had been eliminated. Kennedy spoke to Freeman very briefly at Kennedy's Georgetown home. The house was so crowded that they sought privacy in a bathroom. The only condition Kennedy set was that Freeman choose an Undersecretary from the South, for Kennedy had been under intense pressure to name a Secretary from there. Freeman readily consented and soon named Charles Murphy, a Washington lawyer and onetime special counsel to Truman who had originally come from North Carolina.

Freeman further assuaged Southerners on Capitol Hill by naming Southerners of more recent vintage to several other high posts.[44]

Kennedy was equally uninterested in the Post Office Department. Stories appeared in the press that Congressman William Dawson, an elderly black Congressman from Chicago and a committee chairman, would be named Postmaster General. Dawson, however, was not well regarded by the Kennedys and they arranged an artifice through Chicago Mayor Richard Daley, a friend of theirs and of Dawson. After meeting with Kennedy, Dawson announced that he had been offered the job but had declined because of his health and age. In the end, it went to J. Edward Day, a former associate of Adlai Stevenson who had become an insurance executive in California. Kennedy wanted someone from the West Coast, and he preferred a businessman so as to deemphasize the political aspects of a traditionally partisan position. The appointment was made hastily in order to complete the Cabinet, and the Kennedys later regretted their choice. Day became so suspicious of the Deputy Postmaster General, whose political connections were better than his, that he forced his transfer to another job. Day nevertheless resented his own lack of access to the President and eventually resigned.[45]

The State, Defense, and Treasury Departments concerned Kennedy far more than did Interior, Agriculture, Labor, Commerce, or the Post Office. While the top jobs in the latter departments went to trusted friends and fulfilled regional political interests, the former went to people Kennedy did not know and who were not his partisans. Indeed, their lack of identification with him was an essential requirement of their appointment, for it was through these most prestigious appointments that Kennedy hoped to reassure the country following his razor-thin victory. Whether such reassurance was really necessary is hard to say, but it was understandable in light of the election returns, the Congressional situation, Kennedy's perceptions of the foreign and economic scenes, and his own practical, nonideological approach to governance.

Robert A. Lovett proved to be Kennedy's most important adviser with respect to filling these three posts. Lovett had a unique set of qualifications. He was a Republican who had served as George Marshall's Under Secretary of State and as Secretary of Defense during the Truman administration, and he was an international investment banker on Wall Street. He was a leading establishment figure, a gentleman, a patriot, and a sophisticate. Kennedy barely knew Lovett when he sent Clifford to offer him the Treasury

Department at the end of November. Because he had stomach ulcers, Lovett was reluctant to accept but agreed to consult his physician. Several days later he had lunch with Kennedy in George-town and reported that his physician had confirmed his apprehension and indicated that he might need major surgery soon, which turned out to be the case. Kennedy knew from experience how limiting physical problems could be and was very understanding toward Lovett. In the course of their conversation, Kennedy indicated that he would have been happy to have Lovett at State or Defense but had decided to offer him Treasury because it could be staffed in such a way as to place the least onerous demands on him. "I must confess that this show of trust and confidence," Lovett later revealed, "was a very moving thing and I found it difficult to put into words the appreciation I felt for his attitude."[46]

In this and subsequent conversations, Kennedy and Lovett were clearly charmed by each other. They were both urbane men with a feel for power. Lovett was greatly impressed by Kennedy's apparent indifference to people's political preferences, including Lovett's own, for he had voted for Nixon. He admired Kennedy's thirst for information and was delighted by his wry sense of humor. When Lovett expressed his dislike for serving on committees, they laughed together at the old wartime crack about "a committee being a group of men who, as individuals, can do nothing but who, as a committee, can meet formally and decide that nothing can be done." "No doubt Lovett's urbane realism was a relief from the liberal idealists, like myself," Schlesinger later reflected, "who were assailing the President-elect with virtuous opinions and nominations. Certainly Lovett opened a new sector of talent for him and exerted a quiet influence on his tastes in the next weeks." Since Kennedy was dealing constantly with people ambitious for office themselves or promoting the candidacy of others, Lovett's combination of disinterestedness and experience magnified his influence.[47]

Lovett gave Kennedy his views on the characteristics he thought were needed in the three Cabinet members and the names of people who he believed had them. The Defense Department, in his view, needed someone with a good background in statistical control in order to deal with basic problems of duplication and inefficiency in the Pentagon. He suggested three or four people, including Robert S. McNamara, who had just been named president of Ford Motor Company the day after Kennedy's election, the first nonfamily member to occupy that position. When Lovett was Assistant Secretary of War for Air during World War II, he had brought to the

Pentagon a team of management specialists from Harvard Business School, McNamara among them, and he had performed brilliantly. At war's end, McNamara had planned to return to the Harvard business faculty as a junior professor but had incurred large financial debts as a result of his wife's bout with polio, so he agreed to join Charles B. Thornton and eight other "whiz kids" who sold their services as a package to the ailing Ford Motor Company.

Shriver did further research on McNamara and discovered that he was an unusual man. It was a rare automobile executive who lived in Ann Arbor, an academic town, and who maintained close ties with the academic community. McNamara contributed to liberal causes and participated in great books seminars. "How many other automobile executives or Cabinet members read Teilhard de Chardin?" asked Shriver, who himself did. For recreation McNamara climbed mountains and skied, which made him attractive to the Kennedys, who valued physical vigor and daring. Although nominally a Republican, McNamara had contributed to certain Democratic candidates and was well regarded by Democratic politicians in Michigan and by leaders of the United Auto Workers. O'Donnell later recalled, however, that if McNamara had been Catholic, Kennedy would have stricken his name from the list. Ironically, it would have deprived the first Catholic President of the services of a man he came to regard most highly.

When Shriver first saw McNamara on Kennedy's behalf, McNamara was not very interested in joining the administration. He had just taken over at Ford; a move to Washington would mean a significant financial sacrifice and impose a strain on his family. But Shriver persuaded McNamara to see Kennedy and when he did he began to waiver. He was impressed by Kennedy; he felt he had already made all the money he would ever need; and he believed in public service. He was not interested in the Treasury Department, which Shriver had also raised with him, but in the Defense Department where he had once served and where his industrial experience could be most directly applied. McNamara knew nothing about strategic forces and they were simply not discussed. Indeed, their discussion of all defense matters was exceedingly general.

McNamara did have an excellent grasp of organizations, however, and he asked Kennedy whether he would be able to name his own subordinates, subject to Kennedy's approval, and whether he could reserve judgment on a task-force plan for reorganizing the department. Kennedy readily agreed and assented again several days later when McNamara put these conditions in writing and accepted the Secretaryship. The conditions which Kennedy and McNamara negotiated positioned McNamara to become a strong Secretary. "It was quite clear that he was going to run the Defense Department," Robert Kennedy later recalled, "that he was going to be in charge and although he'd clear things with the President that political interests or favors couldn't play a role in the operation in the Defense Department." Jack was "so impressed with the fact that he was tough about it and strong and stalwart."[48]

McNamara's appointment largely reflected an act of faith in other people's judgment. Likewise, when Kennedy had his first post-election talk with Lovett, Kennedy said that he would have to take his Secretary of State principally on trust because he did not know anyone competent for the job. As things turned out, Kennedy almost did appoint someone he knew quite well, precisely because he did know him, but in the end he chose another stranger, Dean Rusk. But where McNamara proved strong, Rusk proved weak. According to Robert Kennedy, his brother later planned to move McNamara to State to give it the kind of leadership he had brought to Defense.[49]

At the time of Rusk's selection, however, it was not at all clear that Kennedy was looking for muscle at State. Kennedy fashioned himself after the Roosevelt model. "It is the President alone," Kennedy said in a speech the previous January, "who must make the major decisions of our foreign policy." On the other hand, he seemed to understand the difficulties that a President could create. He seemed well aware of Lovett's point that "a Secretary of State is made to look good—or actually to be good—largely by the President and by the degree of backing and trust given the Secretary of State." Lovett and Kennedy also "discussed the dangers inherent in attempting to operate the Department either out of his Presidential hat or as a one-man show in the fashion that Foster Dulles did." All in all, Kennedy knew what he did not want more than he knew what he wanted. He did not want a Cordell Hull who was scorned and undermined by Roosevelt, an Acheson who was unpopular in Congress, or a Dulles, who he mistakenly thought dominated Eisenhower.[50]

Kennedy also knew *whom* he did not want as Secretary of State—Adlai Stevenson, his party's nominee in 1952 and 1956. Stevenson's primary interest was foreign affairs and he had great stature there, more than Kennedy, though that probably did not deter the highly self-confident Kennedy. Although Stevenson retained a large following in the Democratic party and was the sentimental party choice for Secretary, he was not well liked by Kennedy or by people most closely consulted on this job, including Lovett and Acheson. Kennedy respected Stevenson's abilities but regarded him as indecisive. (Suggestively, Robert Kennedy had accompanied Stevenson during the 1956 campaign; he had started out as a great admirer but had ended up so disappointed in him because of his lack of decisiveness that he had quietly voted for Eisenhower.) None of this may have mattered had Stevenson gotten behind Kennedy before his nomination in Los Angeles. Instead Stevenson had allied himself with the "stop Kennedy" movement and had asked Richard Daley, who was backing Kennedy, to switch to him as a favorite son. Stevenson sought to make amends by campaigning hard for Kennedy in the fall, which was no doubt also a campaign for Kennedy's favor when he chose a Secretary of State. But earlier memories lingered on, and Kennedy also resented efforts of Stevenson's supporters to extract a pledge from him on the State Department before the election.

Kennedy explained to Stevenson's supporters that he could not take him as Secretary because he was too controversial. "Oh, he's got too many enemies—they'll chew him alive. They'll call him an appeaser, a Communist," Kennedy was reported to have said. But that was the excuse, not the reason. Through an intermediary, Kennedy offered Stevenson his choice among three other positions, Attorney General, ambassador to the United Kingdom, or ambassador to the United Nations. Gravely disappointed, Stevenson considered declining them all, but his friends persuaded him to take the UN job, where he might make a significant contribution and from which he might hope to exert an influence on Washington. Stevenson had his pride, however, and did not jump at Kennedy's offer. Indeed, after meeting with Kennedy he announced that the job had been offered but that he had not accepted it yet. Primarily Stevenson wanted to know who was going to be Secretary of State. McGeorge Bundy, one of those rumored to be under consideration, was a Republican who had twice voted for Eisenhower. Stevenson could not see how he and Bundy could establish the necessary confidence in one another.

To Kennedy Stevenson's reaction only confirmed his indecisiveness and Kennedy was infuriated, justifiably, in the case of Stevenson's public announcement. He might have had more sympathy for Stevenson, however. After all, Stevenson had twice been chosen their party's nominee and Kennedy had just dashed his other great ambition. Kennedy later believed Stevenson to be doing a good job at the UN, but the circumstances surrounding his appointment left permanent scars. Henceforth, Kennedy had no interest in spending time with Stevenson or in giving him the sort of policy-making role that Stevenson desired and that Kennedy initially promised. Sometimes the chemistry between two people just does not work, and if that was the basic reason for Kennedy's rejection of Stevenson as Secretary he was correct not to take him. But if Kennedy's underlying reason was resentment of Stevenson for nursing his own ambition prior to Kennedy's nomination—and that seems more probable—he was unwise not to rise above these feelings, for he deprived himself of the man most likely to have provided him the wise and strong internal advocacy that Kennedy later realized he wanted from his Secretary of State, and one who had the political standing to do so.[51]

Dean Rusk became Secretary of State through a process of elimination. McGeorge Bundy, the fory-one-year-old Harvard dean, was considered too young and inexperienced. Chester Bowles did have wide government experience and, in contrast to Stevenson, political credits with Kennedy for supporting him early, but Kennedy regarded him as too idealistic, too voluble, and insufficiently tough to negotiate with the Russians. Kennedy came close to selecting David Bruce, an experienced diplomat who had been Under Secretary to Acheson and was regarded as tough enough, but decided against him because he was supposedly too Eurocentric and insufficiently idealistic. Senator J. William Fulbright, chairman of the Senate Foreign Relations Committee, came even closer to appointment. In fact, he was Kennedy's first choice because he knew him well, alone among all the candidates, and he was impressed by his intelligence, common sense, and wisdom. He was popular on the Hill as well. Robert Kennedy, however, persuaded him that Fulbright carried too much heavy baggage. He was a segregationist who had signed the Southern Manifesto against the *Brown* decision. His appointment would give the Russians a propaganda weapon in Africa. "I thought we'd have to spend so much of our time proving ourselves right on it, that we'd even have to take positions that we wouldn't otherwise take just because he was from Arkansas and Secretary of State," Robert Kennedy explained. (Later, when he and Fulbright were allied in opposition to Lyndon Johnson's and Dean Rusk's Vietnam policies, he repented his role.) Fulbright did not resent his rejection, saying that he preferred remaining in the Senate where he thought he could be of greater use.[52]

Rusk had the fewest strikes against him and the most influential

backers, Acheson, and especially Lovett and Robert Kennedy. Rusk
was a Georgian by birth, but an integrationist. He had been
awarded a Rhodes Scholarship, always an impressive credential
with the Kennedys. He was a former college professor, army officer,
and State Department official. In the 1950s he became president of
the Rockefeller Foundation, which did a lot of work in the developing world, where Kennedy hoped to see American influence expand.
He had been for Stevenson, not Kennedy in 1960, and was well
regarded not only by Lovett and Acheson, but by Bowles and Stevenson. He had written an article in *Foreign Affairs* in 1960 entitled
"The President," in which he argued that the President must take
the lead on foreign policy, though he also asserted that the President
should not engage in negotiations, particularly at the summit, and
should leave diplomacy to the diplomats. Rusk had his detractors;
Walter Lippmann told Kennedy that he was a "profound conform-
ist" who would "never deviate from what he considered the offical
view." Lovett gave Rusk only fair marks as an executive, though
high ones as a presiding officer. He recommended him as a man
who would be completely loyal to a President who wished to make
major foreign policy decisions himself.[53]

After Lovett ascertained from Rusk at a Rockefeller board meeting that he would serve if asked, Kennedy invited Rusk to meet with
him. Afterward Rusk told Bowles, prophetically, "Kennedy and I
could not communicate." But equally unprophetic, Rusk concluded
that "if the idea of making me Secretary ever actually entered his
mind, I am sure it is now dead." The very next day Kennedy asked
him to take the job. As Schlesinger later wrote, Kennedy found
Rusk "lucid, competent, and self-effacing." In fact, Rusk was a
hard-working, articulate, and loyal man who was well regarded in
his department, on Capitol Hill, and among foreign diplomats, but
who never fit well into the Kennedy scheme of things. "The system
Kennedy established required an aggressive, assertive Secretary of
State to penetrate the palace guard and make himself heard over the
cacophony in which the President apparently delighted," Warren
Cohen, Rusk's dispassionate biographer has written. "But Kennedy
had knowingly, purposefully chosen a 'gentle, gracious' man who,
wholly lacking in political power, despite his intellectual tenacity,
would not challenge the President."[54]

Rusk saw himself above all as the President's principal adviser
on foreign policy, but he never established the kind of personal
relationship with Kennedy that might have won him the hearing he
wanted. Revealingly, Rusk was the only member of the Cabinet

Kennedy did not call by his first name, and Rusk preferred it that way. Rusk refused to be drawn into policy debates within the administration lest it appear that he had lost a debate on the occasions Kennedy followed someone else's advice. Kennedy later sarcastically put down Rusk's extraordinary reticence by saying that when they were alone Rusk would whisper that there were still too many persons present. Rusk's passivity and administrative indifference should have been plain from the very start, for in contrast to McNamara, he did not insist on being able to name his own subordinates. Kennedy chose Stevenson and Williams before him and then chose his Under Secretaries, Chester Bowles and George Ball. Indeed, Rusk merely named his own executive secretary and the head of Policy Planning. Bowles and Kennedy chose practically all the other appointees, including ambassadors. Some of their choices were inspired, particularly among the ambassadors, but they naturally became Kennedy's people, not Rusk's. Perhaps Kennedy got just what he wanted, being his own Secretary of State much as Roosevelt had been his own, though without the acrimony and contempt that had characterized the Roosevelt-Hull relationship. On the other hand, Kennedy did later recognize the value of having a strong leader in the job, which is why he contemplated moving McNamara to the State Department in his second term.[55]

Indeed, it is not at all clear that Kennedy deliberately set out to be his own Secretary of State. To Lovett he had acknowledged the difficulties of doing so. Rather, he mainly seemed intent on not becoming dependent on one person for foreign policy advice, which is the way he perceived Truman to have been on Acheson. When Kennedy told diplomat George Kennan of his desire to have a small staff of people working directly for him on the foreign policy side, Kennan, who had worked under Acheson, encouraged him to do so. Ironically, the man who headed this staff for Kennedy, McGeorge Bundy, would not have even held this position had there been room for him in the State Department. He only became National Security Assistant after Kennedy's offer of the third Under Secretaryship had to be withdrawn because there were only two such positions and after Bundy declined the job of Deputy Under Secretary for Administration.[56]

When he signed Bundy on, Kennedy did not spell out his duties. In time they came to approximate those of Eisenhower's staff secretary General Andrew Goodpaster, though with more visibility and with greater influence, managing the President's personal day-to-day foreign and defense concerns. Eisenhower's National Security

Assistant had served a planning function and had become the center of a large, complex bureaucracy, which had come under significant fire from Senator Henry Jackson, Professor Richard Neustadt, and others who saw all of its faults and few of its virtues and who were caught in the myth Eisenhower helped create about himself, that he ratified the work of committees. Bundy quickly liquidated that bureaucracy. With just ten to twelve people under him, Bundy eventually created a highly operational staff for the President. In a way, Bundy became Under Secretary to Kennedy as Secretary.

In a 1964 interview, Robert Komer, one of Bundy's deputies, described the flavor of the operation. "Kennedy made very clear we were his men, we operated for him, we had direct contact with him," he said. "This gave us the power to command the kind of results that he wanted—a fascinating exercise in a presidential staff technique, which insofar as I know, has been unique in the history of the presidency." (With Kennedy it became the norm.) The staff acted as Kennedy's "eyes and ears." It monitored diplomatic cables and gave Kennedy advance information and independent judgment on what was brewing in the national security area. Finally, it provided "follow through," working "to keep tabs on things and see that the cables went out and responses were satisfactory, and that when the policy wasn't being executed, the president knew about it and he could give another prod."

Bundy himself remained basically a facilitator, not an advocate; he observed proprieties with Rusk and the two men avoided personal rivalry. But there is no doubt that Bundy and his staff eclipsed Rusk and the State Department in influence. According to Robert Kennedy, his brother "really felt at the end that the ten or twelve people in the White House who worked under his direction with Mac Bundy . . . really performed all the functions of the State Department." This is not how things began; nor did it happen by design. Rather, it derived from Kennedy's desire to be his own Secretary, from certain deep-seeded institutional developments, and from a process of personnel selection by elimination which gave him a passive, reticent, and deliberative Secretary and a National Security Assistant who was eminently capable of providing him with the quick, intelligent, and operational responses he desired.[57]

For Secretary of the Treasury, Kennedy seriously considered only candidates who were likely to reassure the financial community, which was jittery because of a balance-of-payments problem, a gold drain, and Kennedy's election. Neustadt pointed out that any Secretary of the Treasury would end up as a spokesman for the financial community, so he "might as well begin as an effective spokesman *to* them." He suggested that Kennedy look for "a Lovett, a McCloy, a Dillon; a 'Wall Street internationalist,' sophisticated in foreign affairs and prepared for 'positive government.' " After turning down Kennedy's offer to be Secretary, Lovett made it clear that some of Kennedy's economic advisers had no credibility on Wall Street. "I told him," Lovett recalled, "that I thought that Galbraith ranked higher as a novelist than as an economist." He confessed that "during his Presidential campaign his apparent reliance on the views and theories of some of his outer-fringe Harvard economists caused me to look longingly at Republican conservatism without going so far as to wholly embrace Adam Smith or Dr. Milton Friedman of Chicago."[58]

After McNamara also turned down the position, Kennedy considered several other men, all of them acceptable to Wall Street. His ultimate choice, C. Douglas Dillon, was the incumbent Under Secretary of State and was a Republican who had contributed to Nixon's campaign. He was the son of a prominent investment banker in whose firm he had worked before entering government. His candidacy was ardently backed by two of Kennedy's friends in the press, Joseph Alsop and Philip Graham, publisher of the *Washington Post*. "Joe Alsop was a tremendous booster of Douglas Dillon," Robert Kennedy dictated in a memorandum in early 1961. "In view of all the favors that Alsop had done I don't think there's any question that this was a factor. However, obviously if Dillon hadn't shaped up and hadn't impressed Jack the decision would have been quite different." "Politically," he explained, "it was extremely helpful, because taking Dillon, a Republican, a man of considerable responsibility . . . buried the idea that the Kennedy Administration was going to pay no attention to their responsibility in the economic field."[59]

Kennedy's liberal allies were appalled at the prospect of Dillon. "Without knowing Dillon," Schlesinger later recalled, "we mistrusted him on principle as a presumed exponent of Republican economic policies." They tried futilely to come up with a candidate who would be acceptable to them and to Wall Street. Schlesinger told Kennedy there "was no precedent for giving a vital cabinet post to a sub-cabinet official of a defeated administration, especially to an official who had contributed to Nixon's campaign and might well have been Nixon's nominee for the same job." "Oh, I don't care about those things," Kennedy replied. "All I want to know is: is he able? and will he go along with the program?" Kennedy's father had serious doubts about the first matter and his brother Robert worried about the second. What would happen if Dillon resigned in a few months and publicly criticized the administration's financial policies? By prearrangement, Bob Kennedy broke in on a meeting between his brother and Dillon and bluntly asked what he would do if he found himself in disagreement with the policy. Dillon assured him that if he had to resign he would go quietly, and that sealed his appointment.[60]

Interestingly, Eisenhower was almost as bothered as the liberals at the prospect of Dillon's appointment. He did not believe that people who might be destined for Republican party leadership should serve in a Democratic administration, probably because he was concerned at the dearth of potential Republican leaders. He also thought the Democrats stood for the debasement of the dollar. Eisenhower discouraged Dillon from joining the Kennedy administration, but he did not pressure him. "Even if you could have, in advance, a solid guarantee that you would be the sole authority in determining upon matters that fall within the scope of Treasury responsibility," he wrote Dillon, "it is inconceivable to me that any President would in practice, retain only nominal control over these important operations. But without such unbreakable guarantee, you would become a scapegoat of the radicals." After Dillon accepted Kennedy's offer, he informed Eisenhower that Kennedy had "said that fiscal stability was essential to our national security and it was on that he was asking Dillon to take the post." Eisenhower asked if Dillon had gotten Kennedy's complete support. "That was the whole idea," replied Dillon. "It may work out for the good of the country," Eisenhower acknowledged.[61]

John Kennedy's estimate of Dillon proved correct. He was not a mismatch like Durkin. On the contrary, from the start Dillon demonstrated a willingness to be a team player by accepting Kennedy's choices for his principal statutory subordinates. This fit the Rusk model, but Dillon was a wilier bureaucratic infighter than Rusk; he established excellent personal relationships with John and Robert Kennedy, and his Under Secretaries and Assistant Secretaries, though uniformly Democratic, had or acquired their department's rather conservative coloration, so no rebellion developed within the ranks. After his first meeting with Dillon, Walter Heller, the liberal economist who became chairman of the Council of Economic Advisers, recorded that "Dillon is not only very charming (and perhaps disarming), but also open-minded, anxious to rebuild a 'brilliant' treasury staff, and understanding of some of the favorable impacts

of expansionary fiscal policy on the balance of payments problem."
After getting to know Dillon, Schlesinger wrote that "the anomaly
seemed to be, not that he was willing to join the Kennedy administration, but that he ever could have endured the Eisenhower adminstration. He used to describe the cabinet meetings—the opening
prayer, the visual aids, the rehearsed presentations." "We sat
around looking at the plans for Dulles Airport," Schlesinger quoted
Dillon. "They had a model and everything, and we would say why
don't you put a door there, and they would explain why they
didn't. It was great fun if you didn't have anything to do."[62]

Kennedy deliberately set out to balance the more conservative
advice he expected to receive from Dillon with more liberal advice
from the Council of Economic Advisers. When he offered Heller the
chairmanship after Paul Samuelson turned it down to stay at MIT,
he said, "I think Dillon will accept. I need you as a counterweight
to him. He will have conservative leanings, and I know that you are
a liberal." From the beginning there was a tug of war for Kennedy's
favor. The Council, flush with confidence from the development of
sophisticated economic models, favored a tax cut to stimulate the
economy. The Treasury, however, worried about a balanced budget
and inflation, and resisted this proposal. Kennedy wanted economic
expansion *and* he wanted a sound dollar, but the election returns,
the Congressional situation, and his plan to ask the American
people for sacrifice caused him to side with Treasury at the outset.
In 1962, after the modest stimulative measures Kennedy adopted
had failed to bring about the expansion he desired, the economists
persuaded Dillon and Kennedy of the merits of a large tax cut, but
it was not enacted until 1964. The tug of war over economic policy,
it is important to note, though intense, remained friendly, testimony
to the maturity of the participants and to the affection and loyalty
Kennedy commanded.[63]

Kennedy's most controversial Cabinet appointment was that of
his brother Robert as Attorney General. As soon as John Kennedy
floated the appointment as a trial balloon, the *New York Times*
denounced the idea editorially; "It is simply not good enough to
name a bright young political manager, no matter how bright or
young or how personally loyal, to a major post in government that
by rights (if not by precedent) ought to be kept completely out of the
political arena." At thirty-five, he was the youngest Attorney General
since the early nineteenth century when Attorneys General had
merely been private lawyers on Presidential retainer. Some Republicans chafed at his lack of experience as a practicing attorney, but

they could not object very much about his having been campaign manager since Herbert Brownell had been Eisenhower's. Moreover, Robert Kennedy was well respected in the Senate, having been chief counsel to the Senate Rackets Committee. The president of the American Bar Association and J. Edgar Hoover both wrote letters of support. Southern Democrats were lined up in part though the efforts of Lyndon Johnson. Bobby Baker, the influential secretary to the Senate Majority Leader, later quoted Johnson as instructing him: "I want you to lead all our Southern friends in here by their ying-yangs . . . I'm gonna put it on the line and tell 'em it's a matter of my personal survival." The nomination went through the Senate with much less difficulty than Robert Kennedy anticipated.

Ironically, Robert Kennedy accepted his brother's nomination most reluctantly and John, too, had misgivings about making it. Indeed, the position would not have been available had either Ribicoff or Stevenson accepted it. Both brothers feared that the Attorney General would have to do politically unpopular things in the South and that the Kennedy name would suffer there as a result. (They were right.) They had considered schemes whereby Bob would become Under Secretary of Defense to either Lovett or Thomas Gates, the incumbent. In either case, there would have been an understanding that Bob would become Secretary after a year, but McNamara's appointment precluded that. They also considered making Bob an Assistant Secretary of State, but they realized that would create an impossible situation for the Secretary. Bob was not interested in working in the White House because he was used to running his own operation and could not see himself taking orders from his brother on a daily basis. Bob thought about striking off on his own, either in Massachusetts politics or as a college or foundation president. But their father was insistent that he became part of the administration and, in the end, Jack was too.

"In this cabinet," a close friend of Bob's remembered Jack's saying, "there really is no person with whom I have been intimately connected over the years. I need to know when problems arise I'm going to have somebody who's going to tell me the unvarnished truth, no matter what . . . and Bobby will do that." Bob later recalled that he accepted the job "not so much to become Attorney General as to be around during that time." Although he initially declined the job, he could not in the end refuse his brother. Robert recalled what happened next: "He told me to go upstairs and comb my hair to which I said it was the first time the President had ever told the Attorney General to comb his hair before they made an announcement. And then when we were outside he said, 'Don't smile too much or they'll think we're happy about the appointment.' "

Although there are hazards in hiring relatives—for one thing, they are harder to fire—and nepotism never is popular, Bob's appointment proved to be one of John's best personnel decisions. He was a highly effective and important Attorney General who attracted a first-rate staff and breathed new life into the Justice Department. Interestingly, John Kennedy, who always liked to hear more than one opinion, sometimes sought Clark Clifford's views on controversial legal matters, such as whether to prosecute James Landis, a family friend and eminent lawyer. The President's use of outside counsel did not please Bob but nevertheless was a smart thing to do.

In addition to being Attorney General, Bob was his brother's trouble-shooter, confidant, and bureaucratic prodder, particularly, following the Bay of Pigs, in the intelligence and national security areas. Indeed, the only regret that John Kennedy voiced about his brother's appointment in the spring of 1961 was that he had not made him CIA Director. Bob's judgment was sometimes poor, as in his anti-Castro efforts, and sometimes wise, as in the resolution of the Cuban missile crisis. To all he did he brought a unique combination of moral idealism, hard-headed practically, organizational savvy, investigative toughness, and a fierce protectiveness toward his brother's, the President's position. He and McNamara became the two most influential members of the Cabinet.[64]

Before finally agreeing to become Attorney General, Robert Kennedy consulted with (among others) William P. Rogers, the incumbent Attorney General. Rogers did not seem enthusiastic about his taking the job, though he evidently did not explain why. "He wasn't very helpful—no, he wasn't very helpful," Robert Kennedy recalled in 1964. In a 1961 memorandum, he had also noted that Rogers said "there really wasn't much of a challenge because there wasn't a great deal to be done." Kennedy did not know that Rogers had in fact been so upset at the prospect of his appointment that he considered resigning rather than cooperate in the transfer of authority. In some ways this typified relations between the outgoing and incoming administrations—surface cordiality and cooperation masking critical attitudes and hostile feelings.[65]

In contrast to 1952 there was no acrimony between President and President-elect, no prior friendship gone sour. Eisenhower and Kennedy were of different generations, styles, points of view, and political parties. Although Kennedy had never attacked the popular

Eisenhower explicitly in his campaign, his call for getting America moving again through strong Presidential leadership constituted an implicit repudiation of Eisenhower. That in fact was how Eisenhower interpreted the election results himself. "I felt as though 'I had been hit in the solar plexus with a ball bat—' As though eight years of work had been for naught," Eisenhower later recounted. But Eisenhower, a patriot, a planner, and a practitioner of orderly process, had at the ready a telegram to Kennedy saying that he was prepared to meet with him, that he had designated General Wilton Persons, his top assistant, as his liaison, and that he invited Kennedy to name a counterpart, and that his Budget Director and Secretary of State were prepared to assist Kennedy as well. Eisenhower explained to Persons that he wanted "no general invasion of the Executive Department by the Administration—there shall be no direction of staffs by those individuals." Eisenhower had "no objection with the appointee for a Cabinet post sitting down, for example, with the present head of that particular Department."[66]

Kennedy immediately designated Clark Clifford as his liaison, and it was a good choice, for Clifford and Persons were friends, and Clifford was a White House veteran, but not a White House aspirant, and he was diplomatic. He was a better choice for this role than one of Kennedy's immediate staff members, who were all much younger than Persons and itching to get their hands on the levers of power. Clifford and Persons quickly met and established an open line of communications which enabled them to clear up misunderstandings before they became serious. They set up Kennedy's meetings with Eisenhower and with other officials, arranged for his daily intelligence and diplomatic briefings, and provided the intitial contact between Kennedy's top appointees and their counterparts in office.[67]

Persons reported in detail to Eisenhower of his contacts with Clifford, and other officeholders did likewise. Eisenhower himself wrote a long memorandum describing one of his two meetings with Kennedy which he later published as an appendix to his memoirs. The record keeping on the Kennedy side was much less complete and systematic. To some extent, this disparity is attributable to stylistic differences between Eisenhower and Kennedy. Eisenhower, the professional soldier, insisted upon procedural orderlines and formality. Kennedy was the product of a large but informal family and carried over its informality to his career. This disparity in record keeping also fits a pattern in transitions. Outgoing administrations always get busy with self-justifications and with doing things for the record—final budgets, parting public statements, and published memoirs are the most visible aspects of this. With power to get things done ebbing, they suddenly have more time to do things for the record. Incoming administrations, on the other hand, are simply too busy to worry about establishing an internal paper record for future consumption by historians. Nor do they pay much mind to what the incumbents have to tell them either; after all they have just defeated them at the polls. Thus, when it comes to relations between outgoing and incoming adminstrations, the old maxim that history belongs to the winners does not hold.[68]

Often Kennedy's people felt that their briefings by Eisenhower's people were not very helpful, and they came away from them unimpressed with the incumbents' intelligence and industriousness. After spending the morning with Eisenhower's top staff, Myer Feldman recalled, "We had more confidence in our abilities to do the job than we had before. . . . we couldn't believe that anybody in that job (special counsel) could waste three hours the way he had wasted three hours with us." Feldman and Sorensen took pride in the fact that the two of them were taking on the duties of about nine people under Eisenhower. "In talking to General Persons and Jerry Morgan (his deputy), we also got the impression that they weren't so good or they weren't so bright that we had to be cocerned about it."[69]

Kennedy was only slightly more impressed with Eisenhower himself. As they rode together to the Capitol on inauguration day, Kennedy asked Eisenhower what he thought of Cornelius Ryan's highly popular account of D-Day, *The Longest Day*. Robert Kennedy recalled in 1964 that his brother

> was fascinated that Eisenhower never read the book and in fact, hadn't seemed to have read anything. He thought he had a rather fascinating personality, could understand, talking to him why he was President of the United States; that he was a strong personality . . . [who] hadn't done any homework, didn't know a good deal about areas that he should know. I think he always felt that Eisenhower was unhappy with him—that he was so young and that he was elected President and so he always—feeling Eisenhower was important and his election was so close that he went out of his way to make sure that Eisenhower was brought in on more matters and that Eisenhower couldn't hurt the Administration by going off on a tangent and that's why he made such an effort over Eisenhower, not that Eisenhower ever gave him any advice that was very helpful.[70]

Eisenhower seems to have been somewhat more impressed with Kennedy. Prior to his meetings with him after the election, he had considered him a "young whippersnapper," according to a friend. Afterward Persons recalled that Eisenhower found Kennedy personable, attractive, and well briefed. In his memoir, written of course shortly after Kennedy's assassination, Eisenhower confessed "considerable gratification in this visit with the young man who was to be my successor. Throughout the entire proceedings he conducted himself with unusual good taste. Resisting any temptation to flood the White House with his own retinue, he came riding in the back seat of an automobile completely by himself. In our conversations I was struck by his pleasing personality, his concentrated interest and his receptiveness."[71]

Privately, however, Eisenhower sounded a more skeptical note. He wrote a friend lambasting columnist Ralph McGill for selling "himself on a naive belief that we have a new genius in our midst who is incapable of making any mistakes and therefore deserving of no criticism whatsoever." McGill, according to Eisenhower, had

hailed the assembly of brains with which the President-elect is to be surrounded. I think he is possibly correct in his high opinion of Rusk. Everything I have heard about the individual seems good. But when you have a menagerie in the State Department comprising one individual who is no less than a crackpot, another noted for his indecisiveness, and still another of demonstrated stupidity, and finally, one famous only for his ability to break the treasury of a great state, it is very difficult for me to share Ralph's high opinion—either political, economic or social—of such a group.[72]

Although each man had his reservations about the other's judgment or intelligence, they kept such reservations strictly private. Press accounts of their meetings emphasized cordiality, and Kennedy publicly thanked Eisenhower for his cooperation and assistance and let it be known that he had asked Eisenhower if he would be available for some assignments during his administration. For Kennedy such public expressions fit into his strategy of reassurance following his whisker-thin victory. So did his well-publicized and highly unusual visit to Richard Nixon in Florida several days after the election. It won public praise from Nixon as a "very gracious act" which he said was "an excellent example to not only the people of the United States but to the people of the whole world of how our American system works." (O'Donnell, who was present, recalled that "Nixon did most of the talking while Kennedy studied him quietly, as if he was saying to himself, how did I manage to beat a guy like this by only a hundred thousand votes? When we were climbing back into the helicopter to return to Palm Beach, Kennedy said to me, 'It was just as well for all of us that he didn't quite make it.' ")[73]

Kennedy's desire to reassure the public and thereby to resolve the mandate problem through high-mindedness and the avoidance of partisanship made itself evident in his instructions for the preparation of the Inaugural Address. He became dissatisfied with attempts to outline domestic goals because they made it sound too partisan and divisive, too much like the campaign. Kennedy worked very closely with Sorensen in the writing, and many others contributed to the speech or commented on drafts, including Galbraith, Stevenson, Rusk, Bowles, and Lippmann. At Kennedy's insistence it was one of the shortest inaugural addresses in this century (fewer than 1900 words), and it was also one of the most eloquent. Although he was a better public speaker than most modern Presidents, Kennedy was not a great orator; but he did give several great speeches, this among them. It was idealistic, hopeful, sober, and stirring. It was delivered on a cold, clear day following a thick snowstorm which immobilized Washington.

"We observe not a victory of party but a celebration of freedom," Kennedy began. He reaffirmed historic commitments while indicating that a new day had dawned: "Let the word go forth from this time and place, to friend and foe alike, that the torch has been passed to a new generation of Americans, born in this century, tempered by war, disciplined by a hard and bitter peace, proud of our ancient heritage, and unwilling to witness or permit the slow undoing of those human rights to which this nation has always been committed, and to which we are committed today at home and around the world." Kennedy then made a declaration that fit an old pattern of American universalism but that neither he nor the country had the means or the will to fulfill: "Let every nation know, whether it wishes us well or ill, that we shall pay any price, bear any burden, meet any hardship, support any friend, oppose any foe to assure the survival and the success of liberty."

Kennedy spoke reassuringly to our allies, to the United Nations, and to the new nations coming into being. He promised to help the world's poor help themselves "not because the Communists may be doing it . . . but because it is right." "If a free society cannot help the many who are poor," he said, "it cannot save the few who are rich." To Latin America he offered a special pledge, "a new alliance for progress, to assist free men and free governments in casting off the chains of poverty." To those nations who would call themselves an "adversary" (a word Lippmann suggested as a less strident alternative to "enemy"), Kennedy asked for a new quest for peace:

> We dare not tempt them with weakness. For only when our arms are sufficient beyond doubt can we be certain beyond doubt that they will never be employed.
>
> But neither can two great and powerful groups of nations take comfort from our present course—both sides overburdened by the cost of modern weapons, both rightly alarmed by the steady spread of the deadly atom, yet both racing to alter that uncertain balance of terror that stays the hand of mankind's final war.
>
> So let us begin anew, remembering on both sides that civility is not a sign of weakness, and sincerity is always subject to proof. Let us never negotiate out of fear, but let us never fear to negotiate.

Kennedy said that Americans were now summoned to "bear the burden of a long twilight struggle . . . against the common enemies of man: tyranny, poverty, disease, and war itself." In a stirring, often-quoted climax that exaggerated America's peril, Kennedy declared:

> In the long history of the world, only a few generations have been granted the role of defending freedom in its hour of maximum danger. I do not shrink from this responsibility; I welcome it. I do not believe that any of us would exchange places with any other people or any other generation. The energy, the faith, the devotion which we bring to this endeavor will light our country and all who serve it, and the glow from the fire can truly light the world.
>
> And so, my fellow Americans, ask not what your country can do for you; ask what you can do for your country.
>
> My fellow citizens of the world, ask not what America will do for you, but what together we can do for the freedom of man.[74]

Few who heard the speech were untouched by it, particularly the young, whose idealism it stirred. The day after Kennedy was inaugurated, for example, James H. Meredith, a black 28-year-old Air Force veteran, decided to seek admission to the all-white University of Mississippi. He matriculated the following year amidst great controversy and with the assistance of federal troops. A month after the speech was given, a Gallup poll asked Americans if they could think of anything they could do for the country and 63 percent said they could, suggesting a variety of ways. The 1960s were characterized by an unusual amount of social activism which may have occurred under any President, but Kennedy, from his Inaugural Address forward, certainly nurtured it, even if it sometimes went beyond anything he wanted or expected. With respect to the more immediate problem of augmenting—or creating—the mandate that the November returns had failed to provide, the Inaugural Address and the first impressions that Kennedy made after his election and after he took office evidently worked. In mid-February Kennedy received a higher approval rating from the public (72 percent favorable and only 6 percent negative) than did Eisenhower in mid-January (50 percent approval; 27 percent disapproval). Although all newly inaugurated Presidents get high approval ratings, Kennedy preserved his much better than most. (It was 59 percent a month before his death.)[75]

In his first six months as President, Kennedy, like Eisenhower, stayed for the most part in Washington or nearby. He gave few speeches and avoided partisanship as much as Eisenhower had, and he avoided partisan audiences even more. He held news conferences at about the same rate as Eisenhower, averaging two per month, but with the great difference that Kennedy's were telecast live and reached a much wider audience. Kennedy used the press conference to communicate, not merely through the press, but with the public. "For the first time," George Herman of CBS News recalled in 1964, "I saw a President . . . do something which was so professional, from a television man's point of view, and to me obvious what he was doing. When he spoke his set piece on Laos, he didn't look at any reporter in the auditorium, he looked right over their heads into the television camera." "We became spearcarriers in a great televised opera," Peter Lisagor, a veteran newspaper reporter agreed. "We were props in a show, in a performance. Kennedy mastered the art of this performance early, and he used it with great effectiveness."[76]

If Eisenhower was popular because of who he was, Kennedy became popular for what he was—young, physically handsome, rich, Harvard-educated, and smart. He had a beautiful, trend-setting young wife and a little girl and baby boy, at a time when America's population was growing younger; in addition, he had a large, attractive, and highly visible extended family. The Kennedys made great copy on family, society, and fashion pages as well as on front pages. By European standards they were nouveau-riches, but Americans have no prejudice against newly acquired wealth, and they respect the rich when they turn to philanthropy or public service. John Kennedy had long admired and imitated the English aristocracy. When Americans mimic aristocratic manners, they can easily seem snobbish and insincere, but Kennedy never appeared that way. An intellectual's critique of the Kennedy style sold briskly in the early 1980s, but in the early 1960s, most intellectuals, like most Americans, were more often enchanted than offended by Kennedy. In the case of intellectuals, part of the enchantment can be explained by the flattery he gave them.[77]

As a Presidential candidate, Kennedy had assiduously courted the press, with considerable success. "By the last weeks of the campaign," Theodore White reported in his classic account of the 1960 election, "those forty or fifty national correspondents who had followed Kennedy since the beginning of his electoral exertions into the November days had become more than a press corps—they had become his friends and, some of them, his most devoted admirers. When the bus or the plane rolled or flew through the night, they sang songs of their own composition about Mr. Nixon and the Republicans in chorus with the Kennedy staff and felt that they, too, were marching like soldiers of the Lord to the New Frontier."[78]

Kennedy's courting of the press naturally did not cease when he became President. He made himself available often for exclusive and off-the-record interviews, and his brother Robert and many of his top staff members did likewise. In fact, one member of the White House staff who had not worked for Kennedy previously had the experience of turning down an interview request only to get a note from the journalist informing him that the President himself had seen him. In the White House, Kennedy maintained many freindships with journalists and publishers. He followed the press closely, managed the news as much as he could, and objected vocally to critical or unfavorable stories. "Few, if any Presidents, could have been more objective about their own faults or objected more to seeing them in print," Sorensen later wrote. "He wants us as a cheering squad," complained one reporter, prompting Sorensen to write: "Indeed he did." Kennedy collided with the press on news management, self-censorship, and other matters. Many journalists, indeed most, did not become his allies, nor did they lose their independence. He received a normal amount of criticism in print, but despite such criticism and his complaints, he maintained very good relations with the press.[79]

According to one myth about Kenendy, he received little criticism in the press; according to another he was not interested in Congress and failed as a legislative leader. In fact, Kennedy cared a great deal about his legislative program and saw a significant part of it enacted. The myth grew up in part because several controversial measures he sought, particularly Medicare and federal aid to education, were stalled at the time of his death. Actually he had a higher percentage of his legislative requests approved than most recent Presidents, though his immediate successor, Lyndon Johnson, significantly outperformed him and consequently overshadowed him. Johnson was the consummate legislative leader among modern Presidents, but Johnson also benefited significantly from the sympathy generated by Kennedy's assassination and, above all, from the devastating losses in the House and Senate that the Republicans suffered in 1964. Larry O'Brien, who loyally served both Kennedy and Johnson as Congressional liaison chief, later wrote: "I would take nothing from Lyndon Johnson's brilliant and tireless performance with Congress, but I believe that, had Kennedy lived, his record in his second term would have been comparable to the record Johnson established."[80]

In the 1960 election, the Democrats had lost ground in Congress, though they still held majorities in both houses. Few, if any, members of Congress owed their seats to Kennedy's coattails, and the balance of power in the Congress was held by Southern Democrats, many of whom were to the right of Kennedy, particularly on civil-rights issues which had come to the fore in recent years. Kennedy's perilous legislative situation became abruptly clear four days after his inauguration when Speaker of the House Sam Rayburn informed him that he did not have the votes to expand the House Rules Committee when the vote was taken the following day. Kennedy was stunned, for he had earlier agreed to leave this important procedural fight to Rayburn. The Rules Committee under Chairman Howard Smith had been a bottleneck for progressive legislation, and the idea was to dilute Smith's power by adding three new members to it. Although it was Rayburn's fight, it would be Kennedy's loss, both symbolically and actually, so he asked Rayburn to postpone the vote for a week. According to Robert Kennedy, it was a fight that they never wanted to enter; they had been negotiating with Smith to commit himself to report out priority bills in exchange for avoiding the fight over committee expansion altogether, but Rayburn had been insistent. It was a "bitter fight between two old men," Bob Kennedy said, "once we got into it, it was important that we win it."

Publicly, the administration kept a low profile, for it did not want to offend Congressional sensibilities about executive interference in its internal affairs. Behind-the-scenes, O'Brien, Bob Kennedy, and Stewart Udall, a recent House member, worked feverishly to produce a majority. "Support for the new President was our main argument, "O'Brien recalled, "not patronage or arm-twisting." "Let's win this one for Jack, Jackie and little Caroline," he told one congressman. The President himself placed only one phone call, to the head of the North Carolina delegation, but the only result it had was to start rumors that he was busily pleading for votes. White House efforts complemented lobbying by Rayburn, by leaders of the Democratic Study Group, an organization of liberal Democratic House members, and by labor and liberal groups outside the House. The efforts paid off, though just barely, as the House supported Rayburn's measure by a mere five votes. The majority included twenty-two Republicans and only a third of Southern Democrats, which was all the more striking, given the role not only of Rayburn, but of Carl Vinson of Georgia, a very prominent, senior and influential Democratic ally of Rayburn. It was a blunt lesson to Kennedy of the tenuousness of his majority in Congress.[81]

It is also constituted an initiation by fire for O'Brien, who now realized that his job was so demanding that he could not also continue to handle personnel matters. He and Kennedy learned, in addition, that Congressional liaison was going to require extremely careful attention and organization. O'Brien applied his skills as a political organizer to his new work. He had an affable personality, so he overcame the liability of being a stranger to Capitol Hill at the outset. Although his staff numbered only five, he insisted that the Congressional relations directors of forty departments and agencies report to him on their activities and plans, and he strove to make them Presidential agents. He frequently asked President Kennedy to see members of Congress. Kennedy often grumbled about this part of his job; he did not relish it the way Johnson would, but he did it. Many of these meetings were off-the-record and eluded the press. Kennedy's technique was soft-sell; if arms needed twisting, it was up to O'Brien or others.[82]

In his Vice President, Kennedy had a potentially outstanding Congressional relations aide because Johnson had been a unusually effective Senate Majority Leader and had an extraordinary grasp of the workings of Congress. Early signs suggested that he would play an important role in this area. He helped out on the Rules fight, quieted down opposition to Robert Kennedy's nomination, and was elected to the Senate Democratic caucus and made its presiding officer, which was without precedent. But, stung by the fact that some Senators vocally opposed his further participation in the caucus, Johnson dropped out of attendance. Although President Kennedy did from time to time call upon Johnson for advice in the Congressional area, Johnson's potential was never realized. The precise reasons why are not known, but they almost certainly involved personality differences, lack of trust, and the peculiar nature of the Vice Presidency itself. Like most Vice Presidents, Johnson became an observer more than an influence, though he was a particularly unhappy one, for he unlike most others, had been far more influential in his previous job.[83]

Kennedy smoothed relations with Congress at the start of his administration by not requesting civil-rights legislation. The civil-rights issue was the trickiest and most divisive issue for a Democratic President to handle in 1961 because it polarized the party. As a candidate for nomination and election, Kennedy had handled the issue deftly, signaling civil-rights proponents that he sympathized with their cause (such as by calling Coretta King) while reassuring white Southern Democrats that he was moderate and realistic (such as in his selection of Johnson as his running mate). He both carried the Democratic South and won a high percentage of black votes nationwide (black votes made the difference in several Northern and Southern states). In the more liberal Congress of 1960, only the most meager civil-rights legislation had been enacted. With a more conservative Congressional makeup in 1961, Kennedy feared that not only would a fight for civil-rights legislation be an exercise in futility, but that it would make it harder for Southern moderates to support the rest of his program. He was almost certainly right on both counts.

Politically, it was safe for Kennedy to postpone his legislative promise becuse of two related reasons. Neither the four black nor the more numerous liberal white Congressmen were any more confident than Kennedy was that meaningful legislation could be passed. Second, Kennedy did offer civil-rights proponents something in lieu of legislation—executive concern and action in a variety of forms: more vigorous enforcement of existing voting-rights laws by the Justice Department, the appointment of many more blacks to high-level posts then had ever occurred before, access to the White House and Justice Department by civil-rights groups, and rhetorical and symbolic endorsements of civil rights by the President and other members of his administration. There were limits to these actions. The President himself did not mount the "bully pulpit"; he delayed issuing his promised executive order against discrimination in federally assisted housing. He also took pains to avoid offending white sensibilities, in the South, including during the Freedom Rides controversy in May. But Kennedy did enough to retain the friendship of civil-rights proponents, and when he decided that the time was ripe to take much bolder steps two years later, he was at least facing in the right direction.[84]

Kennedy's early legislative successes came in areas where his requests commanded large majorities in his own party, namely anti-recessionary measures, defense, and space. The country was in a recession when he took office; unemployment had risen from 5.3 percent in January 1960 to 6.7 percent in January 1961. Kennedy recommended and Congress quickly enacted liberalized minimum-wage rules and Social-Security benefits along with an area redevelopment program. Kennedy labeled these measures anti-recessionary, but his own economists did not privately expect them to solve the recession. Twice the Council of Economic Advisers and Paul Samuelson made concerted efforts to win Kennedy's approval for a temporary across-the-board tax cut or rebate and twice they failed. (Interestingly, Galbraith, who had not yet left to take up his duties as ambassador to India and who played an important role in the early months of the administration, did not live up to Lovett's worst fears—he opposed his economist friends on cutting taxes.) Kennedy could not see how he could reconcile a tax cut with his sacrifice theme, did not yet comprehend the new economic arguments, and did not believe a tax cut could be enacted because it would be attacked as fiscally irresponsible. "Tell them to count the votes on the Hill," Kennedy told Heller, "and see how far we would get with a tax cut program."[85]

Kennedy and the Congress were forced to revise Eisenhower's final budget upward and to accept a higher deficit in fiscal 1961 than Eisenhower had forecast. It came to $3.9 billion, whereas Eisenhower had projected a surplus of $1.5 billion. The deficit would have been reduced somewhat had Congress adopted Kennedy's program, which would have raised some business taxes, lowered others, and withheld income tax on interest and dividends at the source. Kennedy complained publicly about the excessive optimism of Eisenhower's revenue forecast, while Republicans decried Democratic profligacy. Both had a point. Budget Director Maurice Stans had privately rationalized the rosy forecasts to Eisenhower in part by

noting that "none of us" is "gifted with prophecy," in part through
political considerations: "If, regardless of economic conditions, the
new administration wanted to increase spending, a deficit in your
budget estimates could encourage them to do so quickly and un-
wisely, and they would not have to take the responsibility for causing
the budget to be unbalanced." Congress appropriated close to $95
billion in 1961; Eisenhower, by contrast, had asked for less than $83
billion in new spending authority. But Eisenhower had also be-
queathed to Kennedy a political gift in the form of a record deficit for
one year, 1959, of $12.5 billion. So Kennedy could still appear less
"fiscally irresponsible" than Eisenhower.[86]

The increased spending did not cause the economic upturn that
occurred in the spring of 1961; nor did it stifle it. Meanwhile a
combination of monetary restraint, dictated largely by the balance-
of-payments situation, the weakness of the recovery, and then
wage-price guideposts deterred inflation. In 1962 the Council finally won Kennedy over to a broad-based tax cut. The long Congressional deliberations tended to confirm initial wariness of its
political feasibility, though it was eventually adopted and seemed to
confirm the economists' analysis. It is difficult to say whether Kennedy should have taken his economists' advice at the start of his
administration, but the events well illustrated the political context
in which all economic policy is made.

Although Kennedy avoided blunt partisanship, he framed his appeals for an anti-recessionary program and for changes in national
security and space matters in terms reminiscent of the campaign. In
his early months in office, he painted a bleak picture of America's
condition. "We take office in the wake of seven months of recession,
three and one-half years of slack, seven years of diminished economic
growth, and nine years of falling farm income," he declared in his
State of the Union message. "In short, the American economy is in
trouble." But as bad as the domestic problems were, the foreign ones
were, in his view, worse. "I feel that I must inform the Congress," he
said in that same speech, "that our analysis over the last ten days
make it clear that—in each of the principal areas of crisis—the tide of
events has been running out and time has not been our friend." "Our
problems are critical. The tide is unfavorable. The news will be worse
before it is better."[87]

Some highly visible developments supported Kennedy's pessimistic view. The Soviet Union was clearly ahead of the United
States in space exploration. Large booster rockets that propelled
their larger payloads into space also provided graphic, if misleading,

evidence to the public of their edge in strategic weaponry. In Latin America, Asia, and Africa, new challenges to American interests and ideas had arisen. Eisenhower had canceled a trip to Japan because of peace demonstrations there; Nixon had been physically accosted by anti-American demonstrators in South America. In Cuba, just ninety miles from American shores, anti-government forces under Fidel Castro had toppled a corrupt dictator. Castro proved an even stronger dictator than the one he replaced, but he was also a social revolutionary who would not abide America's historic interference in his country's life, and he found in Moscow a willing new patron. In January 1961 Premier Nikita Khrushchev gave a speech announcing Soviet support for wars of national liberation, and in Southeast Asia such wars were already under way.

Kennedy entered office determined to meet these challenges. His own reputation and, beyond that, his effectiveness impelled him to do so, for he had built his campaign around them. It is impossible to imagine his taking office and announcing that he had been wrong—that America was in solid shape after all, just as Eisenhower had said. A combination of politics, perceptions, and personality produced an excessive concern in Kennedy, however, with always wanting to appear resolute and tough in the face of international challenges. But underneath Kennedy's tough image lay certain mitigating qualities. He was an idealist, though without illusions, as he liked to say, who thought that aiding the world's poor was a worthy goal in itself. He was a war veteran who emphatically believed that war was too important to be left to the generals; indeed, he gave diplomacy high priority and preferred negotiating to fighting. He took a less ideological or Manichean view of the world than Eisenhower or Dulles, had greater respect for neutralism, and welcomed a world of diversity, in which he thought America would be more secure. In other words, he was disinclined to take literally the more universalistic rhetoric of his Inaugural Address. Thus, the picture of Kennedy as a dangerous, uncompromising Cold Warrior that has sometimes been drawn is actually a caricature.

Like all other Presidents since the end of World War II, Kennedy adhered to the containment doctrine. He did not like the way that Eisenhower and Dulles had embellished it with mutual defense pacts with countries of second-order priority and importance, such as SEATO; and on the other hand, he wanted to strengthen NATO. Kennedy did not like "massive retaliation" or the "New Look" either. Like practically all Democrats and some Republicans, he was enamored of the military doctrine of flexible response. Its emphasis on a buildup of conventional forces promised to reduce the risk of nuclear confrontation and exchange. With stronger conventional forces, we could presumably deter attacks that were less than all-out, such as might occur in Berlin, without having to reach for the nuclear button. In addition, he thought we needed to develop a counterinsurgency capability in order to fight guerrilla forces. So Kennedy took office prepared to carry on where Eisenhower had left off, but also with certain notions about changing things. During his first several months in office, he encountered success, failure, and ambiguity. His experiences suggest some clear lessons for future Presidents along with some imponderables.[88]

Several Presidents since Kennedy have set dramatic goals for the country—ending poverty, curing cancer, or making the country energy independent—but Kennedy alone set one that was actually met and met on time, landing a man on the moon before the decade ended. When he entered office, Kennedy knew relatively little about the space program other than that it lagged behind the Soviet Union's, that Eisenhower had treated it parsimoniously, and that American prestige had suffered. The most important job he gave Lyndon Johnson, who knew more about this issue than he did, was to review the space program and look for some spectacular goal at which the United States might be able to beat the Soviet Union. Two events that jarred American prestige hastened Kennedy's adoption of Johnson's recommendation of a lunar landing, the first successful manned orbital flight by Soviet Cosmonaut Yuri Gagarin—to whom Khrushchev boasted, "Let the capitalist countries catch up with our country"—and the shattering defeat at the Bay of Pigs of an anti-Castro force of Cubans, trained, armed, and transported by the United States.

When Kennedy announced the lunar goal in person before Congress in May, he stressed national prestige as the reason. He was less emphatic in arguing that space exploration was an important goal in itself. Congress and the public proved very receptive. Although the lunar program had its critics—and still has—there is no doubt that it commanded a popular majority in this country from start to finish, thanks in considerable part to television, which dramatically brought the developing story into the nation's homes. It certainly also met its original purpose of enhancing American prestige internationally. It harnessed American technological and organizational skill, showed what government could do, and harmed nothing. Some people argued that it drained funds from more pressing objectives, but Kennedy was almost certainly right to observe that Congress would not have appropriated funds for *those* objectives. Indeed, he grew to like it in part because it pumped dollars into the economy that would not have been available otherwise.[89]

The Peace Corps, which Kennedy created by executive order on March 1, 1961, cost far less money than the moon landing, but it also enhanced American prestige internationally. The idea of a peace corps was not new; nor was it original to Kennedy. He adopted it after some equivocation, yet the Peace Corps more than any other initiative came to symbolize his administration in a positive way. It tapped the idealism of thousands of young people and some older citizens who volunteered to go to poor countries as teachers, technicians, health providers, and to fulfill other scarce needs. A key to its early success was that Kennedy put Sargent Shriver in charge of it, and Shriver proved himself to be an unusually able program initiator (which he demonstrated again in 1964 at the Office of Economic Opportunity). Shriver quickly recognized the importance of keeping the Peace Corps independent of the never-popular foreign-aid program, and he got Lyndon Johnson to make a successful last-minute appeal to the President to accomplish this. Its independence of other government bureaucracies, including the CIA, helped give it credibility in the Third World and it allowed Shriver, an excellent lobbyist and publicist, to build broad support for it on Capitol Hill and with the public.[90]

A more ambitious early initiative, the Alliance for Progress, which was intended to accelerate the pace of economic development and social reform in Latin America and thereby improve the image of the United States and reduce the risk of more Castros, proved much less successful than the Peace Corps. Congress made good on Kennedy's promise of a billion dollars of Latin American aid in the Alliance's first year, but that sum was paltry when compared with the continent's needs; in addition, foreign-aid rules and bureaucracy slowed disbursement. More important, many Latin American governments were perfectly content with the status quo in their countries. They welcomed the Alliance's dollars but turned away its social reform. Few countries had governments fully responsive to the aims of the Alliance. Because Kennedy's top priority in Latin America was stopping the spread of communism, he was forced to accept an aid program that achieved far less social reform or economic growth than he set out to produce. Kennedy became a more popular figure in Latin America than Eisenhower in part through the ideals expressed in the Alliance, but his policies there essentially resembled Eisenhower's of the late 1950s. The surface changed more than the substance.[91]

The Alliance's record demonstrated how hard it was to change foreign policy over the long term, while the Bay of Pigs showed how dangerous it can be for a new President *not* to change it in the short term. The Bay of Pigs was Kennedy's great early disaster; no other postwar President has had anything early in his administration to match it in completeness. But Kennedy did learn some valuable lessons from it, and future Presidents, particularly those new to office, can benefit from knowing its history.

From the start Kennedy had reservations about proceeding with the CIA-directed invasion. He was concerned about whether it would succeed and how it might affect his image and America's. That is why he refused to allow overt American involvement in the fighting. It remains a wonder how Kennedy or other high officials ever believed that the United States would be able to maintain plausible "deniability" of involvement in an operation of this scale. There were twelve hundred men in the invading force, and even before they set off from Guatemala for Cuba the press was reporting the American government's role.

Kennedy nevertheless failed to cancel the invasion for several reasons. During the election campaign, he had hurled the loss of Cuba at the Republicans. It therefore would have been politically embarrassing for him to call off an anti-Castro effort that had been hatched in the Eisenhower administration, especially when Allen Dulles, a holdover, endorsed it. Dulles gave it a better chance of success than the overthrow of a leftist government in Guatemala in 1954 which the CIA had engineered. (Closer examination would have revealed that the situations were dissimilar.) Eisenhower had approved the supposedly chancier Guatemala plan, and in one of their two pre-Inaugural meetings he had urged Kennedy to give his "utmost" support to the anti-Castro guerrillas. It is possible that having been stung by Democratic charges of losing ground in the Cold War, Eisenhower took a particularly hard-line stance himself in his talks with Kennedy; it is hard to imagine that Eisenhower ever would have gone along with the particular plan that Kennedy ultimately adopted.

If Kennedy had canceled the invasion he would have had to dispose of the invading forces somehow. They wanted to fight to regain their homeland, so why not let them? Better to send them to Cuba where they wanted to be than let them vent their frustrations and disappointment about a soft President around the United

States. Morover, Richard Bissell, the bright and persuasive CIA advocate of the plan, *his* plan, confidently assured Kennedy that it could not fail. At worst, the invaders could retreat to nearby mountains and wage guerrilla war. Kennedy was reassured when the Joint Chiefs of Staff gave the invasion plans a "fair" chance of success, not knowing that "fair" meant "only fair," not "good." Kennedy was buoyed by an ecstatic report on the military prowess of the invading force by a highly decorated Marine colonel.

Kennedy heard dissenting opinions, particularly from Arthur Schlesinger, Jr., and J. William Fulbright who argued against the invasion on the grounds that it would hurt American prestige, Kennedy's own, and that Castro was only a nuisance, not a major threat. But they were at a rhetorical disadvantage, for while they invoked intangibles like the moral position of the United States and Kennedy's reputation, the plan's proponents struck moral poses and talked of tangibles like fire power, air cover, and landing craft. What is more, the opponents were outnumbered and outranked. Fulbright had clout, but Schlesinger was only a Special Assistant who had just recently been a mere professer, of history at that. As he himself realized, his memos look good on the record, but he had little influence compared with McNamara, Rusk, Dulles, and the Joint Chiefs, all of whom favored the invasion. Kennedy did take Rusk's advice to avoid direct military involvement, and he probably would have followed Rusk's advice to cancel the invasion altogether, but that advice never came. Rusk cut his own department out of what was happening, which was regrettable, for it might well have brought out some of the plan's fallacies such as plausible "deniability." It also would have challenged some of the dreamier assumptions of internal opposition to Castro.

Other factors also contributed to the final go-ahead. Time seemed to be running out as Castro was getting stronger and was beginning to receive Soviet arms. The plan arose so early in the administration that none of the top officials really knew each other. People were less likely to challenge other's credibility, to recognize ambiguity or the difference between advocacy and analysis. Believing that Kennedy was leaning against the invasion, Bundy thought it was his responsibility as a staff member to stress the arguments in favor. Sheer momentum carried things along, particularly since it came from the bright, successful, and persuasive Bissell, with Dulles's full support. Kennedy simply did not know that other high-ranking CIA officials, including Deputy Director Robert Amory and Inspector General Lyman Kirkpatrick had been excluded and had they been asked, almost certainly would have dissented. Finally, Kennedy was affected by his enormous confidence in his own luck. He had overcome the odds and been elected President, and these were heady days when it appeared he could do no wrong. The euphoria that surrounds a person after being elected President can be a dangerous thing.

When the invasion took place on April 17, Murphy's Law ruled the day: if anything can go wrong, it will. The invaders' bombers failed to destroy Castro's planes, which proved more effective than expected and knocked out the invaders' ammunition and communications ships. When things became desperate on the beach, Kennedy relented on his ban on direct involvement and authorized Navy fighters to provide cover for the invading force's bombers, but the fighters arrived and left before the bombers came because of a failure to adjust for differences in time zones. The bombers were shot down or driven off. The invaders fought valiantly, but they were vastly outmanned. What is more, contrary to what Kennedy had been told, they were not trained for guerrilla warfare, and they had landed in a swamp, far away from the nearest mountains. They had been led to expect direct American military support, but retrospectively it became clear that only a full-scale American involvement could have overturned Castro. American air cover might have bought some time, but that is all. Castro's military forces were too strong, his regime too popular, for the invasion to succeed. Most of the invaders were captured, later to be ransomed to the United States, more than a hundred were killed, and a few swam out to sea and were rescued by U.S. Navy vesssels.

Kennedy was stunned, his pain palpable. "How could I have been so stupid?" he wondered. "Deniability," far from being plausible, became instantly and totally implausible. Kennedy had been worried about appearances, but now he appeared foolish, weak, or aggressive, depending on where one stood. Although his decision had proven terrible, he did a good job of picking up the pieces. He consulted with Eisenhower and Nixon and publicly accepted total responsibility for the failure. These steps helped minimize political fallout. He also took care to avoid recriminations within the government. He appointed a panel of inquiry, headed by former Army Chief of Staff Maxwell Taylor, and including his brother Robert, Chief of Naval Operations Arleigh Burke, and Allen Dulles. The inclusion of the last two, who were in effect investigating themselves, signaled the military and the CIA that Kennedy was not looking for scapegoats. The completeness of the debacle at the Bay of Pigs, its timing at the start of the administration, and Kennedy's acceptance of full responsibility helped to produce a rally-round-the-flag effect, and Kennedy's approval rating in a Gallup poll actually rose.

After an appropriate interval, Kennedy did replace Dulles and Bissell. He put Taylor on his staff as a military adviser and in 1962 made him Chairman of the Joint Chiefs of Staff. So Kennedy learned from the Bay of Pigs experience the importance of having his own people at the head of intelligence and the military. Similarly, he began to bring two of those closest to him, Robert Kennedy and Sorensen, into critical foreign policy deliberations. The deliberations prior to Kennedy's decision had been characterized by looseness and disorganization; no one was ever sure where things stood. Kennedy was not about to adopt Eisenhower's committee system, but he did establish oversight and coordinating committees that had not existed before, and he strengthened Bundy's role as a watchdog and channel while also creating an important, analogous role for Taylor. Although the military, including Taylor, looked dimly upon what they regarded as Kennedy's excessive interference, Kennedy drew the opposite lesson from the Bay of Pigs—that he had lost control of the situation, not that he had controlled too much. This lesson served him well during the Cuban missile crisis. Indeed, he came to regard the Bay of Pigs as almost a blessing in that it taught him painful lessons that helped avert much worse catastrophes in the future. Indeed, the Bay of Pigs provides plain lessons for all Presidents in the need for skepticism, caution, and control, particularly in their first months in office when hopefulness, innocence, and bureaucratic and political momentum can weave insidious webs around them.

The Bay of Pigs experience did not teach Kennedy to stop meddling in the internal affairs of a foreign country, only to keep down the "noise level." Prodded by Robert Kennedy and Taylor, the CIA continued to seek Castro's removal. Without the Kennedys' knowledge, the CIA interpreted "removal" to mean assassination. Although its assassination efforts failed, their discovery by Castro may have triggered retaliation in the form of Kennedy's own assassination. We will probably never know. But it is certain that though the Bay of Pigs taught Kennedy the need to control the CIA, he was less than successful in achieving it. The Bay of Pigs also reinforced Kennedy's belief in the need for a better nonconventional and counterinsurgency capability so as to keep future Castros from power in the first place. Latin American governments used counterinsurgency techniques learned from U.S. advisers to crush leftist opposition, though it is debatable whether the long-term interests of the United States were thereby enhanced. But American interests certainly were not well served by U.S. military intervention in South Vietnam, which Kennedy hoped to restrict to counterinsurgency on a fairly small scale but which escalated after his death into something much larger and more conventional.[93]

Laos, which probably occupied more of Kennedy's time than any other issue in his first two months in office, had the potential of becoming another trap, like the Bay of Pigs, but Kennedy never fell into it because he reached an early and wise conclusion that altered the course he inherited. Laos was in crisis when Kennedy came into office, an obscure and murky battleground of political factions, personalities, feudalism, tribal culture, and social revolution set against the background of the Cold War. Eisenhower had backed conservative factions, driving the neutralists into alliance with the Communists. Unfortunately for Washington, its clients had proven so weak militarily and politically that on the eve of Kennedy's inauguration their fate was precarious. In the second pre-Inaugural meeting between Eisenhower and Kennedy, Laos dominated discussion. Although the situation seemed bad enough to Kennedy that he asked how long it would take to put an American division into the country, he did not regard Laos as a land "worthy of engaging the attention of great powers." According to Schlesinger, Kennedy believed "the effort to transform it into a pro-Western redoubt had been ridiculous and that neutralization was the correct policy." But because American prestige had already been committed, Kennedy thought it "essential to convince the Laotian communists that they could not win and to dissuade the Russians from sending further military assistance."[94]

In his first press conference, Kennedy declared his hope that Laos would become a "peaceful country—an independent country not dominated by either side." In his characteristic way, he established a task force and closely monitored Laotian developments. Winthrop Brown, the new American ambassador and a fellow proponent of neutralization, later explained how much help it was "when the President is your desk officer." Meanwhile, the right-wing government's military situation worsened, and Soviet arms continued to flow to the Communist insurgents. Walt Rostow, Bundy's deputy, advocated sending a small American force to bolster the Royal Laotian Army. The Joint Chiefs, on the other hand, either wanted to go all-out, possibly even using nuclear weapons, or they wanted to stay out of Laos. Their all-or-nothing approach and their inability to provide answers to certain questions Kennedy raised shook his confidence in them and helped persuade him to hire Taylor and to step up counterinsurgency training.

Kennedy pursued his objective of neutrality diplomatically with the Soviets and through allies and neutrals. At the same time he placed some American forces on alert, which was done in a way that the Soviets were sure to notice. Kennedy and his advisers concluded that this threat of direct involvement worked; the Soviets did soon begin to sound more cooperative. Indeed, that was the one clear Soviet concession at the Vienna summit meeting. In 1962 a ceasefire and neutralization were achieved. It is important to note, however, that neutralization had always been a professed Soviet objective, so it is possible that the major break in the crisis came with *Kennedy's* policy shift at the very start of his administration. In addition, though Kennedy made it look like he would use force, he did not actually use it; Averell Harriman, who was closely involved in the Laotian crisis, did not know what Kennedy would have done had a ceasefire not later been arranged. In 1965 Schlesinger called Laos a dress rehearsal for the Cuban missile crisis, and that it may have been, not only in its public display of a threat of force, but in its reliance on compromise and diplomacy for resolution.[95]

Fortunately, and unlike the Bay of Pigs, there had been no electoral campaign momentum to carry Kennedy into Laos. In the national defense area, there was a great deal of momentum, not just from the campaign, but from the influential critique of Eisenhower's approach to defense that had developed in the 1950s. The campaign had merely popularized that critique. So it was no surprise that in his first months in office, Kennedy told his Secretary of Defense to consider only what would constitute a sufficient defense and not to worry about how much it might cost, that he ordered a buildup in conventional and counterinsurgency forces, and that he accelerated the construction and deployment of land and sea-based missiles so as to close the alleged missile gap. Stronger conventional forces were needed, Kennedy and the Eisenhower critics argued, to reduce reliance on massive retaliation and to provide for a graduated, flexible response rather than a total response to a Soviet attack, on Berlin for example. Counterinsurgency forces were required, they believed, to fight the new wars of national liberation that the Soviet Union was supporting in former colonies. Additional and less vulnerable missiles were needed to improve America's deterrent; if the United States could survive a Soviet first-strike and launch an effective second-strike, the Soviets would be unlikely to launch a first-strike.

Much controversy continues to surround Kennedy's defense policies. Did the acceleration of the missile program exemplify the ratcheting effect? (We build up on the basis of Soviet capabilities, which we interpret as intentions; they then match our buildup.) Did our buildup scare the Soviets into their desperate attempt to catch up quickly by placing missiles in Cuba, thus precipitating the Cuban missile crisis? Did the expansion of conventional and counterinsurgency forces grease the way toward our military involvement in Vietnam, a country of marginal importance to the United States? In view of the fact that Kennedy accepted Eisenhower's strategic triad of land and sea-based missiles and B-52 bombers, were the changes he wrought even significant? To what extent was Kennedy determining events in the arms race and the Cold War? To what extent were events being shaped in Moscow, by technological and bureaucratic imperatives, and by larger forces of history, ideology, and international relations?

Kennedy's own defense and national security appointees today disagree among themselves about answers to such questions. Analysts outside the government likewise offer conflicting answers. Their elaborate analyses are based on much less than complete evidence on the American side and scanty information on the equally important Soviet side. Yet it does seem likely, for example, that Kennedy accelerated missile deployments more on the strength of campaign momentum than hard intelligence. After hard intelligence from satellite reconnaissance and from a Soviet spy did show irrefutably that there had been an intelligence gap, rather than a missile gap, Kennedy had a high defense official acknowledge the gap's demise, but by then the American buildup was under way. Kennedy, moreover, failed to educate the public on the true nature of the non-existent missile gap.[96]

Although Kennedy appears guilty of certain excesses on defense matters, he also was interested from the very start of his administration in trying to achieve greater rationality, coherence, and control of military decisions. In McNamara he had an excellent person to pursue these goals. Although he had been away from the Pentagon since the end of World War II, McNamara was an extraordinary fast learner and he was a leader. Within his first six months in office, aided by able and quite young civilian appointees, McNamara asked searching questions, imposed systems analysis, demanded greater coherence in weapons procurement, and raised the intellectual level of discussion about nuclear strategy. "Under Eisenhower strategy tended to be a series of presumptions, which were neither exactly stated nor rigorously tested," Michael Mandelbaum has written. "McNamara ushered in strategy by calculation." Not surprisingly, "McNamara's revolution," as it was sometimes called, dismayed some old Pentagon hands and met resistance, some of it successful. Because McNamara enjoyed Kennedy's full backing, however, which strengthened his hand with Congress, he achieved more effective control of the Pentagon than most Secretaries.[97]

The late 1950s and early 1960s were not only years of an arms race and tough public postures by both sides in the Cold War but of direct talks between Soviet and American leaders. Eisenhower met with Soviet leaders in Geneva in 1955 and at Camp David in 1959. Each meeting fostered public hopes of an eventual accord, but neither produced concrete results. The planned summit meeting in Paris in May 1960 was abruptly canceled by Khrushchev after the Soviets shot down a U-2 spy plane and Eisenhower refused to apologize for the overflights which had been going on for three and a half years. "We shall not tolerate insults," Khrushchev declared; "we have our pride and our dignity. We represent a mighty socialist state." Likewise the two sides talked to each other about disarmament and restricting nuclear testing, but the discussions failed to achieve results.[98]

The essential pattern of talking but getting nowhere and sending public signals that were alternately hopeful and ominous continued unchanged in the early part of the Kennedy administration. Kennedy sent a new team with some new concessions to ongoing discussions in Geneva about a nuclear test ban, but they failed to satisfy the Soviets. (Some high Kennedy officials now believe that the United States could have safely accepted virtually any Soviet proposal.) As a goodwill gesture to Kennedy when he took office, Khrushchev released two American airmen whose plane had been downed in the Soviet Union the previous summer. He also indicated to the American ambassador in Moscow that he would like to meet with Kennedy as soon as possible. On the other hand, Khrushchev gave an ominous speech on January 6 in which he made threatening noises about West Berlin, long a bone of contention between East and West, and promised Soviet support for wars of national liberation.[99]

Kennedy met with Khrushchev for two days in Vienna in May. Records of their conversations are still closed, but published accounts by Kennedy administration officials and personal interviews all confirm Kennedy's own public characterizations of the talks as sober and somber. The Vienna meetings were intended to allow the two leaders to get to know each other, but when Khrushchev challenged him verbally, Kennedy had no choice but to respond with equal toughness. Because so little was accomplished at Vienna, some of Kennedy's advisers have concluded that summit meetings should be avoided except when they ratify decisions that have already been reached. On the other hand, there is litle evidence that Vienna actually did great harm. Indeed, it may have been useful for the two men to take each other's measure in person. It reduced the chances of war by miscalculation, which Kennedy appropriately feared as the most likely path to world tragedy.[100]

3

NIXON

☆ ☆ ☆

For a historian writing today, the Presidency of Richard Nixon poses a formidable research problem. Contrary to the popular impression fostered by the release of Watergate tapes, the vast majority of the Nixon administration's records, unlike those of the Eisenhower and Kennedy administrations, remain closed to research, including those having to do with the transition and with the early months in office. In contrast to preceding administrations as well, there are no oral-history collections on which to draw. Many of the key actors, starting with Nixon himself, have written memoirs, and some agreed to be interviewed for the purposes of this book. All oral and written testimony about the Nixon administration from high-level partici-pants, however, comes against the background of the administra-tion's demise. While Kennedy's sudden, tragic death engendered eu-logistic recollections, Nixon's exit in disgrace and the subsequent criminal convictions and jail sentences of his closest aides led to some reminiscences filled with anger and self-justification.

Had Nixon left office in a normal fashion, it is hard to imagine the memoirs of Nixon, Henry Kissinger, H. R. Haldeman, John Ehrlichman, and others reading as they do. Only the Carter admin-istration, where things also turned out unhappily, though not as disastrously, has even approached the Nixon administration in put-ting forth a collection of memoirs whose rule of thumb is "every man for himself." Yet the Nixon administration's memories of itself are among the most revealing (sometimes unconsciously so), self-serving, contradictory, derogatory, *and,* in many ways, fascinating of any Presidential administration. Nixon and his subordinates have, in addition, been scrutinized by accomplished journalists and outside observers, sometimes brilliantly, usually critically, and rarely disinterestedly. The problem comes in trying to derive the salient "facts" from this sea of perceptions, misperceptions, distortions, and missing evidence. What follows therefore must be relatively tentative and speculative, though, it is hoped, dispassionate.

Richard Nixon was elected to Congress from California in 1946 at the age of thirty-three. After achieving national recognition for his successful investigation of the Communist connections of Alger Hiss, a former State Department official, Nixon captured a Senate seat in 1950. Two years later, Eisenhower selected him as his running mate; he was only thirty-nine. He served as Vice President for eight years before narrowly losing the Presidential election to Kennedy in 1960. In 1962 he lost another election, this time to incumbent Pat Brown for governor of California. Afterward he held an impromptu press conference and vented his spleen against the press—"You won't have Nixon to kick around any more because, gentlemen, this is my last press conference."

His political career seemingly over, Nixon moved to New York, where he practiced law and made a substantial income for the first time in his life. He traveled abroad, building upon foreign contacts and expertise acquired in Congress and as Vice President. He also remained a loyal Republican, supporting the conservative leader Barry Goldwater after he captured the Presidential nomination in 1964. Many liberal Republicans such as Governor Nelson Rockefeller of New York, by contrast, sat on the sidelines that fall. In 1966 Nixon campaigned actively and effectively for Republicans of all stripes in helping the party recover from the disastrous results of 1964. In 1968 he showed himself to be his party's favorite by winning a string of primaries. He was perfectly situated in the center of the party but had particularly good relations with southern and conservative factions. At the convention he easily beat back late challenges from Governor Ronald Reagan, on his right, and Governor Nelson Rockefeller, on his left. At the age of fifty-five, he was a young elder-statesman and a seasoned party professional. He had risen phoenix-like from the ashes of defeat of 1960 and 1962; he was nominated and elected President after having been out of office for eight years.

Nixon had grown up in Whittier, California, in a family of modest means which were sapped by a brother's prolonged illness.

He had gone to the local college and then to law school at Duke University. Despite graduating near the top of his class, he had been unable to secure a job in any of the leading New York law firms. He almost became an FBI agent. Instead he returned to Whittier where he practiced law for several years before joining the Office of Price Administration in Washington in early 1942. Six months later he received a Navy commission, eventually serving in the Pacific, though not in combat.

Nixon viewed himself as a self-made man and saw life as a series of struggles, challenges, and crises; indicatively, his first memoir, written after his 1960 defeat, was entitled *Six Crises*. His political career was marked by highs and lows, by near-disasters and stunning rebounds, eventually by resignation and disgrace, now followed by renewed public interest and even respect, as reflected in the large sales of his books. His career first almost came crashing down in the fall of 1952 when a newspaper reported the existence of a private fund businessmen had raised to help him meet Senatorial office expenses. Eisenhower nearly dropped him from the ticket, but Nixon saved himself with a dramatic self-defense on national television. In later years, the "Checkers" speech brought guffaws from college audiences, but when it was originally broadcast, it evoked such an outpouring of public and party sympathy for Nixon that Eisenhower decided to keep him.

Tensions and ambiguities in the Eisenhower-Nixon relationship were evident from that time on, however. Nixon became Eisenhower's loyal messenger and performed numerous party chores, but he never became his protégé or confidant, and his advice was often either not sought or not followed. In 1956 Eisenhower again toyed with dropping Nixon from the ticket; again Nixon saved himself, this time through the support of party regulars. The two men respected one another, sometimes warily, and they occasionally displayed mutual affection, but their public statements about each other were as notable for what they failed to say as for what they said. Eisenhower almost certainly revealed more than he intended when he was asked in 1960 what major ideas Nixon had contributed as Vice President and he replied, "If you give me a week, I might think of one." Likewise, Nixon's failure to include a chapter on Eisenhower in his 1982 book on *leaders* he had known is suggestive.

Nixon embodied more than a few paradoxes and contradictions. He seemed coolly self-confident, apparently subscribing to his reputation as a young but hardworking and adroit elder statesman; yet privately he exhibited insecurity, soaking up reassurance and flattery.

His greatest ambition was to be a peacemaker, but he took pride in his toughness, rigidity, and unpredictability. A global strategist who sought international accord, an end to the Cold War, and a stable world order, a practitioner of *Realpolitik,* Nixon also was—and remains—one of the nation's most influential anti-Communists. Nixon took pride in his decisiveness, and at times he was very decisive, though he also could be utterly indecisive, which he was loath ever to admit. Nixon who abhorred personal confrontation, had his subordinates convey bad news to those affected. Consequently some of those who knew Nixon well, including certain Cabinet Secretaries, simply disregarded the instructions of Nixon's subordinates, safely assuming that Nixon himself would not be able to confront them.

Despite Nixon's long record as a Republican partisan and his repeated invocations of team spirit, he viewed himself as a loner, an outsider, a foe of establishments, real or imagined. Although he regarded himself as a big thinker and a keen student of effective organization, those who worked closest with him often felt he wasted great amounts of time in petty detail and that he lacked managerial sense. Nixon loved the "big play," the political or geopolitical master stroke, and he certainly came up with some. At times he rose above politics and demonstrated a sensitive and generous spirit, but he also had a mean, highly partisan, counterattacking, suspicious, almost paranoid side to him which eventually led to his downfall. Bryce Harlow, who worked closely with both Nixon and Eisenhower, has commented that Ike liked people, so people liked him, whereas Nixon distrusted people, which caused people to distrust him. Although Nixon claimed to be an intensely private and emotionally reserved man, he seemed to relish the limelight and the trappings of office, and his feelings were often plain for all to see. Given these paradoxes and characteristics, it is little wonder that Nixon has become a favorite subject—or target—of psychobiographers.[1]

Nixon became President at a particularly troubled moment in American history. Over a half-million U.S. soldiers were in South Vietnam, participating in a war that had increasingly divided and perplexed the American people, who watched it unfold on television day after day, seemingly endless and unwinnable. Frustrations growing out of the war, including his difficulty in keeping the public united behind it, helped persuade Lyndon Johnson not to seek another term as President. Johnson had, before this, succeeded in greatly broadening the role of the federal government in many areas, including race relations, social welfare, education, and health care. Although these legislative accomplishments had been significant, they had ironically coincided with frightening urban riots by angry blacks and with an increasing crime rate. These unwelcome developments had, in turn, given rise to reaction and white backlash.

Growing numbers of the nation's expanding adolescent and young adult population seemed, meanwhile, to be in open rebellion against traditional values and authorities. Young men's hair was growing longer; young women's hemlines were getting shorter. The nation's youth listened to music that seemed loud, alien and insistent; their language grew coarse, and they increasingly used illegal drugs. Adult America generally was either mystified by what was happening to the young or deplored it. Americans who were used to backing their government during wartime were shocked at the anti-war protests that some of the young and their professorial allies or instigators engaged in; to many, even those who could not understand what this country was doing in Vietnam, anti-war protest smacked of disloyalty. The economy had expanded steadily through the decade and unemployment was low; inflation had begun to rise, but was not widely regarded as an important problem. When Gallup (on January 30, 1969) asked the public what was the most important problem, 9 percent cited inflation; 40 percent cited the Vietnam war; 17 percent, crime and lawlessness; and 16 percent, race relations. If the society was falling apart over a distant war and over racial and generational divisions at home, what difference did economic performance make?[2]

The war, social and racial unrest, and most tragically, violence, spilled over into the electoral process in 1968. Robert F. Kennedy, a leading candidate for the Democratic nomination and a war critic, was assassinated on the morning after he won the Democratic primary in California. During the Democratic Convention in August, Chicago police violently repressed young protestors who had gathered in the city. In the fall campaign, all three major candidates—Nixon, the Democrats' Hubert Humphrey, and Alabama Governor George Wallace of the newly formed American Independent party—criticized protestors; Wallace, who had made his name as an adamant segregationist and who now led a right-wing populist movement, was the harshest of all.

At the start of the campaign, Nixon held a commanding lead in public-opinion polls, but it dwindled as the Democrats, the majority party, began to pull themselves together after the havoc of Chicago. Humphrey, who had been Johnson's surrogate on the war for four years, placed some rhetorical distance between himself and the President, and Johnson helped Humphrey's cause when he declared a bombing halt over North Vietnam shortly before the election, lifting hopes for peace. Wallace's poll ratings slipped meanwhile, but they were still substantial enough as the election approached to raise the possibility of the outcome being thrown into the House of Representatives for the first time since 1876. In the end Wallace probably did siphon more votes from Nixon than from Humphrey, though not enough to deprive Nixon his majority in the electoral college. Nixon won 301 electoral votes to Humphrey's 191 and Wallace's 46 (all in the South.) He received 31,785,000 popular votes to Humphrey's 31,275,000, and Wallace's 9,900,000.[3]

National divisions and the closeness of the election dictated Nixon's main strategy toward transition. If Nixon had been elected by 60 percent of the vote and if there had been no war under way, H. R. Haldeman, his aide, has said, he would have proceeded entirely differently, indeed in somewhat the fashion he adopted in 1972 when he did win by a big margin. But he lacked a strong mandate in 1968, a war was going on which had already debilitated one formerly potent President, the country was in turmoil, and the opposition party controlled the Congress; he was the first newly elected President in 120 years to take office with both houses of Congress controlled by an opposition party. Consequently, Nixon was worried about his very ability to govern. His entirely appropriate and probably inescapable response was to seek national unity. That was the note he struck in a widely quoted statement to the press on the morning after the election:

> I saw many signs in this campaign. Some of them were not very friendly and some were very friendly. But the one that touched me the most was one that I saw in Deshler, Ohio, at the end of a long day of whistle-stopping, a little town, I suppose five times the population was there in the dusk, almost impossible to see—but a teenager held up a sign, "Bring Us Together." And that will be the great objective of this Administration at the outset, to bring the American people together. This will be an open Administration, open to new ideas, open to men and women of both parties, open to the critics as well as those who support us. We want to bridge the generation gap. We want to bridge the gap between the races. We want to bring America together.

It was a noble though difficult objective; how well Nixon met it would go a long way toward determining the success of his transition and his Presidency.[4]

Although national unification became the principal objective of the transition only after the election returns had come in, Nixon's procedural approach to his transition and Presidency had been in formation for many years. "I had strong opinions, many of them derived from my experiences and observations during the Eisenhower years, about the way a President should work," Nixon wrote in his memoirs. "In my view, then and now, the key to a successful Presidency is in the decision-making process. I felt that the matters brought before a President for decisions should be only those that cannot or should not be made at a lower level on the White House staff, or by the Cabinet member responsible for them." That was a lesson Nixon claimed to have learned directly from Eisenhower, "whose staff had too often cluttered his schedule with unimportant events and bothered him with minor problems that drained his time and energy. I knew that I could absorb far more material by reading it than by talking about it, and I have invariably found that staff members will present problems more concisely and incisively in writing than they will in meetings." "A leader's most precious resource is his time," Nixon wrote in *Leaders*. "If he squanders it on the non-essentials he will fail."[5]

These procedural principles did not simply derive from observing Eisenhower, however. On the one hand, they grew out of campaign experience, particularly 1960 and 1962 when Nixon tended to underdelegate authority, and lost. In 1968, by contrast, he delegated far more, buffering and isolating himself in the process. He allowed himself to be managed, packaged, and programmed in ways that he had not permitted in the past, and this time he won. On the other hand, these procedural principles fit Nixon's temperament, for they allowed him to avoid the personal confrontations and disagreements he so disliked. Through memos, Haldeman once said, Nixon could be "perfectly free to turn ideas down without making his decisions personal."[6]

Although Nixon had gotten much political mileage out of his experience as Vice President, when he supposedly observed the decision-making process closely, participated in it, and learned from the masterful Eisenhower, it is suggestive that he, in fact, seemed to have derived more negative lessons than positive ones from his eight years under Ike. In his memoir, in addition to commenting that Eisenhower's time was often wasted on trivial matters, Nixon noted that he "had attended hundreds of Cabinet meetings as Vice President, and I felt that most of them were unnecessary and boring." A more poignant lesson that Nixon had learned during those years was captured in a catch-phrase from his own transition to the Presidency: there was to be "no Sherman Adams, no James Hagerty" in his administration. In typical fashion for Vice Presidents of the past, Nixon had been a kind of lesser Cabinet member who had been effectively outranked by strong Presidential staff members Adams and Hagerty, both of whom he disliked.

Thus, Nixon's perspective from the Eisenhower years was not fundamentally a Presidential one at all, but that of one of the less influential Cabinet members who find themselves being ordered about or denied an appointment with the President by a high and mighty Presidential assistant. Soon after Nixon's election in 1968, a well-informed article in the *New York Times* reported that Nixon planned to "organize the White House staff in a way that will encourage and not inhibit direct communication between his Cabinet officers and the President." Reportedly, Nixon was "eager to avoid the experience of the Eisenhower Administration, in which a small group of men, principally Sherman Adams, regulated the flow of men and ideas from the agencies to the President." People whose egos and status exceed their contact or influence with the President often believe that the reason lies either in the staff member who seemingly controls access, or in a staff system that is exclusionary. That is easier for them to accept than the reality of the situation, which is that all Presidents see and have confidence in whomever they want to, usually a fairly small number of people.[7]

Having spent eight years as second-in-command to Eisenhower, whose several health crises underscored the possibility of his becoming President, and having almost been elected President in 1960, Nixon naturally was thrilled to achieve his goal. In his memoir he described the first moment in which he could savor his triumph alone. It is a characteristic piece of self-revelation from a man who repeatedly proclaims his instinct for privacy:

> When the others had left the library, I went to the record player and selected one of my favorites, the musical score from *Victory at Sea* by Richard Rodgers. I put it on and turned the volume up high. My thoughts meshed with the music. The battle had been long and arduous. We had suffered reverses and won victories. But now we had won the final victory. The music captured the moment for me better than anything I could say or think or write.[8]

Destiny had beckoned, and Nixon went about organizing his administration with the cool detachment of someone who had spent many years as a President-in-waiting and who felt self-assured that he was up to the task. Bryce Harlow, who had worked for George Marshall during World War II and for Eisenhower in the 1950s, was impressed with how relaxed Nixon was in the weeks after his election; it seemed like he had been President for a long time. Nixon himself later wrote:

> As I anticipated becoming President, I found that I was awed by the prospect but not fearful of it. I felt prepared. I had the advantage of experience and of the detachment that comes from being out of office. The "wilderness years" had been years of education and growth.
>
> I had no illusions about either the difficulty of the challenge or about my ability to meet it. I felt I knew what would *not* work. On the other hand, I was less sure what *would* work. I did not have all the answers. But I did have definite ideas about the changes I felt were needed.
>
> As 1968 came to a close, I was a happy man.[9]

For all his vaunted experience and for all his self-assuredness, the fact was that Nixon had never before held a high executive position of real command, the Vice Presidency being a high executive position of no command. Thus, in a sense he came to the Presidency with executive experience that was largely vicarious. In this respect, he resembled Kennedy, not Eisenhower, nor two of his successors, Carter and Reagan. As Nixon went about organizing the White House operation he was eclectic in his approach, seeking to adopt parts of different administrations as needed to suit his style and objectives. Nixon immediately recruited two former Eisenhower staff members, Bryce Harlow and Andrew Goodpaster, to advise him and his staff on White House operations. Harlow had run Eisenhower's Congressional relations office, and Nixon persuaded him to leave the private sector and assume the same duties in his administration. Goodpaster was granted a military leave and helped Nixon's men create a staff secretariat somewhat on the model of the one Eisenhower had used. Nixon visited several times with Eisenhower himself, who was in failing health, but he did not consult with certain other top Eisenhower aides, such as Adams, because of the bad feeling he had toward them.[10]

Nixon came into office with the firm expectation and desire to run foreign policy out of the White House, and in this regard he resembled Franklin D. Roosevelt and John F. Kennedy more than he did Eisenhower, or more accurately, his perception of Eisenhower. "When Eisenhower selected Foster Dulles as his Secretary of

State," Nixon later wrote, "he wanted him to be his chief foreign policy adviser, a role Dulles was uniquely qualified to fill. From the outset of my administration, however, I planned to direct foreign policy from the White House." "I've always thought this country could run itself domestically without a President," Nixon told Theodore White in 1967; "all you need is a competent Cabinet to run the country at home. You need a President for foreign policy; no Secretary of State is really important; the President makes foreign policy." "A mistake in domestic affairs isn't necessarily fatal— but in foreign policy it is fatal," Nixon told White five years later. "Domestic policy," Kennedy likewise often said, "can only defeat us; foreign policy can kill us."[11]

Apparently Nixon found more to emulate in Roosevelt and Kennedy than he did in Eisenhower, whom he presumably knew far better, though in fact may not have either fully understood or appreciated. In particular, he may not have comprehended how in being above politics, Eisenhower may have been practicing a unique, sophisticated, and very successful kind of politics all his own. Roosevelt had a penchant for personal diplomacy, secret negotiations, *Realpolitik,* disregarding his Secretary of State, and playing different parts of his government off against each other. Kennedy ran foreign policy out of the White House, masterfully used rhetoric, public relations, and mass communications and thrived in crises, including the most frightening one of the nuclear age, the Cuban missile crisis. During the Nixon Presidency, all of these tendencies of Roosevelt and Kennedy were prominent. This suggests the value of knowing whom prospective Presidents model themselves after, though, to be sure, they cannot be relied upon for candor in naming them—Nixon would probably have said Eisenhower.

Nixon and his campaign chief of staff, Bob Haldeman, began to focus on White House structures and procedures several weeks prior to the election, when the outcome seemed certain. H. Ross Perot, the Texas businessman, lent them several young executives to serve as staff. Haldeman read books about White House staff operations, and the ones that made the greatest impression were Samuel I. Rosenman's *Working with Roosevelt,* Patrick Anderson's *The President's Men,* and memoirs by Kennedy staff members. They consulted with Harlow and Goodpaster and with a study group on transition based at Harvard's Institute of Politics, headed by Franklin Lindsay, chairman of Itek Corporation. They dismissed both Truman's and Johnson's approaches as too personal and idiosyncratic. Roosevelt's, Eisenhower's, and Kennedy's provided more useful models according to Haldeman, particularly Kennedy's, although it is hard to see how Nixon's operation significantly resembled Kennedy's.[12]

Nixon's principal advisers and assistants as he went about organizing and staffing his administration were John Mitchell, Haldeman, Robert Finch, and Bryce Harlow. Mitchell was a successful New York bond lawyer and law partner of Nixon who became his campaign manager in 1968. Haldeman was a Los Angeles advertising executive who had worked in Nixon campaigns since 1956 and had become his chief of staff in the 1968 campaign. Finch was a former aide and campaign manager for Nixon who had been elected Lieutenant Governor of California in 1966 with substantially more votes than the man who headed the ticket, Ronald Reagan. Bryce Harlow conducted Congressional relations for Eisenhower. Both Finch and Harlow assisted in the 1968 campaign. Nixon also consulted with certain former office-holders whom he respected, including former Attorney General Herbert Brownell and former New York Governor Thomas Dewey, as well as with Congressional leaders. Mitchell, who knew many politicians around the country from his law practice and from running the campaign, was probably the most important adviser on Cabinet selection. When he was away briefly, Brownell spelled him. Haldeman, who had become Nixon's alter ego during the campaign, continued in that role during the transition, which meant that he was with Nixon constantly, listening to his needs, overseeing his schedule, and executing his orders.[13]

Shortly after his election, Nixon flew to Florida and took several aides with him, both to relax and to begin preparing for taking office. Most of the high-level personnel, organizational, and policy work was done out of a small suite of offices at the Hotel Pierre in New York. President Johnson made space available in a federal office building in Washington, but it was used mainly for lower-level personnel work and as a base of operations for New York staff visitors. Under the Presidential Transition Act of 1963, both Nixon and Johnson received federal funds to pay for their transition expenses, to office and to private life respectively, but the amount of money appropriated (about $375,000 for each man) was relatively paltry by later standards, and a large transition bureaucracy was not created.[14].

Although articles based on interviews with Haldeman and others began to appear in the press soon after the election and indicated with some precision just how the White House would operate, there was a fair amount of fluidity in the situation. Within the first several days, a system was created that suited Nixon's particular needs, but Nixon never stopped tinkering with White House operations, with the way policy was formulated and implemented, or with how he related to government officials outside the White House. Nixon had a greater interest in organizational issues than most Presidents and his Presidency was marked by some of the most sweeping reorganization efforts ever proposed, though largely unfulfilled. Nixon's activity in this area derived in part from a deep distrust of bureaucracies.

Nixon's particular personality and style affected his government in other important ways. He would "fall in and out of love" with various members of his staff, as they themselves described the process. Individual staff members would sometimes find themselves literally banished from Nixon's presence, usually without even being aware of what their offense had been, and several months later, they might inexplicably find themselves back in his good graces. Nixon had a habit of complaining to one staff member about another's performance; he was forever working around and behind people, always trying to avoid the direct personal confrontations he abhorred. Because Nixon's own method was so indirect and devious, his subordinates tended to act likewise, and his administration was characterized by a great deal of plotting, feuding, and game playing. All this had its amusing and entertaining side, but it was often counterproductive and wasted much time and energy.[15]

Nixon was initially enamored of the idea of having a staff of five senior generalists, all with equal access to him and all capable of dealing with a variety of concerns. The idea must have been inspired by reading about Roosevelt's and Kennedy's methods. But probably more important, it avoided the Sherman Adams problem, the too powerful "Assistant to the President" Nixon had disliked when he was Vice President. During the transition, Harlow tried unsuccessfully to persuade Nixon that if he did not have a Sherman Adams, he would need to have the equivalent. As things turned out, Harlow proved essentially correct. Several of the people Nixon thought of as generalists were by background and inclination specialists. When he had a Congressional relations matter, Nixon naturally turned to Harlow, an expert, not Haldeman, who had no knowledge of Capitol Hill. Henry Kissinger had such great expertise in the foreign policy area that he completely overshadowed everyone else there. When he needed someone to take care of an administrative problem, Nixon naturally turned to Haldeman, who specialized in such things. Nixon realized he needed someone to guard his door and his time, to keep away from him problems that he regarded as too trivial, such as an airline regulation case that ate up a lot of time soon after he took office, and to keep out appointees he did not want to see. The person who performed these tasks was Haldeman, who became, in effect, the new Sherman Adams, though in modified form.[16]

Although Nixon had tried to avoid creating a too-powerful assistant, he evidently did perceive a need from the beginning to have someone to oversee staff operations and to serve as a "no man." From the start that person was Haldeman, who had performed similar duties with great efficiency during the campaign. Haldeman later recalled that during the transition, Nixon told him a story that explained his decision to choose him for the job. "In 1960, before running for President," Haldeman wrote, "Nixon had visited Eisenhower in the Oval Office. Eisenhower had told him that every President has to have 'his S.O.B.' Nixon had looked over everyone in his entourage and decided that Haldeman was a pluperfect S.O.B. And because of that somewhat unflattering appraisal, my career took a rise." Nixon wrote in his memoirs that they envisaged Haldeman's role to be "administrative rather than substantive":

> He would examine the paperwork to ensure that opposing views were included and then bring the material to me for my decision; he would be a funnel rather than a filter. His intelligence and his capacity for detaching his personal prejudices from the examination of issues made him the ideal man for the job. He would also be the gatekeeper of the Oval Office. This would place him in the unenviable position of having to say no to a lot of people who felt they needed to see me personally and often, but I knew that his strong ego would be able to handle the jealousy and unpopularity such a role inevitably engenders.[17]

Haldeman avoided policy advocacy. He was essentially a broker, and by most accounts a conscientious one, who was Nixon's link to his staff and to the departments and agencies. Although Haldeman was later criticized for isolating Nixon, any isolation that occurred was of Nixon's own making. Haldeman routed all paper into and out of the Oval Office, seeing to it that it was properly staffed out, and constantly jogged other appointees about implementing Nixon's decisions, often through memos that were called Haldeman's "ticklers." He not only guarded the Oval Office

and scheduled Nixon's time, but oversaw the press and public relations operations and general White House administration. He generally kept a low profile, was an "inside man" who took to heart
Louis Brownlow's dictum that Presidential assistants should have a
"passion for anonymity." He did not run a schedule of his own,
was always available to Nixon, and spent enormous amounts of
time with him. Because of his closeness to Nixon, he would sometimes disregard a foolish edict when he knew Nixon was blowing
off steam, though he never led Nixon to believe that he was implementing something he was not, and he was acutely aware that his
position with Nixon would be jeopardized by appearing to be too
soft.[18]

Haldeman acquired a harsh reputation as a tough, ruthless,
brusque, and extraordinarily demanding character, who insisted on
a "zero defects" operation. He was as direct as Nixon was indirect.
With his German name, crew cut, and passion for efficiency, he was
later ridiculed in the press as a "Nazi," Prussian, or martinet. He
developed his own staff of "little Haldemans" whom he later came
to realize he pushed too hard for results. "Because they knew I
wouldn't tolerate failure," he acknowledged, "they used their presumed power in my name to go too far. In many cases, I now
realize, the 'Haldeman wants this done' line was used as a major
threat—often in some matters I knew nothing about."[19]

Invariably during a transition, a sorting out of the President's
staff takes place. Some staff members acquire more power and have
more access than others. Usually this process has already moved far
along during the campaign, with the ones who won the candidate's
confidence remaining on top of the transition and in the White
House. So it was with Nixon, but this meant that certain long-time
staff assistants, old Nixon hands, were disappointed with their rele-
gation to less influential positions than they had wanted and which
they would have gotten had Nixon won in 1960. Rose Mary
Woods, for one, had served as Nixon's personal secretary since
1951. She was given that title in the White House, but for the first
time since Theodore Roosevelt built the West Wing, the President's
personal secretary was not stationed right outside his door. Haldeman had heard how Ann Whitman, Eisenhower's personal secretary, had provided an alternate route into the Oval Office, causing
Sherman Adams difficulties. "Nixon had to break this Haldeman-
first news to Rose personally," William Safire, one of Nixon's
speechwriters later recalled, "a task he hated, and she reacted with
the grief-stricken fury one might have expected of a woman

scorned. Rose and Nixon rode down in the Pierre Hotel elevator afterward and the President-elect spoke to her twice; she would not speak to him; Bryce Harlow, the only other person in that confined space, refers to it as 'the longest elevator ride ever taken by a man who had recently been elected President of the United States.' " "There was a purpose in Haldeman's choice of Rose Woods as the first person with whom to do battle," Safire speculated. "If he could interpose himself between the President and Rose, he could do damn near anything."[20]

In somewhat similar fashion, Herbert Klein, who had known Nixon since 1946 and had served as his press secretary during numerous other campaigns prior to 1968, was passed over as Presidential press secretary in favor of Ronald Ziegler, a twenty-nine-year-old former advertising man from Haldeman's old agency, J. Walter Thompson. During the 1968 campaign, Ziegler had been Nixon's press assistant. According to Haldeman, Nixon feared that Klein would have become too much like James Hagerty. Klein, moreover, was not hostile to the press or paranoid about it, the way Nixon was. Klein was too well known and respected by the press to be able to become what Nixon wanted, a pure spokesman, a role that Ziegler fulfilled perfectly. Ziegler's youth, his background in advertising rather than journalism, and his initial designation as a low-salaried press assistant, rather than press secretary, implicitly sent a message to the press that Nixon held them in a certain contempt. It took Ziegler about a year to get established and win even grudging respect from the White House press corps.

Klein, meanwhile, was superannuated to the newly created position of Director of Communications, from which he talked to reporters and columnists on background and tried to coordinate the press offices of the various departments and agencies. He also traveled a lot. Suggestively, he accepted a Haldeman assistant, Jeb Magruder, as his deputy in the fall. Klein's eclipse related in significant part to Nixon's suspicion of the press, for Klein was too much one of "them." Despite having received generally favorable press treatment during his comeback in the years 1965 through 1968, Nixon was haunted by earlier episodes of what he regarded as the press's hostility toward him. "After the press treatment I received during the Hiss case and the fund episode, and after the flagrant media favoritism for Kennedy in 1960," Nixon wrote in his memoirs, "I considered the influential majority of the news media to be part of my political oposition." Even if Nixon was right that the most influential press and television people opposed him for personal and ideological reasons, a debatable proposition, his very addiction to that view contributed in significant ways to his later downfall. It became a kind of self-fulfilling prophecy during Watergate, a national morality play in which the press and television performed vital roles. Nixon was better off when he treated the media as instruments to be played, which he often did with considerable skill, rather than as enemies to be vanquished.[21]

In the scramble for power and position on the White House staff, old Nixon hands tended to lose, new ones tended to win. Robert Finch, an old hand whom Nixon hoped to groom for high elected office, would probably have lost had he joined the staff, but he preferred to be on his own, and he became HEW Secretary. When he later did go into the White House as counselor to Nixon, he reportedly had little to do. John Ehrlichman, on the other hand, a Seattle lawyer and old friend of Haldeman, went from tour director of the campaign, a logistical job, to White House counsel. This was not Special Counsel in the Charles Murphy, Theodore Sorensen, or Joseph Califano mold, but President's lawyer in the way Bernard Shanley had served Eisenhower. Ehrlichman's assignments included advising appointees on conflict-of-interest, but he also advanced Nixon's February trip to Europe and tried to keep the President's brother, Donald, out of trouble. By the summer, he had moved into an important new role as a referee or broker of the domestic policy debate within the White House.[22]

Nixon, it appears, deliberately set out to create an internal debate on domestic policy, with Daniel Patrick Moynihan on one side and Arthur Burns on the other. Moynihan, a Harvard professor, Kennedy Democrat, and official in the Kennedy and Johnson administrations, became executive secretary of a new Urban Affairs Council, which was supposed to be the domestic equivalent of the National Security Council in foreign affairs. Burns, who had been chairman of the Council of Economic Advisers under Eisenhower and an old friend and adviser to Nixon, was given Cabinet status in a new position as Counselor to the President. "I thought that his conservatism would be a useful and creative counterweight to Moynihan's liberalism," Nixon explained in his memoirs. Several former aides have pointed out that in purposely creating internal conflict, Nixon was consciously modeling himself after Franklin D. Roosevelt. Nixon wanted an interplay of ideas, a debate, out of which would come a product that was stronger, better, and distinctively his own. He operated this way with considerable success with his speech-writing staff, which included a liberal, Ray Price, a centrist,

William Safire, and a conservative, Patrick Buchanan. It is unlikely, however, that Nixon anticipated the polarity of the debate that ensued over domestic policy.[23]

Although the Urban Affairs Council's paternity is uncertain, its stated goal was the development of coherent national policy out of the supposed programmatic chaos of the Johnson years. Its membership consisted of the President, the Vice President, and seven Cabinet members whose departments had responsibilities for programs that dealt immediately with urban or, more precisely, social policy. The Council had nine subcommittees dealing with specific issues, such as the future of the poverty program, with each being chaired by a Cabinet member. In addition it had one committee dedicated to longer-term planning, with the hopeful title, "Transition to Peacetime Economy at the End of Vietnam Hostilities." In his first months in office, Nixon spent much time at Urban Affairs Council meetings, just as he did at National Security Council meetings. That is exactly what its proponents, such as Finch, had had in mind, for they hoped to get Nixon to focus on domestic issues, not just foreign affairs which he preferred.[24]

The selection of Moynihan had a similar purpose, while also demonstrating Nixon's openness, his determination to "bring us together," and his readiness to leaven his campaign staff with dispassionate and experienced outsiders. Although he was a Kennedy Democrat and a Harvard professor, not the usual background of a Nixon aide, Moynihan was no doctrinaire liberal. He had, in fact, publicly chastised liberals for not recognizing the necessity of stability in the social order, for placing too much faith in Washington agencies as the solution to urban problems, and for excusing outrageous behavior by blacks. He had written a controversial report on the black family and was a critic of certain aspects of the War on Poverty. Finally, Moynihan, like Nixon, had humble origins and was a self-made man who believed in traditional values of family, religion, patriotism, and work, so he was a much less incongruous fit than might at first appear.[25]

When Moynihan's name was first brought up, Nixon wondered about his loyalty—"I don't mean Republican. I mean—you know—one of us," Safire recorded Nixon as saying. Nixon nevertheless met with Moynihan to "explore his views and to sound him out about coming to the White House," "Although he quickly made known his opposition to the Vietnam war," Nixon later wrote, "he was clearly interested by the opportunity. Our shared conviction that the current welfare system had to be totally reformed helped to cement the rapport I immediately felt with him." Moynihan was a very captivating, expansive, and witty man, whose historical hyperbole massaged Nixon's grandiosity, as in this early memo:

> It has fallen to you to assume the governance of a deeply divided country. And to do so with a divided government. Other Presidents—Franklin Roosevelt, for example—have taken office in moments of crisis, but the crises were so widely perceived as in a sense to unite the country and to create a great outpouring of support for the President as the man who would have to deal with the common danger. Neither Lincoln nor Wilson, the two predecessors whose situation most resembled yours, in terms of the popular vote and the state of then current political questions, had any such fortune. No one would now doubt that they proved to be two of our greatest leaders, nor yet that their administrations achieved great things. But, alas, at what cost to themselves.. . .
>
> Your task, then, is clear: to restore the authority of American institutions. Not, certainly, under that name, but with a clear sense that what is at issue is the continued acceptance by the great mass of the people of the legitimacy and efficacy of the present arrangements of American society, and of our processes for changing those arrangements.[26]

Nixon had an aide send another of Moynihan's early memos to all Cabinet members on the Urban Affairs Council with the admonition that it was not a final policy paper, "but rather the kind of incisive and stimulating analysis which he feels should constantly be brought to the attention of policymakers." "Daniel Patrick Moynihan bloomed in 1969's spring," Safire wrote, "with his Disraeli books and shibboleth-shattering ideas; Nixon was in love again, we could tell by a look at the log—there was Moynihan in there for long hours, taking Nixon to the mountaintop of social psychology and showing him vistas of Rooseveltian glories." "A volcano in a cornfield," is how Hugh Sidey of *Time* described Moynihan. "Even when I thought Pat Moynihan was wrong about a particular issue or problem," Nixon later wrote, "I found his intellect scintillating and challenging."[27]

Burns, who during the interregnum headed up a series of task forces on issues, was a more reluctant recruit. He had served on the White House staff before and was not interested in doing so again. But he wanted to become chairman of the Federal Reserve Board when that position came open. John Mitchell dangled that prospect before him as an inducement for him to become Counselor in the meantime. Burn's exact duties were vague, though what soon became evident was that he and Moynihan overlapped a great deal and, on issue after issue, clashed. One might have expected Burns to prevail. He was an old Nixon friend, fellow Republican, and closer to him philosophically, yet repeatedly he lost. Nixon has made it clear that he would have preferred to dismantle such Great Society programs as the Office of Economic Opportunity and Model Cities, but he paid heed to Moynihan's warnings that to do so would incite riots and further rend the social fabric. Moving too quickly to kill off even the most unworkable social programs, Moynihan argued, would run counter to Nixon's overarching goal of restoring the authority of American institutions and would leave him vulnerable to the same mob that drove Johnson from office. Moynihan, moreover, seduced Nixon with the idea of becoming an American Disraeli, a conservative reformer, through his ambitious (and ultimately ill-fated) plan for replacing the nation's jumbled welfare programs with a coherent, guaranteed income program, which Nixon boldly proposed in August.[28]

Moynihan probably prevailed over Burns for a complexity of reasons. Each man had a staff, but Moynihan had an institutional vehicle in the Urban Affairs Council. Moynihan controlled the agenda, and Burns could only react. Burns had a job definition that was so large and amorphous that he meandered all over the landscape, while Moynihan was more focused. Moynihan also proved a savvier bureaucratic fighter. While Burns settled into commodious and quiet offices away from the White House, Moynihan fought hard for cramped quarters in the West Wing. "Never underestimate the value of proximity," Moynihan once remarked. Another time he said, "Why, it meant I could piss standing next to Haldeman in the same toilet." Nixon found Moynihan refreshing and "scintillating" whereas Burns was didactic and ponderous. Burns had nothing to counter Moynihan's seductive notion of Nixon as an American Disraeli. And how could Burns prove that dismantling existing programs would not lead to riots and social discord? Finally, the Congressional situation indicated that Nixon proceed cautiously. The Democrats had created the programs and the Democrats retained control of Congress. Many Republicans, moreover, who opposed "big government" in general had grown accustomed to various programs in particular, for they benefited their states, districts, and constituents, too. Nixon simply lacked a mandate to dismantle the social programs created in the 1960s and would have encountered stiff resistance had he tried to do so.[29]

Following the FDR model, Nixon had created a debate within his office, and he evidently enjoyed it at the beginning, but always uncomfortable with acrimony he did not like mediating between Moynihan and Burns. "Before long," Ehrlichman explained, "each was seeing the President behind the back of the other, hoping to gain the final favorable decision on some disputed issues." "For a President to opt for a system of staff conflict," Stephen Hess, Moynihan's deputy, wrote, "he must be prepared to assume a major role in mediation, assignments, and even hand-holding. This Nixon was unwilling to do." The conflict impeded decision making and helped account for the slow pace of Nixon's legislative proposals in his first months in office, a period in which Nixon, like most Presidents, hoped to move fast. Nixon probably also grew weary of the Urban Affairs Council, which took too much of his time and forced him to listen to Cabinet members talk at length about certain domestic policies that did not interest him.[30]

By the summer Ehrlichman was being tried out as a referee of the Burns-Moynihan feud. He proved to be just what Nixon wanted, a dispassionate and efficient broker rather than an ardent advocate. "I believed that the domestic policy staff should be made up of nonadvocates," Ehrlichman later wrote, "whose primary job would be to assemble *all* the facts and *all* the philosophical arguments for the President's consideration." But Ehrlichman has also pointed out that he often did have a policy preference and that one of the great pleasures of his job was that Nixon delegated many decisions to him. In the fall of 1969, Nixon named Burns to the Federal Reserve chairmanship, superannuated Moynihan to Counselor, replaced the Urban Affairs Council with a Domestic Policy Council, and gave Ehrlichman a title to match his functions, Assistant to the President for Domestic Affairs. Ehrlichman, Nixon explained in his memoirs, "had a strong creative streak and a refreshingly acerbic sense of humor, and I considered him to be the ideal choice to bring to domestic policy the same intellectually wide-ranging but organizationally disciplined approach that Kissinger had brought so successfully to foreign policy."[31]

The circumstances of Henry Kissinger's appointment as Assistant to the President for National Security Affairs, like much else in the Nixon-Kissinger relationship, have been described variously by the principals in their memoirs and in the de facto anti-memoirs by Seymour Hersh, the investigative reporter. The Nixon-Kissinger relationship was extraordinarily complicated, and despite all that has been written about it, one can be sure that there is much more to be

known. Historians will undoubtedly be analyzing and debating the
relationship in years to come when documents and transcripts become available, allowing them to test the published accounts by
participants and participant-observers.[32]

Kissinger's Jewish family fled Germany in 1938 when he was
thirteen. He was graduated from Harvard in 1950 *summa cum
laude,* received his doctorate in government in 1954, and subsequently became a professor there and a nationally recognized
foreign policy expert. He had a long association as an adviser to
Nelson Rockefeller, and he served as a consultant to various government agencies in the Eisenhower, Kennedy, and Johnson administrations. In 1967 he played a major role in transmitting a secret
negotiating offer from Washington to Hanoi. He was a very brilliant, energetic, and charming man. (His detractors, Seymour Hersh
most relentlessly, have depicted him as an extraordinarily devious,
deceitful, and Machiavellian one as well.) Kissinger undoubtedly
gave the Nixon campaign some advice on the Vietnam negotiations
under way in Paris in the fall of 1968. How much Kissinger knew,
how much he passed along to the Nixon campaign, and whether he
violated confidences in doing so varies according to who is telling
the story. But it seems certain that Kissinger's cooperativeness
helped establish his bona fides with Nixon.[33]

After his election Nixon found himself short-handed on the
foreign-policy side of things. His foreign-policy research coordinator during the campaign was Richard V. Allen, who was thirty-two
and lacking in experience. Nixon had only met Kissinger once before, but he had liked his popular book *Nuclear Weapons and
Foreign Policy* and knew him by reputation. After the election,
Mitchell arranged for Kissinger to meet with Nixon. The ostensible
purpose was to discuss the recommendations of the Faculty Study
Group on Transition based at Harvard's Institute of Politics. The
actual purpose was to give Nixon a chance to look over Kissinger.
"I had a strong intuition about Henry Kissinger," Nixon recounted
in his memoirs, "and I decided on the spot that he should be my
National Security Adviser." "The combination was unlikely—the
grocer's son from Whittier and the refugee from Hitler's Germany,
the politician and the academic. But our differences helped make
the partnership work," Nixon reflected.[34]

Nixon was undoubtedly beguiled by this brilliant and witty professor, just as he was by Moynihan. Like Moynihan, Kissinger knew
how to flatter as well as advise. Yet, as Kissinger came to realize,
his appointment also served Nixon's political interests. It allowed

him to reach out to normally hostile constituencies and to give himself greater legitimacy. "One of my attractions for Nixon, I understood later," Kissinger wrote, "was that my appointment would demonstrate his ability to co-opt a Harvard intellectual; that I came from Rockefeller's entourage made the prospect all the more interesting." Indeed, Kissinger's appointment was hailed by Kennedy stalwarts like McGeorge Bundy and Arthur Schlesinger and was greeted by a warm editorial in the *New York Times,* which said it "should assure the new Administration of strategic assessments that keep military and political factors in balance." Kissinger's record as a whole indicated, wrote James Reston, the influential *Times* columnist, "that he is a cautious and reflective man who is prudent about the use of military power and does not hesitate to change policies when they seem to be going against the national interest."[35]

At the news conference announcing Kissinger's appointment, Nixon declared that Kissinger was "keenly aware of the necessity not to set himself up as a wall between the President and the Secretary of State or the Secretary of Defense." In the least prophetic and most misleading declaration of his transition, Nixon said, "I intend to have a very strong Secretary of State." Nixon also said that Kissinger would deal with long-range, not tactical issues. Standing at Nixon's side, Kissinger confirmed Nixon's views and refused to discuss policy because he believed that his new job was "inconsistent with making public statements on substantive issues." "But the pledges of each new Administration are like leaves on a turbulent sea," Kissinger later reflected. "No President-elect or his advisers can possibly know upon what shore they may finally be washed by that storm of deadlines, ambiguous information, complex choices, and manifold pressures which descends upon all leaders of a great nation."[36]

As Nixon later acknowledged in his memoirs, he always planned to direct foreign policy from the White House. As both Nixon's and Kissinger's memoirs make clear, Nixon also always planned to use the National Security Assistant and a restructured and revitalized National Security Council as the means toward that end. Nixon had a particular distrust of the State Department, and he gave Kissinger a mandate to revise the policy-deliberating machinery so as to reduce the State Department's role and expand the White House's, which Kissinger and his aides and allies proceeded to do in December. When the Secretary of State-designate protested the changes, Nixon for a time retreated in silence and ambiguity.

But then he went away to work on his Inaugural Address, and Kissinger heard that he had won the first of what would turn out to be a series of victories over the State Department. In his memoir, he described how he heard and what it told about Nixon's operating style:

> Quite unexpectedly, I received a phone call from Haldeman informing me that the President-elect had decided to sign NSDM 2 and that anyone opposing it should submit his resignation. It was all vintage Nixon: a definite instruction, followed by maddening ambiguity and procrastination, which masked the search for an indirect means of solution, capped by a sudden decision—transmitted to the loser by two consecutive intermediaries. It also explains why his White House Assistants came to play such a dominant role. They were the buffer that absorbed unwanted interlocutors, a category including anyone who wanted to express a disagreement face to face. They transmitted unpopular instructions. They bore the weight of departmental wrath.[37]

Most Presidents come into office proclaiming their intention to have a strong Cabinet. By the time they leave office and often well before that, alas, it becomes apparent that that is not how things worked out and that certain White House assistants have proven to be more important than most Cabinet members. As predictable as promises of a strong Cabinet are during campaigns and during transitions are Cabinet nonperformance, impotence, shake-ups, and disillusionment during Presidential terms. It almost invariably turns out that a President has great confidence in only a very few Cabinet members plus a somewhat larger number of Presidential assistants. Nixon fell into this pattern emphatically. During the campaign, he said, "I would operate differently from President Johnson. Instead of taking all power to myself, I'd select Cabinet members who could do their jobs, and each of them would have the stature and the power to function effectively." When he asked individuals to serve in his Cabinet, he created the false impression, if he did not explicitly promise, that they would have direct access to him. In his first Cabinet meeting, he made it sound as if he intended to give its members full freedom to run their departments without White House interference. In fact, Nixon carried out none of these implicit or explicit promises. Power was concentrated in the White House, few Cabinet members enjoyed Nixon's confidence, some were excluded from the Oval Office and many eventually replaced.[38]

Was Nixon insincere? It is easy to argue that he was, and one can use some of his own words and deeds against him. But it is also possible to argue that he was ambivalent or confused about how he wanted to use his Cabinet members (though not about using the Cabinet as a collective body, toward which he was consistently negative) *or* that he entered the Presidency with the simultaneously naïve and disgruntled view of the former junior Cabinet officer that he was, *or* that he was simply caught up in that distinctively American aversion to centralized authority, which tends to manifest itself during campaigns and transitions of all kinds in the expressed hopes of dispersing power and returning it to the people, the departments, states, localities, neighborhoods, or whatever. Most plausibly, Nixon was both sincere and insincere, perhaps naïve in his sincerity and astute in his insincerity.

Nixon's associates offer conflicting testimony on the question of intent. William Safire quotes Haldeman instructing the White House staff at its first meeting. "Our job is not to do the work of government, but to get the work out where it belongs—out to the Departments." "This was not a view that prevailed," Safire reflected, "but it was not a matter of being two-faced—Nixon and Haldeman honestly thought in the beginning that was the way it could and should be done." Haldeman, however, has also recalled trying to dissuade Nixon from making a big thing out of the Cabinet because they were not planning to operate that way. Ehrlichman, meanwhile, has written: "The Cabinet men undoubtedly began their jobs with the euphoric and erroneous idea that Nixon reposed great, almost unbounded confidence in each of them. At the time Nixon probably *believed* that he did, but essentially he didn't. He wanted to be reelected and he wanted a place in history as a great President. Because he wanted these things he couldn't possibly give the Cabinet free reign." John Mitchell, on the other hand, has tacitly acknowledged that Nixon began by saying there would be a strong Cabinet but has emphatically denied that Nixon ever promised Cabinet members access.[39]

Nixon personally involved himself very heavily in Cabinet selection, which supports the notion that he did expect its members to have important roles. Nixon played with his prospective Cabinet like a puzzle, constantly drawing and redrawing it with a multiplicity of combinations until the second week in December, when he dramatically unveiled the entire group to the nation in a live television and radio broadcast from Washington. According to Mitchell, Nixon had fallen for the idea of the one grand announcement on public-relations grounds. It had never been done this way before;

Nixon loved "firsts" and was always seeking public relations masterstrokes. Furthermore, if there were weaknesses in any of the appointments, announcing all of them at once would, Nixon hoped, force the press to assess the Cabinet as a whole and not dwell on the weaknesses. But the media spectacular proved less than spectacular as many of the names had leaked out beforehand, and if the press did not dwell on the weaknesses of individuals, they did play up the homogeneity of the whole—as it turned out, it was a totally white, male, and Republican Cabinet. Moreover, the "hype," including Nixon's lavish introduction, must have built up expectations, both on the part of the public and his appointees of their importance. This was a "first" that has thus far proven to be a "last."[40]

Nixon hoped to have a more broadly representative Cabinet than he in fact got. Because of his narrow mandate, he later explained, he knew that some of his choices for Cabinet posts "would have to serve, even if only symbolically, to unite the country, and 'bring us together.' " He wanted to have some Democrats in the Cabinet, but Hubert Humphrey turned down the UN ambassadorship and Senator Henry Jackson of Washington turned down the Defense Department. According to Ehrlichman, Jackson imposed a condition on acceptance which they were unable to meet—that the Republican Governor of his state, Dan Evans, name a Democrat to succeed him, which Evans refused to do. After Humphrey turned down the UN, Nixon has written, they approached Sargent Shriver for that post, but Shriver made his acceptance conditional on Nixon's not cutting the federal poverty program and Nixon withdrew the offer. Nixon also has claimed that he tried to appoint blacks to the Cabinet, but that Senator Edward Brooke of Massachusetts turned down the UN, and Whitney Young, executive director of the Urban League, declined Nixon's offer to head up the Department of Housing and Urban Development.[41]

Mitchell has said that Nixon drew up his Cabinet with an eye on the 1972 election. Specifically, this meant that he sought to have various parts of the Republican party represented in it. Haldeman has confirmed Nixon's recognition of certain political realities, but also emphasized that he was looking for genuine ability. In addition, Nixon sought ethnic and geographic balance, according to Haldeman, and was determined not to have an eastern establishment Cabinet. Confirming the latter point, Nixon wrote that David Kennedy, who was head of a big Chicago bank, "met my requirement that my Secretary of the Treasury not be part of the New

York–Boston banking establishment that had dominated the department for too long." (In fact, the only Secretary of the Treasury since Nixon entered Congress in 1946 who was either a New York or Boston banker was C. Douglas Dillon. But he was an investment banker whose principal qualification prior to his appointment was that he had been Under Secretary of State.) In a further amusing qualification to Nixon's declared prejudice, moreover, John Mitchell has recalled that Walter Wriston of New York's Citibank turned down Treasury, and Bryce Harlow has insisted that David Rockefeller of New York's Chase Manhattan Bank did likewise. More "establishment" than that one could not get. (According to Mitchell's recollection of the procedure used, it was not a case of turning down Nixon personally, for it was Mitchell's job and occasionally Brownell's to ascertain whether someone would accept an offer before Nixon actually made it.)[42]

Stephen Hess has observed some interesting similarities between the initial Kennedy and Nixon Cabinets, though it is unclear whether they involved anything other than coincidence. "Each President," Hess noted, "chose three Governors, appointed his campaign manager to head the Justice Department, turned to one member of the House of Representatives, gave Treasury to a banker, the Post Office to a businessman, Interior to a Westerner, and Agriculture to a Midwesterner." Each Cabinet contained unknowns, Robert McNamara and George Shultz, who emerged as Cabinet strongmen. Each of the campaign-managers-turned-Attorney General proved to be highly influential advisers in areas outside their jurisdictions. Kennedy succeeded in getting a prominent member of the opposition party to join his Cabinet at the outset; Nixon did not succeed until 1970, when John Connally became Treasury Secretary. In contrast to Kennedy (and probably popular impression), Nixon had two academicians in his Cabinet, Clifford Hardin at Agriculture and Shultz at Labor; Kennedy had none. Three of Nixon's first eleven Cabinet officers had held high positions under Eisenhower. (Secretary of State William Rogers had been Attorney General; Commerce Secretary Maurice Stans had been Budget Director; and Transportation Secretary John Volpe had been Federal Highway Administrator.)[43]

In terms either of Nixon's happiness with them or their effectiveness, it is hard to discern predictively meaningful patterns. Nixon had never met Shultz before, whose administrative experience had been in academics, but he proved to be a star whose influence and responsibilities steadily grew. Another former academic administrator, Hardin, also proved popular in the White House, but none of the three former governors did—Walter Hickel of Alaska at Interior, Volpe of Massachusetts at Transportation, or George Romney of Michigan at HUD. Personal friendship or a background of close political association with Nixon also yielded random results. Mitchell, of course, became a Nixon favorite; Stans retained his confidence, but Rogers and Finch lost it quickly. (Of course, it cannot be assumed that Nixon's interests, on the one hand, or the nation's, on the other, were well served by those who pleased him or ill-served by those who did not.)[44]

Retrospectively, one of the oddest appointments was Rogers. He was probably not Nixon's first choice as Secretary of State; reportedly Robert Murphy, Thomas E. Dewey, and William Scranton were first sounded out and all turned down Nixon's overtures. Rogers was an old personal friend and close political associate to whom Nixon had turned repeatedly for counsel going back to the Alger Hiss days. But there were also certain tensions in their relationship. When they were both in New York practicing law, they rarely saw each other socially. Rogers had taken away some of Nixon's potential clients, and Nixon's friends reminded him that Rogers was a self-server. Hersh reports that many of Rogers's friends, on the other hand, "believe that Nixon was jealous of Rogers' success as a corporate lawyer, and also of his attractiveness to and ease with women." According to Elliot Richardson, who served as Rogers's Under Secretary at the start of the administration, Rogers could "not psychologically bring himself to subordinate himself to Nixon, and that played right into Henry's hands. Rogers felt that in terms of character and judgment he was a better man and he could not subordinate himself, which an effective Secretary of State must do. It's true that Rogers didn't have any inclination to engage in the strategic planning process—but he didn't try." Kissinger shares Richardson's psychological interpretation: "Even less could he [Rogers] face the proposition that he might have been appointed, at least in part, because his old friend wanted to reverse roles and establish a relationship in which both hierarchically and substantively he, Nixon, called the tune for once."[45]

If Nixon appointed Rogers in part to dominate him psychologically, Nixon has never publicly acknowledged it. Nixon has stressed Rogers's intelligence, ability as a negotiator, and demonstrated skill at getting along with Congress and handling the press. "As a personal friend I knew that I could trust him to work with me on the most sensitive assignments in domestic as well as foreign policy."

Mitchell has recalled that Nixon wanted a Secretary of State who would be a mouthpiece and run the State Department for him; in Rogers, he wryly added, he got a partial mouthpiece and the State Department ran him. Haldeman has recalled the importance of Rogers's negotiating skills, while noting the irony that Nixon never used him as a negotiator.[46]

Kissinger has recalled Nixon's telling him just prior to Rogers's appointment that despite the cloud over their relationship that had resulted from their competition for clients, he regarded Rogers as the ideal man for the job:

> Nixon considered Rogers's unfamiliarity with the subject an asset because it guaranteed that policy direction would remain in the White House. At the same time, Nixon said, Rogers was one of the toughest, most cold-eyed, self-centered, and ambitious men he had ever met. As a negotiator he would give the Soviets fits. And "the little boys in the State Department" had better be careful because Rogers would brook no nonsense. Few Secretaries of State can have been selected because of their President's confidence in their ignorance of foreign policy.

"The irony of Nixon's decision to choose as Secretary of State someone with little substantive preparation," Kissinger observed, "was that he thereby enhanced the influence of the two institutions he most distrusted—the Foreign Service and the press." Rather than take his direction from the White House, Rogers, in Kissinger's view, often took his from State Department professionals and the editorial pages of leading eastern newspapers.[47]

Melvin Laird was not Nixon's first choice to be Secretary of Defense—Henry Jackson was, and he was reportedly Laird's first choice as well. But when Jackson declined, Nixon turned to Laird. According to Harlow and Finch, Laird would have preferred to remain in the House of Representatives where he had spent eight terms or he would have liked to become Secretary of HEW. (The latter preference, unusual to say the least, may have been based in part on Laird's interest in running for the Senate in Wisconsin.) Laird was a professional politician who had supported Nixon prior to his nomination in 1968. According to Kissinger, Nixon had "no psychological reservations or old score to settle" with him. Also in contrast to Rogers, Laird had a thorough familiarity with his subject, which he had acquired through long service on the Defense Subcommittee of the House Appropriations Committee. As Secretary, Laird maintained the friendships he had formed in the House, including a very important one with George Mahon of Texas, chairman of the Appropriations Committee. As Kissinger later reflected, "Laird could be ignored by the President only at serious risk." Laird was a great gamesman, who, as Kissinger has written "acted on the assumption that he had a Constitutional right to seek to outsmart and outmaneuver anyone with whom his office brought him into contact. This was partly a game and partly the effort of a seasoned politician to protect his options and garner whatever publicity might be available along the way. Laird was the master of the inspired leak." In these respects, he resembled not only Nixon, but Kissinger.[48]

Outside his immediate staff and department heads, one of the most important appointments a new President makes is his Budget Director (which under Nixon soon became Director of the Office of Management and Budget.) Nixon's first Budget chief, Robert Mayo, proved totally unsatisfactory to him. Mayo was a banker who had worked for David Kennedy. According to Haldeman, Kennedy had made Mayo's appointment a condition of his own acceptance of the Treasury Department; Nixon went along although he had not met Mayo. Unfortunately Mayo never established himself with Nixon, and he quickly alienated the senior White House staff. Nixon always considered Mayo to be Kennedy's man and, to make matters worse, he regarded Kennedy as weak. Ehrlichman has recalled how Nixon was so put off by Mayo's mannerisms and bonhomie during the development of the budget in the fall of 1969 that he simply refused to see or talk to him. By the following summer, Nixon replaced Mayo with Shultz.[49]

Paul McCracken proved to be an influential chairman of the Council of Economic Advisers, though a low-profile one and not as effective a public advocate as Nixon would have liked. Nixon paid mush less attention to his science adviser Lee DuBridge than had his predecessors, particularly Eisenhower and Kennedy, to theirs. The Office of Science and Technology, which DuBridge headed, seemed to be there more by necessity or tradition, and DuBridge was being torn by his constituency, the scientific community, which opposed the Vietnam war. According to Haldeman, the office became bothersome to Nixon, who therefore "backshelfed" it.[50]

In his memoir, Nixon reveals his deep and long-standing distrust of the bureaucracy, which he believed was self-serving, disloyal, mediocre, and predominantly Democratic. He recounts telling his new Cabinet members to "move quickly to replace holdover bureaucrats with people who believed in what we were trying to do." He warned that "if they did not act quickly, they would become captives of the bureaucracy they were trying to change." "We can't depend on people who believe in another philosophy of government to give us their undivided loyalty or their best work," he recalled saying. "For some reason this is something that the supposedly idealistic Democrats have always been better at recognizing then the supposedly hard-nosed Republicans. If we don't get rid of those people, they will either sabotage us from within, or they'll just sit back on their well-paid asses and wait for the next election to bring back their old bosses."[51]

Although there is no reason to doubt that Nixon either said or believed these things, his performance on second-tier personnel was much less partisan, consistent, rigorous, and quick than they would imply. Nixon acknowledged how his exhortations to replace holdover Democrats with Republicans failed to be implemented. "Week after week I watched and listened while even the Cabinet members who had been in politics long enough to know better justified retaining Democrats in important positions in their departments for reasons of 'morale' or in order to avoid controversy or unfavorable publicity." Once the opportunity passed, he recalled, it was too late to correct this failure in his first term. "I could only console myself with the determination that, if I were re-elected in 1972, I would not make the same mistake of leaving the initiative to individual Cabinet members."[52]

To some extent, Nixon's self-described failure may have been attibutable to his own early infatuation with the notion of a strong Cabinet. He gave Cabinet members considerable latitude in naming their subordinates. But it was also caused by the sheer magnitude of the task, by Nixon's aversion to personal confrontations and his lack of directness and toughness in them, and by chaotic, conflicting, and misbegotten efforts to systematize personnel searches. In a later interview for a television documentary on Reagan's transition, Nixon criticized efforts to conduct computerized personnel searches undertaken during the Carter and Reagan transitions; he evidently forgot that it was during his own transition that letters were sent out to the 65,000 people listed in *Who's Who,* including Lyndon Johnson, asking for their nominations of people. The answers were supposed to be coded into a computer for analysis, but the staff that masterminded this effort was inadequate for the task, and most letters lay in piles, unutilized and unanswered. Retrospectively, several of Nixon's top assistants viewed personnel as the most difficult and unsuccessful aspect of Nixon's transition.[53]

Nixon's desire to shake up the bureaucracy and replace Democrats with Republicans may also have been mitigated by his countervailing wish to appear nonpartisan and to bring the country and the government together. Moreover, the fact was that a President appoints relatively few officials and simply has to rely on many career officials. While Nixon gave partisan exhortations to his Cabinet in the early days, he also reportedly told them to fill positions first on the basis of ability and second on the basis of loyalty. In his first months in office, Nixon undertook the unusual mission of visiting all the statutory departments and addressing assemblies of career employees. Repeatedly he praised them for their work and dedication. "Not just because I stand before you today, but because I believe this—and I have often said it publicly and privately—I do think we have the best career service in the world," he told key personnel at the State Department. How utterly different this sentiment was from the ones expressed in his memoir or privately in 1969.[54]

A nonpartisan tone also marked relations between incoming and outgoing administrations, resembling 1960 more than 1952. Although there was no love lost between Johnson and Nixon, the Johnson-Nixon relationship had never been acrimonious either. In September, Nixon had asked Billy Graham, the evangelist, to deliver the message to Johnson that he would never embarrass Johnson after the election, that he respected him as a man and as the President, and that he regarded him as the hardest-working and most dedicated President in 140 years. Graham also told Johnson that Nixon would want Johnson's advice and assistance after the election. Nixon said he would point out some weaknesses and failures of Johnson's administration during the campaign, but that he would never reflect on Johnson personally. When Vietnam was settled, Nixon promised to give Johnson a major share of the credit and to give him a place in history, all because Johnson deserved these things. Johnson, in turn, told Graham that "I intend to loyally support Mr. Humphrey but if Mr. Nixon becomes the President-elect, I will do all in my power to cooperate with him." He was warmly appreciative of the points that Graham conveyed.[55]

"There was," as Johnson pointed out in his memoir, "no reason for restraint on anyone's part and many reasons for establishing a close working relationship." Johnson was probably motivated in part simply by his sense of duty, in part by a desire to leave office

with some additional successes, in part to facilitate favorable treatment after he left the Presidency. Nixon probably hoped to get off
to a better start as a result of cooperation. In addition, the appearance of good relations would help him create the popular impression he sought of bringing the country together. Six days after the
election, Nixon received a national security briefing in the White
House and met with Johnson. Nixon showed himself willing to
cooperate, as it turned out, almost too willing. Nixon was noncom-
mittal on Johnson's desire for a special session of Congress to consider the nuclear nonproliferation treaty, and then several days later
Nixon quietly put out the word that he did not think it a good idea.
But Nixon did promise Johnson that he would present a united
front on Vietnam negotiations and made good on this in a concrete
way in mid-January by going along with Johnson's successful efforts to break up the deadlock on the shape of the negotiating table,
a concession that Kissinger later regarded as their principal mistake
during the transition. Following their meeting, Johnson and Nixon
met the White House press corps and, as Johnson put it, "the
President-elect made an extremely gracious and unexpected gesture." Nixon announced:

> . . . if progress is to be made on matters like Vietnam, the current
> possible crisis in the Mideast, the relations between the United
> States and the Soviet Union with regard to certain outstanding
> matters—if progress is to be made in any of these fields, it can be
> made only if the parties on the other side realize that the current
> administration is setting forth policies that will be carried forward
> by the next administration. . . . I gave assurance in each instance
> to the Secretary of State and, of course, to the President, that they
> could speak not just for this administration but for the nation, and
> that meant for the next administration as well.[56]

In the spirit of bipartisanship, Nixon had foolishly handed
Johnson a blank check. Administration officials were delighted and
amazed. "It will be damned useful," one of them told the *Washington Post,* "because Thieu obviously has been counting on this transition period . . . to bail them out of all sorts of things." Within
days, sober second thoughts evidently prompted Nixon to announce
that he had made the pledge with the understanding that Johnson
would undertake no major foreign policy move without his agreement. Having overstepped one way, Nixon turned around and overstepped the other way. Johnson had no intention of sharing the
Presidency with Nixon and quickly telephoned him. According to

George Christian, Johnson's press secretary, Nixon readily agreed to tell the press that very day that nothing had been agreed to which would weaken Presidential authority. However, Nixon effectively reiterated to the press his expectation of shared decision making. After further behind-the-scenes discussions failed to clarify the matter to his satisfaction, Johnson unambiguously informed the press that he was the sole President until January 20. The next time he was asked about prior approval, Nixon confirmed that no agreement diluting the President's power existed, and the controversy quickly died. For someone as experienced as Nixon, it had been a strikingly maladroit performance, one he does not mention in his memoirs, not surprisingly.[57]

On the other hand, Nixon recounts in his memoirs an abortive idea of Johnson's—which Johnson's memoirs omit. Johnson had proposed that the two men attend a summit meeting in the Soviet Union before Nixon's inauguration. A summit meeting had been planned for August, but the United States postponed it because of the Soviet invasion of Czechoslovakia. After the American Presidential election, former U.S. Defense Secretary Robert McNamara was summoned to the Kremlin by Premier Alexei Kosygin who held forth at length on the need for serious disarmament negotiations. In Washington some viewed this as an encouraging signal to revive the summit idea. One of those who disagreed was Robert Murphy, a retired, highly experienced diplomat respected by Johnson, and also Nixon's liaison with the State Department. Then Johnson hit upon the idea of Nixon's accompanying him to the Soviet Union. It briefly appeared that Nixon was amenable, but then he sent word of his opposition. "I understood his desire to make one last dramatic demonstration of his dedication to peace," Nixon later wrote, "but I saw no solid basis for concluding that the Soviet leaders were prepared to negotiate seriously on any critical issue. Nor did I want to be boxed in by any decisions that were made before I took office." Johnson let the matter drop quietly, though he was disappointed. "Never before had two presidents, one in office and one about to go in office, ever joined in common cause for the good of the nation," Johnson confided to a former aide shortly before his death. "It was one helluva idea." Given Johnson's and Nixon's evident difficulty at either communicating with each other or sharing authority, it was probably fortunate that Nixon decided against it.[58]

Despite these differences, liaison between outgoing and incoming administrations generally proceeded smoothly. In July, Johnson had designated Charles S. Murphy, a highly experienced official, as his central coordinator for transition. Murphy oversaw a large-scale and well-received effort by the various departments and agencies to prepare briefing books for the next administration. He also served as chief liaison officer for the new administration. His counterpart in it was Franklin Lincoln, a law partner of Nixon's. "He and I were congenial and got along well," Murphy later recalled. "We agreed at the outset that when anyone asked us how the transition was going, we were going to say it was going smoothly and it kept going smoothly." Each man tried to extinguish whatever incipient fires broke out. For example, an official of the National Aeronautics and Space Administration informed Murphy that Edward Nixon had requested a briefing on NASA's earth-resources survey program, saying it had been brought to his attention by a Denver businessman and that his brother, the President-elect, had asked him to look into it. Murphy promptly informed Lincoln of the request and Lincoln called John Mitchell in his presence and then told Murphy that he and Mitchell wanted them to continue to discourage any request that had not come through the established channels. Lincoln also indicated that they would see that this request was withdrawn.[59]

All tensions and problems were not resolved, and some resentments lingered on. In his 1971 memoirs Johnson included a personal disclosure that surely must have rankled Nixon: "Mrs. Johnson and I took the Nixons on a tour of the second-floor living quarters of the Executive Mansion. I was surprised to learn that it was the first time either of them had seen that part of the White House, in spite of the eight years they had spent in the Eisenhower administration." Several of Nixon's top aides, though appreciative of the help that everyone from President Johnson on down had provided them, also recalled with a mixture of resentment and amusement how thoroughly Johnson cleaned out the White House—even towels on Air Force One were gone when they arrived. Some partisan members of the new administration were incensed by how much was taken and wanted to publicize that fact as well as certain questionable favors that Johnson had done for himself and for Texas friends. But Nixon himself squelched that idea. He did not want to alienate Johnson, whose silence, if not support, he wanted on foreign affairs. Johnson greatly appreciated the consultations Nixon occasionally had with him, and the frequent national security briefings Nixon arranged for him after he left office. For motives that were probably similarly wary and respectful in nature, Kennedy and Johnson had treated Eisenhower likewise.[60]

Whatever tensions and disagreements existed between Nixon and Johnson remained under wraps during the interregnum. Both men saw it their interests to act in a dignified, respectful, and non-partisan way toward each other, and the cooperative tone they set filtered down. "So smoothly had the personal relations gone," Johnson later wrote with pride, "that on the evening of December 12 an unprecedented event took place. While the Nixon family met with the Johnson family in the Executive Mansion, my Cabinet held a reception for the Nixon Cabinet at the State Department, and my personal staff held a reception for the Nixon staff in the White House mess." Nixon told Raymond Price, the principal writer of his Inaugural Address, that as a matter of basic courtesy he wanted to take care not to "kick the predecessor while he's sitting there on the platform, as Kennedy did in 1960—saying 'the torch has been passed to a new generation' and so forth—but still to get the idea of something new."[61]

Nixon devoted considerable time to preparing his Inaugural Address, for he saw it as a prime opportunity to set the tone and to establish the broad themes of his Presidency. He read every previous Inaugural Address and observed that the most memorable ones were short and therefore resolved to keep his short. The end product of his efforts, though not one of the most memorable inaugurals, as he himself realized before its delivery, was quite good. It conveyed his post-election purpose of unifying the country. He reflected that America faced not a material, but a spiritual crisis. "We find ourselves rich in goods, but ragged in spirit; reaching with magnificent precision for the moon, but falling into raucous discord on earth." He suggested that Americans "lower our voices"; "we cannot learn from one another until we stop shouting at one another." He promised that government would listen and that it would pursue such recent goals as full employment, rebuilding the cities, and protecting the environment. Yet he proclaimed that we were "approaching the limits of what government alone can do." At the same time, he used an idealistic rhetoric reminiscent of Kennedy: "we can build a great cathedral of the spirit"; "I ask you to join in a high adventure"; "until he has been a part of a cause larger than himself, no man is truly whole." These contradictory impulses, skepticism about the ability of central government to solve difficult problems, on the one hand, and the desire to use the Presidency to lead the people to grand and historic goals, on the other, pervaded the Nixon Presidency. All modern Presidents embody some such contradictions, to be sure, but they were especially pronounced under Nixon and then again under Carter.[62]

Nixon's greatest interest and hopes lay in international affairs and his speech reflected that. In tone and substance, it lacked the toughness of Eisenhower's inaugural in 1953 or Kennedy's in 1961, and thereby reflected the imminent arrival of strategic parity between Moscow and Washington, the declining American devotion to universalism as a result of Vietnam, and Nixon's desire to go down in history as a great statesman. "The greatest honor history can bestow is the title of peacemaker," he declared. "This honor now beckons America." Peace, not freedom, was his goal: "Where peace is unknown, make it welcome; where peace is fragile, make it strong; where peace is temporary, make it permanent." "After a period of confrontation, we are entering an era of negotiation." "We seek an open world—open to ideas, open to the exchange of goods and people—a world in which no people, great or small, will live in angry isolation"—an obvious reference to the People's Republic of China, toward which Nixon was already thinking in terms of an opening. To his oath of office, he added a "sacred commitment: I shall consecrate my Office, my energies, and all the wisdom I can summon to the cause of peace among nations." To anyone who might have last heard Nixon in the 1950s when he beat the drum against Communist aggression, the pacific, conciliatory, and hopeful words of his Inaugural Address would surely have come as a surprise.[63]

One of the most striking things about Nixon's early months in office was how little initiative he took in domestic affairs. He did not give a State of the Union speech or even write a message. In terms of a legislative program, it was not a blank page. He did, for example, propose reforms of the postal system at the end of February, taxes at the end of April, and military conscription in May, all of which were enacted. But by the standards of his recent predecessors, it was a rather slow and meager start. In the summer the pace picked up when he proposed several additional reforms, the most notable being the ill-fated Family Assistance Plan. Whether Nixon would have fared better had he proposed FAP and certain other reforms, such as revenue sharing, earlier, during his "honeymoon period," is impossible to determine.[64]

The failure to do so and to produce a genuine legislative program at the start of his term had, it would appear, a multiplicity of causes. First, there was Nixon himself. He preferred foreign affairs, a preference that was understandably reinforced by the country's involvement in a war when he took office. Secondly, Nixon was ambivalent about the role of government and so, for that matter, was the Republican party. He has written that he was "determined to be an activist President in domestic affairs" and that he "had a definite agenda in mind." Although the former statement is undoubtedly true, the precise meaning of the latter was not clear then or now. Thirdly, things moved slowly at first because Nixon had appointed top domestic advisers with sharply opposed viewpoints who battled for his favor. Nixon had in effect created a deadlock within his government, though he would have preferred to call it a debate. Whatever it is called, it moved toward resolution in the summer when Nixon began to have Ehrlichman act as a kind of umpire (though he was also a player) in the domestic policy debate and by which time Mitchell and Shultz had clearly emerged as Nixon's Cabinet favorites. Finally, Nixon faced a Congress controlled by the opposition party, and the country had recently experienced both social unrest and the introduction of many new federal programs. Consequently, it was understandable that Nixon used his first months as a time to take stock, consolidate, and reorganize, rather than innovate or roll back.[65]

In a few areas where the role of the federal government had recently been established, such as in providing food stamps for the poor, Nixon actually expanded an existing program. More often, he merely replaced Democratic administrators with Republican ones, and programs and federal responsibilities continued uninterrupted. In the case of the Office of Economic Opportunity, which had become a target of some conservatives and of Nixon himself during the campaign, Nixon heeded Moynihan's warnings to proceed cautiously. He named a Republican Congressman, Donald Rumsfeld of Illinois, as director, and proposed only relatively minor administrative changes. Bertrand Harding, whom Rumsfeld replaced and who was formerly a career civil servant, wrote Sargent Shriver, OEO's first director: "The truth of the matter is that time ran out on the new boys in trying to answer all the questions inherent in a major reshuffling, and since they had a compulsion to do *something,* they bought the least controversial package available."[66]

In one area of domestic policy, civil-rights enforcement, the early Nixon administration became an absolute battleground. Nixon owed his election in part to the success of his "Southern strategy" which appealed subtly to Southern whites, and for that matter Northern whites, who were unhappy with the rapid pace of racial change and with the role of the federal government in it. After his election, the "Southern strategy" not only held out promise of further Republican gains in the South in the future, including the possibility of attracting Wallace voters in 1972, but it could smooth relations with powerful Congressional Southern Democrats in the present. Meanwhile, federal courts, bureaucrats, and some Nixon appointees and Northern Republicans sought rigorous enforcement, and a weakened but still formidable civil-rights movement did likewise.

Nixon himself equivocated, upholding a commitment to the law and to continued progress one minute, suggesting slower, noncoercive change the next. Gradually, his tilt in the latter direction became clear. In disagreements that arose between Mitchell and Finch and between their respective departments, it was Mitchell and Justice who were in line with Nixon's preferences. Soon HEW employees mounted public protests, and civil-rights sympathizers expressed their dismay with the administration's direction in editorials, letters, speeches, and demonstrations. Despite Nixon's substantive and symbolic retreats on civil-rights enforcement, however, his performance in this area was not totally one-sided. While he took a soft line on federally dictated school desegregation, he sanctioned extensive behind-the-scenes mediation aimed at achieving the same result. He also endorsed the Labor Department's controversial "Philadelphia Plan," which sought to increase black employment in the highly segregated construction industry.[67]

Because the Democrats controlled Congress, Nixon could not expect idyllic Congressional relations, though he could hope for good relations with some Democrats on particular issues, especially Southern Democrats on defense and civil-rights issues. Given the election returns and the Congressional situation, partisanship by Nixon made no sense, and one of Nixon's first steps after the election was to call all the Democratic committee chairmen, telling them he wanted to work together. He avoided making partisan appeals and even avoided making speeches to Republican groups after taking office, and he continued to consult Congressional leaders frequently, many of them Democrats.

Bryce Harlow headed a very experienced Congressional relations office in the White House which constantly had to build coalitions around particular issues because of the lack of a Republican majority. Congress postponed final action on many of Nixon's major requests, some of which were slow in coming in the first place. Not surprisingly, a sharply lower percentage of Nixon's requests (32 percent) were enacted into law in 1969 than were Johnson's in the previous year (56 percent). *Congressional Quarterly* found that Nixon ranked lower in overall suppport, as measured in roll-call test votes, than any previous President in his first year in office since 1953, when it began to do this tabulation. But Nixon, unlike Eisenhower, Kennedy, or Johnson, had a Congress controlled by the opposition party, so his winning percentage of 74 actually looks good next to Eisenhower's 89, Kennedy's 81, or Johnson's 88. In closely contested fights, such as over development of the anti-ballistic missile, which Nixon won, though only barely, in August, or the nomination of Clement Haynsworth to the Supreme Court, on which Nixon lost in November, certain key members of both parties crossed the aisle. From the start of his administration, it should be noted, Nixon had particular difficulty commanding loyalty from six freshmen Republican Senators and from liberal Republicans.[68]

Nixon was somewhat less successful than Kennedy had been in transforming a narrow electoral victory into genuine popularity. In Gallup's survey of Presidential popularity, Kennedy had received 69 percent approval, and 8 percent disapproval ratings after a few weeks in office, 74 percent approval and 11 percent disapproval after five months, whereas Nixon had 59 percent approval and 5 percent disapproval, and 65 percent approval and 12 percent disapproval at comparable junctures. Of course both men undoubtedly benefited from the honeymoon that all Presidents enjoy at the start of their terms. Nixon almost certainly helped himself by acting Presidential and nonpartisan in the months after he was elected. He made a particularly good impression on his trip to Western European capitals in February. "There is an awkward period early in any Presidency when the title and the name do not fit together," Safire wrote, "but the sight of foreign crowds cheering on nightly television helped most Americans accept 'President Nixon.' " Even the press, never Nixon's ally, though at the outset certainly not hostile, credited Nixon with an impressive performance in Europe, in his press conferences, and generally in his conduct of office. It is true that Nixon did not work magic on either the press or a significant part of the public in the manner of Kennedy—it was not in Nixon or perhaps in the times to have done so—but his early record of public and press approval was not to be slighted either.[69]

Much of Nixon's reputation over the long term rested and will continue to rest on how he did in the area that most interested him—foreign policy. In the weeks after his election and in the months following his inauguration, Nixon made decisions and instituted processes in the foreign policy area that were to lead to his greatest successes and to his greatest failures as President. These decisions and processes were so thoroughly woven together, forming such an intricate fabric, that it is not clear whether, if it could all be redone, the successes could be saved while the failures were discarded. Historian John Lewis Gaddis, who finds much to admire in Nixon's approach to foreign policy, has written:

> What this odd alliance of Nixon and Kissinger sought was a strategy that would combine the tactical flexibility of the Kennedy-Johnson system with the structure and coherence of Eisenhower's, while avoiding the short-sighted rigidities that had led to Vietnam or the equally myopic ideological rigidities of a John Foster Dulles. To a remarkable extent, they succeeded, but only by concentrating power in the White House to a degree unprecedented since the wartime administration of Franklin D. Roosevelt. The price was an uninformed, sullen, and at times sabotage-minded bureaucracy, a Congress determined to reassert its eroded constitutional authority without any sense of how far that authority could feasibly extend, and ultimately, the resignation of a president certain otherwise to have been impeached and convicted for abusing the overwhelming power his own system had given him.[70]

Nixon came to office predisposed to reexamine American foreign policy and interested in revising its course. "As I looked at America's foreign policy during the 1960's," he wrote in his memoirs, "I felt that it had been held hostage, first under Kennedy to the cold war and then under Johnson to the Vietnam war. . . . I did not feel that there should be any single foreign policy priority. There were many priorities, moving in tandem, each affecting the other." Nixon had supreme self-confidence in his foreign-policy expertise, and he desired a place in history as a great statesman. Such an aspiration must cross the minds of all new Presidents, but in few has it been so paramount. In Kissinger, Nixon had a close assistant with a sophisticated knowledge of diplomatic history and contemporary international affairs. Kissinger both spearheaded a strategic reassessment and quickly proved an adept tactician, bureaucrat, and negotiator. (What surprised and even angered Nixon about Kissinger was his fabulous ability at building his own reputation with the press, the public, and, eventually, the Nobel Prize committee.)[71]

Nixon also came into office unencumbered by campaign promises in foreign affairs. He had made an issue of the Democrats' inability to end the Vietnam war, and he had promised to end it, though he never indicated how or when. His staunch anti-Communism over the years gave him unusual freedom to negotiate with the Communists, in Vietnam or elsewhere. In 1969, moreover, the Soviet Union was reaching parity in strategic weapons with the United States while its political hegemony within the Communist world seemed shaky. America's Western allies, meanwhile, felt neglected and vulnerable. The United States had committed itself to a costly, lonely, and dispiriting war in Vietnam, a land of little apparent military, political, or economic significance to the United States. In 1968 Johnson had reversed the tide of ever-increasing American military involvement in that war and had begun the process of negotiation and of turning more of the fighting over to the South Vietnamese army. The American public was unhappy about the war, though confused about what should be done and was therefore susceptible to Presidential leadership, particularly from a confident new President with unassailable anti-Communist and foreign policy credentials. All the elements were in place for a sea change in American foreign policy.[72]

In time there was one. Under Nixon, American interests were significantly redefined, and foreign policy became decidedly more "realistic" and less "idealistic," geared to a negotiated balance of power, not to a universal defense of freedom, aimed at international stability, not reform. Under Nixon certain finite limits to American power were recognized. Words like "détente" and "structure of peace" supplanted the "Cold War" and Kennedy's talk of paying "any price," bearing "any burden" "to assure the survival and success of liberty." The old ideological tendencies did not completely disappear, remaining in evidence in American policy in the Third World in particular. But overall, policy did shift markedly. Nixon went to China, negotiated the first Strategic Arms Limitation Treaty with the Soviet Union, withdrew American forces from Vietnam and negotiated an end to that war, or at least to direct American involvement in it. Nixon's landslide reelection in 1972 was in no small measure attributable to his foreign-policy successes. Within two years he left office in disgrace, but nine years after that, a public opinion poll showed that Americans regarded him as the best of any President since FDR in the area of foreign policy.[73]

When Nixon took office he believed that "the relationship between the United States and the Soviet Union would probably be the single most important factor in determining whether the world would live at peace during and after my administration." He took the Communists at their word when they said their goal was world

domination, but he also thought that the Soviets were "too powerful to ignore" and that they never acted out of altruism, only out of
self-interest. "Once this is understood," he later wrote, "it is more
sensible—and also safer—to communicate with the Communists
than it is to live in icy cold-war isolation or confrontation." In his
memoir, Kissinger described Soviet strategy as "essentially one of
ruthless opportunism." "To expect the Soviet leaders to restrain
themselves from exploiting circumstances they conceive to be favorable is to misread history. To foreclose Soviet opportunities is thus
the essence of the West's responsibility. It is up to *us* to define the
limits of Soviet aims." This, Kissinger and Nixon believed, was an
attainable objective.[74]

During the transition period, Nixon and Kissinger together developed a new, central strategy for dealing with the Soviet Union. In
the past, both Moscow and Washington had sought to compart-
mentalize, to reach understandings where they could. Nixon and
Kissinger believed that such an approach failed to modify Soviet
behavior. Therefore, they decided, as Nixon wrote, "to link progress in such areas of Soviet concern as strategic arms limitation
and increased trade with progress in areas that were important to
us—Vietnam, the Mideast, and Berlin." Nixon revealed their new
approach in his first press conference. When he was asked about
starting SALT talks, he replied: "What I want to do is to see to it
that we have strategic arms talks in a way and at a time that will
promote, if possible, progress on outstanding political problems at
the same time—for example, on the problem of the Mideast and on
other outstanding problems in which the United States and the
Soviet Union acting together can serve the cause of peace."[75]

"Linkage was something uncomfortably new and different for
the Soviets," Nixon later wrote, "and I was not surprised when they
bridled at the restraints it imposed on our relationship. It would
take almost two years of patient and hard-nosed determination on
our part before they would accept that linkage with what we
wanted from them was the price they would have to pay for getting
any of the things they wanted from us." Patience and determination
meant, for example, that Nixon refused to go to a summit with the
Soviets until success could be assured and that he delayed for several months the SALT talks the Johnson administration had already
agreed to in principle. It also meant that early in 1969 Nixon began
to worry the Soviets with the prospect of a Sino-American rap-
prochement, well before he knew the Chinese would be receptive to
it.[76]

One of Nixon's greatest difficulties in implementing linkage was his own government's resistance to it. Linkage required a sense of timing and priorities, of seeing individual issues as part of an overall scheme, and it required discipline imposed from above. The foreign affairs and military bureaucracy, however, was organized regionally and functionally, tending to view problems individually, rather than as part of a coherent strategy. Although Nixon needed and used the expertise that these bureaucracies held, he feared their ability and readiness to thwart him through leaks, independent action, and rank insubordination. Nixon found himself flooded by just such devices early in his administration over the question of the timing of SALT talks. "It did not stem the tide that Nixon at a National Security Council meeting on January 25 stressed his determination to control negotiations with the Soviet Union from the White House," Kissinger acerbically recalled. "It did not affect the bureaucratic momentum that the President used every opportunity to emphasize that he did not wish to commit himself to a specific date for talks on arms limitation until he had explored Soviet cooperativeness on political issues, especially Vietnam."[77]

Nixon came to office deeply suspicious of the bureaucracy, and its early behavior did not alleviate his suspicions. "Which came first—Nixon's suspicions of a lifetime or the distrust of him by a government staffed by the opposition for a decade—is a chicken and egg question," Kissinger asserted. Nixon had always planned to run foreign policy out of the White House anyway. Thus, from very early in his administration Nixon sought to segregate the bureaucracy from policy making by carrying on the most sensitive negotiations through back channels, principally through Kissinger and his top aides. Nixon excluded Rogers from his first meeting with Soviet Ambassador Anatoly Dobrynin, and he told Dobrynin that matters of special sensitivity should be taken up with Kissinger first. Rogers was aware of his exclusion and would periodically complain about it, but evidently he was content to have the title of Secretary of State without the influence that the position has sometimes had. Nixon's "administrative approach was weird and its human cost unattractive," Kissinger later acknowledged, "yet history must also record the fundamental fact that major successes were achieved that had proved unattainable by conventional procedures." Whether this was a function more of Nixon than of the system is hard to say. Kissinger's own later service as Secretary of State taught him the advantages of having a strong Secretary, however, in command of a self-confident and self-respecting department.[78]

Linkage had its merits, but it proved of little value in resolving the most pressing foreign problem Nixon had when he became President and one that he hoped and fully expected to resolve quickly—Vietnam. Nixon believed that the key to a Vietnam settlement lay in Moscow and Peking rather than in Hanoi. Without their material assistance, Hanoi would not, he expected, be able to pursue the war for long. Thanks to the Sino-Soviet split, the North Vietnamese supposedly had played off the Soviets and Chinese against each other and won support from both. When Nixon took office, he planned to apply pressure on Moscow to get Hanoi to settle and he did precisely that in his first year in office, but the results were, by his own admission, disappointing. Either the Soviets had less control over their North Vietnamese allies than Nixon assumed, or the Soviets regarded the war as an inexpensive way to extract high costs from the United States. Retrospectively there seems little doubt that the key factors in the prolongation of the war were Hanoi's sheer determination to win control of South Vietnam and Nixon's equal determination not to appear to abandon a prominent commitment.[79]

Although there is less rage than there once was about the Vietnam war, it remains a highly controversial subject. Scholars have been gaining access to documents on American decision making for earlier periods of the war, but not for the Nixon years, where the principal sources are Nixon's and Kissinger's memoirs, on one side, and on the other, accounts by dissenting former aides or by antiwar journalists relying on those aides. However limited access to Washington information has been, access to records and officials in Hanoi, Moscow, and Peking has been infinitely less. Nixon and Kissinger have defended their record on Vietnam as honorable and successful and have attacked the Congress and the press for making it impossible to sustain South Vietnam in 1975 during Hanoi's final, triumphant offensive. Their critics believe they should have cut America's losses in 1969, instead of pursuing a futile and morally, politically, and militarily unsound quest for victory, which wreaked vast destruction in Southeast Asia and political havoc in the United States.[80]

According to Nixon, he began his Presidency with three fundamental premises concerning Vietnam:

First, I would have to prepare public opinion for the fact that total military victory was no longer possible. Second, I would have to act on what my conscience, my experience, and my analysis told

me was true about the need to keep our commitment. To abandon
South Vietnam to the Communists now would cost us inestimably
in our search for a stable, structured, and lasting peace. Third, I
would have to end the war as quickly as was honorably possible.

Nixon's first premise is curious since by early 1969, public opinion
was fractured on the war. In January a Gallup poll found that
Americans by a two-to-one margin agreed that the time had come
to begin monthly troop reductions. In March, while 32 percent
thought we should "escalate war, go all out," 26 percent said we
should "pull out," and 19 percent each favored continuing present
policy or ending the war as soon as possible. Nixon, apparently as
ambivalent as the nation, did not want to "lose" South Vietnam,
nor did he want to keep on fighting indefinitely. The North Vietnamese tenacity to 1969 should probably have made obvious what
subsequent events made crystal clear: the North Vietnamese were
absolutely determined to win and had an excellent chance of doing
so unless American troops were there to prevent them. In the long
run, the United States had to fight on indefinitely, or it had to
accept the probable defeat of South Vietnam. Neither prospect was
acceptable to Nixon, so he clambered out to an unstable middle
ground, gradual withdrawal accompanied by negotiations, increased bombing, and greater material assistance to the South
Vietnamese.[81]

Nixon in effect merely picked up where Johnson had left off
when he began to de-escalate following the Tet offensive of February 1968. In the weeks and months after winning election, Nixon
considered a range of options, including military escalation. He
thought about bombing the irrigation dikes of North Vietnam,
which would have cost hundreds of thousands of lives, and even
about using tactical nuclear weapons or greatly intensifying the
fight on the ground. Nixon rejected both of the bombing options,
he explained, because they would have produced domestic and international uproar and gotten his administration "off to the worst
possible start." "And as far as escalating the conventional fighting
was concerned," he wrote, "there was no way that I could hold the
country together for that period of time in view of the numbers of
casualties we would be sustaining." He also feared that the escalation option "would also delay or even destroy any chance we might
have to develop a new relationship with the Soviet Union and Communist China." (In 1972 America's relations with both countries
were unaffected by U.S. bombing and mining of Hanoi and Hai-

phong, which apparently caused Nixon and Kissinger to regret not
having exercised such a military option at the very outset. One of
the difficulties with linkage is that it is hard to determine cause and
effect relationships, though Nixon and Kissinger make it seem a
precise, scientific exercise in behavior modification.)

In 1969 Nixon also apparently rejected the withdrawal option a
lot more quickly than the escalation option. Withdrawal had political merits at home, Nixon conceded, almost certainly correctly and
in contradiction to his emphasis on a hawkish public. "You didn't
get us into this war," Nixon recalled a Congressional ally telling
him, "so even if you end it with a bad peace, by doing it quickly
you can put the blame on Kennedy and Johnson and the Democrats. Just go on TV and remind people that it was Kennedy who
sent the 16,000 Americans in there, and that it was Johnson who
escalated it to 540,000. Then announce that you're bringing them
all home, and you'll be a hero."

According to Nixon, he rejected this course because he would
not callously abandon an ally to Communist brutalities: "We simply could not sacrifice an ally in such a way." To have done so
would have denied the United States the trust of other nations. It
presumably would have seriously damaged American credibility.
Inded the *manner* in which the United States left Vietnam subtly but
significantly counted more with both Kissinger and Nixon than did
the fate of the Vietnamese. Kissinger wrote:

> We could not simply walk away from an enterprise involving two
> administrations, five allied countries, and thirty-one thousand
> dead as if we were switching a television channel. Many urged us
> to "emulate de Gaulle"; but they overlooked that it took even de
> Gaulle four years to extricate his country from Algeria because he,
> too, thought it important for France to emerge from its travails
> with its domestic cohesion and international stature intact. He
> extricated France from Algeria as an act of policy, not as a col-
> lapse, in a manner reflecting a national decision and not a rout.[82]

One of the most striking things about Nixon's Vietnam policy
making that emerges from his own and Kissinger's memoirs is its ad
hoc nature. Although Nixon regarded himself a global strategist
and methodical planner, Vietnam policy developed on an impro-
vised basis, in response to developments in Southeast Asia and to
political and bureaucratic pressures at home. Thus, when the Communists escalated their attacks early in his administration, Nixon
responded by authorizing air strikes against Communist sanctuaries

inside Cambodia. (The Cambodian raids were kept secret, according to Nixon and Kissinger, in order to save face for the Cambodian
government, and to prevent an international crisis and public outcry
in the United States.) As historian George Herring has observed,
Nixon's Vietnam policy appears to represent "a classic case of the
President appeasing various bureaucratic constituencies by giving
them a bit of what they wanted. The military got the bombing of
Cambodia, Laird his troop withdrawals and Vietnamization, and
the State Department its negotiations."[83]

The policy lacked coherence. "Our policy constantly ran the
risk of falling between two stools," Kissinger conceded. "With Hanoi we risked throwing away our position in a series of unrecipro-
cated concessions. At home, the more we sought to placate the
critics, the more we discouraged those who were willing to support
a strategy for victory but who could not understand continued sacrifice for something so elusive as honorable withdrawal." Nixon's
negotiating position steadily softened, by the summer of 1969 going
beyond what Democratic doves had advocated the year before. The
Vietnamese Communists, who had been at war for many years and
who were prepared to fight for many more, proved obdurate inside
the conference room and wily propagandists outside it. "Hanoi
used every step toward de-escalation or withdrawal as proof of the
validity of its cause and then condemned it as inadequate," Kissinger wrote. "We expended most of our energy in effect negotiating with ourselves." At home Nixon could occasionally rally public
opinion behind the concept of national honor and getting American
POWs home, but more important, he whetted the public's appetite
for peace through troop withdrawals and through reduced American casualties.[84]

At best, Nixon's policy was a prescription for stalemate; at
worst it was a prescription for defeat. The North Vietnamese played
a waiting game until the United States finally agreed in 1972 to
withdraw all of its troops without gaining a comparable pledge
from them. The formal settlement that was reached in 1973 proved,
to few people's surprise, short-lived. It marked the end of direct
American involvement, not of the war itself. When the war did end
two years later in a North Vietnamese victory, some Americans
were sad or bitter, a small number were glad, but most were apa-
thetic. It seems likely that even if Nixon had still been President and
had not been debilitated by Watergate, there would have been relatively little that he could have done to prevent the North Vietnamese victory. Only American ground forces could have done that,

but by then public opinion simply would not have tolerated the reintroduction of ground forces.

That of course is speculative. What is more certain is that despite the ad hoc, incoherent, and unpromising nature of his policy, Nixon approached Vietnam sublimely confident that he could end the war quickly, within six months or a year. Overconfidence is a common malady of newly elected Presidents. In Nixon's case it was reinforced by his belief that Eisenhower had settled the Korean war by sending word diplomatically that he would use nuclear weapons if the North Koreans and Chinese did not settle. Not only did Nixon have the Korean lesson fixed firmly in mind, but he thought that he in particular could exploit it effectively because of his reputation as a hard-line anti-Communist. Before his inauguration, he told Haldeman of his "Mad Man Theory": "I want the North Vietnamese to believe I've reached the point where I might do *anything* to stop the war. We'll just slip the word to them that, 'for God's sake, you know Nixon is obsessed about Communism. We can't restrain him when he's angry—and he has his hand on the nuclear button'—and Ho Chi Minh himself will be in Paris in two days begging for peace."[85]

The Korean settlement provided an inappropriate analogy. As has been shown in the first chapter of this book, it is not clear that a nuclear threat actually did have much to do with ending the Korean war. Eisenhower's concessions on prisoner repatriation and his pressure on Syngman Rhee were probably more important. Like Eisenhower, Nixon also made concessions at the bargaining table, and he placed some pressure on President Thieu of South Vietnam. But there were vast differences between the political and military situations of Korea in 1953 and Vietnam in 1969. The Communists in Korea were militarily contained above a certain line and were prepared to accept the political division that had existed before their invasion. In Vietnam, by contrast, the Communist forces, operating both conventionally and as guerrillas, were dispersed throughout the South and insisted on fundamental changes in the political makeup of South Vietnam, as a prelude, no doubt, to their taking control. In Korea the Communists were contained militarily and accepted political defeat; in Vietnam they were neither militarily contained nor politically defeated.

Nixon nevertheless did apply the lessons of Korea. He sent a "signal" of his "madness" by commencing the secret bombing of Communist sanctuaries in Cambodia in March. Through the Russians, he threatened much worse that summer. But neither the signal nor the threats of worse bombing affected North Vietnam's political position. The air war impeded but could not defeat them. American air power and Vietnamization bought time, but time was not on Nixon's side. That Nixon should have been so confident of his ability to end the Vietnam war within six months or a year of becoming President testifies to the special innocence and hopefulness that accompanies newness to office. It testifies as well to Nixon's particular self-image as a tough, determined, and destined world leader, to the power of faulty historical analogies, and to the unique self-delusionary web that Vietnam had a way of spinning around American policy makers as, in times past, around other outsiders.

Nixon's failure to end the war or, more realistically, to end American involvement in it, had grave repercussions on his Presidency. The criticism he received on the war from Congress, from Democrats, and from the press, and instances of disloyalty by members of his own administration fed his pre-existing suspiciousness and led him and certain of his loyalists to act as if the ends justified the means. The Watergate break-in and cover-up were lineal descendants of the secret bombings, wiretaps, enemies lists, excessive partisanship, and circling of the wagons that accompanied Vietnam policy. Thus, Nixon's worthy transition strategy of bringing the country together, toward which he had made reasonable strides in 1969, was ultimately undermined by his failure to end American involvement in the confounding war he had inherited. Eisenhower had been luckier, more adept, or both.[86]

4

CARTER

☆ ☆ ☆

In the memoir published two years after he left office, Jimmy Carter wrote that of all the Presidents who had served during his lifetime, he most admired Harry Truman. "He was direct," Carter recounted, "somewhat old-fashioned in his attitudes, bound close to his small hometown roots, courageous in facing serious challenges, and willing to be unpopular if he believed his actions were best for the country." Carter observed that many of the problems Truman confronted were also his problems, "the Middle East, China, oil and natural gas, Poland, nuclear weapons, Soviet adventurism, human rights, fights with the Democratic party's liberal wing." Carter probably hoped that like Truman, who also left office unpopular, he too would come to be appreciated in time. "Over the years the American people had come to realize how often his most controversial decisions were, in fact, right," Carter observed. (In the late 1970s Truman became the patron saint of unpopular Presidents, the Republican Ford, no less than the Democratic Carter.)[1]

To date, there has been no sign of a Carter revival. A poll of historians in 1982, for example, placed Carter near the bottom of the "average" Presidents, just behind Ford, just ahead of Harrison. The Truman revival did not, of course, start right after he left office, though by 1962 a poll of historians was already placing him among the "near great." Public nostalgia for Truman began in earnest during the second Nixon term, when scandals made people long for Truman's bluntness, candor, and honesty.[2]

The fluctuating reputations of past Presidents, particularly more recent ones, cautions against predicting what will happen to Carter's in years to come. It will be affected by events that have yet to unfold, by Carter's future role and public profile, any by historical revelation and documentation. One can imagine Carter's stock rising somewhat, particularly on the strength of his diplomatic skills and achievements, his sincerity and intelligence, and his foresight on certain issues. Perhaps some of the scorn that has been heaped upon him will at last yield to sympathy, and he will be seen more as the victim of bad luck than of his own mistakes. In all likelihood, though, a Carter recovery will only go so far. It is hard, for example, to imagine his ever being seen as an inspirational leader or as a masterful politician.

It is tempting to dismiss Carter's transition as aberrant. A highly peculiar set of circumstances, it could be argued, allowed Carter, a complete outsider and dark horse, to be elected President, and his shortcomings in office were so great and uniquely his own that it is not even worth examining how he got started as President. But to skip over Carter would be a mistake, for the problems he faced were similar to those of other newly elected Presidents. If Carter's errors seem particularly egregious, that can actually be instructive for their very scale allows certain general problems to be seen in bold relief. Carter, moreover, did some things well, and future Presidents may wish to emulate him in those respects.

Although Carter will probably never be viewed as an effective politician in office, he was very effective in securing office, most particularly in winning the Democratic nomination in his first try in 1976. If his nomination in 1976 was not a miracle, it was close to it. In contrast to all major party nominees of the last forty years, Carter's name was virtually unknown to the American public a year before his election. Carter had won the Georgia governorship in 1970; the state constitution prevented him from succeeding himself. He had gained some national recognition as one of the "New South" governors who publicly repudiated racism. He was a reasonably successful governor, but his biggest accomplishment, government reorganization, was not the sort of issue to light fires nationally. As a candidate for governor, Carter had laid claim to the populist heritage; as governor, his populism was symbolic, not substantive; he did not battle great corporations or advocate a leveling of wealth and power.[3]

Like all recent nonincumbents who have won major party nominations, Carter began his quest early and worked extremely hard. In the aftermath of Watergate and the resignations in disgrace of Richard Nixon and Spiro Agnew, the public had lost confidence in the nation's political leaders and institutions. This enabled Carter to turn his lack of Washington experience into an asset. "It's time for someone like myself to make a drastic change in Washington," he declared in New Hampshire. "The insiders have had their chance and they have not delivered." He based his campaign on the premise that the public was more interested in personal qualities than in positions on issues. Carter admitted to being a politician, but it was merely one of a number of things he claimed to be in his campaign autobiography, *Why Not the Best?:*

> I am a Southerner and an American. I am a farmer, an engineer, a father and husband, a Christian, a politician and former governor, a planner, a businessman, a nuclear physicist, a naval officer, a canoeist, and among other things, a lover of Bob Dylan's songs and Dylan Thomas' poetry.

He was, of course, not merely a Christian, but a "born again" evangelical Christian, who prayed often, did missionary work, and taught Sunday school. Carter promised never to tell a lie or to make a misleading statement and held out hope for a "government as good and honest and decent and compassionate and filled with love as are the American people."[4]

Although the field of Democratic contenders was large, it was not strong. Neither of the party's most recent nominees, George McGovern or Hubert Humphrey, chose to run; nor did Edward Kennedy, the most prominent liberal. Like McGovern in 1972, Carter benefited from a fast start, winning a straw poll in Iowa and then the New Hampshire primary with 30 percent of the vote, which Carter publicly interpreted as proof that a "progressive Southerner can win in the North." Although Carter had yet to lead in any national polls of Democrats, he quicky became the front-runner in the eyes of the press. Senator Henry Jackson of Washington, who was a centrist like Carter, had decided to stay out of New Hampshire. A week later, Jackson carried far more populous Massachusetts, with Carter finishing a poor fourth, but the press was now focused on the Florida primary, which shaped up as a two-man race between Carter and George Wallace. Although paralyzed by an assassination attempt in 1972, Wallace had for over a decade been a powerful voice for anti-Washington, anti-liberal, and racist sentiments. Carter's victories over Wallace, first in Florida and then in North Carolina and

Illinois, destroyed Wallace's candidacy and pleased liberals and blacks. Some Democrats began to view Carter in a more opportunistic light. No Democrat had ever been elected President without the South; the very liberal McGovern had done poorly there in 1972. Carter might not be as liberal as some Democrats would have liked, but having suffered a crushing defeat in 1972, they were more interested in winning.

Carter defeated the liberal Morris Udall in Wisconsin by a narrow margin and Jackson in Pennsylvania by a more substantial one, though by then some of the bloom was off Carter's rose. Carter's "fuzziness" on the issues, an ill-chosen remark about "ethnic purity," and the late entrance of two fresh faces, Senator Frank Church and California Governor Jerry Brown, slowed Carter's bandwagon in the spring. Church won four western primaries, and Brown prevailed in Maryland and California. But Carter still won more than half the primaries that were held in May and June, including Ohio, which Chicago's powerful mayor, Richard Daley, declared should be decisive. Daley's statement dashed Humphrey's hopes for a draft and assured Carter's nomination before the convention.[5]

With the nomination wrapped up, Carter had the luxury of conducting a careful search for a running mate. Because he lacked Washington experience, Carter decided to focus his search on members of the House and Senate. As governor, Carter had been plagued by a lieutenant governor, Lester Maddox, who was a political opponent. He therefore wanted someone compatible; he also realized that a careful selection process could impress the public with his own Presidential qualifications. Since Carter enjoyed a wide lead in the polls over either of his potential opponents, he did not feel compelled to choose someone who might be able to swing a critical area or constituency in a close election. So Carter consulted widely in the party and held a highly publicized series of meetings with prospective running mates. The publicity was partly intended to bring to the surface any unpleasant surprises about a candidate *before* he was chosen, to avoid repeating the 1972 debacle when McGovern had been forced to drop Thomas Eagleton from the ticket after Eagleton's past psychiatric treatments became known. In the end, Carter selected Walter Mondale, a liberal Senator from Minnesota, who proved a popular choice.[6]

In the summer Carter appeared to be a shoo-in for President. The Democratic party was united to a degree it had not been since 1964. The Republican party had suffered enormous setbacks in the

1974 elections. Gerald Ford, who succeeded Vice President Spiro Agnew and then President Richard Nixon, both of whom resigned in disgrace, was the only nonelected President in the nation's history. Ford's political condition was damaged by his pardoning of Nixon, by the lingering effects of the most severe recession since the 1930s, and by the reputation he acquired as a bumbler. To make matters even worse for Ford, he barely defeated a conservative challenge to his nomination by former California Governor Ronald Reagan. With the polls showing him leading Ford by twenty or thirty points, Carter embarked on the campaign trail expecting not merely to win, but to do so resoundingly, giving him a mandate that would impress Congress.

It was not to be. Ford took advantage of his incumbency, largely staying within the confines of the White House and acting Presidential. His campaign meanwhile ran effective negative advertisements on Carter. Damage to Carter's image was also self-inflicted. Although Carter had won the nomination as an outsider, he then took on the hue of a traditional Democrat, which raised doubts about his consistency and sincerity. In the primaries Carter ran against Washington and stressed his beliefs in balanced budgets, regulatory reform, and government efficiency and reorganization. After he secured the nomination, he embraced not only Democratic candidates everywhere, but certain causes near and dear to particular interests within the party, such as national health insurance, urban aid, welfare reform, and full employment. Carter's loose words also hurt him, the loosest of which came in an ill-advised *Playboy* interview when he said he had "looked on a lot of women with lust. . . . committed adultery in my heart many times."

Luckily for Carter, Ford also made some serious errors, the worst of which came in the second debate when he said there was "no Soviet domination of Eastern Europe," a comment that gave credence to a popular belief that Ford lacked intelligence. It was not a campaign in which issues dominated. Ford and Carter certainly had policy differences, but not clearly philosophical ones. Personality and character loomed far more important, with each campaign casting aspersions on its opponent and many votes being cast *against* one of them rather than *for* one of them. In a low turnout election, Carter eked out a victory, with 49.9 percent of the votes to Ford's 47.9 percent. The electoral count was the closest since 1916, 297 to 241.[7]

Clear election mandates are the exception rather than the rule. Even when they occur, as in 1952 and 1980, they sometimes have as much or more to do with personalities—public adulation of a hero in 1952 or public rejection of a failed President in 1980—as they do with issues or ideology. Like Kennedy in 1960, Carter accentuated the positive. "Although I would have preferred a unanimous vote on Tuesday," Carter told his first press conference after the election, "I think the mandate was broad-based and I think certainly adequate," he averred. "I don't feel timid or cautious or reticent about moving aggressively to carry out my campaign commitments because I only got about 300 electoral votes." Asked about the reasons for his victory, Carter said he did not think it should be interpreted as a vote against Ford personally, though he also said that the public wanted "more aggressive leadership in Washington." The American people, Carter explained, were deeply concerned about "the very high unemployment rate, inflation rate, and the unprecedented budget deficits. I think one of the things that worked to my advantage was my commitment to a businesslike, tough, competent administration of the executive branch itself." Carter noted one additional factor, a "desire on the part of the American people to see some harmony returned to Washington with cooperation between the President and the Congress, provided the President still exercises strong leadership when there's a disagreement between the White House and Congress."[8]

Carter's diffuse explanation of his victory foretold one of his key difficulties—a lack of clarity about his goals. Vagueness is not necessarily a fatal flaw; Eisenhower practically turned it into an asset. But Carter was a Democrat, and Democratic Presidents measured themselves and were measured against the standard of Franklin D. Roosevelt. Following FDR's lead with his New Deal, Truman launched the Fair Deal, Kennedy the New Frontier, and Johnson the Great Society. More in Republican fashion than Democratic, Carter never came up with a single unifying slogan or framework to encapsulate his administration. In a widely noted speech in 1979, Carter acknowledged public criticism of his leadership and observed that America was beset by a "malaise," the very opposite of the potent and hopeful themes sounded by Democratic Presidents or the conservative Republican, though onetime Democrat, who succeeded him. Looking back upon the Carter administration, his closest associates offer conflicting views of its nature—moderate, fairly liberal, fairly conservative, transitional. "I came to think that Carter believes fifty things, but no one thing," James Fallows, his top speechwriter, observed in a widely read magazine article after he left Carter's service in 1978. Fallows also wrote:

> The central idea of the Carter Administration is Jimmy Carter himself, his own mixture of traits, since the only thing that finally gives coherence to the items of his creed is that he happens to believe them all. . . . He holds explicit, thorough positions on every issue under the sun, but he has no large view of the relations between them, no line indicating which goals (reducing unemployment? human rights?) will take precedence over which (inflation control? a SALT treaty?) when the goals conflict. Spelling out these choices makes the difference between a position and a philosophy, but it is an act foreign to Carter's mind.[9]

In fairness to Carter, it is not certain that any Democrat who could have been elected in 1976 would have been able to impose a unifying theme upon the party or the country. In fairness, too, it should be recalled that Carter's Democratic predecessors, including Roosevelt, embodied ambiguities and paradoxes, defied ideological labels, and provoked considerable criticism from within their own party for being insufficiently consistent, visionary, liberal, courageous, and so on. Criticism goes with the job, and Democrats tend to be more critical of their Presidents than Republicans are of theirs. But under Carter such criticism began early and reached record proportions. Within two years of taking office Carter was being compared, not to Roosevelt, but to Roosevelt's *bête noir*, Hoover, the only other engineer to reach the Presidency. It became commonplace to deride Carter as "Jimmy Hoover." As early as the Democratic midterm convention in Memphis, Carter was threatened by the specter of Edward Kennedy, who did offer the party a unifying vision. In 1980 Carter beat back Kennedy's challenge to his renomination, not because Carter had come up with an alternate vision, but through the advantages of incumbency and because of popular doubts about Kennedy's character. It was Kennedy, not Carter, who electrified the 1980 Democratic convention with his words. His party unenthusiastic, plagued by a reputation for weakness, ineffectiveness, and vacillation underscored by high inflation and the prolonged, frustrating hostage crisis in Iran, Carter was crushed at the polls by Ronald Reagan in 1980.[10]

The seeds of Carter's political demise were planted at the very start of his administration. Carter combined inabilities to articulate a clear philosophy or vision and to decide on priorities, with an innocence about Washington and an inattention to the politics of governing. Carter characteristically told his Cabinet and aides merely to provide him with the best policies, irrespective of political considerations, and he would worry about the politics; unfortunately, he regularly failed to do so. Carter thought practically all issues were important, and he found it inherently difficult to downgrade any. When, in the spring of 1977, subordinates asked him about the relationship between proposals for tax reform and welfare reform, both of which would have to travel the same route in Congress, Carter responded in typical fashion for him: "I have no preference; my preference is to move on everything at once." Hamilton Jordan, one of his top aides, has recalled how as the Christmas recess approached in 1977, House Speaker Thomas P. O'Neill came and said Congress could pass three or four administration bills, but not the fifteen or twenty that were pending. Jordan and Mondale submitted a list of three or four to Carter, who restored most of the bills they had left off and returned it to O'Neill.[11]

No one becomes President devoid of political ability, and Carter was very skilled at the use of symbols. At a time of public unease with the "imperial Presidency," candidate Carter symbolically showed that he was a man of the people by staying in the homes of average citizens, introducing himself by his nickname, and participating in town meetings and radio call-in shows. (One of his most effective symbols was the photograph or videotape of him carrying his own bag on his travels. Actually this practice began as a result of his staff's habit of losing his bag, according to James King, a veteran advance man who was later placed in charge of campaign logistics.)[12]

After his election, Carter continued to use symbols effectively, none more so than on Inauguration Day when he left his armored limousine and walked the parade route to the White House accompanied by his wife and children. "I walked to provide a vivid demonstration of my confidence in the people as far as security was concerned," Carter explained in his memoir,"and I felt a simple walk could be a tangible indication of some reduction in the imperial status of the President and his family." In the following months, with great publicity, Carter cut back on White House perquisites for his aides, including limousine service; he attended a town meeting in Clinton, Massachusetts, where he spent the night with a local family; another time he was the guest on a radio call-in show hosted by Walter Cronkite. These manifestations of Carter's openness, informality, and humility were generally well received by the press and the public and help explain Carter's high approval ratings in the spring of 1977.[13]

To some extent Carter's use of symbolic gestures represented a deliberate political strategy of trying to enlarge the slim mandate he had received on election day. Journalists sometimes criticized Carter, as they once had Kennedy, for being too long on symbols and style and too short on substance. But there was a critical difference in the respective Presidential styles. Kennedy traded on the glory and prestige of the office and this gave him the appearance of having greater power than he in fact had, which in turn increased his power; in politics, appearances can become realities. In spelling President with a small "p," Carter, on the other hand, made the office and himself, seem less awesome. Whereas Kennedy dropped his nickname and encouraged the press to refer to him as JFK, an unsubtle reminder of FDR, Carter dropped his formal name altogether, becoming the only President ever to adopt a nickname as his official name. Within a few months of taking office, Carter realized that he may have overreacted "in reducing the imperial Presidency." In response to complaints, he authorized the band to play "Hail to the Chief" on special occasions. But the trend toward a diminished Presidency remained in force under Carter.[14]

In contrast to Kennedy and Reagan, each of whom used rhetoric effectively, and in contrast to Eisenhower and Nixon, each of whom was somewhat less effective with rhetoric but who nonetheless appreciated its importance, Carter neither used it effectively nor appreciated its importance. In the spontaneous setting of a press conference, interview, or meeting, Carter often impressed his listeners with his grasp of issues and with his sincerity. In these settings he could demonstrate humor and sensitivity, though at time defensiveness and hyperbole suggested a certain insecurity. When it came to scripted rhetoric, however, Carter was very weak. He was no orator, often speaking in a singsong, his high voice tending to rise when it should have been falling. His refusal to rehearse a speech or to work on improving his delivery reflected a virtual bias against rhetoric and eloquence. This bias may have been rooted in his aversion to the florid demagogues that his native South produced and in his background as a naval officer and engineer, occupations where precision, not eloquence, was valued. It was also possibly fed by a strong ego running up against modest natural abilities and educational limitations. Most Presidents, of course, have not been great orators, but an ability to inspire and to educate through the spoken word has long been a vital aspect of Presidential leadership, and one which Carter sorely lacked.[15]

Not surprisingly, Carter's speechwriting operation was, according to Jody Powell, always problem-ridden, both when he was governor and in the White House. Carter was often secretive about his speeches and would himself piece together paragraphs from drafts written by people with differing points of view. When Carter had a major speech to give, a frantic last-minute scramble often took place to patch it together and to try to make it coherent. Such a scramble occurred prior to the Inaugural Address, which ended up having the virtue of brevity, though lacking cohesiveness and inspiration. Its most warmly received moment came at the very beginning when Carter graciously thanked Gerald Ford "for all he has done to heal our land."[16]

The Inaugural Address reflected Carter's ambiguity, probably more than he intended. On the one hand, he asked people to lower their expectations and accept modest goals: "I have no new dream to set forth today, but rather a fresh faith in the old dream." "We have learned that *more* is not necessarily *better*, that even our great Nation has its recognized limits, and that we can neither answer all questions nor solve all problems." On the other hand, Carter affirmed his dedication to the lofty goals of his Democratic predecessors ("we will fight our wars against poverty, ignorance, and injustice, for those are the enemies against which our forces can be honorably marshaled"), and he set idealistic goals for America abroad: "There can be no nobler nor more ambitious task for America to undertake on this day of a new beginning than to help shape a just and peaceful world that is truly humane," and "we will move this year a step toward our ultimate goal—the elimination of all nuclear weapons from this Earth." Patrick Caddell later observed that Carter was saved by his walk, for people focused on it rather than on the speech.[17]

Carter's failure or inability to communicate a clear vision did not derive from a lack of idealism. James Schlesinger, who served in high-level positions under Carter, Ford, and Nixon, has recalled that Carter, with whom he had many philosophical discussions about government, truly believed that he had come to Washington to "make the government as good as its people," as one of his campaign slogans promised. At the same time, Carter was a rationalist, though a supremely innocent one. According to Schlesinger and others, Carter took the view of government that he could lay out a problem, propose a solution, and all right-thinking people would see that he was correct and his solution would be adopted. Carter's cast of mind, as Fallows wrote, was technical, not historical; he lacked "curiosity about how the story turned out before." Fallows elaborated:

He wanted to analyze the "correct" answer, not to understand the intangible irrational forces that had skewed all previous answers. When he spoke of cleaning up the bureaucracy, he spoke like a Peace Corps volunteer explaining hygiene in Malaysia, imagining that such scientific insights had never occurred to the listeners before. When he said that, this time, tax reform was going to happen, it was not because he had carefully studied the tales of past failures and learned how to surmount them, but because he had ignored them so totally as to think that his approach had never been tried. In two years, the only historical allusions I heard Carter use with any frequency were Harry Truman's rise from the depths of the polls and the effect of Roosevelt's New Deal on the southern farm.[18]

Carter's rationalism underlay his innovative approach to transition, but his inability to read the political fine print largely thwarted his good intentions. Certain very modest pre-election transition planning had occurred under Eisenhower, Nixon, and Kennedy, but Carter was the first President to divert significant financial resources from his campaign for a transition planning effort. This project was proposed and directed by Jack H. Watson, Jr., a thirty-eight-year-old law partner of Carter's confidant and long-time lawyer, Charles Kirbo. Watson had worked for Carter in the human services area while he was governor, but was not one of his intimates. Operating out of Atlanta, Watson recruited a professional and clerical staff numbering less than fifty. Many of the professional staff members, most of whom were in their thirties, had some Washington experience. All worked long hours for subsistence wages in an atmosphere of idealism, expectation, and ambition. The group focused on policy planning, with an emphasis on the budget and legislative proposals, and on personnel.

The group's existence became publicly known when the Carter campaign sought a ruling from the Federal Election Commission in July exempting transition planning costs from the definition of "qualified campaign expenses." This exemption would have allowed the Watson group's expenses to be met through private contributions rather than out of federally provided campaign funds. The FEC divided along straight partisan lines on the issue, effectively denying Carter's request. Biting the bullet, Carter diverted $150,000 of campaign funds to the group. On the one hand, Carter's action demonstrated his commitment to the endeavor, to good government and to planning. On the other hand, it led to resentment between the Watson group and Carter's campaign organization, headed by Hamilton Jordan, and including Stuart Eizenstat, an Atlanta lawyer who had served in the White House during the latter days of the Johnson administration and who headed Carter's issues staff.

The campaign people hated to see precious financial resources expended on what appeared publicly to be a presumptuous and therefore politically stupid endeavor. To many campaigners who had been with Carter longer, the Watson group seemed like the "new kids on the block" who were trying to steal the older kids' toys, except the "toys" were jobs and influence in the new administration. Several weeks before the election, the Watson group asked the campaign staff for their résumés. With the gap between Carter and Ford narrowing, résumé preparation could hardly be a top priority. But if Carter won, the campaigners nervously wondered, would Watson be handing out the spoils of victory?

Watson and Jordan now attest to mutual admiration and respect, but there can be little doubt that something else characterized their relationship in the fall of 1976—a power struggle. It is possible that, as Jody Powell says, Watson knew better than to try to topple Jordan, that he never would have undertaken a suicide mission. Yet when Harrison Wellford, one of his deputies, warned Watson that bad feeling was developing between the campaign organization and the transition staff, Watson was undismayed, for Carter and Kirbo were giving him such positive signals. Watson's ambition was also being fed by Carter's slide in popularity in September, which was accompanied by horror stories about campaign mismanagement. Rumors circulated that Jordan was in over his head. Finally, Watson was more accessible and more appealing to the press than Jordan, particularly to Washington-based journalists who had not been with the campaign. To Washington journalists, Watson seemed civilized, unlike the "good ol' boys" from south Georgia such as Jordan. Immediately after the election, Watson became a media darling; he was hailed as a boy wonder. When Watson and Wellford arrived at National Airport soon after the election, they were met by such a mob of reporters that the plane taxied to a different gate so that they could escape.

Alas, at the very moment that Watson's star appeared brightest, it was eclipsed by Jordan. Within a matter of days, Jordan prevailed with Carter and had broken off the most crucial part of transition work, personnel. Watson nominally continued to oversee policy planning, liaison, and administration, but even there he began to lose ground to Jordan, Eizenstat, and Mondale's staff. Watson wanted to be chief of staff or the closest thing to it, but he barely managed to stay in the picture, in the end getting a senior White House staff position as Cabinet secretary and assistant for intergovernmental affairs. That he owed to Kirbo, to his own talents and tenacity, and quite possibly to Carter's unwillingness to admit the fecklessness of his highly vaunted transition planning group.

In reality Carter merely did what Presidents-elect normally do, make their top campaign assistants their top White House assistants, though he was loath to admit it at the time. That would have been too political an admission for Carter to make; he believed in his own image as a Washington outsider and idealist who did not play the game according to the old rules. Although Carter effectively settled the power struggle quickly, he did not make the outcome clear to the outside world. Indeed, the very slow manner in which Carter named his senior White House staff and his rejection of a chief-of-staff system in favor of "spokes of a wheel" with Carter at the hub, and Watson and Jordan equal spokes, helped keep the story of a power struggle alive in the press long after Carter had, in fact, ended it in Jordan's favor.

This episode typified Carter's approach to government in important ways. The creation of the Watson group demonstrated his predilection for planning, rationality, and efficiency. But while the idea looked good on paper, it ignored the actual political situation and personal relationships. For the power struggle to have been avoided, Carter either would have needed to decide and reveal the outcome before it began, probably by making Watson subordinate to Jordan, *or* Watson and Jordan would have needed to have trusted and communicated with each other far more than they did, *or* one or both of them would have had to be free of personal ambition, as Clark Clifford had been in 1960. Carter, however, seemed blissfully unaware of the tensions that existed before the election and even after it; though he effectively sided with Jordan, he kept alive the fiction that Jordan and Watson were equals. Finally, the episode received extensive press coverage, which created an unflattering early impression of Carter as President-elect. His transition came across a good deal less efficient, orderly, and idealistic than advertised.[19]

Although pre-election and post-election policy planning sounded good in theory, it was largely a paper exercise until Cabinet members and agency heads themselves were chosen. Not surprisingly, some Cabinet members and agency heads filed its products in their wastebaskets and started all over again with their own people. Where the planning proved fruitful, it usually resulted from the fact that the person who had done it was hired by the Cabinet member or agency head where the work applied. For example, Bert Lance, who became director of the Office of Management and Budget, hired two of Watson's deputies, Harrison Wellford and Bowman Cutter, and their planning work on government reorganization and budget revision, respectively, carried over into the administration.[20]

Although the first federally funded transition took place in 1968, the $2 million Congress appropriated for Carter was over five times the amount Nixon received then. Carter had a transition staff six times the size of Kennedy's in 1960. Unfortunately, the additional funds and staff members did not mean that he had a better transition. The additional resources provided a highly imperfect solution to the old problem of what to do with campaign workers. There were many more campaign workers than there were positions with the transition, and the latter number was reduced even further by Carter's insistence that Watson come in under budget, which he succeeded in doing by $350,000. Naturally, Watson's control of the purse strings only exacerbated feelings against him among the political people. Although the Presidential Transition Act may have caused as many problems as it solved, a newly elected President's most fundamental problems are far more attributable to his own shortcomings than to the availability of relatively modest sums of federal money.[21]

Like his predecessors, Eisenhower, Nixon, and Kennedy, Carter's initial conduct of office reflected his previous experience, reinforced by his perception of how things had gone wrong in the White House shortly before he entered it. In Georgia the Cabinet consisted in part of constitutional officers elected in their own right, so Carter was accustomed to a fairly strong and independent Cabinet. In Georgia he had operated without a chief of staff. Since he had had only three or four personal assistants, he could operate efficiently as his own chief of staff and run a relaxed, informal office. Carter had campaigned on a strong anti-Watergate, anti-imperial Presidency theme. Where Nixon came to rely on a very muscular White House staff giving orders to an impotent Cabinet, Carter was determined to have a strong Cabinet and a modest White House staff. "I would never permit my White House staff to try to run the major departments of government," Carter told his first post-election press conference. "The White House staff would be serving in a staff capacity only— not in an administrative capacity."[22]

Carter found intellectual support for his idealized notion of how to run the government in Stephen Hess's book, *Organizing the Presidency,* and Hess served as a consultant to the transition. Cautionary words came from the Ford administration, which had also wrestled with the legacy of Watergate and which no one accused of having conducted an imperial Presidency. Richard Cheney, Ford's chief of staff, showed Carter's representatives the bent spokes and wheel they kept in the White House as a tangible reminder of how that particular organizational theory had ill-served them. But as usual, advice from a defeated administration fell on deaf ears. It was unusual, however, for an incoming President to react so strongly to his perception of how, not his immediate predecessor but the President before him had gone wrong. Ironically, a major reason that Carter probably dismissed cautionary words from the Ford administration should have raised serious questions in his mind about his own assumptions. Carter believed that the Ford administration had failed to address many urgent national problems. But if Cabinet government and a weak White House had failed Ford, how could they possibly serve Carter, who was determined to grapple with those unmet problems?[23]

It is not clear how many cautionary words Carter heard from his own staff members, several of whose memoranda at the time tend to contradict their memories seven or eight years after the fact. Carter's top assistants (though reportedly not Carter himself), now believe that he started out with a White House staff that was too loosely organized and insufficiently strong and with a Cabinet that was too independent of White House priorities and Presidential interests. Many of Carter's top aides today believe that the original conception of Cabinet government was a mistake and that, in time, the White House operation was strengthened and Cabinet members placed on shorter leashes. That, of course, followed the normal trend of administrations.[24]

During the first Cabinet meetings at Sea Island, Georgia, over the 1976 Christmas holidays, Joseph Califano, who had been Lyndon Johnson's powerful staff assistant in the White House and who became Secretary of Health, Education and Welfare under Carter, was "struck by the ostentatiously nonpresidential ambience of both the new President and his associates. Carter brandished informalities and religion. He slouched in sweater and jeans, spoke softly, constantly appearing to defer to comments by members of the new Cabinet, especially Cyrus Vance." "The odor of naïveté perfumed those two days off the coast of Georgia," Califano later wrote. "The new President evinced little sense of what Washington was like or of the complexities of governing." Califano wondered what Carter meant when he said he wanted welfare reform to be "acted on by the Cabinet." "Did Carter view the Cabinet as a collective decision-making body?" Califano wondered: "Having watched the Cabinet throughout the Johnson administration, I knew it was not. The Secretary of HEW had as little ability to inform a discussion about a major weapons system as the Secretary of Defense had to contribute to a debate on the nuances of the welfare system." As Carter echoed his campaign rhetoric that there would be "no all-powerful palace guard in my White House," Califano remembered Nixon's comparable promises at the Hotel Pierre. "Then the reality of governing produced John Ehrlichman and Henry Kissinger," Califano reflected. "As Carter talked this way, I thought him either naïve or disingenuous, or both."[25]

He was naïve. Had Carter been disingenuous, he would not have insisted on the 30 percent reduction in the size of the White House staff at the start of his administration, nor would he have given Cabinet members great freedom in naming their own subordinates. Sincere though he was, Carter, no less than other modern Presidents, faced problems that cut across department and agency lines and needed a staff to coordinate efforts, mediate differences, and monitor performance. It was not long before Carter's interests were being represented by Hamilton Jordan on political matters or by Stuart Eizenstat on domestic policy matters. Yet authority was often cloudy at the start of his administration, a reflection of Carter's failure to come to grips with how a process that combined strong departments and agencies, Presidential activism, and a humble Presidential staff could actually work. "The president didn't give us any specific guidance as to how he wanted the process handled," said Bert Carp, an Eizenstat deputy who tried to represent Presidential interests on welfare reform.[26]

Carter's hopeful notions of Cabinet government notwithstanding, he had no desire to be a weak or ineffectual President. "After the 1976 campaign," Carter wrote in his memoir, "I was preparing to go to Washington, a place unknown to me, where I would quickly have to learn a new life and a new set of rules. I knew well how crucial the preparation of the budget, dispensing of funds, supervision of the bureaucracy's organization, and management of the government itself had been in my Georgia administration." As governor, Carter had line-item veto authority, and though he did not have that authority as President, he had learned to appreciate the power that comes from presiding over budgets. Through the

budget process, he planned to gain some measure of control over
the individual departments and agencies as well as over the Congress. Carter was an outsider to Congress, and he believed that the
only thing Congressmen ultimately understood was how much
money they were going to get for their programs. Carter also
wanted the Office of Management and Budget to spearhead his
efforts to institute zero-based budgeting, to reorganize the federal
government, and to improve efficiency and coordination within the
departments and agencies.[27]

Because of the importance he attached to OMB, Carter filled its
directorship very quickly and without going through the elaborate
search process he used for other Cabinet-level positions. He chose
one of his closest friends and associates from Georgia, Bert Lance, a
banker who had served as director of the Georgia Department of
Transportation and who in Carter's words was "fiscally conservative like myself." "He was the only one of the Cabinet-level members with whom I had ever worked before and I planned for him to
be the leader on matters dealing with the budget and government
organization," Carter wrote. "It is difficult for me to explain how
close Bert was to me or how much I depended on him. Even my
closest friends in Georgia have never fully understood the extent of
our relationship." Lance and Carter were opposites who attracted.
Lance was big, dark, brash, free-wheeling; Carter small, light, soft-
spoken, constrained. Alone among the Georgians who surrounded
Carter in the White House—and Lance was often in the White
House much as John Mitchell had been early in the Nixon administration—Lance treated Carter as an equal. The other Georgians,
most of whom were much younger than Carter, tended to be
deferential.[28]

Not surprisingly, Lance became a key member of the administration, highly influential within the inner circles on budget, reorganization, economic, and management issues, and an effective, in-
gratiating spokesman to Congress, business groups, and the public.
But Lance had made a fatal mistake at the time he joined the
administration. Rather than place his substantial bank stock holdings in an uninstructed blind trust, Lance agreed to dispose of all of
his stock by October 1977. Public disclosure of its sale during his
confirmation hearings depressed the price of the stock. To spare
him major financial loss, Lance, Carter, and Kirbo worked out a
plan whereby he would place his stock in a blind trust, with the
trustees providing for its sale on a flexible schedule. The plan required Lance to write a letter to the Senate Governmental Affairs

Committee, which had held hearings on his confirmation, to relieve him of his obligation to sell his stock by October. The committee readily consented.

To William Safire, a *New York Times* columnist and Nixon administration veteran, Lance's letter was "artful." "I remembered that kind of writing, Safire reflected and it had "the unmistakable clang of falsity." Safire began what was initially a lonely campaign to investigate Lance's financial affairs, but which in time rivaled the press's activities during Watergate. At first it appeared that Lance would survive, but then came a report from the Comptroller of the Currency to the Senate committee, which, while finding no evidence of criminal wrongdoing, uncovered dubious financial practices. (Later it would be the basis for a criminal indictment of Lance; he was acquitted.) Lance had cut some corners that the average country banker did not cut. Many Americans wished their own banks were as forgiving of overdrafts as Lance had been of his own and were suspicious of a bank president who helped himself so generously to his depositors' funds. Failing to be forewarned by his White House counsel, Robert Lipshutz, another Georgian innocent to Washington life, Carter publicly interpreted the Comptroller's report as a vindication of his friend. "Bert," Carter said before a national television audience, "I'm proud of you."

Sadly for Carter, practically everyone else in Washington who read the report came to the opposite conclusion. Investigative journalists pressed on, and the Lance affair dominated the news through the summer of 1977. In mid-September, with television coverage comparable to Watergate, Lance appeared before the Government Affairs Committee, with the venerable Clark Clifford at his side as counsel. Lance presented himself well, but so much public relations damage had already been done that Senate Democrats had no eagerness to defend Lance. Senate Majority Leader Robert Byrd pointed out to Carter that he was destroying his standing in the country—between August and September, Carter's approval rating, as measured by Gallup, fell from 66 to 54 percent—and he warned that the Lance affair would hurt the party's chances in 1978. Reluctantly, Carter decided that Lance should resign, and he did so in late September.[29]

"It is impossible to overestimate the damage inflicted on my administration by the charges leveled against Bert Lance," Carter reflected after he left office. The Lance affair consumed Carter's time and captured the nation's attention throughout most of the summer of 1977, and related new stories lingered on long after that.

Because Carter had been such a moralist, the affair cost him dearly in terms of credibility and lessened his influence with Congress. For example, Carter's energy legislation had been sailing along quite smoothly until the Lance affair and then it encountered rough seas that significantly delayed its enactment. Losing Lance also deprived Carter of a powerful voice for fiscal conservatism. Lance's successor lacked his standing with Carter and was less politically attuned to Carter's own conservative impulses. Thus, had Lance remained politically unscathed, he might have influenced Carter to pursue more consistent and conservative policies than he did. That is only speculative, of course; on the basis of the blurred positions that Carter took before Lance became the center of controversy, one might come to a different conclusion.[30]

"The ordeal was terrible for us all, and I am not even sure what lessons were taught," Carter reflected sadly in his memoir. One lesson that seems obvious was that Carter needed more politically astute legal advice than he had. Carter's reliance on Kirbo and Lipshutz is understandable, for they had served him well in the past, but Georgia was a world apart from Washington. Although all Presidents need sophisticated legal advice, particularly around ethical issues involving themselves and their top appointees, Carter's needs in this area were magnified. Carter seemed to recognize this fact, for he observed retrospectively: "I had placed such public emphasis on high standards of ethics and morality that I was very vulnerable to political damage from the charges against him [Lance]." Yet for several months Carter clung to a legalistic argument: "I was convinced that it was right and fair to wait for some *proof* of wrongdoing before administering punishment to someone I believed to be innocent." Of course, Carter eventually had Lance resign without such proof. In 1979 Carter hired Lloyd Cutler, a highly experienced and skillful Washington lawyer, to succeed Lipshutz. If Cutler had been there from the beginning, with the requisite authority, the Lance affair might have been prevented in the first place, either by Lance's disqualification or by having him place his bank stock in a blind trust. It is, at least, hard to imagine a Cutler advising Carter that the Comptroller's report cleared Lance.[31]

Carter's handling of the Lance affair thus manifested his provincialism and political innocence, but also a certain self-righteousness and defensiveness. Carter was too close to Lance both personally and financially (he himself had borrowed money from Lance's bank) to take a detached view of the event as it unfolded. Indeed, Carter was overly certain of his own moral rectitude and of the rectitude of those close to him, even though he was evidently surprised that Lance's wealth was not quite as secure as he had assumed.

Carter tended to apply one standard of morality to himself and to his closest associates and another standard to everyone else. For example, when Califano proposed a personal friend as his own trustee, Carter, through Lipshutz, turned him down, requiring Califano to get someone more independent. "When Carter ultimately selected his intimate friend and advisor Charles Kirbo to be his [trustee]," Califano later wrote, "I began to suspect that much of what was going on was for public consumption." Similarly, Carter appeared to have two standards of loyalty to those who worked for him. He had no trouble "cutting losses" when the individuals involved were not members of his inner circle of Georgians, as he did in the cases of CIA nominee Theodore Sorensen or White House assistant Midge Costanza. But when unfavorable publicity swirled around one of his intimates such as Lance, he regarded it as an attack on himself and ordered the wagons to circle—in the best Nixon fashion. As a result, Carter stood by Lance much too long, which, ironically, not only ended up hurting Carter, but Lance as well.[32]

Among the Cabinet-level appointments, Lance's was unusual in not being the product of a methodical, extensive search process. Given his plan to rely heavily on department and agency heads, it followed that Carter would devote a great deal of his time to personnel selection. Indeed, Carter probably paid more attention to it than any President-elect. He used a procedure similar to the one he employed in his selection of Walter Mondale, except this time Mondale was one of his principal assistants, as were Jordan, Kirbo, and Carter's wife, Rosalynn. Carter consulted widely by telephone and held a series of well-publicized interviews with candidates, individually or in groups, usually in Atlanta or at his home in Plains. Some of those examined in this fashion opted out of any further consideration.

The openness of the process generally won praise, and it allowed opposition to surface prior to nomination, but it also subjected Carter to more intense pressure and criticism than Presidents-elect usually face from interest groups. In addition, Carter's rhetoric and promises raised expectations from a variety of groups. At one point, Carter unsuccessfully tried to relieve such pressure by revealing the names of a woman, three blacks, and a Hispanic who had asked not to be considered for Cabinet posts. The open process also led to a protracted and well-publicized struggle over a Labor Secretary.

Carter resented the AFL-CIO's trying to dictate his choice, though he left himself open for it by soliciting its opinion. Ironically, in turning down the labor federation's preferred choice, Carter deprived himself, not of a labor flunky, but of a labor-management statesman, John Dunlop, who had served formerly under Ford. Finally, Carter's open process slowed Cabinet selection. Eisenhower completed his cabinet on the twenty-seventh day after election, Kennedy on the fortieth day, Nixon on the thirty-seventh, and Carter on the fiftieth.

As Carter wished, the Cabinet reflected several kinds of diversity—geographical, gender, and racial. It also embodied considerable Washington experience, as Democratic administrations have been apt to do. Contrary to his campaign commitment to bring in "outsiders," "fresh faces," and names "you've never heard of before," Carter chose a Cabinet of insiders and experienced old hands. That made much sense, particularly for Carter who lacked Washington experience. It made less sense, however, for Carter and his aides to keep certain campaign rhetoric alive well after it had outlived its usefulness. Carter had Eizenstat prepare a book of his campaign promises which reporters then used to document Carter's broken promises. Likewise, Hamilton Jordan was widely quoted as saying that if Cyrus Vance ended up as Secretary of State and Zbigniew Brzezinski as National Security Adviser, he would quit his job because they were the obvious, establishment choices for these positions, and their selection would indicate that the process had failed in its objectives of openness and creativity. Of course, that is precisely what happened, except Jordan did not quit.[33]

Two of Carter's highest-level nominees encountered significant confirmation problems, Sorensen as CIA Director and Griffin Bell as Attorney General. Sorensen, who had been a top assistant to President Kennedy, was a prominent New York lawyer and liberal. He favored reform of the intelligence services. His nomination offended hard-line Senators in both parties who seized upon Sorensen's use of classified documents to write his famous book about Kennedy and on Sorensen's registration for the draft as a conscientious objector. These were nice pretexts; the actual objection was ideological in nature. Opposition to Sorensen certainly should have been anticipated; if it was nothing was done to offset it, and when it arose Carter beat a quick retreat. Several days before the inauguration, Carter told Sorensen that he would continue to support him, but cautioned him that he did not have the committee votes for approval. When Sorensen offered to withdraw, Carter did not try to dissuade him, so Sorensen withdrew. James Schlesinger, a former CIA Director, later reflected that though, in his opinion, the nomination never should have been made, once it had been made, Carter committed a serious mistake by backing down. It was the first such incident in memory to occur in a Senate of the same party as the President-elect, and it made Carter appear to be a weakling. Having taken a patch out of Carter once, hard-liners next went to work on Paul Warnke, Carter's nominee as arms-control negotiator. This time Carter stood firm, and in March Warnke was confirmed by a 58 to 40 vote, nine votes less than the two-thirds that an arms-control treaty would need for ratification, an ominous sign. If Carter had fought for Sorensen and won, it is possible that the struggle over Warnke would not have been so close.[34]

In contrast to his retreat on Sorensen, whom he did not know well, Carter stood firmly behind Bell, whom he had known since childhood. Bell, who had been appointed to the federal bench by Kennedy and who had returned to private practice in 1976, was fully qualified to be Attorney General. As a political supporter of Carter's, a financial backer of his campaign, a friend, and a partner to Kirbo, however, his nomination hardly seems consistent with Carter's campaign pledge of an independent, nonpolitical Attorney General. Bell's selection was certainly no less appropriate than Herbert Brownell's in 1952, Robert Kennedy's in 1960, or John Mitchell's in 1968, and may well have been more so in that at least he was not Carter's campaign manager. But since Watergate, the country had grown concerned about a politicized Justice Department. Because Gerald Ford's Attorney General had been Edward Levi, a nonpartisan and a distinguished academician, Bell's nomination appeared retrograde. Civil-rights groups were upset because of Bell's past associations with segregationists in Georgia, his membership in discriminatory clubs, and his record as a judge. The Senate Judiciary Committee held seven days of hearings, generating a 759-page record. But Carter did not blink this time, Bell admitted during his confirmation hearings that he had learned some things, and liberal Democrats swallowed hard and went along. The Senate confirmed him, 75 to 21, with five liberal Democrats joining sixteen Republicans in the minority. (In office, Bell resisted and resented White House attempts to give his department policy guidance and later wrote about some of his battles with the more liberally inclined White House.)[35]

Although Carter started out hoping that his Cabinet members would serve a full four-year term with him and even won commitments from most of them to do so, few actually did. Indeed, in the summer of 1979, with his own public-approval ratings at depressed levels, Carter presided over the greatest Cabinet shake-up in history, and at the end of his administration only six of the seventeen people Carter initially gave Cabinet rank were still serving in their original posts. The phenomenon of high turnover was certainly not confined to the Carter administration. It had become par for the course in Washington. But Carter started out expecting to score an eagle, and he ended up with a double-bogey, testimony both to his innocence and to flaws in his particular game.[36]

One of the most frequently identified problems with Carter's Cabinet was that it was made up of Washington insiders who were loyal to ideas and interests inimical to Carter's. Griffin Bell reportedly used to say, not entirely in jest, that they should have filled the entire Cabinet and sub-Cabinet with Georgians. But Califano more realistically observed that "widespread loyalty is generated by able leadership," implying that Carter failed to provide that leadership. Often he alternated between giving his Cabinet members little policy guidance and becoming overly involved in the details of their jobs. He did not communicate his vision or priorities to them any better than he communicated them to the nation, or he would tell them one thing and proceed in a contrary fashion. Communications problems were compounded by Carter's unfamiliarity with most of his Cabinet, by his failure to assure that they had people around them who knew him well, and by Carter's naïve belief that he could effectively combine an activist Presidency, a strong Cabinet, and a humble White House staff.[37]

The selection of high-ranking department officials below the Secretary level exemplified and compounded Carter's difficulties. When Cabinet officers took Carter at his word that they could name their own subordinates, they sometimes learned either through leaks in newspapers or more directly that Carter or his political aides, such as Jordan, were displeased with their choices. Both Califano, a liberal Cabinet member, and Bell, a conservative one, have described White House displeasure with appointments they had been told were theirs alone to make. When Brock Adams hired his Congressional staff members to help him run the Transportation Department, Carter did not like it, but did nothing about it; the situation continued to fester and later helped account for Adams's departure. On the other hand, Cabinet Secretaries who were more accommodating in this regard tended to encounter fewer intimations or accusations later that they or their subordinates were disloyal to Carter.[38]

Because Carter gave his Cabinet Secretaries such a free hand in naming their subordinates, he had relatively little patronage to dispense or little ability to recruit people of his own liking to government. According to James King, who became a special assistant for personnel, Carter had only about nine hundred jobs to fill. His appointments were largely confined to the Executive Office of the President, regulatory and independent agencies, boards and commissions, plus whatever largesse Cabinet members or their subordinates relinquished. For this relatively paltry number of jobs, Carter generated over 125,000 names, many of them with accompanying letters, résumés, and recommendations. These came out of the Talent Inventory Program, begun under Watson and continued during the interregnum. They were also stimulated by Carter's public declarations that he was looking for the "best" and by his open invitations for people to nominate themselves or others. On top of this, there were hundreds of campaign workers who had the traditional expectations and over sixteen thousand suggestions from Democratic Congressmen, who had large appetites after eight years of Republican control of the executive branch. It is little wonder, then, that those who tried to exercise responsibility for filling these jobs typically refer to this period of their lives as a "goddamn nightmare."[39]

The personnel situation created difficulties with Congress. Democratic Congressmen at first could not believe that Carter had as little influence over departmental appointments as he claimed, and when they realized it was true, tried to strike their own deals with the departments. As a result, they needed Carter less and also respected him less as a fellow politician. Secondly, by giving away most of the jobs before he even took office, Carter significantly reduced the number of loyalists he could count on throughout the government.[40]

Jordan's involvement in the personnel process had several interesting but little-noted aspects. First, personnel was the primary focus of Jordan's attention during the first six to eight months of the administration. Carter reluctantly gave him this assignment only when he realized he did not have sufficient time to do it himself. Retrospectively, Jordan thought he in turn should have delegated the job to a trusted aide because his time could have been better spent on more important matters. Second, Carter did pressure the Cabinet through Jordan in one area of personnel, affirmative action. Finally, in the various agencies where Jordan had considerable authority, the appointees were decidedly young, activist liberals, which contradicts the view of some Carter partisans that he ended up with a more liberal government than he set out to have because he gave away the store to *Cabinet* officers.[41]

When Carter was asked at his first post-election press conference how he would choose his White House staff, Carter replied, "I'll try to choose them strictly on the basis of merit. I'll use the same procedures that I used to choose the Vice President—getting a lot of advice from people who are knowledgeable about qualifications of those whom I do not know." In his memoir six years later, Carter was more realistic and candid when he wrote that he "had made a private promise to myself to call on some of the talented Georgians who had served me as governor and as a candidate for President." Carter observed that his predecessors "had been criticized for installing their 'cronies' in the White House." "But when I considered the alternative, I decided without any doubt that my predecessors had chosen wisely. The selection of loyal and well-known associates is the result of a need for maximum mutual confidence and a minimum of jealousy and back biting within a President's inner circle."[42]

As the Jordan-Watson struggle demonstrated, however, familiarity does not necessarily breed contentment. More importantly, though all Presidents-elect have transformed their campaign staffs into White House staffs, the individuals involved were usually much more seasoned than Carter's. By filling his White House staff with young and inexperienced Georgians, Carter failed to shore up his own principal weakness as President-elect, his lack of familiarity with Washington. In time Carter did strengthen his White House operation by adding more experienced hands, particularly Lloyd Cutler as counsel, Alonzo McDonald as staff director, and Anne Wexler as assistant for public liaison, so he clearly did learn that he needed to go beyond the "Georgia mafia." In time, too, the Georgians who stayed learned and improved, but it was Carter who paid the costs of their on-the-job training.[43]

According to one school of thought, all Presidents need a chief of staff, and Carter eventually capitulated to this supposed necessity when he named Jordan his chief of staff in 1979. Jordan, however, has pointed out that even after he was designated chief of staff, he still did not function like one. To the end, Carter, like Kennedy, was the hub of a wheel, and like Kennedy the number of spokes merely became reduced over time. A hierarchical staff system suited neither man, and there was no reason either should have tried to have one. Kennedy's Whte House operation was superior to Carter's, however. His key people were generally more talented, more experienced, though no older, and had greater authority. Only Eizenstat among Carter's top aides had Washington experience and even that was very limited. Eizenstat was widely regarded as one of Carter's ablest aides, but his authority was shaky, particularly at the beginning; and he never united policy formulation with public explication the way Sorensen had done so well.[44]

Hamilton Jordan probably justly deserved his reputation as a first-class political strategist, but his exact role and authority, particularly in the early days of the administration, were undefined. Jordan, it has sometimes been said, did not want to be chief of staff, nor did he want anyone else to be. By his own admission he was not a "paper person," nor was he particularly interested in or knowledgeable about policy. He wanted to freelance, but he spent his first eight months tied up in personnel. The impressive skill he later showed in putting together the successful campaign to ratify the Panama Canal treaties could have been put to good use early in the administration, such as in the fight to enact energy legislation.[45]

Kenneth O'Donnell had been the closest counterpart to Jordan in the Kennedy administration. O'Donnell could match Jordan, Haldeman, or anyone else when it came to protecting his President's political interests, but his acts of political loyalty were performed in private, and O'Donnell successfully avoided publicity. By 1977 it was hard for top White House assistants to remain completely in the background; the press would no longer let them. But Jordan contributed to the serious image problems that *he* had by making unwise and umpolitic remarks on the record, by avoiding the Washington social scene, and by not cultivating a more positive image; he became known for wearing cowboy boots and informal clothes to the office. "By the summer of 1979," his colleague and defender Jody Powell has written, "Hamilton had come to be viewed by the large portion of Washington that did not know him personally as a politically astute ne'er-do-well." When Jordan was accused that fall of having used cocaine in a New York nightclub, a large portion of the press readily gave the accusation considerable credence. A special prosecutor later cleared Jordan completely. Although Powell found great fault with the press in its treatment of Jordan, he also acknowledged that Jordan and other staff members made an innocent though serious mistake at the outset:

> It must also be said that we failed to appreciate until too late the repercussions of our failure to socialize in the traditional Washington manner. We missed an opportunity to get to know Washing-

ton better and to separate the sheep from the goats. We failed to
establish personal relationships with individuals who could have
been helpful to us professionally, who would have been there to
defend us against the rumors and half-truths that constantly circu-
late in the nation's capital. Part of Washington felt that we were
being arrogant and interpreted each regret as a snub. Others were
confirmed in their belief that the entire administration, or at least
the White House, had been taken over by the Visigoths.[46]

Although he had never been a reporter, Powell in some respects
proved an effective press secretary, partly because of his very closeness to his principal, partly because of his personality and quick
mind. But as Powell himself acknowledged in his post-administration
book, his lack of familiarity with Washington was hardly an asset,
particularly in the early months of the administration. He developed
a relationship with the press that was much too adversarial, which
contributed to Carter's later problems with unfavorable coverage.
Like Lawrence O'Brien, Frank Moore had no background for the
Congressional liaison job he was assigned. But O'Brien proved good
enough in it to satisfy no less a legislative master than Lyndon Johnson. Moore arrived on the job handicapped by a reputation for ineptitude in the Congress; he had been Carter's liaison to Congressional
Democrats during the campaign but had been so overburdened and
understaffed that he failed to return many phone calls. He was further handicapped by his lack of influence over patronage. His defenders, including Carter and Jordan, assert that Moore eventually
put together an excellent staff and did a fine job; his detractors
disagree. Retrospectively, it does seem clear that in this staff position
above all others, Carter needed an experienced, highly competent
Congressional hand from the very outset.[47]

Carter may have felt that Moore would suffice because he had
Mondale, but though Mondale offered advice on Congress and
served as a trouble-shooter and lobbyist there, he was not interested in becoming a staff member. When Carter early referred to
Mondale as his chief staff person, Mondale recoiled in horror. To
Carter's and Mondale's mutual credit and also because of a gradual growth in Vice Presidential staff during previous years, Mondale's Vice Presidency became the most satisfactory and sensible to
that time and served as a model for the one that followed. Although Presidential promises of a meaningful role to their Vice
Presidents previously had about the same unhappy history as their

promises of Cabinet government, the pattern was broken under Carter. Griffin Bell thought it all a great mistake, for Mondale and his staff members who went to work for Carter had a decidedly more liberal outlook than Carter. "The attempt by Carter and Mondale to gloss over fundamental differences in their political philosophies," Bell wrote, "also helped produce the unclear, all-things-to-all-people voice that the public heard so often from the administration."[48]

Although Bell's criticisms may be dismissed as sour grapes, they are not wrong in identifying a Mondale influence. If Carter proved more susceptible to liberal influence than Bell liked, however, that was probably because Carter was less committed to a distinctly conservative philosophy than Bell thought. Had Carter been as conservative as Bell assumed, he would have made a very different set of appointments, even within his own staff, and he would have pursued quite different policies. To the extent that Mondale exercised a liberal influence, it was because Carter wanted him to. At some critical junctures, Carter reportedly rejected Mondale's advice. It is hard in fact to know when Mondale's advice was taken and when it was rejected because Mondale gave it to Carter in strict privacy, not even telling his aides what he had advised. "Mondale understood who was President," a Carter aide later told Paul Light for his study of the Vice Presidency. "He made his case, made it once, didn't carp about it, didn't tell what happened to outsiders, and never embarrassed the President."[49]

The Mondale Vice Presidency bears favorable comparison with all its predecessors. Mondale was more influential, more involved and thoroughly informed and therefore more prepared to take over than his predecessors had been. Unlike many of them, he was never battered or demeaned by the President or, as more often happened, by his aides. He never became the fire hydrant on the White House grounds or a full-time ribbon-cutter, plights that had often befallen previous Vice Presidents. A variety of factors went into the successful Carter-Mondale relationship: Carter's commitment to making the relationship work and his intolerance of any backsliding by his staff; the personal chemistry, friendship, and trust that developed between Carter and Mondale and between Mondale and Jordan; Mondale's ability to submerge his ego and play a humble, discreet role; lessons Mondale learned from Vice Presidents Hubert Humphrey and Nelson Rockefeller, especially the importance of avoiding line responsibility, serving instead as a generalist; the merging of staffs which had first occurred during the campaign and which

continued in the White House; Mondale's physical proximity to
Carter in a West Wing office, his regularly scheduled meetings with
Carter and his access to virtually all information that Carter received and his inclusion in any meeting he wanted to attend. In the
past, one or more of these factors were present; Spiro Agnew, for
example, had been the first Vice President to have an office in the
White House, but it had done him little good. Under Carter and
Mondale, a number of things came together to make the Vice Presidency a more fruitful and enjoyable experience than it had been
before.[50]

Just as the success of the Carter-Mondale collaboration owed in
part to personal chemistry and to Mondale's experience, so too did
the success of Carter's collaboration with James Schlesinger. Schlesinger's role with Carter paralleled Moynihan's with Nixon. Like
Moynihan, Schlesinger was a refugee from previous administrations
of the opposition party, except Schlesinger had been no less than
CIA Director and Secretary of Defense. Carter seriously considered
Schlesinger for the Defense job in his administration, but evidently
decided that his views were too hard-line. Carter had taken a great
liking to Schlesinger, however, and was determined to find a place
for him, a determination that was reinforced by Henry Jackson, the
powerful Senator from Washington who was a friend and philosophical ally of Schlesinger. So Carter made Schlesinger Secretary-
designate of a new Department of Energy and, pending its creation,
gave Schlesinger a White House base and made him a special
assistant.[51]

"The energy question had rarely come up during the 1976 campaign," Carter later wrote. Yet energy policy became the center-
piece of Carter's program in 1977. In early February Carter fea-
tured the subject in his effective "fireside chat" to the public and
promised that he would have a national energy plan before Congress within ninety days. When that time came, Carter solemnly
declared; "Our decision about energy will test the character of the
American people and the ability of the President and Congress to
govern this Nation. This difficult effort will be the 'moral equivalent of war,' except that we will be uniting our efforts to build and
not to destroy." By year's end, Carter recalled, he had given three
television addresses directly to the nation and another to a joint
session of Congress and all were about energy. "The first session of
the 95th Congress could be said to have had two agendas: energy
and everything else," Carter quoted *Congressional Quarterly*.[52]

The reasons for energy's predominance are not altogether clear. Undoubtedly, the major one was simply as Carter stated it—that he was convinced that national security was at stake. The United States in 1977 was substantially more dependent on uncertain foreign oil supplies than it had been in 1973 at the time of the oil embargo. America was therefore susceptible to potential political blackmail. In addition, Carter pointed out that American enegy consumption was at a record high; we were squandering scarce resources, and we owed it to future generations to conserve and to find replenishable energy supplies if possible. High energy consumption was a cause of inflation and unemployment, in the United States and abroad.[53]

Beyond the objective conditions Carter cited, however, contingencies also conspired to make energy policy his top priority. Because of his abundant experience in government and because of the strong relationship he quickly established with Carter, Schlesinger hit the ground running faster than any other official in the new administration, and Schlesinger's new domain just happened to be energy. Carter was looking for an issue on which he could make his mark quickly, within the "first hundred days" standard set by FDR, and he grabbed hold of energy. Part of the credit went to the weather. It was an extremely cold winter, and the Northeast suffered serious natural gas shortages resulting in school and factory closings. The shortages dramatized the energy problem to a degree it had not been dramatized since the oil embargo of 1973. The speed with which Congress enacted legislation giving Carter emergency powers to deal with the problem of maldistributed supplies encouraged Carter to believe that it would respond similarly were he to seek comprehensive legislation. Indeed, a certain amount of Congressional pressure already existed. Henry Jackson, for example, was preparing to move quickly on an energy department. So, to some extent, it was a case of a President seeing a train leaving the station and his merely hopping on board to try to take control of it.[54]

Unfortunately, the energy train proved to be slow-moving and tended to break down or jump track. The legislation Carter sought was by its nature highly complicated and inherently divisive. The United States was simultanously the world's largest producer and largest consumer of energy. Neither producers nor consumers were satisfied with the compromise that Carter proposed. In the House, Speaker Thomas P. O'Neill appointed a special ad hoc committee under Representative Lud Ashley, and the House approved Carter's

bill on August 5. But Senate rules precluded such a special committee; the legislation was divided up and went to several committees,
the two most important of which were headed by strong-willed and
powerful chairmen with very different outlooks, Russell Long of
Finance and Henry Jackson of Energy and Natural Resources.
Carter later concisely described with some disdain the struggle between special interests that took place:

> In the meantime, [energy industry] spokesmen in the Senate
> were forming a quiet coalition with some of the liberals, who were
> characteristically uncompromising on any of their own demands.
> They did not want any deregulation of oil or gas prices; the pro-
> ducers wanted instant and complete decontrol. The liberals
> wanted all increases from higher prices to go to social programs;
> the producers wanted all the resulting funds retained by the energy
> companies, to be used for increasing producton. The liberals fav-
> ored solar-power projects as a panacea for the world's energy
> woes; the oil producers wanted minimum competition from any
> energy sources they could not control. Some consumer groups saw
> expensive gasoline and restrictive legislation as essential for the
> elimination of the large gas-guzzling vehicles; the automobile com-
> panies wanted low fuel prices and no restraints on the size or style
> of cars. One group wanted to do away with all nuclear power
> plants; another wanted to remove the existing safety regulations,
> which, it claimed, were hamstringing the industry. The environ-
> mentalists wanted ever stricter air pollution standards; the coal
> producers, utility companies, and automobile manufacturers
> wanted to eliminate those we already had.[55]

Although the Congress created the Department of Energy expedi-
tiously, at year's end it was still deadlocked on Carter's comprehensive energy policy. That fact contributed significantly to the image
Carter acquired and never erased for ineffectiveness with Congress.
According to Congressional Quarterly, which has been keeping score
on Presidential success with Congress since 1953, "Carter's success
rate in the Democratic Congress in 1977 outstripped that of his
[immediate]Republican predecessors, but it fell considerably short of
the support given other recent Democratic Presidents." Carter's success rate in his first year was 75.4 percent, compared with Kennedy's
81.0 in 1961 and Johnson's 88.0 in 1964. (Between 1953 and 1977,
the highest Presidential support score was Johnson's 93.0 in 1965
and the lowest was Nixon's 50.6 in 1973.) Carter's 75.4 mark was a

significant improvement over Ford's 53.8 in his last year, but it was only slightly better than Nixon's 74.0 in his first year.[56]

In fairness, it must be recalled that Carter did not face an easy situation in Congress. Through the 1970s the Congress had been growing steadily more fractious, resistant to executive authority, and self-assertive. The large "class of '74," the Watergate class, most of whose members were still present in 1977, had originally been elected on the strength of their opposition to excessive Presidential authority. During the 1970s, subcommittees and Congressional staffs had proliferated, and committee chairmen and party leaders exercised less power than they once did. After eight years of Republic control of the White House, there was much pent-up demand among the Democratic majority for pet programs and for patronage. Few if any members owed their election to Carter's coattails; on the contrary, most Democrats had outpolled him. They had little sense that their fates might be tied to his in the future either. In recent years House and Senate contests had become largely impervious to Presidential contests, though Democrats first elected in 1974 should probably have reflected on how a discredited President had adversely affected the Republicans they defeated.[57]

Carter later claimed that he recognized that his unfamiliarity with Congress and his campaign as an outsider would handicap him and that he sought therefore to establish good relations with Congress by consulting with its leaders and many of its key members during the interregnum and in his first days in the White House. "I had not been in office a week before the top Democratic leaders in both Houses, Speaker Tip O'Neill and Majority Leader Robert Byrd, were complaining to the press that they were not adequately consulted," Carter grumbled, however. "It seemed that Congress had an insatiable desire for consultation, which, despite all our efforts, we were never able to meet. It was not for lack of trying."[58]

However well-intentioned Carter's effort, it clearly failed to meet Congressional expectations or his needs. Carter was hurt by shoddy staff work and by his own lack of familiarity with Congressional sensibilities. For example, when O'Neill paid $300 for his Inaugural tickets and then discovered that they were in the last two rows of the gallery, he figured that it had to be an intentional slight, and he fumed at Jordan. Many of Carter's top aides, including Jordan, Powell, and, of course, Moore, were unfamiliar with members of Congress and made no effort to become acquainted initially. The whole appointment process was a rude shock to many members of Congress. Not only did Senators and Representatives have little leverage through the White House over appointments, but they also sometimes were not given the customary advance notification of appointments from their state or district.

Carter even failed to attend to legislators' creature comforts. "Jimmy Carter had us in that damp pond house of his for five hours and I nearly froze to death," Hubert Humphrey told reporter Haynes Johnson after a pre-Inaugural conference in Plains. "He gave us Coca-Cola and a damned old sandwich with stringy roast beef wrapped in cellophane. We should have been treated better than that." After he was in the White House, Carter served Congressional leaders skimpy Continental breakfasts, which they immediately complained about to the press.[59]

Carter himself had little feel for the Congress or its key figures. Humphrey, who was dying from cancer and was a disinterested observer, elaborated upon this point one spring day in 1977 to Haynes Johnson:

> You see, part of Carter's problems is that he really doesn't know the little characteristics of our colleagues up here. You've got to know what makes 'em tick, you've got to know their wives, you've got to know their families, you've got to know their backgrounds. You know, I used to say Johnson was a personal FBI. The son of a gun was incredible, but so was Kennedy, and so in a sense was Ford. All of the last four presidents were creatures of Congress. Kennedy, Johnson, Nixon, Ford—when they went to the White House, they had connections up here, buddy-buddy connections.

Of course, Ronald Reagan did not have those connections either, but he compensated by hiring aides who did. He also had better interpersonal skills with fellow politicians and was gifted at appealing to the public over the heads of Congress. Carter lacked that gift. Early in his administration, he told Congressional leaders he would go over their heads if need be, and his close associates, Jordan and Kirbo, made the same point with the press and said that was how he had dealt with the Georgia legislature. Not only did Congressional leaders resent such threats and comparisons, but when Carter failed to take his case to the public or did so ineffectively, he was doubly damned.[60]

Looking back upon his record with Congress, Carter in his memoir acknowledged a poor sense of timing: "it would have been advisable to have introduced our legislation in much more careful phases—not in such a rush. We would not have accomplished any more, and perhaps less, but my relations with Congress would have been smoother and the image of undue haste and confusion could have been avoided." Carter practiced management by deadline; he would announce that a policy would be revealed by a certain date and then insist that his subordinates meet that deadline. This practice contributed to inadequate consultation within the administration and with the Congress. On energy policy, for example, Schlesinger tightly controlled policy formulation within the administration, but the lack of internal discussion meant that everybody was not rowing in the same direction. Within five days of Carter's reference to the moral equivalent of war, he downgraded the struggle to a skirmish when he told a press conference that his energy policy would increase jobs, have little inflationary impact, and be a boon to the economy. Apparently, during those five days, Carter heeded advisers with a very different point of view from Schlesinger's. The reversal in tone was widely noticed and did no good for Carter or his proposals.[61]

One of Carter's most costly legislative errors also resulted from undue haste and inadequate consultation. Much as Schlesinger hit the ground running, so did Charles Schultze, chairman of the Council of Economic Advisers and a Budget Director under Lyndon Johnson. During the transition per se, Carter gave Schultze the job of producing an economic recovery program. Such a program would have been undertaken no matter who the CEA chairman was, but Schultze's superior experience allowed him to put one together faster than an inexperienced chairman probably could have and also allowed him to jump the gun on Bert Lance and Treasury Secretary Michael Blumenthal. Before the inauguration Schultze sold Carter on a rebate proposal whereby every taxpayer and dependent would receive a one-time fifty dollar rebate. Schultze argued that this would stimulate the economy, but would not permanently surrender revenues that Carter would later need to bargain for tax reform, which was dear to Carter's heart. Somewhat reluctantly, Carter signed on, though he also adopted a Congressional request for larger public-works spending and Labor Secretary Ray Marshall's proposal for expanded public service jobs and training programs.

Congress was less than enthusiastic about the rebate, but by April several key legislators had put aside their reservations and loyally gotten behind the scheme. By then, however, inflation was threatening to revive, and Lance and Blumenthal were trying to persuade Carter to withdraw the rebate. After a full internal debate, Carter agreed to do so. Not surprisingly, his reversal embarrassed and angered some of the plan's prominent supporters in the Congress, such as Al Ullman, chairman of the House Ways and Means Committee, who had gone out on a limb for Carter. In his memoirs, Carter said he had no regrets about his reversal of field."The obvious inconsistency in my policy," he acknowledged however, "during this rapid transition from stimulating the economy to an overall battle against inflation was to plague me for a long time."[62]

Although Carter was instinctively a fiscal conservative, neither the rebate nor his proposed revisions to Ford's 1978 budget reflected it. On February 22, Carter sent his budget revisions to Congress, and they called for spending $19.4 billion more than Ford had proposed and a deficit almost $11 billion higher than Ford's. The stimulative implications of Carter's budget worried businessmen and conservatives and their worries were delivered to Carter by Lance and Blumenthal, who got Carter back on his own fiscally conservative track. In discussing his reversal on the rebate, Carter implied that he had gone off this track at the start of his administration. "I knew I had made the correct decision," he wrote; "for more than three and a half years, my major economic battle would be against inflation."[63]

Carter's fiscal conservatism together with his strong environmentalism accounted for his assault on thirty-two water resource projects authorized or under construction by the Bureau of Reclamation and the Corps of Engineers. Carter's assault created a furor on Capitol Hill, for these water projects constituted a major pork barrel for senior members of Congress. In the end Carter accepted a compromise proposed by O'Neill. But Carter later regretted having done so, for the compromise bill contained some "wasteful items" which he and his Congressional supporters had opposed. "Signing this act was certainly not the worst mistake I ever made," Carter recalled, "but it was accurately interpreted as a sign of weakness on my part, and I regretted it as much as any budget decision I made as President." Carter's advisers, on the other hand, are divided over whether the water-projects fight should have been undertaken in 1977 and whether Carter could have handled it more effectively and with greater damage-control. In 1978 Carter successfully vetoed the annual public-works bill.[64]

With a 75 percent success rate, Carter obviously did better with Congress than this tale of woe suggests. But his early setbacks, mistakes, and inconsistencies created a negative impression that he would be hard-pressed to erase. Carter's defeats, moreover, tended to attract more attention than his successes. Indeed, Carter had a knack for drawing attention to his defeats and mistakes; he was not a counter attacker like Nixon or a deflector like Reagan. Even Carter's memoirs contain an unusual amount of self-criticism. Admirable though humility is, the simple fact is that Presidential power is enhanced by the appearance of infallibility and invincibility. Finally, closely contested issues where Carter prevailed, such as government reorganization in 1977, or later, energy policy, the Panama Canal treaties, and civil service reform, tended either to have little political payoff or to incur considerable political costs. Although it would be inadvisable for a President to make policy merely or primarily on the basis of expediency, a President needs some popularity in order to govern effectively.[65]

The combination of naïveté and inconsistency that hurt Carter so badly with Congress and public opinion on domestic issues also undermined him on foreign affairs. Ironically, however, Carter's lack of sophistication, striving for bold departures, idealism, and disregard for politics and public opinion, also accounted in some measure for his significant achievements in foreign affairs. As in domestic matters, Carter received little credit for his impressive successes, which included the Camp David agreement between Egypt and Israel, the Panama Canal treaties, human-rights policy, normalization of relations with China, and SALT II negotiations. On the contrary, Carter met defeat in 1980 partly because of the reputation he acquired for vacillation, weakness, and frustration abroad, all symbolized by the Iranian revolution and the extended captivity of American diplomatic hostages in Teheran.

As a candidate for President, Carter became a spokesman for public uneasiness with Nixon's and Kissinger's *Realpolitik*. Although the public generally respected Nixon's and Kissinger's diplomatic feats, segments of it were leery of *Realpolitik*'s seeming amorality. For reasons that lay deeply rooted in the American character and American history, many people yearned for policies based on morality and high ideals. Carter gave voice to that yearning. When he announced his candidacy, Carter spoke of his dream "that this country set a standard within the community of nations of courage, compassion, integrity, and dedication to basic human rights and freedom." That idealistic vision fueled Carter's campaign and motivated him in office. Carter never believed that "we had to choose between idealism and realism, or between morality and the exertion of power." "To me," Carter asserted in his memoirs, "the demonstration of American idealism was a practical and realistic approach to foreign affairs, and moral principles were the best foundation for

the exertion of American power and influence." Brzezinski has recalled that Pope John Paul II commented after meeting Carter:
"You know, after a couple of hours with President Carter I had the
feeling that two religious leaders were conversing." When Brzezinski reported this to Carter, he was immensely pleased. After the
Soviet invasion of Afghanistan had pushed Carter to adopt a hard
line with the Soviets, Brzezinski observed, "Carter seemed to resent
my efforts to make him into a successful Truman rather than a
Wilson."[66]

Carter came to office with considerably less experience in foreign affairs than most new Presidents. But his lack of experience did
not connote a lack of interest or an unwillingness to learn. In the
early 1970s he was an enthusiastic member of the Trilateral Commission, an organization of academicians, businessmen, and former
government officials which had been founded by David Rockefeller
to promote cooperation among North America, Western Europe,
and Japan. It was there that Carter first met Vance and Brzezinski,
its director, who became Carter's top foreign-policy adviser in the
campaign and then National Security Adviser. He became Carter's
tutor. "I was an eager student, and took full advantage of what
Brzezinski had to offer," Carter later unabashedly admitted. "As a
college professor and author, he was able to express complicated
ideas simply. We got to know each other well."[67]

Carter has also recalled that prior to naming Brzezinski to the
White House post, a few people cautioned him that Brzezinski was
aggressive, ambitious, too inclined to speak out, and might be inadequately deferential to the Secretary of State. Carter acknowledged the validity of these observations, but noted that "they
were in accord with what I wanted: the final decisions on basic
foreign policy would be made by me in the Oval Office, and not in
the State Department." Carter was evidently reassured by the fact
that Brzezinski and Vance recommended each other for their respective jobs. In *his* memoirs, however, Vance recalled that he did *not
object* to Brzezinski. Vance believed they could "work together,"
but asked for and received two conditions from Carter—that he,
Vance, would be the President's spokesman on foreign policy and
that, while he would not object to Brzezinski's offering Carter independent advice and would even welcome it, that he be able to
present Carter his "own unfiltered views before he made any foreign policy decisions."[68]

Carter, Vance, and Brzezinski started out with high hopes that
collegiality, mutual trust, and good communications would reign.

And why should they not reign, for they along with Mondale and Defense Secretary Harold Brown agreed on policy objectives? By April of 1977, Brzezinski has written, they had formulated the following ten goals: to promote closer political and economic cooperation among the advanced democracies; to improve political and economic relations with emerging regional powers such as Brazil, Nigeria, Saudi Arabia, and Iran; to develop more accommodating North-South relations; to negotiate a SALT treaty with the Soviet Union and to begin strategic arms reduction talks; to normalize relations with the People's Republic of China; to obtain a comprehensive settlement in the Middle East; to move South Africa toward biracial democracy; to restrict the level of global armaments by reducing American arms sales abroad and by limiting nuclear proliferation and weapons testing; to promote worldwide respect for human rights; to maintain military deterrence vis-à-vis the Soviet Union.[69]

Brzezinski later cited this list of goals as proof that, contrary to the conventional wisdom, the Carter administration did have a defined philosophy and certain priorities. Of course, the very length and ambitiousness of the list could lead a disinterested observer to the opposite conclusion. Vance, moreover, recalled two additional early goals: a Panama Canal Treaty and a sensible energy policy. With so many priorities and ambitious objectives, which would come first? What took priority among the priorities? Carter had a hard time choosing. "Some of Carter's main problems as President," Seyom Brown, a sympathetic critic, has written, "appear to have stemmed from his continuing to display in his executive role the all-things-to-all-people quality that got him elected. . . . Each of Carter's most trusted advisers would sense that the chief was most sympathetic with one's own approach, and would carry back to subordinates and sometimes to the public such presidential guidance as one wanted to (and did) hear."[70]

Given Carter's failure to communicate a consistent and coherent point of view to members of his administration, it is not surprising that he also failed to communicate one to the public. "Although the President had made a point of stressing the need to keep the U.S. public involved in foreign policy making," Brzezinski self-critically wrote, "we failed in our duty to educate the people about what we were doing and where we were heading." Brzezinski also acknowledged that Carter and he paid insufficient attention to the domestic political ramifications of foreign policy. Like many foreign policy experts, Brzezinski tended to think that he rather than the electorate or even politicians could best determine America's national interests, while Carter had populist, somewhat messianic, and Wilsonian tendencies to identify personally with the nation's interests.[71]

One of the most costly features of the Carter administration's handling of foreign affairs was that it had too many spokesmen, each selling his own wares. This problem first became evident when UN Ambassador Andrew Young made public pronouncements about British racism that Carter found it necessary to explain. But the problem gradually took on a more serious dimension as a result of Brzezinski's initial briefings and anonymous "backgrounders" for journalists and later on-the-record speeches and appearances. Vance claims that he warned Carter about the confusion Brzezinski was causing, and claims that Carter repeatedly tried to silence Brzezinski without success. According to Brzezinski, Jordan, Powell, and the President himself, Carter wanted Brzezinski as a spokesman because Vance did not have either the time, talent, or inclination to play this role effectively. Looking back, everyone but Carter regarded Brzezinski's high public profile as a serious mistake. "In retrospect," Brzezinski acknowledged, "it would have been wiser for me to have been the invisible man." Retrospectively, it seems remarkable that Vance's understanding of Carter's intent was at such variance with everyone else's. The situation seems all the more remarkable in light both of Carter's closeness with and respect for Vance and of his campaign criticism of Kissinger as the "Lone Ranger."[72]

For a variety of intermeshed reasons—institutional, personal, and circumstantial—collegiality proved an unobtainable objective. Carter encouraged Brzezinski to come up with new ideas, and Brzezinski was ever wont to do so. He viewed himself as a protagonist in a debate and as a competitor for power, not as a molder of consensus. "Coordination is predominance," Brzezinski characteristically asserted. "And the key to asserting effective coordination was the right of direct access to the President, in writing, by telephone, or simply by walking into his office . . . I was determined to maintain an active and personal dialogue with the President on foreign policy issues because only then could I assert my own authority in a manner consistent with his views." Brzezinski once pointed out to Carter that they were both outsiders, one a Southerner, the other a Pole, and he read him a passage from William Styron's novel, Sophie's Choice, describing "a surprising affinity between Poland and the South, two peoples bred on a history that overcame defeat, on a code of chivalry and honor that proudly compensated for backwardness." On the other hand, Brzezinski acidly observed in his memoirs that Vance, "as a member of both the legal profession and the once-dominant Wasp elite, operated according to their values and rules, but those values and rules were of declining relevance not only in terms of domestic American politics but particularly in terms of global conditions."[73]

The State Department, with its large, professional bureaucracy, tended to be wedded to old ideas and to continuity of policy. Vance cared deeply about the department as an institution. He felt that in recent years, Presidents and Secretaries of State had ignored the department, undermined the morale of the Foreign Service, and failed to embed their policies in the institution. "To be enduring," Vance later wrote, "our policies have to be rooted in the institution charged with implementing them." "The inertia of the department was itself a beneficial restraint on overly rapid action or inadequately assessed plans," Carter commented. "In many ways, Cy Vance mirrored the character of the organization he led. He was intelligent and experienced, thoroughly honorable, sound in his judgments, careful to explore all facets of a question before answering, extremely loyal to his subordinates, and protective of the State Department and its status and heritage."[74]

Kissinger's years as National Security Adviser had made everyone—Vance and Brzezinski, their aides, and the press—far more sensitive to questions of bureaucratic turf and personal influence. Even when Vance and Brzezinski were getting along reasonably well at the start of the administration, people down in the trenches had their bucklers on, ready to do battle. The press, too, immediately went on the prowl for discord and helped generate some all by itself. Within a year, relations between Vance and Brzezinski were quite embittered, a result not only of personal competition for influence with Carter, but pride, bureaucratic pressures, journalistic provocation, and most important of all, philosophical differences. Brzezinski took a more bipolar, geopolitical view of the world, seeing the Soviet Union as America's primary adversary and favoring a form of linkage under the code words, "comprehensive" and "reciprocal." He advocated highly visible human rights and Third World policies, not merely for their own sake, but as anti-Soviet instruments. Vance, on the other hand, was skeptical of grand designs, preferring case-by-case negotiations aimed at narrowing points of difference and developing common interests. He sought to keep strategic arms talks with the Soviets, which he saw as fundamentally important, unlinked to other issues, and preferred to deal with human rights issues with quiet diplomacy. [75]

The conflict led to a certain confusion, incoherence, and inconsistency, but it never froze the policy-making process. Hodding Carter III, the State Department's press spokesman under Vance, later commented that it was widely believed that the President "took speech drafts offered by the State Department and the National Security Council and simply pasted half of one to half of the other. The result was predictably all over the lot, offering the Soviet Union the mailed fist and the dove's coo simultaneously." But there was no lack of foreign policy initiatives. Indeed, Carter's early months in office were marked by greater activism on more fronts than new administrations ordinarily muster. Carter sought to reactivate the stalled Middle East process by holding a series of meetings with Middle Eastern leaders, to win Soviet agreement to arms reductions, to conclude the long-discussed Panama Canal treaties, to infuse new life into NATO, and to promote majority rule in Southern Africa and nuclear nonproliferation and human rights around the world.[76]

The wisdom of taking so many initiatives at the start of an administration can be and has been debated. On the one hand, some initiatives clashed with one another, such as human rights and arms reductions. Carter recalled that in a letter to him on February 25, 1977, General Secretary Leonid Brezhnev "seemed especially provoked by my corresponding with him [on arms reductions] and at the same time sending a letter to Sakharov [Andrei Sakharov, the famous scientist and dissident], who was considered by the Soviet leader to be "a renegade who proclaimed himself an enemy of the Soviet state.' " The sheer volume of initiatives, meanwhile, overloaded the decision-making process and placed great pressure on the President's schedule. In addition, Carter may have depleted his political capital on some issues (the Panama Canal treaties being most frequently cited) that he should have reserved for bigger, more important ones, such as arms control.

On the other hand, it has been argued that it made sense to have many inititatives because there was no way of knowing which would prove successful. With many trees planted, at least some were likely to bear fruit. The decision-making process and the President's schedule may have been strained, but they both survived. Vance has countered the political-depletion argument by asserting that the Panama Canal treaties were of great national importance in their own right and that delay might have led to a weak regime in Panama and to chaos and confrontation, causing the United States much greater problems than it already had in Central America. Vance regarded the notion of a President starting out with a finite amount of political credits as overly simplistic. "The ratification of the treaties," Vance persuasively argued, "showed that the administration was able to take the most contentious foreign policy problem on the national agenda and build a coalition for its resolution."[77]

Newly elected Presidents and their appointees, who have in each instance since 1932 come from the opposite party from their predecessors, want to innovate on foreign policy, to place their own distinctive mark on it. "To be sure," Brzezinski reflected with the benefit of hindsight, "the new men soon discover that the problems they face are more intractable and lasting than they had expected—and the virtues of continuity come to be appreciated more than the merits of innovation." Unfortunately, there are no clear-cut rules on when a new administration should continue along a path laid out by its predecessor and when it should cut a new path. Continuity does not necessarily lead to happy results, as Kennedy learned at the Bay of Pigs. Nixon stayed the course in Vietnam at enormous costs. On the other hand, essential continuity of policy served Eisenhower well in Korea. Discontinuity likewise yields various results. Through innovative approaches at the start of their administrations, both Kennedy and Carter improved U.S. relations with less developed countries. But discontinuity could also be troublesome, as it was in the case of arms negotiations at the start of the Carter administration.[78]

The story of Carter's "deep cuts" strategic arms proposal in March 1977, which Moscow immediately rejected, is long, complex, and informative. It has been well told by Strobe Talbott in his 1979 book, *Endgame,* and more recently Carter, Brzezinski, and Vance have given their versions in their memoirs. A full recounting here would be redundant. But certain aspects of the story are worth recalling because they bear on problems of new administrations generally and on Carter's specifically.[79]

Carter assumed office at a time of significant disillusionment with traditional arms-control measures. The SALT I agreements of 1972 had frozen for five years Soviet and American intercontinental ballistic missiles and submarine-launched ballistic missiles. The Soviets were permitted a numerical advantage of about 2400 to 1700 because the United States had many more long-range bombers, many short-range missiles and bombers in Europe, and a technological advantage. Unfortunately, SALT I had failed to prohibit MIRVs (multiple independently targeted reentry vehicles) so that Carter inherited twice as many warheads in 1977 as had existed five years before. The Soviets, too, had begun to MIRV their missiles, and they had developed a new generation of giant ICBMs. Consequently, they had gained a big lead in "throw-weight," the sheer tonnage of nuclear weapons that could be sent airborne. Meanwhile, the Soviets were producing new Backfire bombers, and the United States had come up with small but hard-to-detect cruise missiles. Thus, it seemed to some people, including Carter, that rather than slow the arms race, SALT I had actually accelerated it. Carter fervently hoped to shift the emphasis from arms limitation to arms reduction and then to nuclear disarmament. "And we will move this year a step toward our ultimate goal," he promised in his Inaugural Address, "the elimination of all nuclear weapons from this Earth."[80]

At Vladivostok in 1974, Ford and Brezhnev had agreed provisionally that each side would be limited to 2400 "strategic delivery vehicles," only 1320 of which could be MIRVed. American long-range bombers would be counted, but not forward-based bombers and missiles. This provisional agreement left unresolved Soviet Backfire bombers and American cruise missiles. At Moscow in early 1976, Kissinger made some concessions on cruise missiles. but Ford backed away from signing an agreement when Kissinger's concessions were attacked by the Pentagon and by hard-line Democrats and Republicans. Moscow rejected an American-proposed "quick fix" that would have deferred resolution of the two most controversial issues, cruise missiles and Backfire bombers. So the arms talks were stalemated through the remainder of 1976 while the arms race continued. In the final budget, Ford called for building a new supersonic bomber, the B-1, and for developing cruise missiles that could be launched from it.[81]

Carter was intent on ending the stalemate and reversing the arms race. In a pre-inaugural meeting, he startled the Joint Chiefs of Staff by asking how few strategic missiles it would take to deter war between the United States and the Soviet Union. Carter himself suggested that each side might get by with two hundred ICBMs. In addition to holding high hopes and ambitious objectives, Carter did not feel bound by the negotiating position of his predecessor, whom he had after all criticized and defeated. Thus, Carter chafed when arms-control experts who had either been carried over from the Ford administration or were new appointees, such as Paul Warnke, advocated trying to get the Vladivostok terms or some minor revision of them signed before moving on to arms reductions.

Carter's desire to try something new was reinforced by political realities and strategic worries. Certain hard-line Democrats, led by Henry Jackson, opposed Vladivostok and wanted deep cuts in heavy missiles, for they regarded the Soviet lead there as very threatening. "Jackson would be a major asset in a future ratification debate if he supported the treaty, and a formidable opponent if he opposed it," Vance later wrote. The strength of potential anti-SALT II opponents was demonstrated by the inauspicious Warnke confirmation vote of 58 to 40 on March 9. But even some people who were more sympathetic to recent arms-control efforts, such as Defense Secretary Brown and Deputy National Security Adviser David Aaron, were worried that the Soviets might be building toward a preemptive first-strike potential, which had graver implications than negating the doctrine of mutual assured destruction that had governed nuclear strategy since the 1960s. In view of increasingly powerful, increasingly accurate, and increasingly MIRVed Soviet ICBMs, were America's land-based missiles becoming vulnerable?[82]

So it was that Carter endorsed the idea of going to the Soviets with a proposal for "deep cuts." Brown and Aaron oversaw the specifics which included significant reductions in the Vladivostok ceilings on both missiles and MIRVs. The proposal cut Soviet heavy missile forces in half, held MIRVed Soviet ICBMs to the same number as their American counterparts, restricted testing of existing ICBMs, and banned the development, testing, and deployment of mobile ICBMs and new ICBMs. Ground-launched cruise missiles, meanwhile, would be allowed to have a range of 2500 kilometers, long enough for them to be fired from West Germany into the Soviet Union; the Soviets had in the past argued for a 600 kilometer limit. The Backfire would have its range restricted and would not be counted as a strategic weapon. Overall, the proposal would have exchanged substantial reductions in existing Soviet forces for marginal cuts in future American ones, such as the MX missile, a mobile ICBM then under consideration. The "deep cuts" proposal was nothing less than a wonderful deal for the United States. "We would be giving up future draft choices in exchange for cuts in their starting line-up," Aaron explained in the terminology of professional American sports.[83]

There were ample signs and warnings that the Soviets would not be receptive to the proposal. They had previously rejected aspects of it. Powerful strategic, bureaucratic, and political reasons made them cling to Vladivostok. In private correspondence with Carter, Brezhnev reacted negatively to Carter's preliminary ideas about arms reduction. As Carter later disclosed, Brezhnev characterized his ideas as "deliberately unacceptable." When Vance briefed Soviet Ambassador Anatoly Dobrynin about "deep cuts," he reacted negatively. Vance himself agreed with the principle of "deep cuts," but believed they would be extremely difficult to negotiate. He favored accepting the Vladivostok framework in the short run and proceeding from there. Vance even persuaded Carter to let him take a form of Vladivostok with him when Vance went to Moscow to talk to Brezhnev and Gromyko, but Carter instructed him to make it "crystal clear" that he preferred "deep cuts."[84]

Although the development of the "deep cuts" proposal was shrouded in secrecy within the American government, Soviet specialists at State and CIA being among those kept in the dark, it was, ironically, exposed to sunlight publicly even before Vance formally presented it to the Russians in Moscow. Carter wanted to practice the open diplomacy he had found so lacking in Kissinger. By going public, Carter also sought to strengthen his hand politically. Indeed, Henry Jackson issued a statement praising the proposal as a step in the right direction, away from what he regarded as the folly of the "Kissinger-Nixon-Ford approach." Carter himself went before the United Nations General Assembly in mid-March and said that the United States was seeking a "deep reduction in the strategic arms of both sides." In a press conference the day before Vance departed for Moscow at the end of March, Carter disclosed that Vance was taking two proposals with him, for substantial reductions and for a Vladivostok-type accord. He observed that previous SALT agreements had not slowed the arms race, however, and expressed his preference for his first proposal. Yet Carter also said that "if we are disappointed, which is a possibility, then we'll try to modify out stance." As Talbott later wrote, that statement "caused even his most loyal and obedient supporters to wince." Carter had invited the Soviets to reject both proposals and to wait for the United States to come up with something better.[85]

Not surprisingly, Vance found the Russians unreceptive to both proposals. They only wanted to negotiate on the basis of Kissinger's plan of January 1976. Vance later recalled being "angered at the vehemence and finality with which" Brezhnev rejected the proposals. In the spirit of open diplomacy, Vance immediately held a press conference. He revealed his disappointment and said that the Soviets had examined both proposals, rejected them, and proposed nothing new. Shortly after Vance left Moscow, Soviet Foreign Secretary Andrei Gromyko held a rare press conference in which he denounced the comprehensive proposal for trying to give the United

States an advantage. He went Vance one better by disclosing the numbers the U.S. had proposed. Then Brzezinski countered with his first on-the-record briefing. The Moscow meeting thus degenerated into an international propaganda match.[86]

Within the Carter administration, finger-pointing got under way immediately, much of it quickly finding its way into print. The authors of "deep cuts" argued that the fault lay not in the proposal, but in the highly public way it was handled, particularly by Vance. State Department officials who had either been leery of "deep cuts" or uninformed of it faulted the proposal itself. Writing in 1979, Talbott enumerated six conflicting reasons why the meeting had been a debacle, which he derived from talking to American officials:

> . . . the old boys in the Kremlin were testing the mettle of the new boys in the White House; the Soviets resented the American attempt to conduct diplomacy out in the open; they resented the new administration's trying to change the rules in a game that had been going on for eight years; they resented the effort to keep them on the defensive; they resented the administration's assumption that it could keep SALT on an even keel while rocking the boat of Soviet-American relations with propaganda about human rights; but most of all they resented what they saw, with justification, as the one-sided nature of the comprehensive proposal itself.[87]

Carter learned from the disappointing experience to proceed in a more cautious, less bold, and less public way. In May, Vance and Gromyko agreed on a three-tier approach and in September some substantive progress was made. But as Vladivostok, rather than "deep cuts," became the basis of bargaining, SALT critics on the right began to be heard from again, and gave the Carter administration renewed reason to regret "deep cuts." "The comprehensive proposal gave a weapon to anti-SALT and anti-détente hard-liners," Vance lamented, "who held up the deep-cuts proposal as the only standard against which to measure the success of the ultimate agreement. A SALT Treaty that contained limitations less stringent than the comprehensive proposal would be attacked as falling short of 'real arms control.' "[88]

That Carter conducted negotiations differently after "deep cuts" showed a willingness to learn, or at least to improve technique. But Carter seemed unaware of larger lessons of politics and leadership that he might have derived from the "deep cuts" debacle. His memoirs did not mention the political costs that Vance accurately described. Carter, it seems fair to say, should have wondered what it would do to his political standing to raise public expectations on arms control and then accept a compromise. He should have wondered about the effects on negotiations and on his own position of his press conference remarks on the eve of Vance's departure. He should have questioned the political wisdom of attaching his prestige to a proposal endorsed by the leading critic of arms control.

Where Kennedy at the Bay of Pigs allowed himself to be carried along by bureaucratic inertia and by the fear of stopping an anticommunist plan that had been hatched by the previous administration, Carter moved along on the special sort of hopefulness and striving for the new that often infects neophytes. Both men were hurt by a lack of vigorous debate among their top advisers, who treaded softly, perhaps fearing to offend their new and unfamiliar boss, the President, and perhaps hoping to earn their spurs with him. Kennedy and Carter were innocents who let themselves believe that nothing very bad could happen to them. But there was an important difference between them. Carter had gone through his own Bay of Pigs and seemingly failed to notice.

5

REAGAN

☆ ☆ ☆

Like Eisenhower, Ronald Reagan did not enter electoral politics until relatively late in life. He was fifty-five when he won his first try for office, the California governorship; Eisenhower was sixty-two when he was elected President. Neither man entered politics from obscurity, however; Eisenhower had been a great military hero, Reagan a motion-picture actor and television host. As a young man Reagan was an ardent liberal and a devotee of Franklin D. Roosevelt; he served six terms as president of a union, the Screen Actors' Guild. In the 1950s he became a celebrity lecturer for the General Electric Company, whose popular television show he hosted, and he moved to the right politically. His exceptional abilities as a political speaker were displayed in the televised appeal he made for Barry Goldwater in 1964, a speech that laid the basis for his own entry into politics two years later.

Political opponents who dismissed Reagan as a mere actor, like those who dismissed Eisenhower as a mere soldier, did so at their peril. In addition to being underestimated by their political opponents, Reagan and Eisenhower shared certain other qualities as well. They were both unusually self-assured and had a knack for making people like them. Campaign buttons in the 1950s proclaimed "I like Ike," and in the 1980s even many of Reagan's political opponents conceded that he was affable, congenial, a "nice guy." Personal popularity helped both men escape blame for setbacks or defeats that in other administrations, such as

Carter's, would have been blamed on the President. Their ability to escape blame was enhanced by their reliance on delegation, which let subordinates take the heat, though delegation also raised questions about each President's knowledge or command. In one way, though, Reagan was more like Kennedy than like Eisenhower: he used humor, including self-deprecation, to good effect.

Although a famous general, Eisenhower, to his own great regret, never saw combat. Reagan contributed to the war effort by acting in training films, but he was imbued with patriotism, and he worshipped heroes. Like Eisenhower, Reagan admired successful businessmen, with whom he established important personal and political friendships, and Reagan, too, was adroit at public relations. Eisenhower was in office when television became widespread; Reagan used television and radio with unusual effectiveness. He relished his nickname as the "Great Communicator," a title that had never been conferred upon Eisenhower, though Eisenhower cared more about communications and was better at them than is often realized.

As a communicator and political leader, Reagan modeled himself after his first political hero, Franklin D. Roosevelt, consciously imitating his style, borrowing from his rhetoric, and seeking to duplicate his achievement. Reagan liked to portray himself as loyal to Roosevelt's early principles, though by citing only a very partial sample, he misrepresented Roosevelt as a conservative. In fact, Reagan devoted himself to reversing the trend toward big government and the welfare state that Roosevelt had initiated. He sought to use Roosevelt's means to achieve Coolidge's ends. Hoover was both stigmatized by the Depression and too progressive to suit Reagan; Coolidge's portrait was given the place of honor in Reagan's Cabinet Room. But it was Franklin D. Roosevelt whom Reagan resembled in his optimism, cheerfulness, theatricality, and ability to dominate the nation's popular agenda.

Roosevelt and Reagan both profited from following weak acts. Their immediate predecessors were able and highly intelligent, but politically maladroit. Hoover suffered from inflexible adherence to certain ideas, while Carter suffered from seemingly limitless flexibility. Roosevelt took command at the nadir of the Great Depression; he did not cure the economy, but he did provide sufficient relief, recovery, and reform to change public expectations of the federal government and to forge an enduring political realignment which Republicans through Reagan struggled to undo. The economic situation that Reagan inherited was less dire than it had been in 1932, though probably worse than any new elected President had faced since then.

Roosevelt raised public expectations not only about the role of the federal government but about the Presidency; the fourteen years preceding Reagan's term were difficult ones for American Presidents. Johnson, who for a few years seemed a reincarnation of Roosevelt, fell victim to the political consequences of Vietnam. Nixon, after a triumphant reelection in 1972, was enveloped in scandal and then resigned in disgrace. Ford, the only unelected Vice President to succeed to the Presidency, served only two years before losing to Carter, who in turn lost to Reagan. In 1980, political observers were asking: Can a President govern? Reagan emphatically showed that one could.

Reagan's supporters often attribute his success to his devotion to a distinctive political ideology or philosophy. It served him well, they argue, not only because his particular beliefs were valid but because any philosophy is better than none. Reagan's immediate predecessors supposedly lacked firm beliefs and were consequently buffeted about by events. Undoubtedly, Reagan's conservatism did lend a coherence and provide a direction that had recently been missing. But before concluding that ideology is the essential ingredient of a successful Presidency, it should be noted that ideology also accounted for significant problems and mistakes under Reagan and that Reagan's impressive successes with Congress had much to do with his willingness to negotiate and to compromise. It should also be recalled that Hoover was cursed by an excessive devotion to dogma while Franklin Roosevelt was blessed by flexibility and experimentalism.[1]

Before winning the nomination in 1980, Reagan unsuccessfully sought it twice before, in 1968 when his last-minute candidacy failed to stop Nixon, and in 1976, when he waged a long campaign to try to wrest the nomination from President Ford. With Ford on the sidelines in 1980, Reagan overcame a crowded field and then named his strongest rival, George Bush, as his running mate. There was jubilation in the Carter White House, for Reagan seemed a vulnerable candidate on account of his long identification with conservatism. "At the time," Carter later wrote, "all my political team believed he was the weakest candidate the Republicans could have chosen." But Carter and his aides underestimated Reagan's ability to reassure the public of his good sense, decency, and desire for peace. They also underestimated public dissatisfaction with Carter himself. In one of the most memorable moments of the 1980 Presidential debates, Reagan captured the national mood when he said more sorrowfully than angrily, "There you go again," when Carter attacked him.[2]

The election became a referendum on Carter, and Carter had lost public confidence in his second year in office and failed to regain it on a sustained basis. (In July 1980 Carter's approval rating, according to Gallup, was 21 percent, a record low for any President.) The nation's high inflation rate and the long, frustrating, and highly publicized captivity of American hostages in Iran served as constant reminders of Carter's ineffectiveness. Consequently Carter did worse than any incumbent President seeking reelection since Hoover, winning only 41 percent of the vote to Reagan's 50.7 percent and John Anderson's 6.6 percent. (Anderson was a liberal Republican who ran as an independent.) The electoral vote was 489 to 44, with Reagan prevailing in every region of the country. Reagan's coattails and the backlash to Carter significantly affected the partisan makeup of Congress. For the first time since 1954, the Republicans, who picked up twelve seats, gained control of the Senate, and they reduced the large Democratic majority in the House by thirty-three votes.[3]

Survey research and post-election analysis indicated that the results were more a repudiation of Carter than they were a mandate for conservatism. At the same time, the public was well aware that the change Reagan offered would move the country in a more conservative direction. "They are willing to go along with that," William Schneider, a political scientist observed, "not because they were convinced of the essential merits of the conservative program, but they were willing to give conservatism a chance. It is as if, having got nowhere for the past four years with Jimmy Carter at the wheel, the voters turned to Ronald Reagan and said, 'O.K.— you drive.' "[4]

Reagan quickly and wisely laid claim to having won a mandate for change, and he used it to maximum effect in commanding his party and in winning support among those Democrats, especially Southern House members, who were not far away from him ideologically and whose support he needed to forge a working majority in the House. At the same time, the appearance of a mandate helped him to take firm control of his own party and to steamroll Democrats who were far away from him ideologically, many of whom were dispirited after election day. Yet Reagan knew, in part because his pollster Richard Wirthlin told him, that on many particular issues the public did not share his views, even on the need for tax reduction.

To a greater extent than any of the other four Presidents considered here, Reagan deliberately set out to exploit and build upon the momentum that was generated by the election itself, to use his mandate, ambiguous or not. (Franklin D. Roosevelt and Lyndon Johnson had done likewise, and among the other four Presidents considered here, Kennedy came closest to Reagan.) Among the several groups Reagan established after his election, none assumed greater importance than the one on political strategy headed by Wirthlin. It worked out a plan whereby Reagan could demonstrate his effectiveness at governing within the first one hundred days and thereby lay a basis for future successes. In specific terms, the strategy was fairly simple and came directly out of the campaign and out of Reagan's convictions—to restore the economy by reducing government spending and taxes and to enhance America's international security by increasing defense spending, both in absolute terms and relative to the rest of the budget. That meant shrinking the role of the federal government domestically, particularly in social welfare and regulatory matters, and it meant expanding its military power.

Once Reagan had demonstrated his effectiveness, it was hoped, he would be able to move the country and the Congress along on other issues, such as the cluster of social issues that animated a fervent minority. Supposedly, the expansion of America's military power would make America's adversaries in the world more restrained and tractable. Everything did not work out according to plan. After four years of a military buildup by Washington, it was hard to discern actual gains in either American security or the tractability of its foes; U.S.–Soviet relations were worse than they had been for many years. The timing of economic events, meanwhile, did not follow expectations. A steep recession brought Republican reversals in the 1982 elections, which made it harder for Reagan to have his way with Congress. With respect to Reagan's own reelection campaign, on the other hand, the timing could not have been much better, for by then the economy had rebounded while inflation remained in check, though budget deficits set new records.

Despite the failure of things to work out precisely according to plan, suggesting flaws in underlying assumptions and ideology, it made sense for Reagan to have a strategy, a sense of priorities and of overarching objectives. The strategy came easily to Reagan because he thoroughly believed in its priorities and objectives. It reflected Reagan's ideal of a President as an inspirational leader—during the

transition he read Edmund Morris's popular biography of Theodore
Roosevelt and was impressed anew with the importance of the "bully
pulpit" which the Republican Roosevelt had pioneered—and it
played to Reagan's facility as a communicator. The strategy was
reinforced and partly driven by lessons that Reagan and his aides
derived from the Nixon and Carter experiences. Nixon, they believed, had squandered his honeymoon by failing to take the initiative at the start of his administration. (A similar lesson could be
derived from the Eisenhower experience, though apparently it was
not.) Carter, they believed, had tried to do too much at the start of
his administration, had utterly lacked priorities, lurching from issue
to issue. Carter's Presidency in particular constituted a negative role
model which they were determined to avoid following.[5]

Reagan had received a better preparation for the Presidency as
governor of California than Carter had received as governor of
Georgia. California, the nation's most populous state, came much
closer to being a microcosm of the United States than did Georgia, a
relatively small state. Its population was much more heterogeneous
than Georgia's, its economy vastly larger and more complex. Its
budget was among the largest of any government in the world. In
California Reagan had learned to work with a legislature controlled
by the opposition party; Georgia was a one-party state. In contrast
to Georgia where governors could not succeed themselves, in California they could and Reagan did, winning by a substantial margin,
though it was less substantial than his first. Four years later he left
office with his popularity intact. Carter initially tried to govern the
United States the same way he had governed Georgia—with no
thought to his reelection.[6]

During his governorship and campaigns for President, Reagan
developed a certain administrative style. He preferred a collegial
staff to a rigidly hierarchical one, and he twice fired top aides who
had assumed too much authority, most recently in February 1980,
when he dumped John Sears as campaign manager. Reagan wanted
to hear opposing points of view from his staff but he was uncomfortable with acrimony, wanting everyone to get along. He preferred working with small groups of aides, and he resisted becoming
overly dependent on any one aide. Reagan liked to delegate, and he
guarded himself against overwork and immersion in detail. He
viewed himself as a chairman of the board who made and articulated all the big decisions, while leaving lesser decisions and implementation to others. Reagan's needs and style reportedly fostered
an atmosphere among his staff of surface congeniality and subsur-

face warfare. One staff member likened the atmosphere to a Shake-spearean tragedy where, at the end, the battlefield was littered with the dead and wounded, victims of each other's knives, while hovering above, untouched by it all, the smiling apparition of Reagan.[7]

Reagan evidently learned an important lesson from his transition to the governorship and from having observed Carter's experience in the White House. When he became governor, Reagan was an amateur in state government who in turn depended heavily and at considerable cost on inexperienced staff members. When Carter became President, he filled the upper echelons of his staff with fellow Georgians who were as new to Washington as he was. Before his election in 1980, Reagan had decided not to surround himself exclusively with a "California mafia." He wanted to retain such long-time aides as Edwin Meese III and Michael K. Deaver, but he also wanted to bring in people who could provide administrative talents and interest and Washington experience that he and his veteran aides lacked. In effect, he recognized his weakness as a newcomer to Washington and decided to compensate for it.[8]

In a remarkably shrewd and unusual move, Reagan named James A. Baker III, a relatively new acquaintance, as his chief of staff. A wealthy Houston lawyer, Baker was a superb political tactician who had served as Gerald Ford's chief delegate hunter in 1976. He managed his friend George Bush's Presidential campaign in 1980. Thus he had twice worked against Reagan, though he subsequently earned his spurs as Reagan's negotiator of the debates with Carter. Baker, whose responsibilities under President Reagan included legislative affairs, public liaison, communications, press, personnel, and the White House legal counsel, in turn hired people according to ability, experience, and how they would work with him, not according to past association with Reagan. Thus Baker brought into the White House many veterans of the Nixon and Ford administrations, including Max Friedersdorf, David Gergen, and Richard Darman. It is suggestive that of the twenty-seven original members of the legislative affairs office, for example, only two had worked in the Reagan campaign. Baker and many of those he appointed were distrusted by conservative and supply-side ideologues, including some members of the administration, but Reagan self-confidently and wisely assumed their loyalty and got off to a much more effective start because of their inclusion.

His title as chief of staff notwithstanding, Baker was actually part of a troika with Meese and Deaver, who reportedly had convinced Reagan to hire Baker. Together the three reported to Reagan and oversaw the rest of the executive branch. Meese became Counselor to the President and had Cabinet rank; he oversaw policy. Both National Security Assistant Richard Allen and Domestic Policy Adviser Martin Anderson reported to him, and he also ran the system of Cabinet councils which he created. Deaver, whose title was deputy chief of staff, was in charge of scheduling and of Nancy Reagan's office and served as a free-lance and troubleshooter. He was closest to the Reagans personally and looked after a variety of their needs. Baker, Meese, and Deaver got along personally, and for the first year at least the system seemed to work reasonably well.

The Meese-Baker-Deaver staff system was established within a few days of the election. Although many details remained to be ironed out and subordinate players chosen, it proved invaluable for Reagan to have these top aides in place quickly. Though expressing public and private affection for "Cabinet government," Reagan was already showing that he was not so enamored of it that he would neglect the White House or downplay its role as Carter had initially done. The early attention Reagan paid to his own staffing needs both forecast and contributed to the strong Presidential leadership he was able to exert at the start of his administration. The prompt establishment of clear lines of authority at the top also spared Reagan the confusion and appearance of confusion that the Jordan-Watson struggle had caused Carter.[9]

Reagan likewise created no ambiguity over who was to direct the transition itself. On election day he named Meese transition director. Thus for the period between election and inauguration, Meese was a first among equals, though Baker and Deaver were hardly shunted aside. Both played critical roles in Cabinet selection, for example, and Baker hired the staff for the many important areas of responsibility which he would control. Meese's selection as transition director probably had to do with his penchant for organization, his closeness to Reagan on policy, and his prior involvement in transition planning.

Meese had been thinking about the problem of Presidential transition since Reagan's 1976 campaign, when he had several conversations with Nixon and Ford veterans about it. In the fall of 1979, he asked E. Pendleton James, a friend of over thirty years, to begin planning how to put together an administration. James had spent his career in executive search and had been a deputy to Frederic Malek, Nixon's personnel director, who had been given the job of correcting the personnel mistakes that had been made during Nixon's transition. In the spring and summer of 1980, James did a

small amount of preliminary planning while still running his business. When Meese wanted to expand this endeavor, William Casey,
the campaign manager, objected. He was concerned that such an
effort would distract campaign workers from their overriding mission and that its disclosure by the press would make Reagan appear
presumptuous. Casey acknowledged the importance of planning,
though, and went along with the effort which Meese agreed to keep
quiet.[10]

Pre-election transition planning was modest in scope and clan-
destine in style. The planning task force was headed by James, with
Helene Von Damm, Reagan's secretary, as his deputy. It focused on
identifying appointive positions and the kind of qualifications each
demanded, and it generated lists of names of prospective appointees. It rented office space in Alexandria which by coincidence had
previously housed George Bush's Presidential campaign. James used
the cover of his executive search business, which he was still operating, to travel around the country and talk to people; periodically he
reported to Meese secretly at 6:00 a.m. at Bob's Big Boy restaurant
in Arlington. In mid-September the New York Times revealed the
group's existence on its inside pages, though without identifying
any of its personnel. "We're not looking for high visibility," Meese
told Adam Clymer, the Times reporter. Transition planning, Meese
indicated, was not going to be allowed "to diminish, even one
scintilla from the campaign effort." The story attracted little
attention.[11]

These early planning efforts gave way after the election to the
most elaborate transition machinery in history. The Reagan transition operation spent the full $2 million appropriated by Congress
plus an additional $1 million or more that was raised privately and
funneled through a specially created trust fund and foundation.
Reagan's transition organization occupied a large federal office
building several blocks from the White House, employed over a
thousand people, and utilized many volunteers. "It is marvelous
how the people who most bewail bureaucracy so often turn out in
practice to be the worst bureaucratizers of all," Arthur Schlesinger,
Jr., chided in the Wall Street Journal. "The true-hearted conservatives conducting the transition in Washington are staging a bureaucratic orgy that those ancients who recall the transition from Eisenhower to Kennedy in 1960 can only watch with stupefaction and
incredulity." In self-defense, Reaganites often explained, either with
conviction or sheepishly, that it required a large bureaucracy to try
to take control of a runaway one.[12]

The very scale of the transition operation, with its numerous task forces and volunteers, created a somewhat misleading impression of chaos and confusion. What residents and observers of Washington often saw was the blizzard of task forces, committees, and teams that Meese devised in part to reward, flatter, and occupy the conservative faithful. Like Kennedy's outside task forces in 1960, some of Reagan's in 1980, such as the Heritage Foundation's detailed work, proved useful and their policy recommendations were adopted, either immediately or eventually. Some of those engaged in such efforts were also later appointed to office; indeed, as ever, personal ambition helped account for the large number of willing volunteers. But in 1980, as in 1960 and every other transition, the key decisions about personnel, policy, and organization were made by the President-elect with a relatively small number of aides and advisers.[13]

As usually happens, those who occupied important positions in the Presidential campaign moved laterally into the transition. William Casey, the former campaign chairman, now chaired a senior advisory committee and encouraged the utilization of people with Washington experience. But in fact many of those who held senior positions in the transition and then in the Reagan administration already possessed such experience. William Timmons, who headed the section on executive branch management, which sent teams into seventy-three agencies and departments in Washington, had previously been an aide to Nixon and Ford and was a highly successful Washington lobbyist. Casper Weinberger, who oversaw the budget initially, had been Director of OMB, among other posts, and before that had served as state finance director under Reagan. Pen James in personnel, Richard Allen in national security affairs, and Martin Anderson in domestic policy had all served under Nixon, albeit briefly. Likewise, Tom Korologos, who initially covered Congressional relations, Fred Fielding, who handled conflict of interest, and Edwin Harper, who assisted Anderson on domestic policy, were veterans in these areas from previous Republican administrations. It was a highly seasoned team.[14]

Some top campaign aides, such as Stuart Spencer, voluntarily moved into the background during the transition, and others who played important roles in it, including Timmons, Wirthlin, and Korologos, were unwilling to serve in an official capacity much beyond it. (It is not cynical to observe that their politically related businesses stood to profit handsomely from their visible connections to the administration.) Others such as Weinberger wanted to return to government, but not to the jobs they had formerly held. Some who joined the Reagan administration were quite ambivalent about doing so, supposedly including Deaver and Reagan's former press secretary and political aide Lyn Nofziger. Perhaps because of the strong business ethos of the Reagan administration and the lack of an equally strong commitment to public service, combined with relatively low government salaries and lucrative private possibilities, top campaign assistants were somewhat less desirous of joining this new administration than is usually the case. Yet signs abounded that the love of power, the appeal of public service, and devotion to a political leader, cause, or patriotic duty still animated people, disclaimers to the contrary notwithstanding.

Reagan selected his three top staff aides and then left it largely to them to choose the rest of the White House staff, including even the press secretary, a decision that Presidents usually make for themselves. He did, however, play a large role in selecting his department and key agency heads. Adhering to the normal pattern of new Presidents, Reagan favored Cabinet government, so he naturally wanted to choose its members. Indeed, his sincerity about Cabinet government was suggested by his initial reliance on a group of senior advisers rather than his own staff for recommendations. Yet the inevitable limitations of Cabinet government were suggested by the fact that his staff actually developed the criteria for selecting Cabinet members, drew up lists of prospective candidates, and were at Reagan's side when he made his decisions. In the White House, his aides would play large roles in evaluating Cabinet members and in determining and implementing Presidential policy.[15]

Prior to the election, Meese laid out for James the criteria for selecting the Cabinet which would later be used for the sub-Cabinet as well: philosophical commitment to Reagan; integrity; competence; toughness, by which was meant the ability to withstand pressure from special interest groups; and team play. The list was unexceptionable as such things go. As in the past, all the criteria did not carry equal weight in practice, philosophical commitment to Reagan being more important than the others. Nor did this list constitute the totality of what Reagan sought. Like other Presidents, Reagan wanted his Cabinet to achieve a certain geographic, racial, and gender balance, though he was less committed to such representativeness than a Carter or a Kennedy had been, and he found it hard to achieve. Very few blacks met the important criterion of commitment to Reagan's philosophy; at least one who did was not interested in serving. According to James, two women turned down

Cabinet posts. Like other Presidents before him, Reagan discovered that though there were plenty of aspirants, he could not get everyone he wanted.[16]

When he was elected governor, Reagan turned to a group of friends—conservative businessmen—who had promoted and sponsored his candidacy to help him choose his Cabinet. When he was elected President he turned once again to this group, the "kitchen cabinet," somewhat enlarged and now chaired by William French Smith, Reagan's personal attorney and business adviser. Its membership included Holmes Tuttle, Justin Dart, William Wilson, Earle Jorgenson, Theodore Cummings, Jack Wrather, Alfred Bloomingdale, Joseph Coors, Daniel Terra, Henry Salvatori, Casper Weinberger, and Charles Wick. Meeting at Smith's law firm soon after the election, with Reagan present but saying very little, the kitchen cabinet whittled down the lists James provided to three or four candidates for each post, though names were shuffled around and new ones added. The kitchen cabinet played an important role in Cabinet selection, but Reagan made his final decisions after consulting with a separate group of seven aides, advisers, and the Vice President-elect, Meese, Baker, Deaver, Casey, James, and Senator Paul Laxalt of Nevada, Reagan's closest friend in the Senate.

As always, the press was filled with speculation about who was to be named and why or why not. Meese's standard response to such speculation still holds true today—"those who know aren't talking and those who are talking don't know." But several interesting things can be observed about the process and the results. First, it is striking how many of those involved in the selection process actually received appointments—Smith became Attorney General; Weinberger, Secretary of Defense; Casey, CIA Director; Wick, USIA Director, and several others, ambassadors. It is not known whether these appointments had been predetermined, were "done deals" in Reagan parlance. It is also true that all Presidents-elect have appointed friends and political allies to key posts. But Reagan's advisers hardly gave the appearance of being disinterested in the manner of a Lucius Clay, Clark Clifford, or Robert Lovett. The process also reflected Reagan's preference for delegation. Reagan made the final decisions, but, like Eisenhower, he appeared to make them from a fairly short list of options that the kitchen cabinet and his aides supplied. He did not do his own staff work or interview candidates the way Carter had. Like Kennedy, though not to the same degree, he sought advice from friends in the press such as William F. Buckley, Jr., and George Will. Finally, Reagan distanced himself from the announcement of appointments, most of which were made by Meese in Washington, sometimes while Reagan was in California.[17]

The Cabinet reflected the great importance attached to political loyalty and compatibility. Before selecting Alexander Haig to be Secretary of State, Meese, Baker, James, and Laxalt grilled him on his ambition to be President. Had he not satisfied them that he no longer entertained such an ambition, he would have been rejected. Haig proved to be an ill-fit anyway, for his ego and pride were too big to be contained within an administration that set a high premium on team play, loyalty, and collegiality. Reagan showed more foresight in steering clear of two other Republican powerhouses, John Connally and William Simon. Henry Kissinger had meanwhile been ruled out on ideological grounds—Reagan had attacked him in 1976 for conducting too weak a foreign policy.

Haig had the biggest name in the Reagan Cabinet and not surprisingly lasted the shortest period of time. The rest of the Cabinet did not exactly consist of household names, but that is often the case. As usual, some would become well known because of their roles as public spokesmen and their obvious importance within the administration, especially OMB Director David Stockman and Treasury Secretary Donald Regan. Interior Secretary James Watt, on the other hand, achieved notoriety because of his confrontational style and his imprudently expressed views, while Labor Secretary Raymond Donovan achieved it on account of allegations of corruption against him. (He later became the first incumbent Cabinet officer in history to be criminally indicted.) Secretary of Energy James Edwards remained in the background and left the administration early, while HUD Secretary Samuel Pierce, the only black, was a quiet figure who endured.

The turnover rate among Cabinet officers was as high as had now become usual, with Haig, Edward, Watt, Transportation Secretary Drew Lewis, and Health and Human Services Secretary Richard Schweiker all gone before the end of Reagan's first term. Smith, too, resigned but agreed to stay on pending resolution of Reagan's controversial nomination of Meese to be Attorney General. Their record of performance in office from a Presidential perspective appears also to have been normal, with stars, flops, and the rest performing somewhere in between. The one characteristic all Cabinet members shared was philosophical agreement with Reagan. Even Haig, who published a withering memoir after Reagan fired him, had no serious philosophical disagreements with Reagan.

United Nations Ambassador Jeane Kirkpatrick, the only woman and the only Democrat in Reagan's original Cabinet, was a vocal supporter of Reagan's election in 1980.[18]

Although the process of choosing Cabinet members began earlier than usual, with James getting underway in the summer, it took longer to complete than ever. Reagan did not name his last department head until January 8, Terrel Bell as Secretary of Education. (It does not appear that Reagan's promise to abolish the Department of Education, along with the Department of Energy, had anything to do with the delay; it is also worth noting that Reagan never made good on either promise.) The slowness of appointments was caused in small part by the complex new financial disclosure and conflict-of-interest requirements of the Ethics in Government Act of 1978. But it also related to the large number of advisers used and the elaborate clearance system. Certainly the process moved slower than Reagan expected or wanted, but new Presidents are customarily frustrated by how long it takes to make appointments.[19]

Delay was even more characteristic of sub-Cabinet appointments for which an elaborate sign-off procedure was established before nominations went to Reagan. After Cabinet Secretaries and the White House personnel office had settled on a candidate, he or she would have to be cleared by Anderson or Allen, Nofziger, White House Counsel Fred Fielding, the White House Congressional liaison office, and James, Baker, Meese, and Deaver. Then the appointment went to Reagan for his approval. Other than Reagan, only Baker, Meese, and Deaver had veto power. Nofziger, the political affairs adviser, strove to reward the faithful and block the unfaithful and exercised considerable influence, but lacked veto power. The process was prolonged by the sheer number of sub-Cabinet appointments; the new legal requirements; the slow motion of bureaucracy, with legally required Internal Revenue Service checks often taking weeks; and the elaborate system of clearances itself. The White House sometimes deliberately delayed filling certain jobs as ways of signaling or impeding bureaucracies it disliked. Delays in the White House also evidently were used to put independent Cabinet officers in their place. Haig, for one, suspected that the White House staff sat on some nominations that had to be sent to the Senate for confirmation.

Drawing a lesson mainly from Nixon's experience but also from Carter's, Reagan was determined not to lose control of the sub-Cabinet. After Reagan asked individuals to serve in the Cabinet, James or usually Meese would explain to them that sub-Cabinet appointments came under the President and that Reagan intended to exercise his authority fully. Initially no Cabinet member resisted this idea in theory, though some later resisted it in practice. Cabinet designees were assured that they would be involved in the selection process and that they would not be forced to take anyone they could not tolerate. They were then assigned someone from James's office to work closely with them on personnel.

The end results were an unusually centralized personnel operation, tight Presidential control of the sub-Cabinet, and an ideologically cohesive government. When everything went according to expectations, Cabinet members and White House personnel officers worked cooperatively together, and there was little pride of authorship over particular appointees. Yet expectations sometimes went awry, and Cabinet officers could end up with subordinates they had not wanted and had trouble commanding. The system also made it harder for Cabinet officers to attract the highest-caliber deputies. Some very able and experienced people wanted no part of such a centralized and politicized system.[20]

As usual there was no shortage of applicants for jobs. James constantly reminded his staff that filling a government job was easy—one had only to answer the telephone or open the mail. But most applicants lived around Washington, and many had Congressional sponsors, though Congressional Republicans were probably less grasping on the whole than their Democratic counterparts had been four years previously, for they were chastened by what had happened to Carter and some Democratic Congressmen: defeat at the polls. James tried to get his staff members to adopt a search mentality and gave them a hard time when they came up with candidates who lived around Washington.

As a conservative who had long campaigned against big government, Reagan looked favorably upon businessmen and said after his election that he wanted people to take government jobs who did not need or even want government jobs and who would tell him when their jobs were no longer necessary. "I want people who are already so successful," Reagan told *Time*, "that they would regard a government job as a step down, not a step up." In the private sector, Reagan said, "there's an awful lot of brains and talent in people who haven't learned all the things you *can't* do." In actuality, James found it relatively easy to get businessmen to serve as Cabinet or agency heads or as ambassadors. (Reagan reversed Carter's practice of appointing a heavy preponderance of ambassadors from the Foreign Service; under Reagan, ambassadorships once again became largely the province of rich and well-connected amateurs.) On the other hand, the administration found it harder to attract outstanding young people from business. Many were reluctant to leave the fast track in their chosen fields for the comparatively low pay, lack of privacy, and difficulties of public life. If they were not predisposed to begin with, it was hard to infect them with the bug of public service. Reagan's philosophy itself placed a much higher value on private endeavor than on government or public service.[21]

Although Reagan undoubtedly did bring in some talented new people who will probably be heard from in years to come, it does not appear that those in the sub-Cabinet and other appointive positions were of the quality of Roosevelt's New Dealers or Kennedy's New Frontiersmen. While Reagan succeeded in hiring like-minded followers whose mission was to bring their agencies into line with his policies and way of thinking, they were probably less successful in doing so than is commonly realized. Some of Reagan's appointees turned out merely to have the right ideology, but not the requisite knowledge, experience, management skill, or personality to be effective. Three years into the administration, political scientist Laurence Lynn studied the impact of Reagan appointees at the head of five agencies and found "some gains, some losses and much movement in place." In the scandal-ridden and controversial Environmental Protection Agency, Reagan eventually had to clean house entirely and bring back the agency's first director, William D. Ruckelshaus, to restore public and Congressional confidence.[22]

The Reagan administration's strong business ethos had certain negative implications. Baldly stated, some officials failed to understand and respect the difference between private interest and public trust. The vast majority of Reagan's appointees were law abiding and honest, but some failed to recognize that they had to be like Caesar's wife, above suspicion. Hence, the Reagan administration compiled the worst record of conflict-of-interest allegations and scandals since the Eisenhower administration.

Beginning with the transition, there was in-house counsel to advise appointees on conflict of interest and to explain the new legal requirements of the Ethics in Government Act. Unfortunately, the counsel's office did not appear to have sufficient authority or muscle, though it was headed by Fred Fielding, who had been a deputy to John Dean during Watergate and knew how damaging the mere suspicion of wrong-doing could be. The basic problem here may well have been a combination of naïveté, stubbornness, and blindness in Reagan himself. He too readily accepted his comrades' assertions of innocence. Although his willingness to stand behind them demonstrated an admirable sort of personal loyalty, such steadfastness was also destined to hurt him politically and weaken his cause.[23]

Reagan's appointees, it could be said, fell into two categories: pragmatists and ideologues. Appointees in either category, however, tended to be to the right of center; right and far right, said some approvingly, others contemptuously. Liberal Republicans were a scarce commodity in the Reagan administration; in the party and in the Congress they constituted a diminished, loosely organized, and weak minority. But there was a highly organized, well-financed, and powerful conservative movement from which the Republican party and Reagan himself recently had derived much vitality and considerable financial and organizational muscle. The conservative movement comprised a range of ideological, religious, and economic interests, many of them organized in reaction to liberal trends in such areas as abortion, school prayer, economic and environmental regulation, taxation, and foreign policy.

Among Reagan's department heads, only James Watt qualified as a bona fide member of the conservative movement; all the others were merely Republicans. Certain spokesmen of the conservative movement including Richard Vigurie and John Lofton decried the appointment of Nixon and Ford "retreads," including Pen James, and were particularly distressed by the appointment of Frank Carlucci, a career civil servant, as Deputy Secretary of Defense. The conservative groups beat the drum for more "Reaganites," by which they actually meant more of their own. In the absence of counter pressure, the pragmatists, being pragmatists, accommodated to right-wing pressure; after the inauguration there was a noticeable increase in the number of appointments that went to the right. Within the administration, it was sometimes known as "throwing bones to the right." Several very conservative nominees failed to win Senate confirmation.

Prior to the election, the planning group had identified eighty-seven appointive positions in the economic policy area that Meese targeted as Reagan's top priority should he be elected. Because of the establishment of this priority, economic-policy jobs were filled fairly quickly, enhancing Reagan's ability to get his economic program in place early. Taking a leaf from the corporate world, the planning group had recognized that new employees need orientation. Prior to the inauguration, a full day of orientation was held for Cabinet members in which Meese played a prominent role and Reagan a supporting one. There was also a plan developed for orienting sub-Cabinet members, but little came of it until well after they were already settled in their jobs, when Meese arranged for the Kennedy School of Government at Harvard to conduct a series of seminars in public management.

The planning group also hoped to establish a system whereby all of the administration's sub-Cabinet appointees would have occasional contact with the President, but several years later, sub-Cabinet officials generally felt remote from the President and the White House. If Reagan's appointees in the departments and agencies were less likely to "go native" than their counterparts in prior administrations, that probably had more to do with the selection process than it did with the White House's ability to establish close contact with them. Those of Reagan's appointees who were newcomers to the federal government typically had a dim view of career civil servants, whom they assumed were indolent, liberal, and self-serving. Experience caused them to drop such stereotypical views and almost invariably taught them to respect career officials. An orientation program at the outset might have challenged some of their assumptions, allowed them to make better use of career officials, and avoid ill-conceived and damaging clashes with them. The warfare that sometimes erupted between appointees and career officials in Interior, EPA, and Energy usually helped no one.[25]

Liaison between outgoing and incoming administrations followed the norm, with both sides vowing that it would be the "best" in history, which it could have been, still without being very good. For the second time in a row, a challenger from the opposition party defeated an incumbent, but there was probably even less love lost between Carter and Reagan than between Ford and Carter. Reagan has not published his version of his post-election relationship with Carter, but Carter has. He portrays Reagan in their only substantive meeting as detached and uninterested in the important information Carter gave him orally. "Some of the information was quite complex," Carter wrote, "and I did not see how he could possibly retain all of it merely by listening. I asked him if he wanted a pad so that he could take some notes, but he responded that he could remember what I was saying." Carter proceeded with his report and when he paused, Reagan then asked if he could have a copy of Carter's notes. "They were extremely brief reminders—just a few words on one 3 x 5 card—to prevent my overlooking any of the fifteen or twenty subjects, but I quickly had my secretary make a copy for him."

Carter was of course implying that he knew and could remember a lot more than Reagan. With obvious disdain, Carter recalls Reagan's "first real comment" in the discussion: "He expressed with some enthusiasm his envy of the real authority that Korean President Park Chung Hee had exercised during a time of campus unrest, when he had closed the universities and drafted the demonstrators." It is possible to imagine Reagan's some day writing that Carter lectured to him in a patronizing and boring way about policy matters that they had publicly debated previously and that had been settled in Reagan's favor by the electorate. The Carter-Reagan relationship appears to have been about as uncomfortable as the Truman-Eisenhower one, though without the face-to-face hostility.[26]

Elsewhere in the White House, liaison tended to be more amicable and perhaps even more productive. Meese later spoke warmly of the cooperation he received from Hamilton Jordan and Jack Watson, who had finally become Carter's chief of staff and was his designated transition chief. According to Meese, they gave him and his people as much detailed information as they requested. Watson offered some "dos and don'ts" that Meese found helpful. The plethora of Reagan transition teams and advisers caused some problems and confusion, and Carter administration officials occasionally found themselves mediating between competing Reagan groups. At the same time, several of Carter's top people were impressed with the competence and experience of their counterparts in the Reagan team, in such people as Meese, Baker, Friedersdorf, Timmons, and Stockman; they openly acknowledged that they were a stronger cast of characters than they themselves had been four years before. Some of Reagan's people were so sure of their superiority that they were not interested in what their predecessors might be able to tell them; their attitude was: "We know what we're doing; just be sure to be out of your offices at the proper time."[27]

The experience around the departments and agencies varied considerably. At Transportation, Secretary Neil Goldschmidt advised Drew Lewis to acquire a staff quickly and never to look at his "in" box because it would always be filled and the department's bureaucracies would consume all his time. He suggested that Lewis establish a few priorities and go after them. Lewis followed Goldschmidt's advice and was glad of it. A key element in Stockman's fast start at OMB was not advice he received from his predecessor, but his highly effective use of its career staff which he had

access to by late December. According to Glenn Schleede, a Stockman deputy and former career official at OMB, many of the career
people there were fiscal conservatives who felt that Carter had given
away the store. They provided invaluable assistance in Stockman's
drive to pare the federal budget.[28]

At the State Department, Robert Neumann led a Reagan transition team that raised the hackles of both appointees and career
officials. The Neumann group seemed answerable to no one and
through its inquisitorial style raised fears of purges and recrimina-
tion. Within a couple days of his designation as Secretary, Alexander Haig held a meeting with the outgoing Secretary, Edmund
Muskie, in which he apparently made all the right noises of reassurance with regard to the Foreign Service. Then after meeting with the
transition team and receiving its report, Haig dismissed it. That
dismissal made Haig into something of an instant hero at State, and
he was toasted in the *Washington Post*. In his memoirs Haig indicated that his dismissal of Neumann had been misunderstood; he
actually thought Neumann and his committee had done an excellent
job, and he appointed six of its members, including Neumann, to
important posts. "It was nice to be loved, however briefly, by the
Washington Post," Haig later reflected. "But the right wing of the
Reagan constituency, and the hardliners on his staff, could not have
been pleased to think that my first act as Secretary-designate was to
punish Reaganites and rescue liberals. It did not make me look like
a team player." Richard Allen, meanwhile, was much more the
team player as he cleaned house among the National Security Council Staff; he found replacements at a slow pace, however, and his
appointees tended to be more ideological and less able than their
predecessors.[29]

Although Carter and Reagan publicly pointed out that Carter
had full legal authority until Reagan took the oath of office, power
inevitably began to shift on election day. New Presidents obviously
lack formal authority, but they can begin to engage in diplomacy
either directly or by sending signals, messages or emissaries abroad.
Eisenhower, Kennedy, Nixon, and Carter all did so, and Reagan did
as well. Thus Allen held two discussions with Soviet Ambassador
Dobrynin, and Reagan held a highly publicized meeting with Mexi-
can President José Lopez Portillo on the border between the two
countries. Lopez Portillo and Reagan warmly embraced each other,
and both men reaped favorable publicity from the encounter. It
showed Reagan to be deft at personal diplomacy with a leader of a
neighboring country who had not gotten along well with Carter.

Reagan also met briefly in Washington with West German Chancel-
lor Helmut Schmidt, with whom Carter had had even more strained
relations.[30]

The minutes of these several meetings have not been made public, but it can be safely assumed that the conversations did not
merely concern the weather. Nor were these by any means the only
contacts with foreign governments or agencies; the main thing
Meese and Allen were trying to prevent was *unauthorized* contact.
When the International Energy Agency became worried about possible oil shortages as a result of the explosive situation in Iran, for
example, Carter's Department of Energy urged the imposition of
quotas. With Meese's approval, Glenn Schleede, who was working
in the energy area of the transition, quietly passed word to the
agency through a British embassy friend that Reagan opposed quotas and the agency fell in line.[31]

During the interregnum the Carter administration was engaged
in delicate negotiations to secure the release of the American hostages in Iran. It was in Reagan's interest that these negotiations be
successfully concluded before he took office. In late December,
when the negotiations appeared to be stalemated over the large
amount of money the Iranians were demanding, Meese issued a
helpful warning to the Iranians that they should not expect a better
deal from Reagan. When a settlement was reached two days before
the inauguration, Reagan gave his assurances that he would honor
it. The hostages were in fact released moments after the inaugural,
overshadowing it as a news story yet enhancing a spirit of hopefulness and of a new beginning that played perfectly into Reagan's
scheme of things. Reagan wisely asked Carter to fly to West Germany to meet the hostages, which Carter readily consented to do.
"This arrangement," Haig later wrote, "had the virtue of giving
Carter public credit for the deliverance of the hostages while separating him from the nearest media center by the width of the Atlantic and the Rhine." (Haig apparently overlooked satellite communications.) In the first meeting of the National Security Council on
January 21, Haig was appalled that Reagan even entertained the
suggestion from his aides that the United States abrogate the agreement with the Iranians.[32]

Reagan was lucky not to have to deal with the hostage situation
in his first days in office, much as Carter had been unlucky to have
to contend with it through the last year of his administration and to
be unable to resolve it before the election. But while this was a
prime example of how Reagan just seemed to get better breaks from

Dame Fortune than Carter did, Reagan's courtship of Washington reflected superior political skills and intelligent planning. Both men had run as outsiders who promised to be the people's champion in a capital dominated by remote and powerful institutions. In contrast to Carter, who continued to keep Washington at arm's length after his arrival, Reagan plunged right into the life of the city, determined to show that he did not have horns and that he was a charming, politically astute man who was ready, willing, and able to work with and through the city's institutions and leaders to achieve his purposes.

In mid-November, Reagan paid a carefully orchestrated and highly successful visit to Washington in which he met and socialized with leading members of Congress, including Democrats Thomas P. O'Neill and Edward Kennedy, the press, the Teamsters' union, the Supreme Court, and community leaders. "There is only one letter separating 'President' from 'resident',", Reagan told a social gathering at the F Street Club that included more Democrats than Republicans, "and I intend to be both." "Government is a partnership," said James Baker, "that's something Jimmy Carter never understood." "Tour Meant To Spotlight the Contrast to Carter," headlined the *Washington Post,* which gave Reagan's visit favorable coverage. The return of formal entertaining and high style to the White House pleased Washington society generally, though the opulence of the Reagans and their friends also came in for sharp criticism when they were contrasted to the lifestyles of the poor and, after a recession hit, of middle-income Americans.[33]

While Carter had started off lecturing powerful members of Congress, Reagan began by listening to them, which flattered them, even if he had no intention of following their advice. All of Reagan's new acquaintances seemed to agree that he was personable and charming. Carter had threatened to treat the Congress like the Georgia legislature and to appeal directly to the people; Reagan never threatened this—he merely did it when he had to. Reagan's ability and willingness to play an insider's game were shared by key members of his staff, particularly Baker, who already knew his way around town, but also Deaver, who quickly became familiar with it, and to a lesser extent, Meese.

Reagan and his staff recognized the importance of good press and public relations and were masterful at both, not always, of course, but often. Reagan himself held an unusually small number of press conferences—about half the number that Carter had held and a quarter of the number that Eisenhower had held in his first term. But that connoted a recognition that the press conference did not show Reagan at his best—he tended to make misstatements and to fall victim to rhetorical overkill. It did not in the least suggest a lack of interest in getting his story out. Through radio and television speeches primarily, Reagan got his story out to the people directly, often and effectively. A top priority of staff meetings, meanwhile, was how to put the proper "spin" on that day's news, particularly its televised news, something that they often achieved. If Reagan was less available to the press than his recent predecessors had been, moreover, his top aides were more available than theirs. Haig and Paul Craig Roberts, a devout supply-sider at Treasury, later wrote bitterly about leaking by Reagan's top aides. In the Reagan administration, news management, leaking, and image making were sometimes raised to art forms.[34]

Although the Reagan administration departed from Carter's in many of its procedures, it largely continued the role for the Vice President that had been carved out by Mondale under Carter. In fact, the Mondale Vice Presidency very much served as the model for the Bush Vice Presidency except that Bush rejected one piece of Mondale's advice and sought certain line responsibilities such as overseeing task forces on regulatory relief and on crime. Like Mondale, Bush remained largely a generalist who was kept well informed and attended virtually any meeting he wanted. Like Mondale, he was discreet about what he advised the President and succeeded in avoiding becoming a White House target, in part because the White House staff was headed by his good friend Baker. He maintained an office in the White House, though he also spent considerable time in a larger one across the street. During the transition, Bush received some helpful advice from Robert Finch, who had been lieutenant governor under Reagan during his first two years in Sacramento. Finch recommended that he have a regular lunch date alone with Reagan, who consented, and the time they spent alone together reportedly proved important in cementing their friendship.[35]

Like Carter, Nixon, and Eisenhower, Reagan came into office promising "Cabinet government." According to Meese, "Cabinet government" was a given, for Reagan had used it in California and was determined to use it in Washington. It was something he discussed with prospective Cabinet members when he was recruiting them. According to Meese, Malcolm Baldridge would not have left Scovill Corporation, where he was making close to a million dollars a year, unless he could be an important Secretary of Commerce and not just a figurehead. Similarly, Donald Regan would not have left Merrill Lynch for the Treasury Department if some staff person in the White House or chairman of the Council of Economic Advisers were going to call the signals. During the transition, Meese had Weinberger draw up plans on how to make "Cabinet government" work, and the two of them had many discussions about it; Weinberger had designed the system of Cabinet government that Reagan used in Sacramento.[36]

Partly on the basis of the California experience, partly on the basis of an abortive plan by Nixon at the start of his second term, Meese and Weinberger originally came up with a scheme for a "super cabinet," consisting of the four most senior department heads—State, Defense, Treasury, and Justice—and a like number of senior White House aides. It would be a board of directors over which Reagan would preside. Reportedly, it was Baker who sank this scheme, pointing out that it would be unworkable for the Secretaries of State and Defense, for example, to spend their time reviewing decisions from Interior, Health and Human Services, and Labor. In place of the "super cabinet," Meese then developed the "cabinet council" system which was instituted. Under it there were first five and later seven subcommittees of the Cabinet—Economic Affairs, National Resources and the Environment, Commerce and Trade, Human Resources, Food and Agriculture, Legal Policy, and Management and Administration. Two precursors of this system were the Economic Policy Board that had operated during the Ford administration and the National Security Council which had been in existence since 1947.[37]

Both the "super cabinet" plan and the "cabinet council" gave important roles to Reagan's top staff members. In fact, that is the way the government has often worked in the modern era, and Reagan's administrative plans merely formalized that reality. Since the President's senior assistants were going to be equal in influence to Cabinet members, why not seat them at the table right from the start? That is what happened both literally and figuratively as the three aides moved into chairs at the Cabinet table rather than around the periphery as custom dictated. Meese even chaired the cabinet council on management and administration. There was nothing inherently wrong with any of this and much that was right, but Reagan apparently did fail to communicate to prospective Cabinet members that this was how things were going to be. Thus, not for the first time, a newly elected President raised false expectations among his appointees with loose talk about Cabinet government.

For most of his Cabinet Secretaries, especially those who had worked with Reagan before, talk of Cabinet government followed by a prominent role for White House staff caused no difficulty, but Haig, for one, never adjusted to it.[38]

The cabinet councils were a notable institutional innovation of the Reagan administration. In the administration's first sixteen months or so, the full Cabinet met on the average of three times a month, while council meetings were held at a rate of nearly twelve per month. Some councils were much more active than others and certain officials much more likely to attend than others. The Economic Affairs council met a hundred times, while in the same period, the Human Resources council met fifteen times and the Food and Agriculture council met ten times. The President himself attended 14 percent of council meetings while the most regular attenders were Martin Anderson, 65 percent; CEA Chairman Murray Weidenbaum, 60 percent; Donald Regan, 59 percent; Malcolm Baldridge, 53 percent; Drew Lewis, 49 percent; and George Bush, 43 percent.

The councils, along with full Cabinet meetings, served Reagan's purposes in several ways. They fit his preference for group discussion and multiple advocacy over one-on-one meetings and single advocacy; one of Reagan's favorite words was "roundtable," which he and his closest associates used as a verb. Full Cabinet meetings were reserved for general discussions about philosophy, strategy, and budget while council meetings covered more narrow and specialized topics. But Reagan used both kinds of meetings not only to acquire information, but to communicate his views and philosophy and to forge a consensus. The council meetings served as a means for shooting down bad ideas, for thwarting parochial interests, and for integrating White House staff work with that of the departments. On the other side of the coin, the councils provided members a sounding board and gave them added legitimacy and stature in their departments and before Congress.[39]

Although the cabinet councils were on the whole a worthwhile innovation, their importance should not be exaggerated. Government never operates strictly according to organization charts. Paul Craig Roberts, later wrote that though the cabinet council on Economic Affairs was chaired by Treasury, Donald Regan "himself seemed to have little control" over it. "The council functioned as a forum for the economic policy views of OMB and CEA," explained Roberts. "Treasury was supposed to receive the agendas, review the papers that were to be presented, and prepare comments for the secretary, but in practice it was often bypassed." Outside the council framework, important deals were struck, alliances forged, crises responded to, and initiatives developed. Cabinet officers sometimes went directly to the President or to the troika. As always, much depended on personal relationships, on the momentum generated by past decisions, on the Congress, and on public opinion. Particular circumstances, not the council system, explained how and why the administration, without incurring political costs, succeeded in breaking the air traffic controllers union when it went on strike illegally or how the administration suffered an embarrassing defeat when it tried to impose limits on Social Security. The councils did not account for how "voluntary" auto-import restrictions triumphed over free trade or for the public-relations debacle that resulted from implementation of new disability regulations.[40]

It was moreover, the Legislative Strategy Group, not the cabinet councils, that was responsible for guiding the President's program through Congress. The Legislative Strategy Group was initiated in February by Richard Darman, who pointed out that Treasury, OMB, and the White House legislative office were going off in three different directions and therefore needed coordination and control. Baker and Meese were nominally cochairmen, but Baker became de facto chief. Its membership included Darman, Cabinet Secretary Craig Fuller, Friedersdorf, Gergen, Regan, and Stockman. Reportedly, it became the single most influential committee, setting the priorities, cutting the deals, and communicating the message that allowed Reagan to prevail on his program. By playing such a critical role on tactics, the group inevitably became deeply involved in policy. The original division of authority between Meese, the formulator of policy, and Baker, the implementer of policy, began to break down. It is suggestive of formal structure's limited importance that when the White House organizational chart was redrafted in 1982, the Legislative Strategy Group did not appear among the thirty-five interconnected boxes.[41]

Nor did White House organizational charts reveal the extent of OMB's influence in the early days of the administration, an influence that had several sources. Reagan's philosophy and program called for reducing the scope of the federal government's activities and their size, for reducing taxes, and for eliminating the deficit and reducing the national debt. By so doing, Reagan believed, individuals and businesses would have the incentive to work harder and produce more, the economy would grow, inflation would be tamed, and people at all income levels would benefit. Given Reagan's ideology, it followed that any Director of OMB he appointed could have been expected to play a large role. But a combination of things allowed Stockman to expand that role even further.

Stockman had a remarkable grasp of the budget, acquired first during his days on Capitol Hill, but then expanded through prodigious work in the months following his designation. Stockman simply knew more than most people, could recite chapter and verse on details of the budget with ease, and was extremely well prepared, all of which gave him an advantage. In addition, Stockman came to office with the right political credentials and sponsorship. Congressman Jack Kemp, the most effective spokesman for supply-side economics among politicians, was an ally and sponsor. Kemp had been the conduit for a much-leaked memorandum Stockman wrote before his appointment entitled "Avoiding a GOP Economic Dunkirk," which depicted the economic situation as even more dire than Reagan portrayed it in the campaign. The memo also urged Reagan to declare a national emergency, and warned that unless strong action were taken, inflation and high interest rates would persist and Reagan would suffer political reversals in 1982. In it Stockman presciently forecast polarization in Republican ranks between supply-side tax cutters and the more fiscally orthodox.[42]

Stockman made effective use of OMB's career staff, though some also complained about OMB's politicization and its loss of professional integrity under him, and he hired able deputies like Edwin Harper, Glenn Schleede, and Edwin Dale, a highly respected reporter from the *New York Times* who handled OMB's press and public affairs. Stockman himself was an articulate and self-assured spokesman. After the President, he became the administration's most visible and effective advocate for its economic program, appearing with great frequency before Congressional committees, on the nightly news, and in interviews. He also spent considerable time with print journalists and was to be badly burned by a series of interviews he gave one, William Greider, which Stockman, for reasons that have never been clear, failed to make "off-the-record."

When his remarks to Greider came out in a highly publicized and widely quoted article in *The Atlantic* in November 1981, Stockman appeared to have been much less certain privately than he ever publicly acknowledged about all his numbers. He admitted that "Kemp-Roth was always a Trojan horse to bring down the top rate" on taxes. "It's kind of hard to sell 'trickle down'," Stockman volunteered, "so the supply-side formula was the only way to get a tax policy that was really 'trickle down.' Supply-side is 'trickle down' theory." Democratic opponents of the administration naturally relished such "confessions," and devout supply-siders who had already been growing suspicious of Stockman because of his way-wardness on taxes became ever more so. Stockman survived the uproar, though there can be little doubt that his credibility and effectiveness were damaged.[43]

But that was all to come. In the early months of the administration, Stockman was in the saddle. He and his staff hunted for $40 billion in cuts in a budget running over $700 billion. Reagan promised not to cut the so-called "social safety net," which actually meant the broad-based entitlement programs such as Social Security, Medicare, veterans' benefits, and government-sponsored pensions. He was also firmly committed to increasing defense spending, so most reductions had to come in a variety of domestic programs in agriculture, housing, urban development, job training and public service employment, transportation, energy, natural resources, education, and health and human services.

By the time of Reagan's inauguration, Stockman's staff had prepared a series of policy papers outlining various cuts which were then presented to Cabinet members during their first week in office. A budget working group was established which was stacked in Stockman's favor. Before most Cabinet officers could even become familiar with their departments or learn how to defend their turf, they were handed a fait accompli on their budgets, the fundamental policy document for their departments. It was for this reason that it could be said that in the first year of the Reagan administration, OMB made domestic policy.

Stockman did not win on everything. Thanks to his Congressional background, Schweiker knew the Health and Human Services budget intimately and was able to protect certain areas from Stockman's knife, including Head Start and medical research, both of which also happened to enjoy great popularity on the Hill. Haig managed to get projected cuts in foreign aid restored. Baldridge and U.S. Trade Representative William Brock succeeded in restoring funds to the Export-Import Bank. But overall, Stockman prevailed, for he hit the ground running faster than the department heads, and he had the President's full support—except when it came to the Defense budget, which Stockman got around to later. There he hit a stone wall in Weinberger and Reagan. Even those Cabinet officers who were more able to defend turf, such as Schweiker, were reluctant to go to the mat on more than a few items. They had, after all, been chosen for their loyalty to Reagan and for their team play, and the budgetary review process served to reinforce those attributes.[44]

Stockman's effective behind-the-scenes work was matched by Reagan's ability to sell his program to the public and to Congress. The selling of the program, both budget cuts and tax cuts, proceeded in a highly visible fashion and in private, through superbly crafted speeches by Reagan to the nation and through an intensive lobbying effort largely out of public view. Reagan himself held numerous meetings with Congressmen and made hundreds of phone calls. In addition, the White House organized a major campaign to bring pressure to bear on Congressmen and Senators in their districts and states. Businessmen and business organizations were marshaled in support of a President's program to an unprecedented degree, and they were potent allies.

Reagan addressed the nation twice from Capitol Hill, and his second speech, at the end of April was especially effective and memorable. It marked his recovery from being wounded in an assassination attempt a month before. It hardly seems like good luck to have been shot and nearly killed, but in several ways the attempt on his life actually was a break for Reagan. The shock of his wounding, which was captured on videotape and shown repeatedly on television, and the gracious, courageous, and good-humored way he responded to it earned respect and admiration. His one-liners and quips endeared him to many. Even before the shooting Reagan had impressed people with his personal ease and charm. "When he displayed that same wit and grace in the hours after his own life was threatened," wrote David Broder, one of the country's most influential reporters, "he elevated those appealing qualities to the level of legend." The physical assault on him actually made him less vulnerable to political attack. It is impossible to measure with precision, but the assassination attempt almost certainly extended Reagan's honeymoon with Congress by several months and it created a store of public good will and respect that endured long after that.[45]

Reagan always referred to his program as bipartisan, which it was in the sense that a minority of Democrats supported it. In fact, Texas Democrat Phil Gramm became principal sponsor of Reagan's budget bill while another Texas Democrat, Kent Hance, was designated principal author of the administration's tax bill. The prominent role given to these Democrats was not mere magnanimity on Reagan's part. Rather, it was dictated by cold reality, for without the support of the "boll weevils," conservative Democrats principally from the South and West whose districts had heavily supported Reagan, his program could not have been passed. It is easier to talk about forging a bipartisan majority than to achieve one, however, so Reagan deserves much credit for actually doing the latter. (A couple of "boll weevils" later changed parties, and Gramm went on to win a Senate seat as a Republican in 1984.)

Reagan and the Republican leadership were also effective in maintaining party discipline, a sine qua non for the program's passage. Senate Republicans, for example, voted with Reagan on 80 percent of the roll calls *Congressional Quarterly* used in its annual scoresheet of Presidential success in Congress, the highest such score it had ever recorded. The explanation for Republican loyalty lay partly in the fact that many Republicans were chastened by having witnessed the results of Democratic disunity under Carter. It also related to the skillful leadership of Howard Baker in the Senate and Robert Michel in the House and to the impact of the election returns, to Reagan's salesmanship, organized pressure, and competent staff work. Very important, too, Reagan showed a willingness to compromise with "gypsy moths" from the Northeast and Midwest who sought restoration of cuts in certain programs and with business-oriented and fiscally orthodox Congressmen who either added Christmas ornaments to the tax bill or delayed its effect.[46]

Judged in political terms, Reagan was highly successful. No President since Lyndon Johnson and, before that, Franklin D. Roosevelt, so dominated the Congress and the nation's political agenda. Although a severe recession beginning in 1981 damaged Reagan's public standing and his influence with Congress in 1982 and 1983, the economy began to recover in 1983, and by the election of 1984 Reagan had recovered politically as well. His ability to take credit for the recovery stemmed from the strong impression of leadership that he made at the start of his term. Indeed, public perception of Reagan's leadership went a long way toward explaining his landslide win over Walter Mondale, who never escaped the shadow of Carter's legacy of weak leadership. Reagan's political impact could also be seen in the Democrats' eschewal of expensive new spending programs in 1984 and in their essential acquiescence in the budgetary reordering that Reagan had engineered in 1981. In 1984 Mondale zeroed in on the budget deficit while Reagan trumpeted economic growth, a reversal of traditional roles for Democrats and Republicans and one which boded well for the Republicans. The seeds of that reversal were planted by Reagan in his first months in office, a compelling example of the political opportunity posed by a transition.[47]

The economic consequences of Reagan's program, on the other hand, tend to be more illustrative of the perils of transition. Relatively little in the economy went according to plan. Reagan hoped that tax cuts would spur savings and investment; over the next several years, at least, savings were essentially flat. More generous depreciation allowances and investment tax credits may have boosted investment, yet their positive effects were also largely offset by interest rates kept inordinately high by record deficits. Cuts in individual tax rates fueled the recovery in 1983, but that was traditional Keynesianism, not supply-side theory, at work. The tax cuts were supposed to lead to such growth as to raise revenues and balance the budget, but Reagan in fact presided over the biggest deficits in history, accumulating vast amounts of debt with ominous long-term implications. Reagan was also wrong about the timing of economic events. Instead of the economic growth he anticipated early in his administration, Reagan got the worst recession since 1938. Economists affiliated with the Democrats later rued the difference between Carter and Reagan, which was that Carter got his good economic news early in his term and his bad news late in it, while Reagan luckily had it the opposite way.

The recession that occurred under Reagan succeeded in beating back inflation. Between 1980 and 1983, consumer price inflation fell from 12.4 percent to 3.8 percent, one of Reagan's proudest achievements. But it was the 1979 decision of the Federal Reserve Board under Paul Volcker to impose tight monetary restrictions that many economists believe caused the recession. Reagan merely acceded in a policy that had been adopted during the Carter administration and to which Carter himself had agreed. By retarding worldwide demand for oil, the recession caused a drop in oil prices, whose earlier rise had been the single most important factor in inflation. The recession was so severe, however, incurring such costs in lost productivity and in human terms, that it is reasonable to ask whether the Reagan administration should have taken steps, including tighter fiscal policies, to persuade the Fed to ease up on the money supply in 1981. The Fed's relaxation of the money supply the following year led to the recovery.[48]

Reagan failed to achieve his original goal of reducing federal spending to 19 percent of GNP. In 1984, it was 25 percent of GNP; in the last year of the Carter administration, it had been 23 percent of GNP. Reagan's failure to come closer to his goal owed primarily to the necessity of having to service a growing national debt at high interest rates. Secondarily, it resulted from increased defense spending and from Reagan's reluctance to tackle government-sponsored pensions and insurance in 1981. Three years later, Stockman told

Fortune magazine that our "biggest failure was that we didn't create a much bigger and better package of spending cuts in the beginning. We should have gone after the big boulders—the social insurance programs." In fairness, Reagan did seek substantially more budget cuts than Congress approved, and he even took a pass at Social Security, but it was poorly handled and allowed Congress to go on record unanimously against it. The following year Reagan took refuge in a bipartisan commission on Social Security.[49]

Although the 1981 budget reductions did not shrink federal spending nearly as much as Reagan hoped, there is no question that he achieved significant reductions in the domestic budget and halted its long growth. If there was a "Reagan revolution," that was it, and most of it was achieved as a result of his 1981 offensive. "During each of the five 4-year periods between 1960 and 1980," the Council of Economic Advisers pointed out in its 1984 report, spending for all nondefense activities except Social Security and Medicare "rose between 11 percent and 38 percent even adjusting for inflation. But comparable spending for the 1980–1984 years fell by 12.5 percent." "After a period of unremitting expansion in domestic spending, we have had zero growth in real terms since 1980—leaving aside defense and interest," Stockman said in 1984. "No new programs, no new entitlements, no new claims on the taxpayers' dollars."[50]

At the same time, there can be no question that domestic budget cuts fell disproportionately on the poorest, most vulnerable, and least powerful members of American society. Means-tested entitlements were cut the most, either through stricter eligibility requirements, through reduced funding, or both. The Congressional Budget Office later demonstrated that low-income programs were reduced more than twice as deeply as social programs not concentrated on the poor. Significant reductions occurred in programs providing the poor with food and nutrition, housing, health care, and employment and training. The effects of these cuts were soon compounded by the recession. Between 1980 and 1982 the number of Americans living below the poverty line increased by 5.5 million. Economic conditions, budget cuts, and the 1981 tax reduction, whose benefits were regressive, together meant that the gap between the richest and poorest families in America widened for the first time in decades. Hundreds of thousands of Americans, including a disproportionately large number of children, experienced hunger, malnutrition, homelessness, and despair, notwithstanding the administration's assurances about the long-term benefits of economic growth and about preserving the social safety net.[51]

In addition to reversing the trend toward an expanding domestic budget, Reagan accelerated one that had begun under Carter toward increased military spending. The buildup under Carter had come in response to fears of growing Soviet military spending, including the development and deployment of new generations of missiles, and in response to Soviet activism abroad, in Africa and Afghanistan particularly. It had resulted as well from perceived threats to Western oil supplies in the Persian Gulf. In his final proposed budget for 1981, Carter projected a defense spending increase in real dollars of 5 percent a year. In his revisions to Carter's budget, Reagan proposed increasing that number to 7 percent. He added $26 billion to Carter's proposed defense budget, a 14.6 percent increase.[52]

Reagan's increases were not based on new strategic departures, however. Reagan did revive the B-1 bomber, which Carter had opposed, and he created a bigger navy with more aircraft carriers, but he rejected the "quick fixes" to America's strategic arsenal which certain conservative advisers, such as William Van Cleave, proposed in order to close America's alleged "window of vulnerability." Weinberger deemed Van Cleave's "quick fixes" excessively costly, and many military experts regarded them as technically unfeasible. Like the "missile gap" of 1960, the "window of vulnerability" turned out to be effective campaign rhetoric but to have no substantive merit. Weinberger later said that the administration deliberately avoided a full-fledged strategic review at the outset because such reviews in the past had been followed by pronouncements that "prejudged and oversimplified reality; they put blinders on our vision." Samuel P. Huntington, a Harvard professor, military expert, and former member of the Carter administration, correctly pointed out that the Reagan administration's "strategy was essentially the upside strategy the Carter administration had outlined." The difference, Huntington noted, was that Reagan made a much more concerted effort to make that strategy a reality; Reagan matched strategy with dollars.[53]

Reagan believed that a military buildup was essential to restore American influence and power, which in his view had been declining relative to the Soviet Union in recent years and seemingly long before that. He believed that the only thing that impressed the Soviets was military capability and the will to use it. He viewed the world strictly in bipolar terms, as a struggle between the Soviet

Union and the United States, between communism and capitalism, between totalitarianism and freedom. Reagan regarded the détente of the Nixon years and the human-rights emphasis of the Carter years as having weakened American resolve and diverted it from the essential task of halting Soviet expansionism. In his first press conference as President on January 29, Reagan plainly stated his long-held views of Soviet methods and intentions:

> Well, so far détente's been a one-way street that the Soviet Union has used to pursue its own aims. I don't have to think of an answer as to what I think their intentions are. They have repeated it. I know of no leader of the Soviet Union since the revolution and including the present leadership that has not more than once repeated in the various communist congresses they hold, their determination that their goal must be the promotion of world revolution and a one world socialist or communist state, whichever word you want to use.
>
> Now, as long as they do that and as long as they at the same time have openly and publicly declared that the only morality they recognize is what will further their cause, meaning they reserve unto themselves the right to commit any crime, to lie, to cheat, in order to attain that, and that is moral, not immoral, and we operate on a different set of standards. I think when you do business with them, even as a détente, you keep that in mind.[54]

These were the harshest words used by an American President in public to describe Soviet behavior since Truman, and they were deliberate, reiterated by Reagan in subsequent weeks, and fully shared by his key appointees in the national security area. It was permissible to negotiate with the Soviets as long as American diplomats understood that negotiation was the continuation of confrontation by other means. Reagan himself avoided contact with the Soviets, spurning a summit conference which they sought. Haig and other members of the administration spoke to Soviet representatives, but took a hard line, pressing them to demonstrate their willingness, as Haig put it, to "behave like a responsible power." "That was the basis of our early policy toward Moscow," Haig later wrote. The chilly relations that were established in the beginning never warmed up over the next four years.[55]

The most dangerous part of the U.S.–Soviet relationship obviously was that it could lead to cataclysmic nuclear war, to the end of civilization and perhaps of human life. Over the previous twenty years, leaders of both countries had recognized that possibility and had sought to regulate and control nuclear arms and had reached some agreements. Reagan believed that the two SALT treaties, the first ratified, and second unratified (though observed, even by Reagan) had contributed to American military inferiority and had not lessened the number or destructive power of nuclear weapons anyway. (Strategic inferiority or superiority is largely irrelevant since what matters is having a *sufficient* deterrent, and the United States clearly had that; Reagan was correct that past agreements had failed to prevent an arms race, but how much worse would the arms race have been without them?) Reagan thus came into office not believing in traditional arms control and hoping that an American buildup would somehow encourage the Soviets to reduce their weaponry, an unrealistically hopeful expectation. "Arms before arms control" became the administration's guiding principle. It was one which, Strobe Talbott demonstrates in *Deadly Gambits,* virtually assured the failure to reach any agreement once arms talks did, because of European and Congressional pressure, take place. The net effect of the policies adopted by Reagan was to promote an arms race without any new restrictions on it.[56]

Reagan actually paid little attention to arms control in his first months in office, which was not surprising given his attitude toward it. He did, however, pay a good deal of attention to El Salvador, where a leftist guerilla insurrection was threatening a civilian/military regime that was dominated by the military. The Carter administration had backed that regime, but pressured it to institute land reform and to stop the military's savage treatment of civilians, a campaign the military waged much more relentlessly than its fight against the guerillas (where it often exhibited cowardice). The military's savagery was brought home to Americans by the uncovering of a mass grave in December 1980. In it were found the bodies of four American nuns who had been raped and murdered by Salvadoran soldiers. Because of its concern for human rights, the Carter administration suspended aid to El Salvador. But human rights were a low priority under Reagan. A few weeks after becoming Secretary of State, Haig postulated the incredible theory that the nuns may have tried to run a roadblock.[57]

Haig, in fact, took the lead both within the councils of government and publicly for a more vigorous, higher profile, and more military solution to the problem of leftist insurrection in Central America. Haig quickly retired Robert White, the American ambassador to El Salvador, who favored a negotiated settlement and who soon became one of the Reagan administration's harshest critics.

White was replaced by Dean Hinton, whom Haig characterized as more "tough-minded." In late February the State Department issued a White Paper which concluded that "Cuba, the Soviet Union, and other Communist states . . . are carrying out . . . a well-coordinated, covert effort to bring about the overthrow of El Salvador's established government and to impose in its place a Communist regime with no popular support." A week later the Reagan administration sent twenty additional military advisers to El Salvador and indicated that it would promptly send $25 million in military assistance.[58]

Haig's attempts to make El Salvador a top priority, however, encountered significant resistance. Journalists in *The Nation,* the *Washington Post,* and the *Wall Street Journal* exposed the White Paper itself as a "textbook case of distortion, embellishments, and exaggeration," as Raymond Bonner, a leading reporter on Central America for the *New York Times* later characterized it. Many members of Congress were uneasy at the administration's lack of concern for human rights and were worried about direct American military involvement. Having had its reputation damaged by Vietnam, the military itself was wary of entering wars that would prove unpopular at home. As Haig later revealed, the President's own advisers were in two camps. In one was Haig. In the other camp, "which favored a low-key treatment of El Salvador as a local problem and sought to cure it through limited amounts of military and economic aid—which would be granted step by step—along with certain covert measures, were the Vice President, the Secretary of Defense, the Director of Central Intelligence (with reservations), the President's aides, Richard Allen, and most of the others."[59]

Reagan's troika, according to Haig, wanted to protect him from anything that might damage his popularity or sidetrack his legislative agenda. Whatever the precise reasons, El Salvador did not become the top priority issue that Haig desired, though Reagan, Weinberger, and other administration officials did accept Haig's dubious premise that Central America belonged essentially in a cold war context rather than a local context. In accepting that premise, they closed their eyes to the region's particular history and to past U.S. involvement in it, and they closed their ears to what the Soviets themselves were telling them. Remarkably, Haig revealed that his conversation with Soviet Ambassador Anatoly Dobrynin convinced him "that Cuban activities in the Western hemisphere were a matter between the United States and Cuba." One wonders how Haig could have been convinced of that and still seen Salvadoran insurrection as part of a Soviet design.[60]

Much as domestic considerations got in Haig's way on El Salvador, they tripped him up on the grain embargo that Carter had imposed on the Soviet Union in January 1980 in reaction to its invasion of Afghanistan. During the campaign Reagan had criticized the embargo for imposing an inequitable burden on American farmers and promised to lift it. Reagan's Secretary of Agriculture, John Block, naturally pressed him to keep that promise, and Meese did too. Haig failed to persuade Block, Meese, and ultimately, Reagan, that the embargo was an important foreign policy issue. With the United States lecturing the Soviets not to interfere in other countries, with Warsaw pact troops maneuvering along Polish borders, and with the military government in Warsaw making ominous noises toward Solidarity, it was hardly the right moment, Haig argued, to lift the embargo. When Haig realized he was getting nowhere with Reagan, he urged delay through which he hoped to wring some advantage or at least to limit the damage that would ensue. When the embargo was finally lifted, however, it came with suddenness and as a surprise to Haig, who was disgusted that a valuable bargaining chip could just be given away for nothing.[61]

The day after Reagan lifted the embargo, Haig told the press that if the Soviet Union invaded Poland, the Reagan administration would impose a total ban on all trade with the Soviet Union, including grain. According to Haig, he "made this statement with the President's blessing, and though it constituted nothing more than a restatement of established U. S. and NATO policy, it created a flurry in the White House. Clarifications were issued by James Baker's White House spokesmen, which raised doubts that I had been speaking for the President in this matter." Reagan was upset by this latest flurry in the media and questioned his staff. "They had told him that they had attempted to moderate" Haig's remarks "because they weren't aware that these reflected the President's position." Haig elaborated: "The President, they explained to the President, had been having private telephone conversations with me and they didn't know the resulting decisions and had had no guidance. In other words, they had been prevented from policing the chief executive's relationship with me and, therefore, could not be held responsible for any unfortunate results." This did not end matters, according to Haig, for Baker's messengers then sent rumors of "Haig's imminent resignation or dismissal through the press."[62]

This was just one of a series of seriocomic episodes involving Haig, most of which were played out on the airwaves and in newspapers. "In its public face," wrote I.M. Destler, Leslie Gelb, and

Anthony Lake, "Ronald Reagan's first year was history repeating itself as farce. Predecessors had seen bitter inner disputes, courtiers and barons fighting over serious policy stakes. But now, a President who had denounced the infighting under Jimmy Carter found himself, within a year of the election, on the telephone with columnist Jack Anderson about whether there really was a 'guerrilla' in the White House out to get the Secretary of State." Haig began with the publicly stated intention of being the President's "vicar" on foreign policy, but he often seemed little more than an errant and somewhat ridiculous country parson. His troubles began early when his ambitious organizational plan for taking over foreign policy got permanently "lost" in Meese's briefcase. Although Haig scored some successes, especially in the salutary influence he exerted on administration policy toward Western Europe and China, they were overshadowed by bureaucratic and personality struggles over his authority, ultimately culminating in Reagan's firing him in July 1982.[63]

To some extent, the Haig fiasco was simply a matter of personal chemistry, as Meese and Pen James have characterized it, of Haig's not being the right kind of personality for this administration. But Reagan knew or ought to have known what Haig was like before he appointed him. Indeed, he appointed him precisely because he wanted or thought he wanted a vigorous, experienced, and tough figure at State—Haig's military background was a big plus. George Shultz, the other leading candidate, was rejected, despite his more soothing personality, because of his reputation as an "extreme moderate." (Another factor in Shultz's rejection was public relations; Shultz worked for the Bechtel Corporation, the same privately held company with large interests in Saudi Arabia that employed Weinberger.) As Robert Lovett once observed to John F. Kennedy: "a Secretary of State is made to look good—or actually to be good—largely by the President and by the degree of backing and trust given the Secretary of State." Here is where Reagan failed; although he promised Haig his backing from the time he appointed him and repeated that pledge to him periodically, Reagan either allowed or directed his aides—it is not known which—to undercut Haig and to undermine his authority and effectiveness. Among the poor and unworkable relationships that recent Presidents have had with their Secretaries of State, this was surely the worst.[64]

Although this will have to be a matter for future biographers to resolve, it appears likely that a major source of the problem was Reagan's own lack of interest, knowledge, self-confidence, and experience in foreign policy. Reagan at the start did not seem comfortable with the subject. Rather than try to compensate for his weakness by hiring, learning from, and working closely with top-caliber professionals, Reagan was content to surround himself with lesser lights and to tolerate bureaucratic warfare and confusion. Although Reagan quite appropriately did not turn over foreign policy completely to Haig, he did not assume command of it himself either. It was a sorry aspect to a transition, which in many other respects demonstrated high political skill.[65]

CONCLUSION:
HISTORICAL PATTERNS
AND LESSONS

In less than three months, newly elected Presidents prepare for the assumption of power. It is a brief and unique period, one in which those who are about to take over the largest, most complex, and important institution in the world must consider in much more concrete and specific terms than is possible in a campaign what they want to accomplish and how, when, and with whom they hope to accomplish it. It is not a time for quiet contemplation, however. Critical decisions are made at a rapid pace, and those decisions are both perilous and rich in opportunity. During the interregnum and then in their first months in office, Presidents-elect choose the highest officials of the executive branch, set lines of authority and organization, and determine substantive domestic and foreign policies. The attention they command allows them to set a tone, to create an important first impression at home and around the world. Although Presidents make changes in policy, personnel, and organization as they go along, they usually prefer adjusting course to reversing it, so the course they set initially must be chosen well.

No two Presidents are exactly alike, and the conditions, circumstances, and personalities that future Presidents encounter will not precisely duplicate those of their predecessors. Therefore, it is not profitable to lay out a narrow set of rules for future Presidents to follow. But there are important similarities between Presidencies and there have been recurring patterns in transitions, and from these similarities and recurring patterns certain broad lessons as well as suggestions and warnings may be derived.

Presidential transitions and the administrations that follow are the shadow of the man—or, someday, the woman—who heads them. They silhouette his past experience and future goals, strengths and weaknesses. Like shadow and background, the strengths and weaknesses often exist side by side. Eisenhower thus profited from being above politics, but his newness to politics also sometimes hurt him, as in his failure to engage Congress in a program of his choosing. Reagan's ideology gave him a clear vision of what he wanted to achieve, but it also blinded him at times to economic and international realities. Kennedy's newness to executive office helped him to generate an atmosphere of promise, change, and excitement, but his lack of executive experience also damaged him, most particularly at the Bay of Pigs. Nixon's eight years as Vice President broadened him, but they also fostered a certain overconfidence and gave him a somewhat skewed perspective on the Presidency. Carter's very lack of Washington experience encouraged him to reach high, but it also made it harder for him to attain his goals.

Presidents-elect, therefore, should take a good hard look at themselves and determine how to compensate for their weaknesses—their strengths just naturally assert themselves. Carter was a stranger to Washington who surrounded himself with aides who were also strangers. As his aides became familiar with Washington, they improved, and Carter also later brought in some more experienced people to buttress them. But he should have taken this step at the very outset. Reagan, another outsider to the capital, wisely did use experienced Washington hands from the beginning, including Baker, Timmons, and Friedersdorf. Yet Reagan did not adequately compensate for his lack of familiarity with foreign policy. On the contrary, he distanced himself from it early in his administration. In this regard, Carter did much better, becoming a diligent student of foreign policy soon after his election.

Similarly, Eisenhower could have benefited from greater attention to and stronger staffing in domestic politics, and Kennedy from something comparable on how the executive branch worked. Nixon's greatest weakness arguably was a flawed character, not the sort of thing that people perceive in themselves. Yet perhaps even that problem might have been ameliorated had Nixon recognized the need to have someone, perhaps Haldeman, who served as a "no" man, not just to the rest of his administration, but to Nixon himself.

The weeks and months after a Presidential election are not times when humility reigns in the victor's camp. Rather it is one when confidence, hope, sometimes arrogance, hubris, and a sense of infallibility run high, characteristics that contribute to, if they do not directly cause, some of the mistakes that are made. This atmosphere, reinforced by the fact that in every instance since 1932 the new President has defeated either the incumbent or his putative successor, largely explains why new Presidents have been unable or unwilling to learn from their predecessors. What is true of new Presidents frequently obtains for their top appointees with *their* immediate predecessors as well. Relations between outgoing and incoming Presidential administrations have usually been civil, occasionally uncivil or nonexistent, but rarely productive or educational. Although incumbent administrations sometimes provide useful information on pending matters—and incoming administrations are wise to devour it—in no known case has a newly elected President acquired insight into the office or its problems from his predecessor; in no known case has he altered how he was planning to proceed as a result of something he learned from his predecessor.

Not only do newly elected Presidents regularly fail to learn from their predecessors, but they often do things in reaction to some perceived error in his ways. This reactiveness is in part a healthy outgrowth of the political process; if the people wanted the old ways, they would have voted differently. But new Presidents frequently overreact to a perceived flaw in their predecessor. In reaction to Truman, Eisenhower was too anti-political. In reaction to Eisenhower, Kennedy was too anti-organizational. In reaction to Nixon, Carter was too "anti-imperial." In reaction to Carter, Reagan was too ideological.

Only Nixon did not overreact in this manner. Nixon, however, did not foresee that Vietnam would cause him the political woes it caused Johnson, that Vietnam would become "Nixon's war" in much the same way it had been "Johnson's war." That he was wrong on this count only illustrates the larger point that new Presidents and those around them, buoyed by their recent electoral victory, tend to believe that bad things cannot happen to them. But bad things do happen. Some Presidents are reelected, but all Presidents leave office with significant amounts of scar tissue. Directly pertinent to transitions themselves, all Presidents have made decisions at the start of their administrations that they later regarded as serious mistakes or should have so regarded.

Several lessons can be derived from these particular patterns.

Future Presidents would be wise to dampen down excessive optimism and avoid hubris by looking closely at some of their predecessors' errors. The humility that comes from understanding history does not necessarily imply inaction, and might possibly save them from making similar mistakes themselves. In addition, they should try to learn from their predecessors, not merely about pending matters, but some of the larger lessons they learned from being President. That sort of understanding has occasionally been achieved between high officials other than Presidents. Comparable understanding in Oval Office meetings might spare future Presidents the sort of overreaction that has sometimes led them astray in the past.

More candid discussions with their predecessors might disabuse Presidents-elect of illusions about organizational reform. In particular, new Presidents are prone to toss around the chestnut of "Cabinet government," about which little is heard by the time they leave office. Only Kennedy refrained from promising Cabinet government, and that was because he operated under the illusion created largely by Eisenhower himself that the Cabinet in the 1950s actually made important decisions. Partly in reaction to the perception of Eisenhower as a kind of passive chairman of the board, Kennedy downplayed the Cabinet as an institution.

The United States will never have Cabinet government unless it adopts parliamentary government, a far-fetched possibility. The Cabinet in the United States has never been a decision-making body, nor has it exercised much collective influence in recent years. Obviously Presidents cannot conduct all of the business of government themselves, however; they depend upon the various bureaucracies. At the same time, Presidents never regard all the bureaucracies or their heads equally. In every administration some appointed officials have emerged as more influential and respected by the President than others. This is a function, not simply of the quality or characteristics of individual appointees, but of a President's priorities, interests, background, and personality, and of the relationships that develop between a President and his individual appointees. Thus, Dean Rusk did not change, but his standing in the Oval Office certainly did as a result of a change in *its* occupant.

Cabinets can be and sometimes have been useful sounding boards and sources of advice, as they were under both Roosevelt and Eisenhower. Because Cabinets have become so large and reflect such a disparity of interests and expertise, the streamlined cabinet councils instituted by Reagan offer a practical alternative to the full-scale Cabinet session. At the same time, the inclusion of White

House aides in the Cabinet councils points to an inevitable fact of life—the importance of the White House staff in the modern American system. It is unwise and inefficient for White House staffs to try to operate the departments and agencies, to take over or replicate their work on a day-to-day basis. But Presidents should and inevitably do use their staffs to assure that their policies are being carried out within the departments and agencies, to develop and coordinate policies that cross organizational lines, as many of the most important ones do, and to help resolve differences that arise between and among bureaucracies.

The principal mischief caused by loose talk about Cabinet government and other reorganizational schemes at the start of administrations is that they raise false hopes and fuel unrealistic expectations about what they might accomplish. New Presidents need to be straightforward with individual Cabinet members about their expectations. In hiring someone for an area they expect to be a low priority, for example, they ought to let their prospective appointee know that unambiguously. Similarly, if a President plans to be his "own Secretary of State," as several of them acknowledged after the fact, it would be prudent for him to apprise prospective appointees of that intention and to conduct careful discussions about precisely what that means. Indeed, relations between Presidents and Secretaries of State have frequently been unsatisfactory and deserve greater care and attention than they have been receiving.

Congress's recognition of problems in the operation of foreign policy has partly motivated periodic proposals to subject the President's National Security Adviser to Senate confirmation. Whatever the merits of these proposals, Senate confirmation does not hold promise of improving the relationship dramatically. In the face of understandable Presidential resistance to Congressional incursions on Presidential appointment authority, Senate confirmation is unlikely to be instituted anyway. Presidents ought to pay as careful attention to the selection of senior White House aides, including national security advisers, as they do to their Cabinet members, however, for experience has repeatedly shown that these individuals will play vitally important roles. The press, likewise, should scrutinize White House appointees as closely as it does Cabinet nominees, and new Presidents can, in turn, pick up warning signs from the press of shortcomings and problems in their own staffs.

All Presidents-elect rely on their closest associates and aides to staff their offices during the interregnum. The people who help them win election are the same ones who help them prepare to assume office. In the one instance where a President-elect went outside his inner circle for top staff assistance on the day after his election, Carter with Watson, he soon returned to the usual pattern, though with a certain lingering ambiguity. Presidents-elect have also sometimes paid attention to disinterested outside advisers, most notably Kennedy with Lovett, Clifford, and Neustadt. For assistance in finding and selecting top personnel, Presidents-elect have turned in addition to trusted friends (in every instance), relatives (in several instances), their Vice Presidents (in the cases of Carter and Reagan), journalists (in the cases of Kennedy and Reagan), and professional recruiters (Reagan with James, though several incumbent Presidents had also used professional recruiters after they were settled in office).

Transitions qua transitions are a growth industry. Both pre- and post-election transition planning have grown steadily more elaborate over time, thanks in part to the advent of federal financing in 1968, but also because of private contributions, the proliferation of "think tanks," and the growing sophistication of a multitude of special interests. Eisenhower and Kennedy ran sparse and lean operations compared with those of Carter and Reagan. That did not mean that the latter Presidents had substantially better transitions overall; nor did it mean they had substantially worse ones. Both Eisenhower, on one end of the time spectrum, and Reagan, on the other, did some things well and other things less well or poorly. The high and low ends are probably attributable to each man's particular strengths and weaknesses.

But there is a middle ground which transition planning and machinery occupy; they can elevate the highs and moderate the lows. Although it is impossible to measure with any precision, it does appear that Reagan, with his greater planning and more substantial transition machinery, enjoyed an advantage over Eisenhower, particularly in being able to enunciate and implement domestic policies quickly. He also had an advantage over Carter, who planned, but undercut himself by inadvertently setting up the harmful competition between Jordan and Watson, which, among other things, negated much of Watson's planning. No power struggle took place under Reagan, at least not during the transition, with Meese in charge from start to finish. The lesson in this is obvious— clear lines of authority must emanate from the prospective President himself.

Like big government, big transitions are not apt to shrink significantly in the foreseeable future. It is suggestive that the President most opposed to big government ran the biggest transition ever. But to place the matter in perspective, the federal government spends substantially more money on ex-Presidents than it does helping newly elected Presidents get ready to assume office. Large corporations devote infinitely more time and money to finding, recruiting, and orienting people for senior management positions than Washington does for positions with substantially greater responsibilities. The federal government does not even pay moving expenses for noncareer appointees while orientation programs for them have only been sporadic. Given the magnitude of the task, therefore, just one part of which is filling hundreds of upper-echelon executive jobs within the space of a few months, Presidents-elect need all the help they can get. Indeed, it would be worthwhile for Presidents in the future, perhaps in cooperation with former Presidents, to determine what additional institutional, financial, and informational resources and devices they could have used to improve their own transitions.

Most former Presidents and their top aides would probably agree that personnel is the single most time-consuming, frustrating, and difficult part of transitions. People who have helped run personnel operations in new administrations often do not remember that time of their lives with any fondness. There is always a flood of job-seekers, but finding the right people is another matter entirely. Although Presidents-elect routinely assert they are looking only for the most qualified people, competence or brilliance either in a substantive area or in management is not necessarily all that is involved. They also look for such things as personal loyalty, team play, toughness in being able to withstand bureaucratic or special interest pressure, creativity, and skills in press, public, and Congressional relations. Different jobs require different combinations of such attributes.

In addition, new Presidents, to one degree or another, invariably want their appointees to represent or reflect various parts of their constituency or of constituencies they hope to acquire—Catholic, ethnic, black, female, business, union, western, southern, and so on. They want as well to avoid appearing to overrepresent a certain constituency—had McNamara been Catholic, Kennedy would have dropped him from consideration; Shultz was dropped from consideration in part because the Reagan Cabinet already had one Bechtel executive. Then, too, Presidents are under intense pressure to reward the faithful, both their own and their party's and all Presidents recognize the need to relieve some of that pressure from time to time. Although Presidents have been known to boast that no one ever turned them down for a job, promising candidates for appointment sometimes remove themselves from consideration well before an offer is made and occasionally after it has been made. Add to this mix campaign commitments and resentments, acceptability to Congress and to affected constituencies, conflict-of-interest problems, personal friendship, and human chemistry, and it is easy to see why filling jobs will always be an extraordinarily complicated affair.

It also has extraordinarily unpredictable outcomes. In every administration, some strangers or relative newcomers have won the President's confidence and become key actors while others have failed to win his confidence and become short-time or bit players. Similarly, Presidents have been pleased with the performances of some old friends and long-time associates and disappointed by others. The presence or absence of prior Washington experience likewise fails to forecast an individual's performance accurately. There have been newcomers to Washington from business, academics, law, state politics, and elsewhere who starred and others who flopped, and the same has held true for old Washington hands. Yet despite the lack of clear-cut rules, first dozens, then hundreds of jobs are filled at a rapid pace with no certainty of results. "I must make the appointments now"; Kennedy observed, "a year hence I will know who I really want to appoint."

Retrospectively, Presidents or their partisans have sometimes regretted early loss of control of sub-Cabinet appointments, which has occurred either through design or happenstance. Nixon and his aides came to believe that too many of his Cabinet officers had "married the natives," the department's bureaucrats and permanent interests, and that many sub-Cabinet officials had loyalties primarily to the Cabinet Secretary who appointed them rather than to the President. Some Carter partisans believe his Presidency suffered greatly from allowing Cabinet officers to name people who lacked political allegiance to Carter and who were out of step with him philosophically. To assure political loyalty and philosophical consistency, the Reagan transition established an unusually centralized appointment operation. It succeeded in reestablishing the principle that sub-Cabinet officials were *Presidential* appointees, but even so, some Cabinet officers enjoyed a good deal of latitude.

Between the extremes of absolute Presidential control of sub-Cabinet appointees and absolute control by Cabinet officers exists a large middle ground of negotiation and give and take in which neither side gets everyone it wants but neither side feels the other has forced appointees upon them whom they do not approve or cannot abide. Indeed, the absence of such a process can signal further problems down the road. For example, a Cabinet officer who passively acquiesces to a President's naming all the people around him is not apt to provide strong leadership. A President who abandons all control of sub-Cabinet appointments, on the other hand, runs the danger of encouraging renegades and self-serving departments and agencies.

A mixture of centralized and decentralized personnel operations for choosing the sub-Cabinet makes the most sense. Indeed, new Presidents and their Cabinet officers should start to worry if either one dictates sub-Cabinet selections. In addition, Presidents and their Cabinet officers should cast the recruitment net widely and obviously should not just follow the comfortable route of hiring friends, past employees, and acquaintances. The goal should always be to find highly qualified and competent people who will be dedicated to public service. The techniques for finding such people have varied, from Kennedy's eclectic consultations and the efforts of the Shriver group to Reagan's use of James, an executive-search professional in charge of a large staff.

New Presidents should also bear in mind that finding excellent people for available positions is not all they are required to do on the personnel front. Although often overlooked or shortchanged, orientation can play an important part in welding an administration together, in helping strangers get to know one another and to begin working together in a common purpose. The days Eisenhower spent on the *Helena* with members of his administration-to-be, for example, proved very valuable in this regard. Newcomers to Washington also need to get to know its more permanent inhabitants, particularly those in Congress and the media. In contrast to Carter and his Georgians, Reagan and his Californians promptly and profitably began to socialize with some of Washington's most influential and powerful residents.

New administrations must beware of conflict-of-interest and Senate confirmation problems. Presidents therefore need smart, tough, technically proficient lawyers with plenty of Washington savvy, and they must give these lawyers enough authority to be effective. Because of the Ethics in Government Act of 1978, most appointees today require legal counsel. Some appointees will need to be saved from themselves; occasionally appointments will need to be withdrawn, the earlier and more quietly, the better. Most important, new Presidents need protection from avoidable confirmation headaches such as those caused by Charles Wilson—although some confirmation battles such as Charles Bohlen's are worth fighting and winning—and they need to be spared impropriety and scandal.

Inevitably, some appointees will not work out as hoped. When that happens, Presidents and their personnel advisers need to ask themselves what went wrong. Was it the wrong person for the job, or did impossible demands and expectations accompany the job? If a person was miscast, can he or she contribute to the administration in some other capacity? Although no administration ever has as many high-level jobs to fill as it does at the outset, it continues to have a substantial number. Presidents and their personnel advisers should therefore learn from the mistakes and disappointments that originated in the administration's early days. In addition, despite the demands of daily events, they should pay attention to the benefits that can accrue from a serious approach to evaluation and education of their appointees.

Often new administrations tend to ignore career officials when they are making appointments, but then pay greater attention to them as time goes by. The slighting of career officials at the start of administrations grows out of the anti-Washington, anti-bureaucratic rhetoric of recent campaigns, lack of familiarity with their abilities, and suspiciousness toward those who have worked closely with and are perhaps loyal to the political opposition. The greater respect administrations give career officials later comes from having gotten to know them. Then they appreciate their talents and competence and realize that their great loyalty is to public service, not to political party.

New administrations should take heed of career officials, not only as potential appointees, but because of the help they can provide and, conversely, the roadblocks they can put up. Career officials, along with appointees who are carried over from one administration to the next, possess valuable institutional memory that newcomers lack. Although old hands have a natural tendency to continue along existing paths, they can also caution new hands to hidden dangers lurking in departures in policy and organization. They can keep them from reinventing the wheel, and they can show them where the actual levers of change are located and how to get the simple tasks accomplished. Alternatively, career officials, who see appointees come and go, can decide to sit quietly by while the newcomers flounder, and they can thwart and undermine them in a variety of ways.

Although they must beware of entrapment in policies they are committed to revising or would be wise to scrap, such as the nascent plan to invade Cuba that Kennedy inherited in 1961, new Presidents and their appointees should, for reasons both of self-interest and the national interest, establish effective, working relations with career officials and carry-overs as soon as possible. The purge of the State Department in 1953 not only damaged morale, but hurt the administration's image and proved costly to the country over the long term. A much more positive model, meanwhile, has been provided by the way in which new administrations have dealt with the budget bureau or office. Perhaps because of the instant and powerful need new administrations have for preparing budgets, they have very quickly established effective working relationships with career budget officials. It has both helped new administrations get started and maintained a high professional élan in that organization.

Although all new administrations enter office well stocked with campaign promises of dramatic change in national policy, continuities, not discontinuities, between administrations tend to be the more striking. This holds true not only in domestic policy, but in foreign policy, where Presidents have somewhat greater freedom of action. Indeed, American foreign policy fickleness is sometimes exaggerated by critics. On the overarching objective of containing communism, United States policy has been essentially constant for forty years. Even changes in strategy, tactics, and tone have often been incremental, frequently beginning in one administration and extending into the next, sometimes many more. For example, America's struggle to defeat communism in Vietnam carried through six administrations. Carter adopted a tough stance toward the Soviet Union and began an arms buildup in 1979 which Reagan carried forward and accelerated in 1981. Trade policy, commitments to the security of allies, and foreign aid, among other things, have changed marginally if at all when the government has changed hands. Symbols and rhetoric tend to change much more than does the substance of policy.

There are a variety of restraints to actual shifts in national policy, most of which find expression in law and are based in the Constitution. In order to alter existing institutions or create new ones—in taxation, expenditure, or regulation, infrastructure, entitlements, or defense—Presidents must marshal public opinion and lead Congress. Although Presidents have some leeway in how they execute the laws, even there they cannot run afoul of public opinion, Congress, or the courts. In foreign policy, where Presidents have more leeway, their power can be undermined by an unhappy public and by an uncooperative Congress. It is Congress that appropriates money for foreign aid and for national security and that ratifies treaties. Thus, Presidential power can largely be understood as the power to persuade.

The first days and months in office present a rich opportunity to exercise that power. Although a long-term view would lead to skepticism about the likelihood of much changing when the Presidency changes hands, Presidents-elect, the press, the public, and even Congress are apt to take a more hopeful view. Man's innate and Americans' especial fondness for the new, relief at the end of a partisan season and the passing of a fatigued administration, and celebration for the orderly transfer of democratic authority together create an atmosphere rife with possibility, which newly elected Presidents should prepare for, nurture, and exploit. The first few months in office are popularly called the President's honeymoon, and like real honeymoons they often do not quite live up to expectations.

Eisenhower and Nixon had the special situation of inheriting wars which they hoped to end quickly on favorable terms. Eisenhower did so, which ranks as the single most successful accomplishment of any of these five Presidents in their transitions. Nixon thought he could do the same, but the situations were less similar than he understood, and his failure had grave repercussions for his Presidency. The wars, however, only partially explain why both Eisenhower and Nixon were initially so inactive on the domestic front. Uncertain about what to do, Eisenhower and Nixon treated their first months in office as a time for study and planning. Some of the study and planning eventually bore fruit, but the crop could have been more bounteous had the planning occurred much earlier and been implemented during the honeymoon.

Living with the activist legacy of their mythic fellow Democrat, Franklin D. Roosevelt, Kennedy and Carter got rolling more quickly. Carter expected and tried to do too much. Some of his initiatives, especially in foreign policy, eventually paid off, but after filling the atmosphere with the symbols of a diminished Presidency and failing to communicate clear directions, he did not even get much credit for those. Kennedy did better. He filled the air with the symbols and rhetoric of a revitalized and more muscular Presidency, yet was more realistic than Carter. He asked for less and got credit for more. He even withstood with relative impunity the worst pratfall of any of these new Presidents.

A former Democrat, Reagan consciously modeled himself after

FDR, though striving to halt the very expansion of government that Roosevelt had initiated. He set priorities during his transition, articulated them clearly, and stuck to them tenaciously. He took over the domestic political agenda as no President since Johnson, another Roosevelt imitator. Reagan's program, like Roosevelt's, is subject to criticism for having gone too far, not far enough, or being misconceived, but there can be no doubt that Reagan used his transition to assert political command. As in 1933, foreign policy took a back seat to domestic policy, but it was more tolerable to let foreign policy slide in 1933 than it was in 1981, and in addition to that, Roosevelt came to office with greater sophistication and self-confidence in diplomacy than Reagan had.

Although transitions hand new Presidents a superb opportunity for creating the appearance and possibly the reality of movement and change, they need not be their only opportunity. In other words, the importance of transitions should not be exaggerated. Presidents have in fact turned things around to their favor and instituted significant changes at later points, especially in their third year in office, though not only then. In this regard, it is worth recalling Kennedy's tax, civil-rights, and test-ban proposals, Nixon's opening to China, détente with the Soviet Union, and imposition of wage and price controls, or for that matter, Roosevelt's "Second Hundred Days." On the other hand, if a President starts off, as Carter did, with embarrassing setbacks, it becomes difficult to turn things around later. It is better to set some early priorities and accomplish them and to avoid highly visible defeats; success breeds success and failure breeds failure.

Finally, it is important to bear in mind that *all* Presidents make serious mistakes. That is guaranteed by the sheer speed of events, the difficulty of the job, and human fallibility. What happens next is most important. Does the new President try to understand his mistake and learn from it? Does he merely compound it? Does he ignore it or deny that it has occurred? Answers to these questions will go a long way toward determining how well he does in the rest of his term, for Presidents should have the capacity to recognize their mistakes and learn from them. Kennedy posed the right question after the Bay of Pigs when he asked: "How could I have been so stupid?"

NOTES

CHAPTER 1: EISENHOWER

1. Bernard Montgomery, *Memoirs* (Cleveland: World Publishing Co., 1958), 484.

2. *The Eisenhower Diaries*, ed. Robert H. Ferrell (New York: Norton, 1981), 162.

3. On Eisenhower's military career and his beliefs, see especially: *Eisenhower Diaries;* Dwight D. Eisenhower, *Crusade in Europe* (Garden City: Doubleday, 1948); Dwight D. Eisenhower, *At Ease: Stories I Tell to Friends* (Garden City: Doubleday, 1967); Stephen E. Ambrose, *Eisenhower,* Vol. 1, (New York: Simon & Schuster, 1983); Robert Griffith, "Dwight D. Eisenhower and the Corporate Commonwealth," *American Historical Review* 87 (Feb. 1982), 87–122.

4. *Eisenhower Diaries*, 161–62; Robert J. Donovan, *Conflict and Crisis: The Presidency of Harry S Truman, 1945–1948* (New York: Norton, 1977), 86–87, 338, 389–90; Herbert S. Parmet, *Eisenhower and the American Crusades* (New York: Macmillan, 1972), 33–56.

5. James T. Patterson, *Mr. Republican: A Biography of Robert A. Taft* (Boston: Houghton Mifflin, 1972), 409–578; Ambrose, *Eisenhower,* Vol. 1, pp. 497–541; Parmet, *Eisenhower,* 57–117.

6. Parmet, *Eisenhower,* 118–49; Ambrose, *Eisenhower,* Vol. 1, pp. 550–71; Barton J. Bernstein, "Election of 1952," *History of American Presidential Elections, 1789–1968,* Vol. 4, ed. Arthur M. Schlesinger, Jr. (New York: Chelsea House, 1971), 3215–66.

7. Lucius D. Clay, Columbia Oral History (henceforth COH) (1967), 50; Herbert Brownell, COH (1967), 93–94, 110; Herbert Brownell, Memorandum for Governor Adams (1958), Whitman File, Administration Series, Box 10, Dwight D. Eisenhower Library, Abilene, Kansas (henceforth EL); Patterson, *Mr. Republican,* 582–85; *New York Times,* Nov. 8, 1952; confidential source; Robert A. Taft to

Richard B. Scandrett, Jr., Dec. 3, 1952, Robert A. Taft Papers, Box 404, Library of Congress.

8. See, for example: Fred I. Greenstein, *The Hidden-Hand Presidency: Eisenhower as Leader* (New York: Basic Books, 1982).

9. Clay, COH (1967), 50–86; Brownell, COH (1967), 87–137; Brownell, COH (1971), 11–15; Brownell, Memorandum for Governor Adams (1958), Whitman File, Administration Series, Box 10, EL; confidential source; Herbert Brownell interview, July 29, 1960, Laurin L. Henry Papers, Box 3, John F. Kennedy Library, Boston, Mass. (henceforth KL); Dwight D. Eisenhower, *Mandate for Change, 1953–1956* (New York: Doubleday, 1963), 82–87, 89–92; Sinclair Weeks, COH (1967), 43–44; Appointment records for November, 1952, Whitman File, Dwight David Eisenhower Diary Series, Box 2, EL.

10. Clay, COH (1967), 51–52; Lucius D. Clay, John Foster Dulles Oral History Project (henceforth DOH) (1965), Princeton University Library (henceforth PUL), 7–22; Brownell, COH (1967), 94–98; Herbert Brownell, DOH (1965), 17–22; Milton S. Eisenhower, COH (1967), 13–14; Townsend Hoopes, *The Devil and John Foster Dulles* (Boston: Little, Brown, 1973), 114–36; Dwight D. Eisenhower, DOH (1964), 6–7; Robert A. Divine, *Eisenhower and the Cold War* (New York: Oxford University Press, 1981); Patterson, *Mr. Republican,* 583; Stephen Ambrose, *Eisenhower,* Vol. 2 (New York: Simon & Schuster, 1984), 20–22.

11. Brownell, COH (1967), 98–100; Henry Cabot Lodge, *As It Was* (New York: Norton, 1976), 28–29, 47.

12. Brownell, COH (1967), 101; Eisenhower, *Mandate,* 86; confidential source; Lodge, *As It Was,* 48.

13. Clay, COH (1967), 57–61, 93–94; Eisenhower, *Mandate,* 87; Parmet, *Eisenhower,* 183–84; Patterson, *Mr. Republican,* 583–84.

14. Clay, COH (1967), 63–66; Brownell, COH (1967), 105, 115, 118, 124; Eisenhower, *Mandate,* 87–89, 92; Patterson, *Mr. Republican,* 583.

15. Brownell, COH (1967), 111, 137; Brownell, COH (1971), 15; Sherman Adams, COH (1967), 135–36; Dwight D. Eisenhower, COH (1967), 38; Eisenhower, *Mandate,* 90–91.

16. Lodge, *As It Was,* 51–52; *New York Times,* Dec. 3, 1952; Patterson, *Mr. Republican,* 584–85.

17. Eisenhower, *Mandate,* 92; Sherman Adams, *Firsthand Report* (New York: Harper & Brothers, 1961), 61; Minutes of Cabinet Meetings for 1953, Whitman File, Cabinet Meetings Series, Box 1, EL.

18. Eisenhower, *Mandate,* 87–89; Lodge, *As It Was,* 48–49; confidential source.

19. Adams, *Firsthand Report,* 50–53; Eisenhower, *Mandate,* 89; Clay, COH (1967), 92; Parmet, *Eisenhower,* 177–79.

20. Adams, COH (1967), 137–39; Adams *Firsthand Report,* 53–58; Gabriel Hauge, COH (1967), 50–51, 79; Bernard Shanley, Oral History (henceforth OH) (1975), EL, 71; Bernard Shanley Diaries, Box 1, EL; Wilton B. Persons, COH (1970), 26–27, 49; confidential source; *New York Times,* Jan. 14, 1953; Diary entry for Feb. 17, 1953, Files of Eben A. Ayers, Box 17, Harry S Truman Library, Independence, Missouri (henceforth TL).

21. Truman to Eisenhower, Eisenhower to Truman, Aug. 14, 1952; Truman to Eisenhower, Aug. 16, 1952; Eisenhower to Truman, Aug. 19, 1952, all in

Papers of Harry S Truman (henceforth Truman Papers), President's Secretary's Files, Box 118, TL.

22. Harry S Truman, *Memoirs,* Vol. 2 (New York: Doubleday, 1956), 501–5; Eisenhower, *Mandate,* 84; confidential sources.

23. *Off the Record: The Private Papers of Harry S Truman,* ed. Robert H. Ferrell (New York: Harper & Row, 1980), 274–75; Eisenhower, *Mandate,* 85.

24. Lodge, *As It Was,* 31–38; Memorandum of Meeting at the White House Between President Truman and General Eisenhower, Nov. 18, 1952, Truman Papers, President's Secretary's Files, Box 118, TL; Harold Stassen to Eisenhower, Nov. 8, 1952; Eisenhower to Stassen, Nov. 10, 1852, both in Whitman File, Administration Series, Box 38, EL; Truman, *Memoirs,* Vol. 2, pp. 516–21; *Washington Post,* Nov. 20, 1952.

26. Interviews with Sherman Adams, John Steelman, in Laurin L. Henry Papers, Box 3, KL.

26. *Off the Record,* 275; Elmer B. Staats, COH (1967), 16–20; Roger W. Jones, COH (1967), 9–11, 18–20.

27. Roger Jones, COH, 13–14.

28. Interview with Marion B. Folsom, Henry Papers, Box 3, KL; John Snyder to President Truman, January 2, 1953, Truman Papers, President's Secretary's File, Box 160, TL.

29. Dean Acheson, Memorandum for the President, Jan.12, 1953, Truman Papers, Official File, Box 1235, TL; Memorandum of conversation with John Foster Dulles, Dec. 24, 1952, Dean Acheson Papers, Box 67, TL; Interviews with Dean Acheson and David Bruce, Henry Papers, Box 3, KL.

30. Roderic L. O'Connor, DOH, 28, 58; John W. Hanes, Jr., DOH, 9, 124–26; Herbert Brownell, DOH, 27; Hoopes, *The Devil and John Foster Dulles,* 138–53.

31. *New York Times,* Jan. 6, 8, 9, Dec. 10, 1953; O'Connor, DOH, 26–27; Hoopes, *The Devil and John Foster Dulles,* 145–46.

32. Donald B. Lourie, DOH, 1–21, 30–31; Donald B. Lourie to John Foster Dulles, Dec. 23, 1952, Dulles Papers, Subject Series, Box 8, PUL; Loy Henderson, COH (1967), 30–31.

33. Hanes, DOH, 125–30.

34. David Bruce interview, Henry Papers, Box 3, KL; Hoopes, *The Devil and John Foster Dulles,* 146–48.

35. Interviews with William C. Foster, Herbert Brownell, Don K. Price, William Schaub, Henry Papers, Box 3, KL; C. E. Wilson to the President, Feb. 13, 1953, Whitman Files, Legislative Meetings Series, Box 1, EL; Memorandum of calls with C. E. Wilson, Dec. 30, 1952, Jan. 8, 1953, Whitman Files, Administration Series, Box 44, EL; Lodge, *As It Was,* 30, 48; *New York Times,* Dec. 24, 1952.

36. Sherman Adams interview, Henry Papers, Box 3, KL; Sherman Adams to Milton Eisenhower, Dec. 10, 11, 1952, Central Files, Official, Box 460, EL; *Washington Post,* Dec. 24, 1952; James M. Lambie, Jr., to Halliday Clark, March 1, 1953, Lambie Papers, Box 3, EL; James M. Lambie, Jr., COH, 2, 6; *New York Times,* Jan 18, 1953.

37. Wilton B. Persons, COH, 12–14; Parmet, *Eisenhower,* 150–53; Mark W. Clark, *From the Danube to the Yalu* (New York: Harper & Bros., 1954), 231.

38. Eisenhower, *Mandate,* 93–95.

39. Clark, *From the Danube*, 233; Lodge, *As It Was*, 39; Persons, COH, 16; *Washington Post*, Dec. 6, 1952.

40. Ellis Briggs, COH (1972), 53–55; Ellis Briggs, *Farewell to Foggy Bottom: The Recollections of a Career Diplomat* (New York: David McKay, 1964), 229–31; Clark, *From the Danube*, 238–39.

41. Eisenhower, *Mandate*, 96; Parmet, *Eisenhower*, 155–57; George Humphrey, DOH, 1–3; confidential source; *New York Times*, Dec. 9, 1952.

42. Confidential source; *New York Times*, Dec. 10, 11, 12, 1952; New York *Herald Tribune*, Dec. 11, 1952; *Eisenhower Diaries*, 46, 47, 49, 51–54; George H. Gallup, *The Gallup Poll*, Vol. 2 (New York: Random House, 1972), 1113.

43. *New York Times*, Dec. 18, 1952; Douglas MacArthur, "Memorandum on Ending the Korean War," Dec. 14, 1952, Dulles Papers, Subject Series, Box 8, PUL. It is published in Douglas MacArthur, *Reminiscences* (New York: McGraw-Hill, 1964), 410–12.

44. Eisenhower, *Mandate*, 180–81; Eisenhower, DOH, 8–10.

45. *Eisenhower Diaries*, 189; Eisenhower, *Mandate*, 430–31; *Washington Post*, Dec. 24, 1952; *New York Times*, Dec. 24, 1952. Eisenhower did not see Hoover again until July on the occasion of one of Eisenhower's stag dinners.

46. Anthony Eden, *Full Circle* (Boston: Houghton Mifflin, 1960), 24–25, 36–37; Eisenhower's schedules for November and December, Whitman File, DDE Diary Series, Box 2, EL; Dulles to Eisenhower (2), Nov. 14, 1952, Whitman File, Dulles-Herter Series, Box 1, EL.

47. *Eisenhower Diaries*, 222–24; Richard E. Neustadt, *Alliance Politics* (New York: Columbia University Press, 1970).

48. Patterson, *Mr. Republican*, 585–87; *New York Times*, Jan. 1, 3, 1953; *Eisenhower Diaries*, 234, 240–42.

49. *Eisenhower Diaries*, 218–21, 227; *Washington Post*, Dec. 19, 27, 1952; *New York Times*, Dec. 19, 1952; Eisenhower, *Mandate*, 116, 190–95; Leverett Saltonstall, COH, 71; Joe Martin, *My First Fifty Years in Politics* (New York: McGraw-Hill, 1960), 223–27.

50. Marion B. Folsom, COH, 32–36; *New York Times*, Jan. 5, 28, 1953; Eisenhower, *Mandate*, 201–2.

51. Dwight D. Eisenhower to Milton Eisenhower, Nov. 6, 1953, Whitman File, Name Series, Box 12, EL; *New York Times*, Jan. 7, 10, 1953; *Washington Post*, Jan. 10, 1953; Eisenhower, *Mandate*, 192–95; Interviews with Sherman Adams, Herbert Brownell, Gabriel Hauge, Laurin L. Henry Papers, Box 3, KL; Parmet, *Eisenhower*, 156–57; confidential source.

52. Proceedings, Cabinet Meeting, Jan. 12, 1953; Notes on Commodore "Cabinet Meeting," Jan. 13, 1953, Whitman File, Cabinet Meetings Series, Box 1, EL.

53. Eisenhower, *Mandate*, 110–12; *New York Times*, Jan. 16, 17, 18, 1953; Leverett Saltonstall, COH, 79–80; confidential source; Brownell, DOH, 102, 122–23; Hearings before the Committee on Finance, U.S. Senate, 83d Cong., 1st sess. on Nomination of George M. Humphrey, Secretary of the Treasury-designate.

54. Elie Abel, COH, 3.

55. *Eisenhower Diaries*, 226–27; Eisenhower, *Mandate*, 111–12; David A. Frier, *Conflict of Interest in the Eisenhower Administration* (Baltimore: Penguin, 1970); Aaron Wildavsky, *Dixon-Yates: A Study in Power Politics* (New Haven: Yale University Press, 1962).

56. Eisenhower, *Mandate*, 100–101; Truman, *Off the Record*, 287; Edward Folliard, COH (1967).

57. Dwight D. Eisenhower, *Public Papers of the Presidents*, 1953, pp. 1–8; Eisenhower, *Mandate*, 100–102; Emmet John Hughes, *The Ordeal of Power: A Political Memoir of the Eisenhower Years* (New York: Atheneum, 1963), 52–53; Notes on writing of the Inaugural Address, White House, Office of the Staff Secretary, L. Arthur Minnich Series, Box 1, EL; John F. Kennedy, *Public Papers of the Presidents*, 1961, 1–3.

58. *Eisenhower Diaries*, 226; Parmet, *Eisenhower*, 176.

59. *Eisenhower Diaries*, 225; Eisenhower, *Mandate*, 107, 112–13.

60. Eisenhower's friendships are documented in the Whitman File, Name Series, EL; Milton S. Eisenhower, COH (1967); Eisenhower, *Mandate*, 270–72; Minnich note on President, Personal Life, Feb. 25, 1953, White House Office, Office of the Staff Secretary, Minnich Series, Box 1, EL; Ambrose, *Eisenhower*, Vol. 2, pp. 73–75.

61. Dwight D. Eisenhower to E. E. Hazlett, July 21, 1953, Whitman File, Name Series, Box 18, EL; Minnich note, The President—Relaxation, May 19, 1953, White House Office, Office of the Staff Secretary, Minnich Series, Box 1, EL; Eisenhower, *Mandate*, 266–68.

62. Diary of Eben Ayers, Feb. 27, 1953, Truman Papers, Files of Eben A. Ayers, Box 17, TL; Adams, *Firsthand Report*, 71–75; Adams, COH, 213; Adams, DOH, 6–7; Parmet, *Eisenhower*, 176–79; Bernard Shanley Diaries, Box 1, EL.

63. Adams, *Firsthand Report*, 75; confidential source; Dwight D. Eisenhower to Edgar Eisenhower, April 3, 1953, Whitman File, DDE Diary Series, Box 3, EL; Edgar Eisenhower to Dwight D. Eisenhower, Whitman File, Name Series, Box 11, EL; Robert J. Donovan, *Eisenhower: The Inside Story* (New York: Harper & Bros., 1956), 71.

64. Dwight D. Eisenhower to E. E. Hazlett, July 21, 1953, Whitman File, Name Series, Box 18, EL.

65. Eisenhower, *Public Papers*, 1953, pp. 11–509, quotation on p. 42; *Eisenhower Diaries*, 271–72.

66. Gallup, *The Gallup Poll*, Vol. 2, pp. 1116, 1123, 1137, 1142, 1145, 1150.

67. Eisenhower, *Mandate*, 194–95.

68. *Eisenhower Diaries*, 226; Notes for C. D. Jackson, Dec. 30, 1952, DDE: Diaries, Box 1, EL; Notes on the State of the Union Message, Feb. 27, 1953, White House Office, Office of the Staff Secretary, Minnich Series, Box 1, EL.

69. Eisenhower, *Public Papers*, 1953, pp. 12–34; *New York Times*, Feb. 3, 1953; Charles E. Bohlen, *Witness to History, 1929–1969* (New York: Norton, 1973), 309–10.

70. Notes on Controls, Feb. 19, 1953, White House Office, Office of the Staff Secretary, Minnich Series, Box 1, EL; Eisenhower, *Mandate*, 124–26; H. Scott Gordon, "The Eisenhower Administration: The Doctrine of Shared Responsibility," in Crauford D. Goodwin, ed., *Exhortation and Controls: The Search for a Wage Price Policy, 1945–1971* (Washington, D.C.: Brookings Institution, 1975), 94–134.

71. Eisenhower, *Public Papers*, 1953, p. 21; *Eisenhower Diaries*, 235–36; Patterson, *Mr. Republican*, 600; Supplementary Notes, Legislative Leadership Meeting, Feb. 9, 1953; Notes on Legislative Leadership Meeting, April 30, 1953; Supplementary Notes, Legislative Leadership Meeting, May 12, 1953, all in Whitman File, DDE Diary Series, Box 4, EL.

72. Eisenhower, *Mandate,* 126–33, 201–2; Gary W. Reichard, *The Reaffirmation of Republicanism: Eisenhower and the Eighty-third Congress* (Knoxville: University of Tennessee Press, 1975), 97–108; *Congressional Quarterly Almanac,* 1953, pp. 130–31; Parmet, *Eisenhower,* 220–22; Supplementary Notes, Legislative Leadership Meeting, May 12, 1953, Whitman File, DDE Diary Series, Box 4, EL; J. M. Dodge, "A Few Notes of Concern . . . " Aug. 5, 1953, DDE Confidential Files, Subject Series, Box 10, EL; Herbert Stein, *The Fiscal Revolution in America* (Chicago: University of Chicago Press, 1969), 284–99.

73. Parmet, *Eisenhower,* 222–25; Notes on the President's Meeting with Congressional Leaders, Jan. 26, 1953, Whitman File, Legislative Meetings Series, Box 1, EL; Sherman Adams to Dodge, Feb. 12, 1953, Whitman File, DDE Diary Series, Box 4, EL; Adams to Dodge, March 10, 1953, Whitman File, Legislative Meetings Series, Box 1, EL; Minnich, Supplementary Notes, Legislative Leadership Meeting, March 23, 1953, Whitman File, DDE Diary Series, Box 4, EL. Henry Lee explained the long-term consequences of this legislation to me.

74. Eisenhower, *Mandate,* 133–35; Notes on Reorganization Act, Feb. 3, 1953, White House Office, Office of the Staff Secretary, Minnich Series, Box 1; Summary of the Principal Activities of PACGO, Jan. 1953 through Jan. 1961; DDE Central, Official File, Box 461; Supplementary Notes, Legislative Leadership Meeting, May 25, 1953, Whitman Files, DDE Diary Series, Box 4; "Special Committee on Government Organization," Jan. 13, 1953, O. C. Hobby Papers, Box 16, EL; Various notes on Legislative Leadership Meetings for 1953, in Whitman File, DDE Diary Series, Box 4, and in Whitman File, Legislative Meetings Series, Box 1; all of the preceding in EL.

75. Minnich Notes on Department of Health, Education and Welfare, White House Office, Office of the Staff Secretary, Minnich Series, Box 1; O. C. Hobby to Alvin Bentley, April 6, 1953, to Joseph McCarthy, March 20, 1953, to James E. Murray, March 25, 1953, O. C. Hobby Papers, Box 16; Joseph Dodge to the President, March 12, 1953, DDE Central, Official Files, Box 460; all in EL.

76. *Eisenhower Diaries,* 227; Parmet, *Eisenhower,* 325–27.

77. Adams, *Firsthand Report,* 303; Patterson, *Mr. Republican,* 590; DDE Personal Diary entry, Oct. 8, 1953, Whitman Files, DDE Diary Series, Box 9, EL; Parmet, *Eisenhower,* 326–30.

78. Minnich note on appointments, May 15, 1953, White House Office, Office of the Staff Secretary, Minnich Series, Box 1, EL.

79. Confidential memorandum, July 7, 1953, DDE Confidential Files, Subject Series, Box 4, EL. For some comparative statistics on the backgrounds of Presidential appointees, see David T. Stanley, Dean E. Mann, Jameson W. Doig, *Men Who Govern: A Biographical Profile of Federal Political Executives* (Washington, D.C.: Brookings Institution, 1967), 9–40.

80. Memorandum of call with C. E. Wilson, Jan. 8, 1953, Whitman Files, Administration Series, Box 44, EL; telephone conversation with Gov. Adams, April 6, July 17, 1953, Telephone Conversations memoranda, both in Dulles Papers, Box 10, PUL; telephone conversations with Leonard Hall, May 6, 1953, Dulles Papers, Box 1, PUL; E. Frederic Morrow, *Black Man in the White House* (New York: Coward-McCann, 1963).

81. Minnich Notes on appointments and patronage, Feb. 10, 1953, May 15, 1953, July 9, 1953, White House Office, Office of the Staff Secretary, Minnich Series, Box 1, EL.

82. *Ibid.;* Charles Willis to Gov. Adams, May 28, 1953, DDE Official File, Box 896, EL; Minnich note on patronage, July 17, 1953, White House Office, Office of the Staff Secretary, Minnich Series, Box 1, EL.

83. Eisenhower to Dulles, March 18, 1953, Dulles Papers, White House Memoranda Series, Box 1, PUL.

84. Parmet, *Eisenhower*, 214–15; Don Price interview, Henry Papers, Box 3, KL.

85. Eisenhower, *Public Papers*, 1953, pp. 13–14; Hughes, *Ordeal of Power*, 85–88; Athan G. Theoharis, *The Yalta Myths: An Issue in U. S. Politics, 1945–1955* (Columbia: University of Missouri Press, 1970), 154–65; Supplementary Notes, Legislative Leadership Meeting, March 2, 1953, Whitman File, DDE Diary Series, Box 4, EL.

86. *Eisenhower Diaries*, 233–34; Eisenhower to E. E. Hazlett, July 21, 1953, Whitman File, Name Series, Box 18, EL; Hughes, *Ordeal of Power*, 92–97; Parmet, *Eisenhower*, 247–53; Harold Stassen, DOH, 32; Eisenhower, DOH, 11–12; Ambrose, *Eisenhower*, Vol. 2, pp. 55–59.

87. Hoopes, *The Devil and John Foster Dulles*, 4–6, 151–58; Truman to Acheson, Aug. 11, 1952, Acheson Papers, Box 67, TL; John W. Hanes, Jr., DOH, 15–16; Bohlen, *Witness to History*, 311–12; Loy Henderson, COH, 26–29.

88. Richard M. Fried, *Men Against McCarthy* (New York: Columbia University Press, 1976), 277–78; Lourie, DOH, 30.

89. Hoopes, *The Devil and John Foster Dulles*, 157–58; Bohlen, *Witness to History*, 335–36; Ambrose, *Eisenhower*, Vol. 2, pp. 64–65; David M. Oshinsky, *A Conspiracy So Immense: The World of Joe McCarthy* (New York: Free Press, 1983), 261–64.

90. Gary May, *China Scapegoat: The Diplomatic Ordeal of John Carter Vincent* (Washington, D.C.: New Republic Books, 1979), 262–94.

91. George F. Kennan, *Memoirs, 1950–1963*, Vol. 2 (Boston: Little, Brown, 1972), 170–80.

92. Bohlen, *Witness to History*, 312–14.

93. *Ibid.*, 314–36; telephone conversations of March 19, 20, 24, April 3, 1953, and Dulles to McLeod and McLeod to Dulles, March 20, 1953, Dulles Papers, White House Memoranda Series, Box 8, PUL; telephone conversations of March 19, 20, Dulles Papers, White House Memoranda Series, Box 10, PUL; telephone calls, March 23, 1953, Whitman Files, DDE Diary Series, Box 4, EL; Notes on Bohlen, April 4, 1953, White House Office, Office of the Staff Secretary, Minnich Series, Box 1, EL; Thomas C. Reeves, *The Life and Times of Joe McCarthy: A Biography* (New York: Stein and Day, 1982), 468–76; Patterson, *Mr. Republican*, 595–96; Parmet, *Eisenhower*, 241–46; Ambrose, *Eisenhower*, Vol. 2, pp. 61–62; Oshinsky, *A Conspiracy So Immense*, 286–93.

94. Patterson, *Mr. Republican*, 596–97; *Eisenhower Diaries*, 233–34.

95. Reeves, *Life and Times of Joe McCarthy*, 476–91; Oshinsky, *A Conspiracy So Immense*, 265–85.

96. Dwight D. Eisenhower to Edgar Eisenhower, March 27 and April 7, 1953, Whitman Files, Name Series, Box 11, EL; Eisenhower to Dulles, April 1, 1953, Whitman File, Dulles-Herter Series, Box 1, EL; Dulles to Eisenhower, June 27, 1953, Whitman File, DDE Diary Series, Box 4, EL; telephone calls, June 20, 23, 1953, Whitman File, DDE Diary Series, Box 4, EL; Eisenhower, DOH, 16–18; Herman Phleger, DOH, 14–24; Minutes, Cabinet Meetings, Feb. 20, March 13,

20, 27, April 3, May 8, June 5, July 3, 17, 1953, Whitman File, Cabinet Meetings Series, Box 1, EL; Parmet, *Eisenhower,* 306–12.

97. Reichard, *Reaffirmation of Republicanism,* 63–96; various notes, Legislative meetings for 1953 in Whitman File, Legislative Meetings Series, Box 1, and Whitman File, DDE Diary Series, Box 4, EL; Minutes of Cabinet Meetings, April 3, 10, 17, May 1, July 17, 1953, Whitman File, Cabinet Meetings Series, Box 1, EL.

98. Eisenhower, *Public Papers,* 1953, p. 13.

99. Eisenhower to Alfred Gruenther, Feb. 10, 1953, Whitman File, DDE Diary Series, Box 3, EL.

100. John Lewis Gaddis, *Strategies of Containment: A Critical Appraisal of Postwar American National Security Policy* (New York: Oxford University Press, 1982), 128–29; Richard H. Immerman, "Eisenhower and Dulles: Who Made the Decisions?" *Political Psychology* 1 (Autumn 1979), 3–20; James Hagerty, DOH, 15–17; *Eisenhower Diaries,* 237.

101. C. L. Sulzberger, *A Long Row of Candles: Memoirs and Diaries, 1934– 1954* (New York: Macmillan, 1969), 706–7; Gaddis, *Strategies of Containment,* 136–45, 156–59; Kermit Roosevelt, *Countercoup: The Struggle for the Control of Iran* (New York: McGraw-Hill, 1979); Richard Immerman, *CIA in Guatemala: The Foreign Policy of Intervention* (Austin: University of Texas Press, 1982); *Foreign and Military Intelligence,* Book I, Final Report of the Select Committee to Study Government Operations with Respect to Intelligence Activities, U.S. Senate, 94th Cong., 2d sess. (Washington, D.C.: U.S. Government Printing Office, 1976), 97–115.

102. Ambrose, *Eisenhower,* Vol. 1, p. 76; Ambrose, *Eisenhower,* Vol. 2, pp. 94–96; Hughes, *Ordeal of Power,* 100–112; Eisenhower, *Mandate,* 143–49; Parmet, *Eisenhower,* 275–81; C. D. Jackson to Robert Cutler, March 4, 1953, Whitman File, Administration Series, Box 32, EL; Special Estimate, Central Intelligence Agency, March 10, 1953, OSANSA, NSC Series, Subject Subseries, Box 5, EL.

103. Eisenhower, *Mandate,* 147; Eisenhower, *Public Papers,* 1953, 179–88; Ambrose, *Eisenhower,* Vol. 2, pp. 94–96.

104. Bohlen to Sec. of State, April 25, 1953, DDE Confidential File, Subject Series, Box 66, EL; Text of *Tass* Report on President Eisenhower's Speech, Aug. 1, 1953; Bohlen to Secretary of State, April 18, 1953, DDE Confidential File, Subject Series, Box 65, EL; Parmet, *Eisenhower,* 279–82; *Khrushchev Remembers* (Boston: Little, Brown, 1970), 315–41.

105. Eisenhower, *Public Papers,* 1953, pp. 306–18.

106. Gaddis, *Strategies of Containment,* 145–97; Glenn H. Snyder, "The 'New Look' of 1953," in Warner H. Schilling, Paul Y. Hammond, Glenn H. Snyder, *Strategy, Politics and Defense Budgets* (New York: Columbia University Press, 1962), 383–524; Douglas Kinnard, *President Eisenhower and Strategy Management: A Study in Defense Politics* (Lexington: University Press of Kentucky, 1977); Eisenhower to Secretary of Defense, November 30, 1953, Whitman File, Administration Series, Box 44, EL; Joseph Dodge to the President, Sept. 30, 1953, Whitman File, DDE Diary Series, Box 3, EL; telephone calls, Dec. 2, 1953, Whitman File, DDE Diary Series, Box 5, EL.

107. Robert Cutler, *No Time for Rest* (Boston: Little, Brown, 1965), 293– 313; *Organizing for National Security,* Hearings before the Subcommittee on Na-

tional Policy Machinery of the Committee on Government Operations, U.S. Senate (Washington, D.C.: U.S. Government Printing Office, 1961), Vol. 1, pp. 577–603, Vol. 2, pp. 159–89.

108. Cutler, No Time for Rest, 295–96, 317–20.

109. Cutler, No Time for Rest, 307–10; Gaddis, Strategies of Containment, 145–46; Kennan, Memoirs, Vol. 2, pp. 181–82.

110. Gaddis, Strategies of Containment, 146, 161–97; Cutler, No Time for Rest, 296–97; Melanie Sue Billings-Yun, "Decision Against War: Eisenhower and Dien Bien Phu, 1954" (Ph.D. dissertation, Harvard University, 1982); Ambrose, Eisenhower, Vol. 2, passim.

111. James Shepley, "How Dulles Averted War," Life 40 (Jan. 16, 1956), 71; Memorandum of Restricted Meeting of Chiefs of Delegations, Bermuda, Dec. 7, 1953, Whitman Files, International Meetings Series, Box 1, EL; Donovan, Eisenhower: The Inside Story, 115–16; Edward Friedman, "Nuclear Blackmail and the End of the Korean War," Modern China 1 (Jan. 1975), 75–76; Adams, Firsthand Report, 48–49; Eisenhower, Mandate, 181.

112. Friedman, "Nuclear Blackmail," 75–91; Barton J. Bernstein, "New Light on the Korean War," International History Review 3 (April 1981), 256–77; David Rees, Korea: The Limited War (Baltimore: Penguin 1970), 402–20; Alexander L. George and Richard Smoke, Deterrence in American Foreign Policy: Theory and Practice (New York: Columbia University Press, 1974), 235–40; John L. Gaddis, Russia, the Soviet Union and the United States: An Interpretive History (New York: Wiley, 1978), 214–15; James F. Schnabel and Robert J. Watson, The History of the Joint Chiefs of Staff: The Joint Chiefs of Staff and National Policy, Vol. 3, The Korean War, Part 2 (Wilmington, Del.: Michael Glazier, Inc., 1979), 962–82; Hildreth, Karachi to the Secretary of State, Cable 1772, May 22, 1953, Whitman File, Dulles-Herter Series, Box 1, EL; Foreign Relations of the United States, 1952–1954, (hereafter Frus), Vol. 15, Korea (Washington, D.C.: U.S. Government Printing Office, 1984), 817–18, 886–92.

113. Minnich notes, Legislative Leadership Meeting, Whitman File, DDE Diary Series, Box 4, EL; Memorandum of Discussion at 131st Meeting of the NSC, Feb. 11, 1953, Whitman File, NSC Series, Box 4, EL; Memorandum of Discussion at the 139th Meeting of the NSC, April 8, 1953, Whitman File, NSC Series, Box 4, EL; Frus, Vol. 15, Korea, 769–70, 825–27, 892–94.

114. Notes by the Executive Secretary to the NSC, "Analysis of Possible Courses of Action in Korea," April 2, 1953, OSANSA, NSC Series, Policy Papers Subseries, Box 4, EL; Eisenhower, Mandate, 180; Bernstein, "New Light on the Korean War," 273–74; Frus, Vol. 15, Korea, 845–46, 977, 1065.

115. Adams, Firsthand Report, 118; Frus, Vol. 15, Korea, 1068–71; Hildreth, Karachi to the Secretary of State, Cable 1772, May 22, 1953, Whitman File, Dulles-Herter Series, Box 1, EL; Chester Bowles, Ambassador's Report (New York: Harper & Bros., 1954), 242; Bernstein, "New Light on the Korean War," 271.

116. Eisenhower, Mandate, 181–85; Clark, From the Danube to the Yalu, 261–81; Schnabel and Watson, History of the Joint Chiefs, 983–1009; Maxwell D. Taylor, Swords and Plowshares (New York: Norton, 1972), 142–45; Dulles to the President, June 14, 1953, Whitman File, Dulles-Herter Series, Box 1, EL.

117. Eisenhower, Mandate, 185–87; Minutes of Cabinet Meeting, June 19, 1953, Cabinet Meetings Series, Whitman File, Box 2, EL; Minnich Notes of Legis-

lative Leadership Meeting, June 24, 1953, Whitman File, DDE Diary Series, Box 4, EL.

118. Dulles to Rhee, June 22, 1953, Whitman File, International Series, Box 32, EL; Schnabel and Watson, *History of the Joint Chiefs*, 1017.

119. Walter S. Robertson, COH (1967), 58–61; Clark, *From the Danube to the Yalu*, 284–88; Schnabel and Watson, *History of the Joint Chiefs*, 1017–29.

120. Schnabel and Watson, *History of the Joint Chiefs*, 1020–33; Taylor, *Swords and Plowshares*, 147.

121. Schnabel and Watson, *History of the Joint Chiefs*, 1027–54; Eisenhower, *Mandate*, 187–89; Taylor, *Swords and Plowshares*, 146; Walter G. Hermes, *Truce Tent and Fighting Front* (Washington, D.C.: Office of the Chief of Military History, 1966), 470–97.

122. Robert Murphy, COH (1972), 44; Ellis Briggs, COH (1972), 72; Taylor, *Swords and Plowshares*, 137; Clark, *From the Danube to the Yalu*, 297; Eisenhower, *Mandate*, 190–91; Ambrose, *Eisenhower*, Vol. 2, pp. 104–7.

CHAPTER 2: KENNEDY

1. Robert Dallek, *Franklin D. Roosevelt and American Foreign Policy, 1932–1945* (New York: Oxford University Press, 1979), 164; Michael R. Beschloss, *Kennedy and Roosevelt: The Uneasy Alliance* (New York: Norton, 1980).

2. The best source on Kennedy's life before he became President is Herbert S. Parmet, *Jack: The Struggles of John F. Kennedy* (New York: Dial, 1980).

3. Theodore H. White, *The Making of the President, 1960* (New York: Atheneum, 1961); Memorandum for speechwriters, July 23, 1960, Theodore C. Sorensen Papers, Box 26, John F. Kennedy Library, Boston, Mass. (henceforth KL).

4. White, *Making of the President, 1960*, 387–409; Theodore C. Sorensen, *Kennedy* (New York: Harper & Row, 1965), 211–23, 339–40.

5. Sorensen, *Kennedy*, 218–23; Arthur M. Schlesinger, Jr., *A Thousand Days: John F. Kennedy in the White House* (Boston: Houghton Mifflin, 1965), 118–19; confidential sources; Arthur M. Schlesinger, Jr., *Robert Kennedy and His Times* (Boston: Houghton Mifflin, 1978), 219–20.

6. Sorensen, *Kennedy*, 227–28.

7. *Ibid.*, 229; Schlesinger, *Thousand Days*, 120–21; unsigned and undated memorandum, Clark Clifford Papers, Reel 1, KL.

8. Schlesinger, *Thousand Days*, 122–24; author's conversation with Richard Neustadt, Nov. 1, 1982.

9. Sorensen, *Kennedy*, 230–31; Clifford Memorandum on Transition, Nov. 9, 1960, John F. Kennedy Papers, Pre-Presidential, Box 1071, KL.

10. Schlesinger, *Thousand Days*, 120.

11. Schlesinger, *Thousand Days*, 123–24; Richard E. Neustadt, Memorandum on Staffing the President-Elect, Oct. 30, 1960, JFK Papers, Pre-Presidential, Box 1072, KL; Clifford Memorandum on Transition, Nov. 9, 1960, JFK Papers, Pre-Presidential, Box 1071, KL.

12. Interview note, Richard E. Neustadt, Dec. 22, 1960, Laurin L. Henry Papers, Box 3, KL; Frederick G. Dutton, Kennedy Library Oral History, John F. Kennedy Library, Boston, Mass. (henceforth KOH), 45; Charles Bohlen, KOH, 4; George F. Kennan, KOH, 34–35.

13. Neustadt, "Memorandum on Organizing the Transition," Sept. 15, 1960,

Personal Files of Richard E. Neustadt, John F. Kennedy School of Government, Cambridge, Mass.

14. Neustadt, "Memorandum on Staffing the President-Elect," Oct. 30, 1960, JFK Papers, Pre-Presidential, Box 1072, KL; Clifford Memorandum on Transition, Nov. 9, 1960, JFK Papers, Pre-Presidential, Box 1071, KL; Clark Clifford, KOH, 63 (in Clifford's possession.)

15. Sorensen, *Kennedy*, 230 and *passim;* Pierre Salinger, *With Kennedy* (New York: Doubleday, 1966); Kenneth P. O'Donnell and David F. Powers, with Joe McCarthy, *"Johnny, We Hardly Knew Ye": Memories of John Fitzgerald Kennedy* (Boston: Little, Brown, 1972), 81ff.

16. Salinger, *With Kennedy*, 53–59; Sorensen, *Kennedy*, 322–26; George H. Gallup, *The Gallup Poll: Public Opinion, 1935–1971*, Vol. 3 (New York: Random House, 1972), 1765.

17. Salinger, *With Kennedy*, 64–65; O'Donnell and Powers, *"Johnny,"* 226–27; Mary McGrory, "The Right-Hand Men—Pierre Salinger, Lawrence O'Brien, and Kenneth P. O'Donnell," *The Kennedy Circle,* ed. Lester Tanzer (Washington, D. C.: Luce, 1961), 75–81.

18. Sorensen, *Kennedy*, 234–44; Memo, Special Counsel to the President, undated, Sorensen Papers, Box 31, KL; Myer Feldman, KOH, 304–12; Hugh Davis Graham, "Short-Circuiting the Bureaucracy in the Great Society: Policy Origins in Education," *Presidential Studies Quarterly* 12 (Summer 1982), 407–20.

19. Hugh Sidey, "Brother on the Spot," *The Kennedy Circle,* 209; Schlesinger, *Robert Kennedy,* 193.

20. Salinger, *With Kennedy,* 64; Schlesinger, *Robert Kennedy,* 228; Frederick G. Dutton, KOH (1965).

21. Salinger, *With Kennedy,* 64–72; confidential sources.

22. Salinger, *With Kennedy,* 64–72; Sorensen, *Kennedy,* 258–65; confidential sources; Dutton, KOH (1965); Walt W. Rostow, KOH, 12–14.

23. Robert F. Kennedy, interviewed by John Bartlow Martin (1964), KOH, 37–38; Lawrence F. O'Brien, *No Final Victories: A Life in Politics from John F. Kennedy to Watergate* (Garden City, N. Y.: Doubleday, Inc. 1974), 97–101; John Hart, "Staffing the Presidency: Kennedy and the Office of Congressional Relations," *Presidential Studies Quarterly* 13 (Winter 1983), 101–10.

24. O'Donnell and Powers, *"Johnny,"* 234–35; Sorensen, *Kennedy,* 254–55; Harris Wofford, *Of Kennedys and Kings: Making Sense of the Sixties* (New York: Farrar, Straus and Giroux, 1980), 67.

25. Neustadt, "Staffing the President-Elect," Oct. 30, 1960, JFK Papers, Pre-Presidential, Box 1072, KL; Robert Kennedy, interviewed by Martin, 51, and interviewed by Anthony Lewis, IV, KOH, 22; Schlesinger, *Robert Kennedy,* 259; Parmet, *Jack,* 91–92, 510–11, 523.

26. Robert Kennedy, Martin interview, KOH, 51; Neustadt, "Staffing the President-Elect," Oct. 30, 1960, JFK Papers, Pre-Presidential, Box 1072, KL; Clark Clifford, Memo for file, Nov. 10, 1960, Clark Clifford Papers, Reel 1, KL.

27. Schlesinger, *Robert Kennedy,* 244–60; David J. Garrow, *The FBI and Martin Luther King, Jr.: From "Solo" to Memphis* (New York: Norton, 1981); confidential sources.

28. Peter Wyden, *Bay of Pigs: The Untold Story* (New York: Simon + Schuster, 1979), 95–96, 98–100, 268–69; Schlesinger, *Robert Kennedy,* 443–54; Robert Kennedy, Martin interview, KOH, 51, 70–71; Richard Bissell, KOH

(1967), 1–6; Chester Bowles, KOH (1970), 62–63; *The Memoirs of Richard Nixon* (New York: Grosset & Dunlap, 1978), 233.

29. Sorensen, *Kennedy*, 254–56; Adam Yarmolinsky, KOH (1964), 20.

30. Sorensen, *Kennedy*, 255; Robert Kennedy, Martin interview, KOH, 1–40; Robert A. Lovett, KOH (1964); Clifford, Memorandum of Conversation with Sen. Kennedy, Nov. 30, 1960, Clark Clifford Papers, Reel 1, KL; confidential sources.

31. Memorandum, Sorensen to O'Brien, n.d., Sorensen Papers, Box 31, KL.

32. Yarmolinsky, KOH (1964), 1–26; Myer Feldman, KOH (1965), 312–14; Harris Wofford, KOH, 87–99; Wofford, *Of Kennedys and Kings*, 67–97.

33. Wofford, *Of Kennedys and Kings*, 11–28, 43–97; confidential sources; Carl M. Brauer, *John F. Kennedy and the Second Reconstruction* (New York: Columbia University Press, 1977), 46–51.

34. Yarmolinsky, KOH, 17–21; Wofford, *Of Kennedys and Kings*, 70–86; Wofford, KOH, 87–98; confidential sources.

35. Confidential sources: Yarmolinsky, KOH, 15–26; Robert Kennedy, Martin interview, KOH, 14–15; Feldman, KOH, 320–23.

36. Sorensen, *Kennedy*, 251–58; David T. Stanley, Dean E. Mann, Jameson W. Doig, *Men Who Govern: A Biographical Profile of Federal Political Executives* (Washington D. C.: Brookings Institution, 1967), 24, 130, 132–33; confidential sources; Hugh Heclo, *A Government of Strangers: Executive Politics in Washington* (Washington, D. C.: Brookings Institution, 1977), 103–5.

37. John Kenneth Galbraith, *Ambassador's Journal: A Personal Account of the Kennedy Years* (Boston: Houghton Mifflin, 1969), 7.

38. Wofford, *Of Kennedys and Kings*, 71–72; David E. Bell, KOH, 2–10; Philip S. Hughes, KOH, 1, 14; Richard E. Neustadt, "Memorandum on Staffing the President-Elect," Oct. 30, 1960, JFK Papers, Pre-Presidential, Box 1072, KL; confidential sources; Maurice Stans to Eisenhower, Jan. 18, 1961, Whitman File, Transition Series, Box 3, Dwight D. Eisenhower Library, Abilene, Kansas; Sorensen, *Kennedy*, 263; Larry Berman, *The Office of Management and Budget and the Presidency, 1921–1979* (Princeton: Princeton University Press, 1979), 67–73; Feldman, KOH (1968), 37–38.

39. O'Donnell and Powers, *"Johnny,"* 227, 229; Robert Kennedy, Martin interview, KOH, 17.

40. Transcript of Brookings interview with Clark Clifford, Feb. 24, 1961, Clifford Papers, Reel 1, KL; Robert Lovett, KOH, 11; Schlesinger, *A Thousand Days*, 130; *New York Times*, Dec. 2, 1960; *Washington Post*, Dec. 2, 1960.

41. Robert Kennedy, Martin interview, KOH, 19–20; Brauer, *Kennedy and the Second Reconstruction*, 30–60; Luther Hodges, KOH, 1–3.

42. Schlesinger, *Robert Kennedy*, 225–26; Clifford Memorandum of Conversation with Sen. Kennedy, Nov. 30, 1960, Clifford Papers, Reel 1, KL; Stewart L. Udall, KOH (1970), 31–36. Anderson, not surprisingly, tells the story differently. See Clinton P. Anderson, KOH (1967), 35–37.

43. Schlesinger, *Robert Kennedy*, 227; Robert Kennedy, Martin interview, KOH, 17; Neustadt memorandum on "Cabinet Departments: Some Things to Keep in Mind," Nov. 3, 1960, President's Office Files, Box 64, KL.

44. Schlesinger, *Robert Kennedy*, 226–27; Schlesinger, *A Thousand Days*, 143–44; Orville Freeman, KOH (1964), 14–19.

45. Schlesinger, *Robert Kennedy*, 227; Robert Kennedy, Martin interview, KOH, 15–16; Feldman, KOH (1965), 345–51, (1968), 42–44.

46. Clifford Memorandum of Conversation with Sen. Kennedy, Nov. 30, 1960, Clifford Papers, Reel 1, KL; Lovett, KOH (1964), 1–6.

47. Schlesinger, *Thousand Days,* 129; Lovett, KOH, 20.

48. Lovett, KOH, 14–17; Schlesinger, *Robert Kennedy,* 224–25; Robert Kennedy, Martin interview, KOH, 6; Yarmolinsky, KOH, 15–18; Wofford, *Of Kennedys and Kings,* 70–71; O'Donnell and Powers, *"Johnny,"* 236–38; Schlesinger, *Thousand Days,* 131–33; Henry L. Trewhitt, *McNamara,* (New York: Harper & Row, 1971), 4–11; confidential sources.

49. Lovett, KOH, 9; Robert Kennedy, Martin interview, KOH, 27–29.

50. Schlesinger, *Robert Kennedy,* 233; Lovett, KOH, 9–10.

51. Schlesinger, *Robert Kennedy,* 133–36; John Bartlow Martin, *Adlai Stevenson and the World* (Garden City, N.Y.: Doubleday, 1977), 556–65; Robert Kennedy, Martin interview, KOH, 10–12; O'Donnell and Powers, *"Johnny,"* 178.

52. Schlesinger, *Robert Kennedy,* 222–23; Robert Kennedy, Martin interview, 7–9; O'Donnell and Powers, *"Johnny,"* 235–36; Wofford, *Of Kennedys and Kings,* 80–82; confidential sources.

53. Schlesinger, *Robert Kennedy,* 223–24; Robert Kennedy, Martin interview, KOH, 8–10; Schlesinger, *Thousand Days,* 140–41; Lovett, KOH, 17–18; confidential source; Ronald Steel, *Walter Lippmann and the American Century* (Boston: Little, Brown, 1980), 523–24.

54. Lovett, KOH, 18–20; Chester Bowles, *Promises To Keep: My Years in Public Life, 1941–1969* (New York: Harper & Row, 1971), 299–300; George W. Ball, *The Past Has Another Pattern: Memoirs* (New York: Norton, 1982), 170–71; Schlesinger, *Robert Kennedy,* 223; Robert Kennedy, KOH, 9, 15–16; Warren I. Cohen, *Dean Rusk* (Totowa, N. J.: Cooper Square Publishers, 1980), 101.

55. Cohen, *Dean Rusk,* 94–107; Bowles, *Promises to Keep,* 301–35; Sorensen, *Kennedy,* 270; confidential sources; Robert Kennedy, Martin interview, KOH, 28–29.

56. George F. Kennan, KOH (1965), 33–34; confidential source.

57. Confidential sources; I. M. Destler, "National Security Management: What Presidents Have Wrought," *Political Science Quarterly* 95 (Winter 1980–81), 578–80; I. M. Destler, "A Lost Legacy? The Presidency and National Security Organization" (April 1982), unpublished; Robert Kennedy, Martin interview, KOH, 28; I. M. Destler, Leslie H. Gelb and Anthony Lake, *Our Own Worst Enemy: The Unmaking of American Foreign Policy* (New York: Simon + Schuster, 1984), 182–95.

58. Richard E. Neustadt, Memorandum on Cabinet Departments, Nov. 3, 1960, President's Office Files, Box 64, KL; Lovett, KOH, 23–24.

59. Schlesinger, *Robert Kennedy,* 225; Schlesinger, *Thousand Days,* 135; O'Donnell and Powers, *"Johnny,"* 238–39; Sorensen, *Kennedy,* 255; confidential sources.

60. Schlesinger, *Thousand Days,* 134–35; Schlesinger, *Robert Kennedy,* 225; Robert Kennedy, Martin interview, KOH, 12–14.

61. Dwight D. Eisenhower, *Waging Peace, 1956–1961* (Garden City, N.Y.: Doubleday, 1965), 603; Eisenhower to Dillon, Dec. 15, 1960, Whitman File, DDE Diary Series, Box 55, EL; telephone calls, Dec. 15, 31, 1960, Whitman File, DDE Diary Series, Box 55, EL; "a" to Eisenhower, Nov. 14, 1960, Whitman File, DDE Diary Series, Box 54, EL.

62. Walter W. Heller, Notes on First Ten Days in Washington, Jan. 13, 1961,

Walter W. Heller Papers, Box 3, KL; Schlesinger, *Thousand Days,* 135–36; confidential sources.

63. Heller, Recollections of early meetings with Kennedy, Jan. 21, 1964, Heller Papers, Box 5, KL; Council of Economic Advisers Oral History, KOH, esp. 107–254 and James Tobin's notes.

64. Schlesinger, *Robert Kennedy,* 228–36, 452; Clark Clifford, KOH (1974), 42 (1975), 27–28.

65. Robert Kennedy, Martin interview, KOH, 24; Schlesinger, *Robert Kennedy,* 231; Note initialed by Eisenhower, Nov. 9, 1960, Whitman Files, DDE Diary Series, Box 54, EL.

66. Unsigned notes, Nov. 9, 10 (1960), Whitman File, DDE Diary Series, Box 54, EL; Notes on conversation of the President and General Persons, Nov. 3, 1960, Whitman File, Transition Series, Box 1, EL; Eisenhower, *Waging Peace,* 601–2.

67. Wilton B. Persons, Columbia Oral History, 137–41; Unsigned memorandum, n.d., Clifford Papers, Reel 1, KL.

68. Eisenhower, *Waging Peace,* 712–16; Persons, COH, 143; Whitman Files, Transition Series, Boxes 1, 3, EL; Clifford Papers, Reel 1, KL.

69. Feldman, KOH (1965), 342–43; confidential sources.

70. Robert Kennedy, Martin interview, KOH, 49–50.

71. Clifford, KOH, 49–50; Persons, COH, 144; Eisenhower, *Waging Peace,* 603.

72. Eisenhower to "Bob," Jan. 3, 1961, Whitman File, DDE Diary Series, Box 55, EL.

73. *New York Times,* Nov. 13, Dec. 7, Jan. 20, 1961; "a" to the President, Nov. 14, 1960, Whitman File, DDE Diary Series, Box 54, EL; O'Donnell and Powers, *"Johnny,"* 299; Stephen E. Ambrose, *Eisenhower,* Vol. 2 (New York: Simon + Schuster, 1984), 606–8.

74. Sorensen, *Kennedy,* 240–45; Galbraith, *Ambassador's Journal,* 15–17; John F. Kennedy, *Public Papers of the Presidents,* 1961, pp. 1–3.

75. James Meredith, *Three Years in Mississippi* (Bloomington: Indiana University Press, 1966), 50–59; Gallup, *The Gallup Poll,* Vol. 3, p. 1707, 1850; Thomas E. Cronin, *The State of the Presidency,* 2d Ed. (Boston: Little, Brown, 1980), 328–29.

76. Kennedy, *Public Papers,* 1961, pp. 1–525; Gallup, *The Gallup Poll,* Vol. 3, p. 1765; Mary McGrory, Peter Lisagor, George Herman, KOH, 52–53.

77. Gary Wills, *The Kennedy Imprisonment: A Meditation on Power* (Boston: Little, Brown, 1982).

78. White, *Making of the President, 1960,* 338.

79. Sorensen, *Kennedy,* 310–22; confidential source; Salinger, *With Kennedy,* 84–143; Robert Kennedy, Martin interview, KOH, 41; Benjamin C. Bradlee, *Conversations with Kennedy* (New York: Norton, 1975); President's Appointment Books, 1961, KL.

80. Cronin, *State of the Presidency,* 171–72; O'Brien, *No Final Victories,* 104.

81. O'Brien, *No Final Victories,* 105–7; Robert Kennedy, Martin interview, KOH, 43–45; Richard Bolling, *House Out of Order* (New York: Dutton, 1965), 215–20.

82. O'Brien, *No Final Victories,* 107–12; Richard Bolling, *Power in the House* (New York: Dutton, 1968), 209–10; Hart, "Staffing the Presidency."

83. Bobby Baker, *Wheeling and Dealing: Confessions of a Capitol Hill Opera-*

tor (New York: Norton, 1978), 133–43; Clifford, KOH, 67–68; Leonard Baker, *The Johnson Eclipse: A President's Vice Presidency* (New York: Macmillan, 1966); O'Donnell and Powers, *"Johnny,"* 5–11, 192–98.

84. Brauer, *Kennedy and the Second Reconstruction,* 30–125.

85. *Congressional Quarterly Almanac,* Vol. 17, (1961), 63, 70–71; Stein, *Fiscal Revolution,* 372–453; Walter W. Heller to Whom It May Concern (esp. Messrs. Tobin, Gordon and Solow), March 27, 1961, Heller Papers, Box 3, KL; Heller to the President, and CEA, "A Second Look at Economic Policy in 1961," both March 17, 1961, President's Office File, Box 63a, KL; CEA, KOH.

86. *Congressional Quarterly Almanac,* 1961, pp. 72–73; Stein, *Fiscal Revolution,* 370–71, 387–95; Sorensen, *Kennedy,* 412–21; Memorandum, Maurice Stans to the President, Robert B. Anderson to the President, both Dec. 12, 1960, Whitman File, DDE Diary Series, Box 55, EL.

87. Kennedy, *Public Papers,* 1961, pp. 19–28.

88. See, generally Sorensen, *Kennedy;* Schlesinger, *Thousand Days;* Roger Hilsman, *To Move a Nation: The Politics of Foreign Policy in the Administration of John F. Kennedy* (Garden City, N.Y.: Doubleday, 1967); Schlesinger, *Robert Kennedy,* 417–42; John Lewis Gaddis, *Strategies of Containment: An Appraisal of Postwar American National Security Policy* (New York: Oxford University Press, 1982), 198–236. For an example of a critical view of Kennedy, see Bruce Miroff, *Pragmatic Illusions: The Presidential Politics of John F. Kennedy* (New York: David McKay, 1976).

89. John M. Logsdon, *The Decision to Go to the Moon: Project Apollo and the National Interest* (Cambridge: MIT Press, 1970), 93–130; Sorensen, *Kennedy,* 523–29; O'Donnell and Powers, *"Johnny,"* 410, and for a critical view, see Walter A. McDougall, ". . . *The Heavens and the Earth: A Political History of the Space Age* (New York: Basic Books, 1985), 302–24.

90. Wofford, *Of Kennedys and Kings,* 243–84; Gerard T. Rice, "Kennedy's Children: The Peace Corps, 1961–3" (Ph.D. dissertation, Department of Modern History, University of Glasgow, 1980).

91. Schlesinger, *Thousand Days,* 186–205, 759–93; Jerome Levinson and Juan DeOnis, *The Alliance That Lost Its Way: A Critical Report on the Alliance for Progress* (Chicago: Quadrangle Books, 1970); Milton S. Eisenhower, *The Wine Is Bitter: The United States and Latin America* (Garden City, N. Y.: Doubleday, 1963).

92. This account of the Bay of Pigs draws upon the following sources: Ambrose, *Eisenhower,* Vol. 2, pp. 608–10, 637–41; Schlesinger, *Thousand Days,* 237–97; Schlesinger, *Robert Kennedy,* 442–49; Peter Wyden, *Bay of Pigs: The Untold Story* (New York: Simon + Schuster, 1979); Neustadt, *Presidential Power,* 220–25; *Operation ZAPATA: The 'Ultrasensitive' Report and Testimony of the Board of Inquiry on the Bay of Pigs* (Frederick, Md.: University Publications of America, 1981); Maxwell D. Taylor, *Swords and Plowshares* (New York: Norton, 1972), 178–203; Handwritten notes of meeting between Eisenhower and Kennedy, Jan. 19, 1961, Clifford Papers, Reel 1, KL; Maxwell Taylor, KOH, (1964), 3–17; Richard Bissell, KOH and COH; Robert Kennedy, Martin interview, KOH, 48, 55–89; confidential sources; Memos to the President from McGeorge Bundy, Feb. 8, 9, 18, 1961 and from Arthur Schlesinger, April 10, 1961, National Security Council Files, Box 35, KL.

93. Schlesinger, *Robert Kennedy,* 442–98, 533–58, 614–17; Robert Kennedy,

Martin interview, KOH, 89–92; Herbert S. Parmet, *JFK: The Presidency of John F. Kennedy* (New York: Dial, 1983), 213–21.

94. Schlesinger, *Thousand Days,* 323–29; Clifford's handwritten notes of meeting between Eisenhower and Kennedy, Jan. 19, 1961, Clifford Papers, Reel 1, KL.

95. Schlesinger, *Thousand Days,* 329–42; Rostow to the President, March 9, 1961, Bundy to the President, May 1, 1961, President's Office Files, Box 121, KL; Rostow, KOH, 44–80; confidential sources; Hilsman, *To Move a Nation,* 91–141; W. W. Rostow, *The Diffusion of Power: An Essay in Recent History* (New York: Macmillan, 1972), 265–68.

96. Desmond Ball, *Politics and Force Levels: The Strategic Missile Program of the Kennedy Administration* (Berkeley: University of California Press, 1980); Gaddis, *Strategies of Containment,* 198–273; Richard Aliano, *American Defense Policy from Eisenhower to Kennedy: The Politics of Changing Military Requirements* (Athens: Ohio University Press, 1975); confidential sources.

97. Michael Mandelbaum, *The Nuclear Question: The United States and Nuclear Weapons, 1946–1976* (Cambridge: Cambridge University Press, 1979), 69–189, quotation on 73; William W. Kaufman, *The McNamara Strategy* (New York: Harper & Row, 1964); Lawrence J. Korb, *The Joint Chiefs of Staff: The First Twenty-five Years* (Bloomington: Indiana University Press, 1976), 111–21; Trewhitt, *McNamara.*

98. Khrushchev quoted in John Lewis Gaddis, *Russia, the Soviet Union and the United States: An Interpretive History* (New York: Wiley, 1978), 229.

99. *Ibid.,* 231–33; Schlesinger, *Thousand Days,* 301–6, 344–47; Glenn T. Seaborg, *Kennedy, Khrushchev and the Test Ban* (Berkeley: University of California Press, 1981), 30–60; confidential sources.

100. Schlesinger, *Thousand Days,* 347–78; Sorensen, *Kennedy,* 541–50; *Khrushchev Remembers: The Last Testament* (Boston: Little, Brown, 1974), 486–501; Charles E. Bohlen, *Witness to History, 1929–1969* (New York: Norton, 1973), 479–93; confidential sources.

CHAPTER 3: NIXON

1. Bryce Harlow, author's interview, June 14, 1983; H. R. Haldeman, author's interview, June 8, 1983. For psychobiographies of Nixon, see: David Abrahamsen, *Nixon vs. Nixon: An Emotional Tragedy* (New York: Farrar, Straus and Giroux, 1977); Fawn M. Brodie, *Richard Nixon: The Shaping of His Character* (New York: Norton, 1981); Bruce Mazlish, *In Search of Nixon: A Psychohistorical Inquiry* (New York: Basic Books, 1972). Richard Nixon's own books include: *Six Crises* (Garden City, N.Y.: Doubleday, 1962); *Memoirs* (New York: Grosset & Dunlap, 1978); *The Real War* (New York: Warner, 1980); *Leaders* (New York: Warner, 1982). Valuable memoirs by Nixon aides include: John Ehrlichman, *Witness to Power: The Nixon Years* (New York: Simon + Schuster, 1982); H. R. Haldeman with Joseph DiMona, *The Ends of Power* (New York: Times Books, 1978); Henry Kissinger, *White House Years* (Boston: Little, Brown, 1979); Herbert G. Klein, *Making It Perfectly Clear* (Garden City, N.Y.: Doubleday, 1980); Raymond Price, *With Nixon* (New York: Viking, 1977); William Safire, *Before the Fall: An Inside View of the Pre-Watergate White House* (Garden City, N.Y.: Doubleday, 1975). On the 1968 election, see: Theodore H. White, *The Making of*

the President, 1968 (New York: Atheneum, 1969); Lewis Chester, Godfrey Hodgson, Bruce Page, An American Melodrama: The Presidential Campaign of 1968 (New York: Viking, 1969); Joe McGinniss, The Selling of the President, 1968 (New York: Trident Press, 1969). Probably the most interesting book about Nixon by a journalist is Garry Wills, Nixon Agonistes: The Crisis of the Self-Made Man (Boston: Houghton Mifflin, 1969). For Eisenhower's views of Nixon, see Stephen E. Ambrose, Eisenhower, Vol. 2 (New York: Simon + Schuster, 1984)

2. George H. Gallup, The Gallup Poll: Public Opinion, 1935–1971 Volume 3 (New York: Random House, 1972), 2180. For a valuable analysis of American public opinion on the Vietnam war, see: John E. Mueller, War, Presidents, and Public Opinion (New York: Wiley, 1973).

3. Chester et al., An American Melodrama; White, Making of the President, 1968.

4. Haldeman, author's interview, June 8, 1983; Nixon, Memoirs, 334–35; John Ehrlichman, author's interview, May 26, 1983; New York Times, Nov. 6, 1968.

5. Nixon, Memoirs, 337–38; Nixon, Leaders, 334.

6. Klein, Making It Perfectly Clear 12, 352–53; Nixon, Six Crises, 501; Lou Cannon, "The Forces that Forged the Future: 'He Didn't Want to Stay in Yorba Linda'," in The Fall of a President, by the staff of the Washington Post (New York: Delacorte Press, 1975), 62; Richard Whalen, Catch the Falling Flag (Boston: Houghton Mifflin, 1972), 61; Kissinger, White House Years, 45; and for Haldeman quotation, Allen Drury, Courage and Hesitation (Garden City, N.Y.: Doubleday, 1971), 73.

7. Nixon, Memoirs, 337–38; New York Times, Nov. 11, 1968; Author's interviews with Haldeman, Harlow, and Robert Finch, June 9, 1983.

8. Nixon, Memoirs, 335.

9. Ibid., 361; Harlow, author's interview.

10. Author's interviews with Haldeman, Finch, Harlow.

11. Nixon, Memoirs, 340; White, Making of the President, 1968, 147; Theodore H. White, The Making of the President, 1972 (New York: Atheneum, 1973), 354; Arthur M. Schlesinger, Jr., A Thousand Days: John F. Kennedy in the White House (Boston: Houghton Mifflin, 1965), 426.

12. Author's interviews with Haldeman, Harlow; Theodore H. White, Breach of Faith (New York: Atheneum, 1975), 96; Safire, Before the Fall, 109, 152; Price, With Nixon, 62–66.

13. Author's interviews with Haldeman, Finch, Harlow, and John Mitchell, June 14, 1983.

14. Haldeman, author's interview; Washington Post, Nov. 7, 1968; New York Times, Nov. 7, 1968; Franklin B. Lincoln, Jr., "Presidential Transition, 1968–1969," American Bar Association Journal 55 (June 1969), 529–33.

15. Author's interviews with Haldeman, Ehrlichman; Haldeman, Ends of Power, 58–64; Ehrlichman, Witness to Power, 75–86, 212–20; Safire, Before the Fall, 497–98; Richard P. Nathan, The Plot That Failed: Nixon and the Administrative Presidency (New York: Wiley, 1975).

16. Author's interviews with Haldeman, Harlow, Ehrlichman; Safire, Before the Fall, 281.

17. Nixon, Memoirs, 337; Nixon, Leaders, 335; Haldeman, Ends of Power, 53–54.

18. Author's interviews with Haldeman, Ehrlichman, Harlow, Finch; Halde-

man, *Ends of Power,* 45–65; Safire, *Before the Fall,* 278–93; Klein, *Making It Perfectly Clear,* 110–11; Price, *With Nixon,* 97.

19. Haldeman, *Ends of Power,* 52–55.

20. Safire, *Before the Fall,* 113–14; Jeb Stuart Magruder, *An American Life: One Man's Road to Watergate* (New York: Atheneum, 1974), 56–71.

21. Nixon, *Memoirs,* 354–55; Safire, *Before the Fall,* 341–65; author's interviews with Haldeman, Herbert Klein, June 9, 1983; Klein, *Making It Perfectly Clear,* passim.

22. Author's interviews with Finch, Ehrlichman, Haldeman; Ehrlichman, *Witness to Power,* 58–59, 169–78, 191–92.

23. Nixon, *Memoirs,* 342; Safire, *Before the Fall,* 99–104; author's interviews with Haldeman, Finch.

24. Daniel Patrick Moynihan, *The Politics of a Guaranteed Income: The Nixon Administration and the Family Assistance Plan* (New York: Random House, 1973), 73–75; Finch, author's interview.

25. Author's interviews with Finch, Haldeman; Douglas Schoen, *Pat: A Biography of Daniel Patrick Moynihan* (New York: Harper & Row, 1979), 1–186.

26. Safire, *Before the Fall,* 108; Nixon, *Memoirs,* 341–42; Daniel P. Moynihan to the President-elect, Jan. 3, 1969, George A. Romney Papers, HUD Series, Box 87, Bentley Historical Library (hereafter BHL), Ann Arbor, Mich.

27. John C. Whitaker for Cabinet Members of the Urban Affairs Council, Jan. 29, 1969, and attached memo by Moynihan to Nixon, Jan. 9, 1969, Romney Papers, HUD Series, Box 87, BHL; Safire, *Before the Fall,* 497; Sidey quoted in Dan Rather and Gary Paul Gates, *The Palace Guard* (New York: Harper & Row, 1974), 105; Nixon, *Memoirs,* 342.

28. Author's interviews with Mitchell, Ehrlichman, Haldeman; Drury, *Courage and Hesitation,* 357; Rowland Evans, Jr., and Robert Novak, *Nixon in the White House* (New York: Random House, 1971), 14, 18; Nixon, *Memoirs,* 424–26; Moynihan to Nixon, Jan. 3, 1969, Romney Papers, HUD Series, Box 87, BHL; Moynihan, *Politics of a Guaranteed Income,* 69–148.

29. First Moynihan quotation, Rather and Gates, *The Palace Guard,* 69; second Moynihan quotation, White, *Breach of Faith,* 114; author's interviews with Harlow, Mitchell; Stephen Hess, *Organizing the Presidency* (Washington, D.C.: Brookings Institution, 1976), 121–22.

30. Ehrlichman, *Witness to Power,* 246–47; Hess, *Organizing the Presidency,* 123; Moynihan, *Politics of a Guaranteed Income,* 74; authors interviews with Haldeman, Ehrlichman.

31. Ehrlichman, *Witness to Power,* 82–83, 207–8, 242–43; author's interviews with Ehrlichman, Haldeman; Nixon, *Memoirs,* 434.

32. Nixon, *Memoirs,* 340–41; Kissinger, *White House Years,* 7–16; Seymour M. Hersh, *The Price of Power: Kissinger in the Nixon White House* (New York: Summit Books, 1983), 11–24.

33. Nixon, *Memoirs,* 323–28, 340; Kissinger, *White House Years,* 10; Hersh, *The Price of Power,* 11–24; author's interviews with Mitchell, Haldeman.

34. Author's interviews with Mitchell, Haldeman; Nixon, *Memoirs,* 34–41; *Washington Post,* Dec. 3, 1968.

35. Mitchell, author's interview; Kissinger, *White House Years,* 12; *New York Times,* Dec. 4, 1968.

36. *New York Times,* Dec. 3, 1968; Kissinger, *White House Years,* 16.

37. Nixon, *Memoirs*, 340; Kissinger, *White House Years*, 38–48; Hersh, *Price of Power*, 27–36; I. M. Destler, Leslie H. Gelb, and Anthony Lake, *Our Own Worst Enemy: The Unmaking of American Foreign Policy* (New York: Simon + Schuster, 1984), 202–8.

38. Nixon quoted in Stephen Hess, "Is There a Republican Approach to Government," *Washington Monthly*, Feb. 1969, p. 61; Haldeman, author's interview; Ehrlichman, *Witness to Power*, 87–88.

39. Safire, *Before the Fall*, 116; author's interviews with Haldeman, Mitchell; Ehrlichman, *Witness to Power*, 88.

40. Author's interviews with Finch, Haldeman, Mitchell; Ehrlichman, *Witness to Power*, 87; *New York Times*, Dec. 9, 10, 11, 12, 1968; *Washington Post*, Dec. 9, 10, 11, 12, 1968; *Time*, Dec. 20, 1968, pp. 10–18.

41. Nixon, *Memoirs*, 338–39; *New York Times*, Dec. 10, 13, 1968; Hubert H. Humphrey, *The Education of a Public Man: My Life and Politics* (Garden City, N.Y.: Doubleday, 1976), 432–33.

42. Author's interviews with Mitchell, Haldeman, Harlow; Nixon, *Memoirs*, 339–40.

43. Hess, *Organizing the Presidency*, 115.

44. Author's interviews with Haldeman, Ehrlichman; Ehrlichman, *Witness to Power*, 87–112.

45. Author's interviews with Haldeman, Finch; Nixon, *Six Crises* (paperback edition, published by Warner in 1979), 24, 91, 156–58; Evans and Novak, *Nixon in the White House*, 21–23; Kissinger, *White House Years*, 26, 28; Hersh, *Price of Power*, 32–33 (Richardson quotation on p. 33).

46. Nixon, *Memoirs*, 339; author's interviews with Mitchell, Haldeman.

47. Kissinger, *White House Years*, 26–28.

48. *Ibid.*, 32–33; author's interviews with Harlow, Finch, Ehrlichman.

49. Ehrlichman, *Witness to Power*, 88–91; author's interviews with Ehrlichman, Harlow, Haldeman.

50. Haldeman, author's interview.

51. Nixon, *Memoirs*, 26, 351–52.

52. *Ibid.*, 355–56.

53. Author's interviews with Haldeman, Ehrlichman, Mitchell; Transcript of interview with Richard Nixon, n.d., WGBH, Institute of Politics, Harvard University; Klein, *Making It Perfectly Clear*, 145–46; Whalen, *Catch the Falling Flag*, 224–25; George Christian, *The President Steps Down* (New York: Macmillan, 1970), 244; Memorandum for Files, Bill Blackburn, Nov. 27, 1968, Central File, FG 11–8, Box 69, Lyndon B. Johnson Library, Austin, Texas.

54. Author's interviews with Haldeman, Ehrlichman, Mitchell; Evans and Novak, *Nixon in the White House*, 66; Richard Nixon, *Public Papers of the Presidents*, 1969, pp. 24–28.

55. Lyndon Baines Johnson, *The Vantage Point: Perspectives of the Presidency, 1963–1969* (New York: Holt, Rinehart + Winston, 1971), 555; Notes by Billy Graham, n.d., White House Famous Names, Box 6, Johnson Library.

56. Johnson, *Vantage Point*, 555–56; Christian, *The President Steps Down*, 121–24; Kissinger, *White House Years*, 52–53; *Washington Post*, Nov. 12, 1968; "Meeting with the President," Nov. 11, 1968, Johnson Library.

57. *Washington Post*, Nov. 12, 16, 1968; Christian, *The President Steps Down*, 124–31; Johnson, *Vantage Point*, 556–57.

58. Nixon, *Memoirs,* 345–46; Kissinger, *White House Years,* 49–50; Christian, *The President Steps Down,* 144–46; Jack Valenti, *A Very Human President* (New York: Norton, 1975), 372–73.

59. Charles S. Murphy, interviewed by Thomas S. Baker, May 7, 1969, Johnson Library, II, 17–23; Lincoln, "Presidential Transition," 529–33; Memorandum, Charles S. Murphy to the Files, Nov. 20, 1968, and attached Memorandum for the Record by Willis H. Shapley, Nov. 19, 1968, Central Files, FG 11–8, Box 69, Johnson Library.

60. Johnson, *Vantage Point,* 556; author's interviews with Haldeman, Mitchell, Ehrlichman; Bobby Baker, with Larry L. King, *Wheeling and Dealing: Confessions of a Capitol Hill Operator* (New York: Norton, 1978), 263–64; Merle Miller, *Lyndon: An Oral Biography* (New York: Putnam, 1980), 545.

61. Johnson, *Vantage Point,* 558–59; Charles Murphy, Johnson Library Oral History, II, 22; Price, *With Nixon,* 42–43.

62. Price, *With Nixon,* 42–49; Nixon, *Public Papers,* 1969, pp. 1–4.

63. Nixon, *Public Papers,* 1969, pp. 1–4.

64. *Congressional Quarterly Almanac,* 1969, pp. 107–16, 1040–42.

65. Nixon, *Memoirs,* 414; author's interviews with Haldeman, Ehrlichman; Herbert Stein, *Presidential Economics* (New York: Simon and Schuster, 1984), 133–53; Price, *With Nixon,* 70–80.

66. Nixon, *Public Papers,* 1969, pp. 112–12, 350–54; Bertrand Harding to Sargent Shriver, March 6, 1969, Bertrand Harding Papers, Box 59, Johnson Library.

67. Author's interviews with Mitchell, Finch, Ehrlichman, Haldeman; Harry S. Dent, *The Prodigal South Returns to Power* (New York: John Wiley & Sons, 1978), 73–156; Leon Panetta and Peter Gall, *Bring Us Together: The Nixon Team and the Civil Rights Retreat* (Philadelphia: Lippincott, 1971).

68. Harlow, author's interview; Nixon, *Public Papers,* 1969; *Congressional Quarterly Almanac,* 1969, pp. 107–16, 1040–42.

69. *Gallup Poll,* 1959–1971, Vol. 3, pp. 1703, 1722, 2181, 2198; Safire, *Before the Fall,* 132–33; Klein, *Making It Perfectly Clear,* 107; author's interviews with Haldeman, Klein.

70. John Lewis Gaddis, *Strategies of Containment: A Critical Appraisal of Postwar American National Security Policy* (New York: Oxford University Press, 1982), 275.

71. Nixon, *Memoirs,* 343; Kissinger, *White House Years,* 54–70; Haldeman, *Ends of Power,* 84, 94–97.

72. *Gallup Poll,* 1959–1971, Vol. 3, pp. 2172–73, 2179.

73. Gaddis, *Strategies of Containment,* 274–344; Harris poll reported in *Boston Globe* Aug. 26, 1983.

74. Nixon, *Memoirs,* 344; Kissinger, *White House Years,* 119.

75. Nixon, *Memoirs,* 346; Kissinger, *White House Years,* 126–30.

76. Nixon, *Memoirs,* 346; Kissinger, *White House Years,* 130–38, 169, 187.

77. Gaddis, *Strategies of Containment,* 302–3; Kissinger, *White House Years,* 134–38; Henry A. Kissinger, *Years of Upheaval* (Boston: Little, Brown, 1982), 414.

78. Kissinger, *White House Years,* 822, 841, 138–44; Nixon, *Memoirs,* 369–70; Hersh, *Price of Power,* 40–43; Kissinger, *Years of Upheaval,* 414–46.

79. Nixon, *Memoirs,* 345–46, 390–414; Kissinger, *White House Years,* 265–69.

80. For an excellent survey of recent writing on the war, see Fox Butterfield, "The New Vietnam Scholarship," *New York Times Magazine,* Feb. 13, 1983, pp. 26–35, 45–61.

81. Nixon, *Memoirs,* 349; *Gallup Poll,* 1959–1971, Vol. 3, pp. 2179, 2189.

82. Nixon, *Memoirs,* 347–49; Kissinger, *White House Years,* 227–28.

83. Kissinger, *White House Years,* 235–311; Nixon, *Memoirs,* 380–82; George C. Herring, "The Nixon Strategy in Vietnam," a paper presented at the Woodrow Wilson Center, Washington, D.C., Jan. 6, 1983.

84. Kissinger, *White House Years,* 254–65.

85. Haldeman, *Ends of Power,* 82–83; author's interviews with Haldeman, Ehrlichman; George C. Herring, "Nixon, Kissinger, and Madman Diplomacy," paper presented to Organization of American Historians, April 10, 1980.

86. Author's interviews with Haldeman, Ehrlichman; Jonathan Schell, *The Time of Illusion* (New York: Knopf, 1976).

CHAPTER 4: CARTER

1. Jimmy Carter, *Keeping Faith: Memoirs of a President* (New York: Bantam Books, 1982), 65–66.

2. Robert K. Murray and Tim H. Blessing, "The Presidential Performance Study: A Progress Report," *Journal of American History* 70 (Dec. 1983), 535–55.

3. On Carter's background and governorship, see: Betty Glad, *Jimmy Carter in Search of the Great White House* (New York: Norton, 1980); Gary M. Fink, *Prelude to the Presidency: The Political Character and Legislative Leadership Style of Governor Jimmy Carter* (Westport, Conn.: Greenwood Press, 1980).

4. Jimmy Carter, *Why Not the Best?* (Nashville, Tenn.: Broadman Press, 1975), 9–10; Eugene H. Roseboom and Alfred E. Eckes, Jr., *A History of Presidential Elections,* 4th Ed. (New York: Collier, 1979), 315–20; Jules Witcover, *Marathon: The Pursuit of the Presidency, 1972–1976* (New York: Viking, 1977), 106–18, 222–39.

5. Jonathan Moore and Janet Fraser, eds., *Campaign for President: The Managers Look at '76* (Cambridge, Mass.: Ballinger, 1977), 78–116; Roseboom and Eckes, *History of Presidential Elections,* 321–26; Witcover, *Marathon,* 119–354.

6. Carter, *Keeping Faith,* 36–37; Witcover, *Marathon,* 359–66; Moore and Fraser, *Campaign for President,* 110–13; Hamilton Jordan, author's interview, Jan. 19, 1984; Richard Moe, author's interview, Nov. 29, 1983.

7. Witcover, *Marathon,* 361–656; Moore and Fraser, *Campaign for President,* 117–57; Roseboom and Eckes, *History of Presidential Elections,* 325–37; Stuart Eizenstat, author's interview, Dec. 8, 1983.

8. Pre-inaugural press conference transcript, Nov. 4, 1976, reprinted in *Presidency, 1977* (Washington, D.C.: Congressional Quarterly, 1978), 91A–93A.

9. James Fallows, "The Passionless Presidency," *The Atlantic,* May 1979, p. 42; William E. Leuchtenburg, *In the Shadow of FDR: From Harry Truman to Ronald Reagan* (Ithaca, N.Y.: Cornell University Press, 1983), 197–99; Jody Powell, author's interview, Dec. 8, 1983; Patrick Caddell, author's interview, Nov. 29, 1983; Eizenstat, author's interview, Bert Lance, author's interview, Nov. 22, 1983; Jordan, author's interview; Jack Watson, author's interview, Nov. 22, 1983; Har-

rison Wellford, author's interview, Dec. 8, 1983; Landon Butler, author's interview, Feb. 3, 1984.

10. Author's interviews with Eizenstat, Caddell, Butler, Charles Schultze, Feb. 1, 1984; Leuchtenberg, *In the Shadow of FDR*, 199–208.

11. Author's interviews with Caddell, Moe, Jordan, James Schlesinger, Feb. 1, 1984, Gail Harrison, Jan. 27, 1984; Laurence E. Lynn, Jr., and David F. Whitman, *The President as Policymaker: Jimmy Carter and Welfare Reform* (Philadelphia: Temple University Press, 1981), 125 (quotation).

12. Author's interviews with Caddell, James King, Dec. 6, 1983.

13. Carter, *Keeping Faith*, 17–18; Robert Shogan, *Promises To Keep: Carter's First Hundred Days* (New York: T. Y. Crowell, 1977), 96–164; George H. Gallup, *The Gallup Poll: Public Opinion, 1972–1977*, Vol. 2, 1976–1977 (Wilmington, Del.: Scholarly Resources, 1978), 994–96, 1036, 1063; "Maestro of the Media" (three articles), *New York Times Magazine*, May 15, 1977.

14. Shogan, *Promises to Keep*, 96–164; "Maestro of the Media," *New York Times Magazine*, May 15, 1977; Carter, *Keeping Faith*, 26–27; author's interviews with Powell, Caddell; Caddell's "Initial Working Paper on Political Strategy" was entered in *Congressional Record*, Senate, June 21, 1977, pp. 20100–20109.

15. Author's interviews with Powell, Caddell; Fallows, "The Passionless Presidency"; Don F. Hahn, "The Rhetoric of Jimmy Carter, 1976–1980," *Presidential Studies Quarterly* 14 (Spring 1984), 265–88.

16. Author's interviews with Powell, Caddell; Jimmy Carter, *Public Papers of the Presidents*, 1977, Vol. 1, p.1; Fallows, "The Passionless Presidency."

17. Carter, *Public Papers of the Presidents*, 1977, Vol. 1, pp. 1–4; Caddell, author's interview.

18. Fallows, "The Passionless Presidency," 44; author's interviews with Schlesinger, Jordan, Powell; Joseph A. Califano, Jr., *Governing America: An Insider's Report from the White House and the Cabinet* (New York: Simon + Schuster, 1981), 24–25; Leuchtenburg, *In the Shadow of FDR*, 200–201.

19. Author's interviews with Jordan, Watson, Powell, Wellford, Eizenstat, Harrison, Moe, King; Charles Kirbo, author's interview, Jan. 19, 1984; James Gammill, author's interview, Nov. 9, 1983; Shogan, *Promises to Keep*, 74–81; Bruce Adams and Kathryn Kavanagh-Baran, *Promise and Performance: Carter Builds a New Administration* (Lexington, Mass: Lexington Books, 1979), 11–25; "Report of the Study Group on Presidential Transition; Special Annex: The 1976 Transition," Institute of Politics, John F. Kennedy School of Government, Harvard University, Oct. 1980, pp. 1–10.

20. Author's interviews with Jordan, Wellford, Lance; Anthony Lake, author's interview, Feb. 6, 1984; David Aaron, author's interview, January 5, 1984.

21. "Report of the Study Group on Presidential Transition; Special Annex: The 1976 Transition," 1, 36–38; Watson, author's interview.

22. Author's interviews with Lance, Powell, Jordan; *Presidency, 1977*, 94-A.

23. Stephen Hess, *Organizing the Presidency* (Washington, D. C.: Brookings, 1976); author's interviews with Jordan, Powell, Moe, Watson.

24. Memo, Jack Watson to Jimmy Carter, Nov. 3, 1976; Memo, Stuart Eizenstat to President-elect Carter, n.d., both in Stuart Eizenstat's possession; author's interviews with Eizenstat, Jordan, Powell, Watson, Moe.

25. Califano, *Governing America*, 24–27.

26. Author's interviews with Powell, Lance, Jordan, Eizenstat; Carp quoted

in Lynn and Whitman, *The President as Policymaker,* 52. This book is an intensive examination of one early and unsuccessful policy initiative of the Carter administration.

27. Carter, *Keeping Faith,* 128; Lance, author's interview; Zbigniew Brzezinski, *Power and Principle: Memoirs of the National Security Adviser, 1977–1981* (New York: Farrar, Straus and Giroux, 1983), 21.

28. Carter, *Keeping Faith,* 127–28; author's interviews with Lance, Schlesinger, Wellford, Harrison.

29. Carter, *Keeping Faith,* 129–36; William Safire, *Safire's Washington* (New York: Times Books, 1980), 260–82; Richard E. Neustadt, *Presidential Power: The Politics of Leadership from FDR to Carter* (New York: John Wiley & Sons, 1980), 225–31; author's interviews with Schlesinger, Lance, Moe; *Presidency, 1977,* 1–2.

30. Carter, *Keeping Faith,* 127; author's interviews with Lance, Schlesinger, Wellford.

31. Carter, *Keeping Faith,* 130–37; author's interviews with Butler, Schlesinger, Schultze.

32. Califano, *Governing America,* 25.

33. Carter, *Keeping Faith,* 47–49; author's interviews with Jordan, Schultze, Moe, Watson, Kirbo; "Report of the Study Group on Presidential Transition; Special Annex: The 1976 Transition," 19–21, 50–51; Adams and Kavanagh-Baran, *Promise and Performance,* 24–42; Cyrus Vance, *Hard Choices: Critical Years in America's Foreign Policy* (New York: Simon + Schuster, 1983), 30.

34. Author's interviews with Schlesinger, Powell, Aaron; Adams and Kavanagh-Baran, *Promise and Performance,* 157–59; "Report of the Study Group on Presidential Transition; Special Annex: The 1976 Transition," 24.

35. Adams and Kavanagh-Baran, *Promise and Performance,* 158; Clark R. Mollenhoff, *The President Who Failed: Carter Out of Control* (New York: Macmillan, 1980), 35–46; Griffin B. Bell with Ronald J. Ostrow, *Taking Care of the Law* (New York: Morrow, 1982), esp. 21–50.

36. Bell, *Taking Care of the Law,* 45–48; Carter, *Keeping Faith,* 49.

37. Author's interviews with Jordan, Watson, Butler, Powell, King, Eizenstat, Lance, Caddell; Califano, *Governing America,* 29.

38. Califano, *Governing America,* 27–41; Bell, *Taking Care of the Law,* 40–42; author's interviews with Jordan, King.

39. Author's interviews with King, Jordan, Butler, Gammill; "Report of the Study Group on Presidential Transition; Special Annex: The 1976 Transition," 26–28; Adams and Kavanagh-Baran, *Promise and Performance,* 51–58.

40. Author's interviews with King, Jordan, Caddell.

41. Author's interviews with Jordan, King, Gammill, Butler, Kirbo, Caddell; Califano, *Governing America,* 41.

42. *Presidency, 1977,* 93-A; Carter, *Keeping Faith,* 40–41.

43. Author's interviews with Schlesinger, Schultze, Watson, Butler.

44. Author's interviews with Jordan, Powell, Schlesinger, Schultze.

45. Author's interviews with Jordan, Watson, Powell, Schultze, Butler, Moe.

46. Jody Powell, *The Other Side of the Story* (New York: Morrow, 1984), 109–11.

47. *Ibid.,* 50–53; confidential sources; Haynes Johnson, *In the Absence of Power: Governing America* (New York: Viking, 1980), 24–25, 156, 163, 165,

175–78; Shogan, *Promises to Keep*, 207–22, 254–55; author's interviews with Jordan, Schlesinger, Schultze.

48. Author's interviews with Jordan, Moe, Eizenstat; Bell, *Taking Care of the Law*, 24.

49. Author's interviews with Jordan, Moe; Paul C. Light, *Vice Presidential Power: Advice and Influence in the White House* (Baltimore: Johns Hopkins University Press, 1984), 213.

50. Light, *Vice Presidential Power*, esp. 201–22; author's interviews with Jordan, Moe.

51. Author's interviews with Jordan, Schlesinger.

52. Carter, *Keeping Faith*, 91–101.

53. *Ibid.*, 91–93.

54. Author's interviews with Schlesinger, Eizenstat, Butler, Schultze.

55. Carter, *Keeping Faith*, 97–99.

56. *Presidency, 1977*, 31; Paul C. Light, *The President's Agenda: Domestic Policy Choice From Kennedy to Carter* (Baltimore: Johns Hopkins University Press, 1982), 44–45.

57. Johnson, *In the Absence of Power*, 26–30; author's interviews with Powell, Jordan, Caddell, Schultze.

58. Carter, *Keeping Faith*, 71.

59. Johnson, *In the Absence of Power*, 20, 48, 177–78; Shogan, *Promises to Keep*, 124–26; Carter, *Public Papers of the Presidents, 1977*, Vol. 1, photograph following p. 692.

60. Johnson, *In the Absence of Power*, 43, 166; Light, *The President's Agenda*, 46–49; Shogan, *Promises to Keep*, 210–11; Schultze, author's interview; William F. Mullen, "Perceptions of Carter's Legislative Successes and Failures: Views from the Hill and the Liaison Staff," *Presidential Studies Quarterly* 12 (Fall 1982), 522–33.

61. Carter, *Keeping Faith*, 87; author's interviews with Schlesinger, Eizenstat, Schultze; Shogan, *Promises to Keep*, 237–38.

62. Carter, *Keeping Faith*, 78; Shogan, *Promises to Keep*, 226–31; W. Michael Blumenthal, "Candid Reflections of a Businessman in Washington," *Fortune*, Jan. 29, 1979, p. 22; *Congressional Quarterly Almanac, 1977*, pp. 97–106; author's interviews with Schultze, Lance, Eizenstat.

63. Carter, *Keeping Faith*, 78; *Congressional Quarterly Almanac, 1977*, pp. 213–16.

64. Carter, *Keeping Faith*, 79; *Congressional Quarterly Almanac, 1977*, p. 608; Shogan, *Promises to Keep*, 212–15, 227–28; author's interviews with Jordan, Lance, Moe.

65. Author's interviews with Jordan, Powell, Lance, Watson, Wellford.

66. Seyom Brown, *The Faces of Power: Constancy and Change in United States Foreign Policy from Truman to Reagan* (New York: Columbia University Press, 1983), 451–63; Carter, *Keeping Faith*, 141–43; Brzezinski, *Power and Principle*, 27, 30–31; John Lewis Gaddis, *Strategies of Containment: A Critical Appraisal of Postwar American National Security Policy* (New York: Oxford University Press, 1982), 345–48.

67. Carter, *Keeping Faith*, 51, Brzezinski, *Power and Principle*, 5–10; Brown, *Faces of Power*, 455.

68. Carter, *Keeping Faith*, 52; Vance, *Hard Choices*, 34; Brzezinski, *Power and Principle*, 10–11.

69. Brzezinski, *Power and Principle*, 36–37, 48–56; Vance, *Hard Choices*, 35; author's interviews with Aaron, Lake.

70. Vance, *Hard Choices*, 44; Brzezinski, *Power and Principle*, 56–57; Brown, *Faces of Power*, 456; Aaron, author's interview.

72. Vance, *Hard Choices*, 35–36; Brzezinski, *Power and Principle*, 29–30, 37–40; Carter, *Keeping Faith*, 53–54; Carter, *Public Papers*, 1977, Vol. 1, pp. 600, 647; author's interviews with Jordan, Powell, Aaron, Lake.

73. Brzezinski, *Power and Principle*, 18–31, 43, 63–64; Aaron, author's interview.

74. Vance, *Hard Choices*, 39–44; Carter, *Keeping Faith*, 53; author's interviews with Aaron, Lake.

75. Author's interviews with Aaron, Schlesinger, Lake; Brown, *Faces of Power*, 451–63; Brzezinski, *Power and Principle*, passim; Vance, *Hard Choices*, passim; I. M. Destler, Leslie H. Gelb, and Anthony Lake, *Our Own Worst Enemy: The Unmaking of American Foreign Policy* (New York: Simon + Schuster, 1984), 216–20.

76. Hodding Carter quoted in Brown, *Faces of Power*, 458; Brzezinski, *Power and Principle*, 81–190; Vance, *Hard Choices*, 45–190.

77. Carter, *Keeping Faith*, 146; Brzezinski, *Power and Principle*, 81; Vance, *Hard Choices*, 156–57; author's interviews with Aaron, Lake.

78. Brzezinski, *Power and Principle*, 81.

79. Strobe Talbott, *Endgame: The Inside Story of SALT II* (New York: Harper & Row, 1979).

80. Talbott, *Endgame*, 21–31; Carter, *Keeping Faith*, 212–18; Carter, *Public Papers*, 1977, Vol. 1, p. 3; Ernest R. May, draft chapter on "Deep-Cuts."

81. Talbott, *Endgame*, 31–37.

82. *Ibid.*, 38–59; Vance, *Hard Choices*, 47–51; Brzezinski, *Power and Principle*, 151–61; Aaron, author's interview.

83. Talbott, *Endgame*, 60–61.

84. Carter, *Keeping Faith*, 218–19; Vance, *Hard Choices*, 52–53; Talbott, *Endgame*, 60–63.

85. Talbott, *Endgame*, 63–67; Vance, *Hard Choices*; 53–55; Carter, *Public Papers*, 1977, Vol. 1, pp. 498, 503.

86. Vance, *Hard Choices*, 53–55; Talbott, *Endgame*, 68–75; Brzezinski, *Power and Principle*, 162–64.

87. Talbott, *Endgame*, 75–78; author's interviews with Aaron, Lake.

88. Vance, *Hard Choices*, 55–63; Talbott, *Endgame*, 78–87; Brzezinski, *Power and Principle*, 164–70.

CHAPTER 5: REAGAN

1. Ronald Reagan with Richard G. Hubler, *Where's the Rest of Me?* (New York: Duell, Sloan and Pearce, 1965); Lou Cannon, *Reagan* (New York: Putnam, 1982); Bill Boyarsky, *Ronald Reagan: His Life and Rise to the Presidency* (New York: Random House, 1981); William E. Leuchtenburg, *In the Shadow of FDR: From Harry Truman to Ronald Reagan* (Ithaca: Cornell University Press, 1983), 209–35.

2. Cannon, *Reagan*, 186–303; Jimmy Carter, *Keeping Faith: Memoirs of a President* (New York: Bantam Books, 1982), 542.

3. Austin Ranney, ed., *The American Elections of 1980* (Washington, D.C.: American Enterprise Institute for Public Policy Research, 1981); Gerald M. Pomper, *The Election of 1980: Reports and Interpretations* (Chatham, N.J.: Chatham House, 1981); Jonathan Moore, ed., *The Campaign for President: 1980 in Retrospect* (Cambridge, Mass.: Ballinger, 1981).

4. William Schneider, "The November 4 Vote for President: What Did It Mean?" in Ranney, ed., *The American Elections of 1980*, 248; *New York Times*, Nov. 6, 1980.

5. Author's interviews with Edwin Meese, III, Aug. 30, 1984, Martin Anderson, May 30, 1984, David Gergen, March 20, 1984; Elizabeth Drew, "A Reporter at Large: Early Days," *The New Yorker*, March 16, 1981, pp. 84–99.

6. Cannon, *Reagan*, 119–86; author's interviews with Meese, Hamilton Jordan (Jan. 19, 1984).

7. Cannon, *Reagan*, 241–58, 304–5, 371–401; Boyarsky, *Ronald Reagan*, 106–9; Gergen, author's interview; Paul Craig Roberts, *The Supply-Side Revolution: An Insider's Account of Policymaking in Washington* (Cambridge: Harvard University Press, 1984).

8. Cannon, *Reagan*, 119–31; Meese, author's interview.

9. Author's interviews with Meese, Gergen, Pendleton James (June 27, 1984), Edwin Harper (June 29, 1984); confidential sources; Cannon, *Reagan*, 306–8; Laurence I. Barrett, *Gambling with History: Ronald Reagan in the White House* (Garden City, N.Y.: Doubleday, 1983), 74–79, 94–106.

10. Author's interviews with Meese, James.

11. *Ibid.*; *New York Times*, Sept. 14, 1980, p. 32.

12. *Wall Street Journal*, Jan. 7, 1981; *Washington Post*, December 13, 15, 22, 1980, June 1, 1984; *New York Times*, Dec. 21, 22, 1980, June 7, 1984; Report by the Comptroller General to the Chairman, Committee on Energy and Commerce, House of Representatives, "The Reagan-Bush Transition Team's Activities at Six Selected Agencies," Jan. 28, 1982; author's interviews with Meese, Harper, Anderson.

13. Organizational charts of Reagan transition, in possession of Institute of Politics, John F. Kennedy School of Government, Harvard University, Cambridge, Mass.; Charles L. Heatherly, ed., *Mandate for Leadership: Policy Management in a Conservative Administration* (Washington, D.C.: Heritage Foundation, 1981); *Washington Post*, Nov. 15, 16, 1980.

14. Author's interviews with Meese, James, Harper, Gergen, Anderson; *Washington Post*, Nov. 7, 11, 15, 1980.

15. Author's interviews with Meese, James, Gergen; Fred Barnes, "Who's in Charge?" *The Washingtonian*, Aug. 1983, 124–33; G. Calvin Mackenzie, "Personnel Selection for a Conservative Administration: The Reagan Experience, 1980–1981" Department of Government, Colby College, Waterville, Maine; Barrett, *Gambling with History*, 75–76; Transcripts of interviews with Pendleton James, William French Smith, Edwin Meese, William Timmons, for WGBH-TV documentary on Reagan transition, Institute of Politics.

16. Author's interviews with James, Meese; Mackenzie, "Personnel Selection for a Conservative Administration"; Barnes, "Who's in Charge?"; *Washington Post*, Dec. 15, 1980; *New York Times*, Dec. 18, 1980.

17. Author's interviews with Meese, James, Gergen, William Tucker (Aug. 30, 1984); Meese, James, Smith interviews for WGBH; Transcripts of Meese press

briefings for Dec. 1980 at Institute of Politics; *Time,* Dec. 15, 1980; clippings from *New York Times, Washington Post, National Journal,* for late November, early December, at Institute of Politics.

18. Alexander M. Haig, *Caveat: Realism, Reagan, and Foreign Policy* (New York: Macmillan, 1984), 11; author's interviews with Meese, James, Gergen, Tucker; Margaret Jane Wyszomirski, "Roosevelt and Reagan: Cabinet Recruitment and Performance," paper delivered at the 1984 Annual Meeting of the American Political Science Association, Washington, D.C., 1984.

19. *New York Times,* Dec. 6, 1980, Jan. 8, 1981; *Washington Post,* Jan. 22, 1984; Dick Kirschten, "Wanted: 275 Reagan Team Players; Empire Builders Need Not Apply," *National Journal,* Dec. 6, 1980, pp. 2077–79; author's interviews with James, Meese, Tucker.

20. Author's interviews with James, Meese, Tucker, Drew Lewis (June 25, 1984), Richard Schweiker (June 28, 1984); confidential sources; Mackenzie, "Personnel Selection for a Conservative Administration"; Haig, *Caveat,* 67–68; Ronald Brownstein and Nina Easton, *Reagan's Ruling Class: Portraits of the President's Top 100 Officials* (Washington, D.C.: Presidential Accountability Group, 1982), 289–96 and *passim; Time,* May 11, 1981, p. 9.

21. Author's interviews with James, Meese, Tucker; confidential sources; J. Jackson Walter, "The Ethics in Government Act, Conflict of Interest Laws and Presidential Recruiting," *Public Admininstration Review* 41 (Nov./Dec. 1981), 659–65; *Time,* Nov. 17, 1980.

22. Laurence E. Lynn, Jr. "The Reagan Administration and the Renitent Bureaucracy: A Study of Public Management in Five Federal Agencies," 1983 (Kennedy School of Government), 38; Paul Portney, "Natural Resources and the Environment: More Controversy Than Change," in John L. Palmer and Isabel V. Sawhill, eds., *The Reagan Record* (Cambridge: Ballinger, 1984), 141–75; Donald Lambro, *Washington—City of Scandals: Investigating Congress and the Big Spenders* (Boston: Little, Brown, 1984), 251–88.

23. *National Journal,* Jan. 14, 1984, pp. 92–93; author's interviews with James, Gergen, Tucker, Glenn Schleede (June 22, 1984); Brownstein and Easton, *Reagan's Ruling Class,* passim.

24. Mackenzie, "Personnel Selection for a Conservative Administration"; author's interviews with James, Meese, Tucker, Gergen; *Reagan's First Year* (Washington, D.C.: Congressional Quarterly, Inc., 1982), 43, 81–85.

25. Author's interview with James; Haig, *Caveat,* 76; unpublished research conducted by Dorothy Robyn and William Kristol, Kennedy School of Government, Summer 1984; *Reagan's Ruling Class* contains many examples of the warfare between appointive and career officials; Edward Preston, "Orienting Presidential Appointees," *The Bureaucrat* 13 (Fall 1984), 40–43. (This journal contains a variety of other articles that pertain to relations between political appointees and civil servants.)

26. Carter, *Keeping Faith,* 577–78.

27. Author's interviews with Meese, Tucker, Gergen, Harrison Wellford (Dec. 8, 1983), Jack Watson (Nov. 22, 1983).

28. Author's interviews with Meese, Tucker, Lewis, Schleede, Harper.

29. Haig, *Caveat,* 71–72; *Washington Post,* Dec. 24, 1980; confidential sources.

30. Barrett, *Gambling with History,* 85–87; *Washington Post,* Dec. 11, 29,

1980, Jan. 6, 1981; Brzezinski, *Power and Principle,* 23, 26–27; *New York Times,* Jan. 6, 1981; *Time,* Dec. 1, 1980, Jan. 12, 1981.

31. *Washington Post,* Jan. 7, 1981; *New York Times,* Dec. 2, 1980; Schleede, author's interview.

32. Frederick C. Mosher, "Presidential Transition and Foreign Policy" (Charlottesville, Va.: White Burkett Miller Center of Public Affairs, 1983), 152–53; *Washington Post,* Jan. 21, 1981; *New York Times,* Jan. 21, 1984; Haig, *Caveat,* 77–79.

33. *Newsweek,* Dec. 1, 1980; *Time,* Dec. 1, 1980; *Washington Post,* Nov. 19, 1980; Cannon, *Reagan,* 339–42.

34. Author's interviews with Meese, Gergen; Steven R. Weisman, "The President and the Press: The Art of Controlled Access," *New York Times Magazine,* Oct. 14, 1984; Roberts, *Supply-Side Revolution,* 98–124; Haig, *Caveat,* 92–94; Cannon, *Reagan,* 372–74; Sidney Blumenthal, "Marketing the President," *New York Times Magazine,* Sept. 13, 1982.

35. Author's interviews with Peter Teeley (Dec. 14, 1983), Gergen; Paul C. Light, *Vice Presidential Power; Advice and Influence in the White House* (Baltimore: Johns Hopkins University Press, 1984), 260–69.

36. Author's interview with Meese.

37. *Ibid.,* Barrett, *Gambling with History,* 72–73; Chester A. Newland, "The Reagan Presidency: Limited Government and Political Administration," *Public Administration Review* 43 (Jan./Feb. 1983), 6–7; Edwin Meese, III, "The Institutional Presidency: A View from the White House," *Presidential Studies Quarterly* (Spring 1983), 197.

38. Author's interviews with Meese, Lewis, Schweiker; Haig, *Caveat,* 80–83.

39. Newland, "The Reagan Presidency," 6–10; author's interviews with Meese, Anderson, Schleede, Lewis, Harper.

40. Roberts, *Supply-Side Revolution,* 122–24, 142 (quotation), 259–77; author's interviews with Lewis, Schweiker; Barrett, *Gambling With History,* 9–93, 155–58; Dick Kirschten, "Reagan's Cabinet Councils May Have Less Influence Than Meets the Eye," *National Journal,* July 11, 1981, pp. 1242–47.

41. Author's interviews with Gergen, Harper, confidential sources; Barrett, *Gambling with History,* 89, 151–53, 156–63; Dick Kirschten, "Reagan's Legislative Strategy Team Keeps His Record of Victories Intact," *National Journal,* June 26, 1982, pp. 1127–29; Roberts, *Supply-Side Revolution,* 254.

42. Barrett, *Gambling With History,* 134–35; Cannon, *Reagan,* 339; author's interviews with Harper, Schleede; Newland, "The Reagan Presidency," 11–12.

43. William Greider, "The Education of David Stockman, *The Atlantic,* Dec. 1981, pp. 105–28; William Greider, *The Education of David Stockman and Other Americans* (New York: Dutton, 1982); Barrett, *Gambling with History,* 187–93; Cannon, *Reagan,* 346–48; Roberts, *Supply-Side Revolution,* 161–212.

44. Greider, "The Education of David Stockman," 108–26; author's interviews with Schweiker, Lewis, Schleede, Anderson, Harper.

45. Cannon, *Reagan,* 331–36, 402–7; Barrett, *Gambling with History,* 146–72; Gergen, author's interview.

46. *Reagan's First Years,* 73–76; Stephen J. Wayne, "Congressional Liaison in the Reagan White House: A Preliminary Assessment of the First Year," in *President and Congress: Assessing Reagan's First Year,* ed. Norman J. Ornstein (Washington, D.C.: American Enterprise Institute for Public Policy Research, 1982), 44–65.

47. William Schneider, "Performance is the Big Campaign Issue, and That Gives Reagan a Big Edge," *National Journal*, Oct. 6, 1984, pp. 1894–95; William Schneider, "Half a Realignment," *New Republic*, Dec. 3, 1984, pp. 19–22; *The Harris Survey*, 1984, no. 97, Nov. 1, 1984; *The Gallup Report*, Aug./Sept. 1984, pp. 15–29.

48. The economic consequences of Reagan's policies have been much debated; I have been influenced in these conclusions by discussions at the Institute of Politics with Paul Samuelson and Francis Bator and by the columns that appeared in the *Boston Globe* in 1984 by Martin Feldstein, Alan Blinder, Lester Thurow, and James Tobin; by Isabel V. Sawhill and Charles F. Stone, "The Economy: The Key to Success," and Perry D. Quick, "Businesses: Reagan's Industrial Policy," both in *The Reagan Record*, ed. Palmer and Sawhill; and by Herbert Stein, *Presidential Economics* (New York: Simon +Schuster, 1984), 235–376.

49. Peter W. Bernstein, "David Stockman: No More Big Budget Cuts," *Fortune*, Feb. 6, 1984, p. 54.

50. *Economic Report of the President*, 1984, pp. 28–29; Bernstein, "David Stockman," 55.

51. Congressional Budget Office, *Major Legislative Changes in Human Resources Programs Since January 1981*, Aug. 1983, p. viii; *End Results: The Impact of Federal Policies Since 1980 on Low Income Americans* (Center on Budget and Policy Priorities, Sept. 1984, Interfaith Action for Economic Justice, Washington, D.C.), 1–16; D. Lee Bowden and John L. Palmer, "Social Policy: Challenging the Welfare State," 177–215; Marilyn Moon and Isabel V. Sawhill, "Family Incomes: Gainers and Losers," 317–46, both in Palmer and Sawhill, eds., *The Reagan Record*.

52. *Congressional Quarterly Almanac*, 1981, pp. 191–92; Samuel P. Huntington, "The Defense Policy of the Reagan Administration, 1981–1982," in Fred I. Greenstein, ed., *The Reagan Presidency: An Early Assessment* (Baltimore: Johns Hopkins University Press, 1983), 86–87.

53. *Congressional Quarterly Almanac*, 1981, pp. 191–92; Huntington, "The Defense Policy of the Reagan Administration," 88–99; William W. Kaufmann, "The Defense Budget," in Joseph A. Pechman, ed., *Setting National Priorities, the 1982 Budget* (Washington, D.C.: Brookings Institution, 1981), 133–83.

54. *Reagan's First Year*, 138.

55. Seyom Brown, *The Faces of Power: Constancy and Change in United States Foreign Policy from Truman to Reagan* (New York: Columbia University Press, 1983), 568–73; Haig, *Caveat*, 95–107.

56. Strobe Talbott, *Deadly Gambits: The Reagan Administration and the Stalemate in Nuclear Arms Control* (New York: Knopf, 1984).

57. Raymond Bonner, *Weakness and Deceit: U. S. Policy and El Salvador* (New York: Times Books, 1984), 74–76.

58. Haig, *Caveat*, 117–28, 138–40; Bonner, *Weakness and Deceit*, 252–54.

59. Bonner, *Weakness and Deceit*, 255–61; Haig, *Caveat*, 128–30; Gergen, author's interview; confidential sources.

60. Bonner, *Weakness and Deceit*, 260–69; Walter LaFeber, *Inevitable Revolution: The United States in Central America* (New York: Norton, 1983); Haig, *Caveat*, 131.

61. Haig, *Caveat*, 110–14.

62. *Ibid.*, 115–16.

63. I. M. Destler, Leslie H. Gelb, and Anthony Lake, *Our Own Worst Enemy: The Unmaking of American Foreign Policy* (New York: Simon + Schuster, 1984), 225–32; Haig, *Caveat, passim;* confidential sources.

64. Author's interviews with Meese, James; Barrett, *Gambling with History,* 68; Robert Lovett, Kennedy Library Oral History, 9–10.

65. Confidential sources; Talbott, *Deadly Gambits.*

INDEX

☆ ☆ ☆